Alastair
Sawday's

Special Places
to Stay

French Châteaux
& Hotels

4   Contents

The major trend I have to report is: the British still love France. The dark clouds over France now have a wide silver lining; the gloom seems to have lifted a little and people are slipping back into France as travellers and tourists. Nobody ever doubted that they would, because the Lady is indisputably seductive, but it is good to know that she has not been neglected for long.

Hoteliers are working hard to tempt guests in too. Once suspected of serving high-priced meals, driving people to eat 'prix fixes' menus elsewhere, many now have realistic Menus du Jour which make the most of local and fresh produce. They are even beginning to embrace the organic theme — more remarkable than you might think, for the French have always been so proud of their food that

Photo: Tom Germain

they found it hard to imagine why there was a need to take on 'new' ideas.

Another trend is last-minute booking — driving poor owners nuts — but at least the visitors come. All this spontaneity might be a side effect of the internet — and we've played our part — you can swiftly find the information you need, browse photos, scour reviews and trust what you find. The result is we're able to book up at the last minute in ways that were unheard of a decade ago. We used to pore over maps and guide books for weeks before making decisions.

As ever, I am touched by the exhilarating variety of these Special Places.

Here are a few examples: a château in Normandy that regularly receives theatre groups, another in the Midi-Pyrénées that has the most wonderful treehouse, often used by couples on their wedding night, and there is a Dordogne château that has a handsome kitchen where you can learn by osmosis while chefs cook your dinner. Then there are the utterly fabulous hotels: find one in Landes in Art Nouveau/contemporary Basque style, a place in the Pas-de-Calais with wildly funky, fabulous, interiors and another in Burgundy described as "stunning" by the inspector. These 'Special' châteaux and hotels just get better and better, and we are delighted to ride on their coat tails.

Alastair Sawday

How do we choose our Special Places?

It's simple. There are no rules, no boxes to tick. We choose places that we like and are fiercely subjective in our choices. We also recognise that one person's idea of special is not necessarily someone else's so there is a huge variety of places, and prices, in the book. Those who are familiar with our Special Places series know that we look for comfort, originality, authenticity, and reject the insincere, the anonymous and the banal. The way guests are treated comes as high on our list as the setting, the architecture, the atmosphere and the food.

Inspections

We visit every place in the guide to get a feel for how both house and owner tick. We don't take a clipboard and we don't have a list of what is acceptable and what is not. Instead, we chat for an hour or so with the owner or manager and look round. It's all very informal, but it gives us an excellent idea of who would enjoy staying there. If the visit happens to be the last of the day, we sometimes stay the night. Once in the book, properties are re-inspected every few years, so that we can keep things fresh and accurate.

Feedback

In between inspections we rely on feedback from our army of readers, as well as from staff members who are encouraged to visit properties across the series. This feedback is invaluable to us and we always follow up on comments. So do tell us whether your stay has been

a joy or not, if the atmosphere was great or stuffy, the owners and staff cheery or bored. The accuracy of the book depends on what you, and our inspectors, tell us.

A lot of the new entries in each edition are recommended by our readers, so keep telling us about new places you've discovered too. Please use the forms on our website, www.sawdays.co.uk.

However, please do not tell us if your starter was cold, or the bedside light broken. Tell the owner, immediately, and

8

simply because we like them. Our opinions and tastes are ours alone and this book is a statement of them; we hope you will share them. We have done our utmost to get our facts right but apologise unreservedly for any mistakes that may have crept in. The latest information we have about each place can be found on our website, www.sawdays.co.uk.

You should know that we don't check such things as fire alarms, swimming pool security or any other regulation with which owners of properties receiving paying guests should comply. This is the responsibility of the owners.

get them to do something about it. Most owners, or staff, are more than happy to correct problems and will bend over backwards to help. Far better than bottling it up and then writing to us a week later!

Using this book
Finding the right place for you

All these places are special in one way or another. All have been visited and then written about honestly so that you can take what you want and leave the rest. Those of you who swear by Sawday's books trust our write-ups precisely because we don't have a blanket standard; we include places simply because we like them. But we all have different priorities, so do read the descriptions carefully and pick out the places where you will be comfortable. If something is particularly important to you then check when you book: a simple question or two can avoid misunderstandings.

Subscriptions

Owners pay to appear in this guide. Their fee goes towards the high costs of inspecting, of producing an all-colour book and of maintaining our website. We only include places that we find special for one reason or another, so it is not possible for anyone to buy their way onto these pages. Nor is it possible for the owner to write their own description. We will say if the bedrooms are small, or if a main road is near. We do our best to avoid misleading people.

Disclaimer

We make no claims to pure objectivity in choosing these places. They are here

Maps

Each property is flagged with its entry number on the maps at the front. These maps are a great starting point for

planning your trip, but please don't use them as anything other than a general guide – use a decent road map for real navigation. Most places will send you detailed instructions once you have booked your stay.

Ethical Collection

We're always keen to draw attention to owners who are striving to have a positive impact on the world, so you'll notice that some entries are flagged as being part of our 'Ethical Collection'. These places are working hard to reduce their environmental footprint, making significant contributions to their local community, or are passionate about serving local or organic food (see p. 429).

Symbols

Below each entry you will see some symbols, which are explained at the very back of the book. They are based on the

information given to us by the owners. However, things do change: bikes may be under repair or a new pool may have been put in. Please use the symbols as a guide rather than an absolute statement of fact and double-check anything that is important to you – owners occasionally bend their own rules, so it's worth asking if you may take your dog even if they don't have the symbol.

Wheelchair access – Some châteaux and hotels are keen to accept wheelchair users into their hotels and have made provision for them. However, this does not mean that wheelchair users will always be met with a perfect landscape, nor does it indicate that they have been officially assessed for such a status. You may encounter ramps, a shallow step, graveled paths, alternative routes into some rooms, a bathroom (not a wet room), perhaps even a lift. In short, there may be the odd hindrance and we urge you to call and make sure you will get what you need.

Limited mobility – The limited mobility symbol 👤 shows those places where at least one bedroom and bathroom is accessible without using stairs. The symbol is designed to satisfy those who walk slowly, with difficulty, or with the aid of a stick. A wheelchair may be able to navigate some areas, but these places are not fully wheelchair friendly. If you use a chair for longer distances, but are not too bad over shorter distances, you'll probably be OK; again, please ring and ask. There may be a step or two, a bath or a shower with a tray in a cubicle, a good distance between the car park and your room, slippery flagstones or a tight turn.

Pets – Our 🐕 symbol shows places which are happy to accept pets. It means they can sleep in the bedroom with you, but not on the bed. It's really important to get this one right before you arrive, as many places make you keep dogs in the car. Check carefully: Spot's emotional wellbeing may depend on it.

Owners' pets – The 🐈 symbol is given when the owners have their own pet on the premises. It may not be a cat! But it is there to warn you that you may be greeted by a dog, serenaded by a parrot, or indeed sat upon by a cat.

Practical Matters
Types of places

Hotels can vary from huge, humming and slick to those with only a few rooms that are run by owners at their own pace. In some you may not get room service or have your bags carried in and out; in older buildings there may be no lifts. In smaller hotels there may be a fixed menu for dinner with very little choice, so if you have dishes that leave you cold, it's important to say so when you book your meal. If you decide to stay at an inn remember that they can be noisy, especially at weekends. If these things are important to you, then do check when you book.

Photo: Château du Guilguiffin, entry 156

Rooms

Bedrooms – these are described as double, twin, single, family or suite. A double may contain a bed which is anything from 135cm wide to 180cm wide. A twin will contain two single beds (usually 90cm wide). A suite will have a separate sitting area, but it may not be in a different room. Family rooms can vary in size, as can the number of beds they hold, so do ask. And do not assume that every bedroom has a TV.

Bathrooms – all bedrooms have their own bathrooms unless we say that they don't. If you have your own bathroom but you have to leave the room to get to it we describe it as 'separate'. There are very few places in the book that have shared bathrooms and they are usually reserved for members of the same party. Again, we state this clearly.

Prices and minimum stays

We quote the lowest price per night for two people in low season to the highest price in high season. Only a few places have designated single rooms; if no single rooms are listed, the price we quote refers to single occupancy of a double room. In many places prices rise higher when local events bring people flooding to the area.

The half-board price quoted is per person per night unless stated otherwise, and includes dinner, usually three courses. Mostly you're offered a table d'hôte menu. Occasionally you eat à la carte and may find some dishes carry a small supplement. There are often great deals to be had, mostly mid-week in low season.

Meals

Breakfast is included in the room price unless otherwise stated.

Some places serve lunch, most do Sunday lunch (often very well-priced), the vast majority offer dinner. In some places you can content yourself with bar meals, in others you can feast on five courses. Most offer three courses for €25-€50, either table d'hôtes or à la carte. Some have tasting menus, occasionally you eat communally. Some large hotels (and some posh private houses) will bring dinner to your room if you prefer, or let you eat in the garden by candlelight. Always ask for what you want and sometimes, magically, it happens.

Most small hotels do not accept one-night bookings at weekends. Small country hotels are rarely full during the week and the weekend trade keeps them going. If you ring in March for a Saturday night in July, you won't get it. If you ring at the last moment and they have a room, you will. Some places insist on three-night stays on bank holiday weekends.

Booking and cancellation

Most places ask for a deposit at the time of booking, either by cheque or credit/debit card. If you cancel — depending on how much notice you give — you can lose all or part of this deposit unless your room is re-let.

It is reasonable for hotels to take a deposit to secure a booking; they have learnt that if they don't, the commitment of the guest wanes and they may fail to turn up.

Some cancellation policies are more stringent than others. It is also worth noting that some owners will take the money directly from your credit/debit card without contacting you to discuss it. So ask them to explain their cancellation policy clearly before booking so you understand exactly where you stand; it may well avoid a nasty surprise. And consider taking out travel insurance (with a cancellation clause) if you're concerned.

Arrivals and departures

Housekeeping is usually done by 2pm, and your room will usually be available by mid-afternoon. Normally you will have to wave goodbye to it between 10am and 11am. Sometimes one can pay to linger. Some smaller places may be closed between 3pm and 6pm, so do try and agree an arrival time in advance or you may find nobody there.

Smoking

It is now illegal to smoke in public areas and few hotels in this guide permit smoking in bedrooms. Bars, restaurants and sitting rooms have all become smoke-free; smokers must make do with the garden.

Closed

When given in months this means for the whole of the month stated. So, 'Closed: November–March' means closed from 1 November to 31 March.

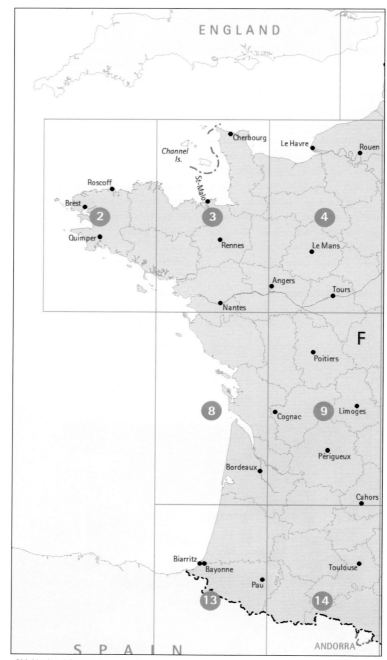

©Maidenhead Cartographic, 2012

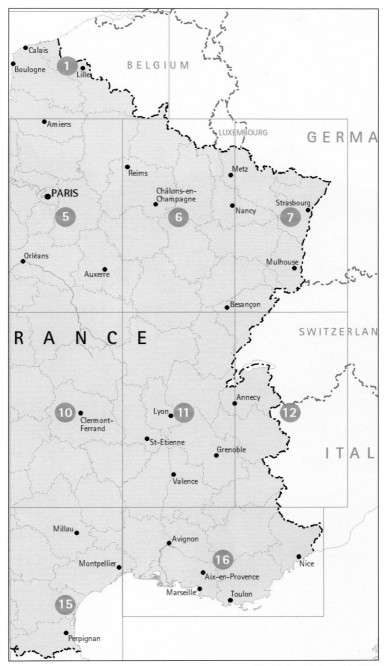

British Hotels & Inns

Dog-friendly Breaks in Britain

Italy
Ed. 7, pub date April 2012

French Bed & Breakfast

Alastair
Sawday's

Special Places to Stay

Seventh edition
Copyright © 2012
Alastair Sawday Publishing Co. Ltd
Published in 2012
ISBN-13: 978-1-906136-55-0

Alastair Sawday Publishing Co. Ltd,
The Old Farmyard, Yanley Lane,
Long Ashton, Bristol BS41 9LR, UK
Tel: +44 (0)1275 395430
Email: info@sawdays.co.uk
Web: www.sawdays.co.uk

The Globe Pequot Press,
P. O. Box 480, Guilford,
Connecticut 06437, USA
Tel: +1 203 458 4500
Email: info@globepequot.com
Web: www.globepequot.com

Series Editor Alastair Sawday
Editorial Angharad Barnes,
Géraldine Roul
Editorial Director Annie Shillito
Content & Production Manager
Jackie King
Senior Editor Jo Boissevain
Production Coordinator Alex Skinner
Writing Alex Baker, Angharad Barnes,
Sarah Baxter, Jo Boissevain,
Ann Cooke-Yarborough, Annaliza Davis,
Monica Guy

Inspections Kate Anderson, Rose Angus,
Richard & Linda Armspach,
Angharad Barnes, Isabelle Browne,
Ann Carisso Haine, Annaliza Davis,
Penny Dinwiddie, Georgina Gabriel,
Monica Guy, Diana Harris-Sawday,
Nikky Hilyer, Rosie Jackson,
Susan Luraschi, Caroline Renouf,
Alex Skinner, Charles Skipwith,
Victoria Thomas, Jo Wilds, Elizabeth Yates
Thanks also to those people who did an
inspection or write-up or two.

Thanks to Ann Cooke-Yarborough for her
invaluable help and support.

Marketing & PR 01275 395433

*We have made every effort to ensure the accuracy
of the information in this book at the time
of going to press. However, we cannot accept
any responsibility for any loss, injury or
inconvenience resulting from the use of
information contained therein.*

Maps: Maidenhead Cartographic Services
Printing: Butler, Tanner & Dennis, Frome
UK distribution: Penguin UK, London
Production: Pagebypage Co. Ltd

Cover photo credits 1. La Maison du Paradou, entry 339 2. Les Moulins de Vontes, FBB entry 361
3. istockphoto.com/mendelewski

Map 1

17

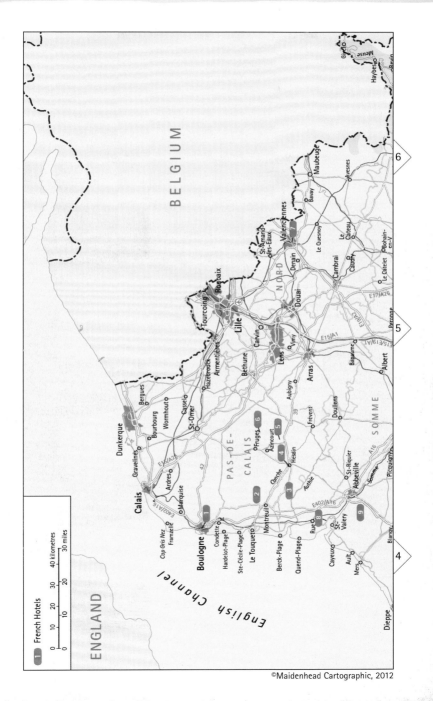

©Maidenhead Cartographic, 2012

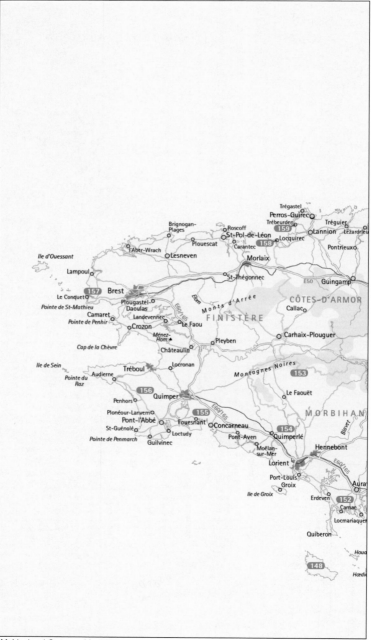

Map 3

19

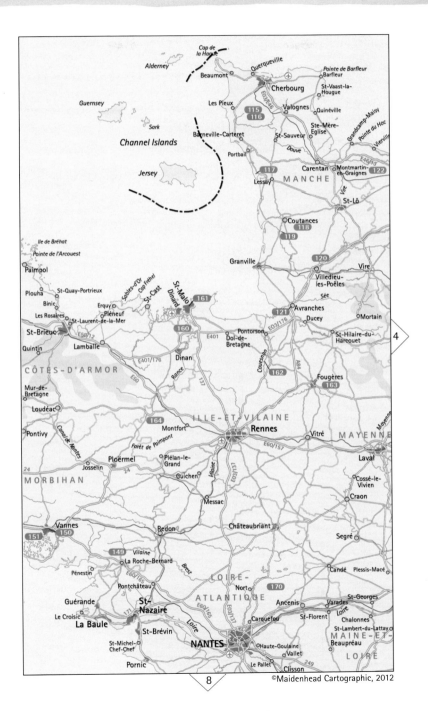

©Maidenhead Cartographic, 2012

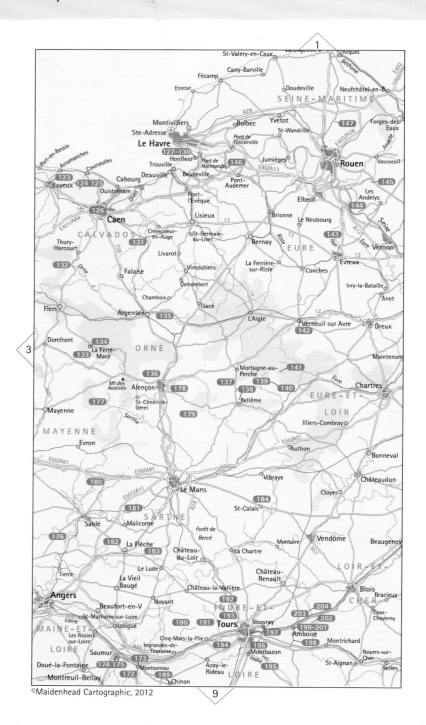

Map 5

21

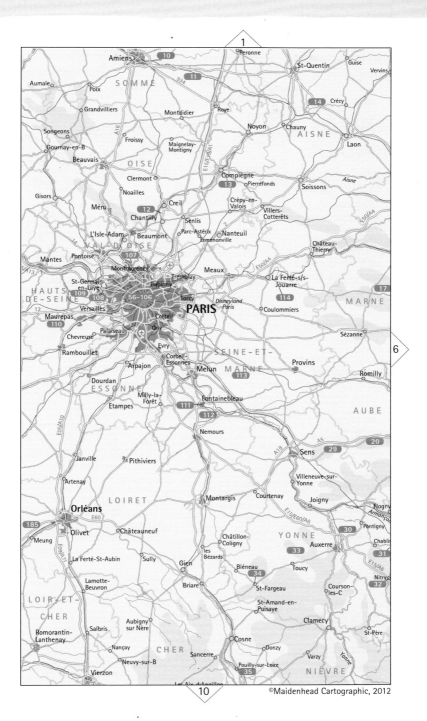

©Maidenhead Cartographic, 2012

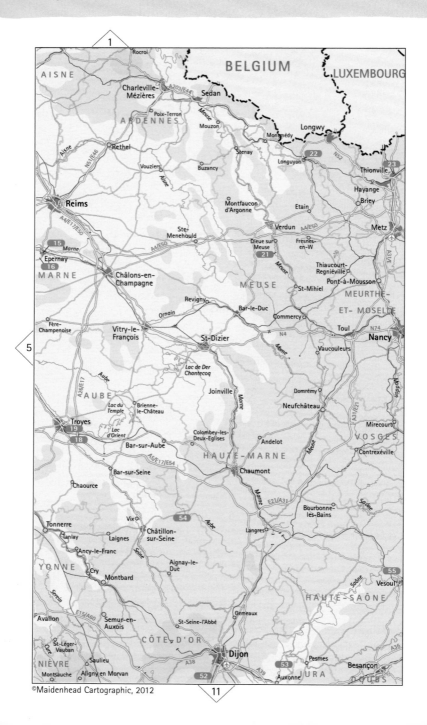

Map 7   23

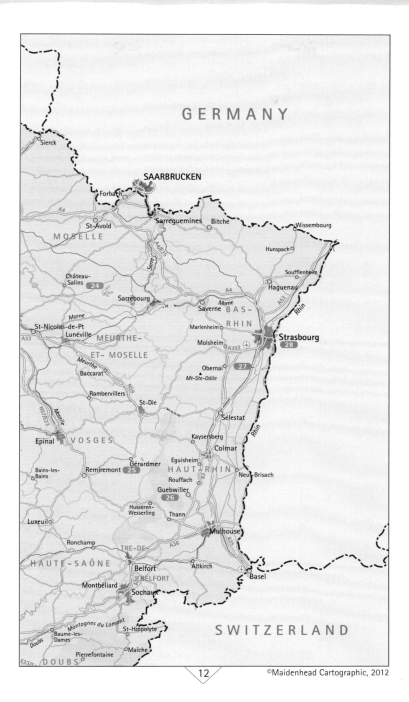

©Maidenhead Cartographic, 2012

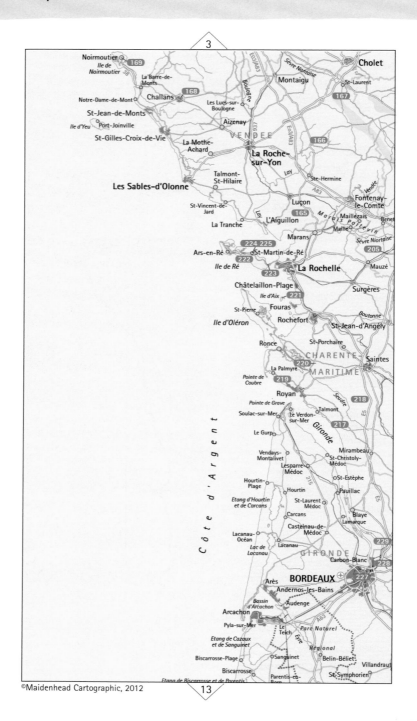

Map 9

25

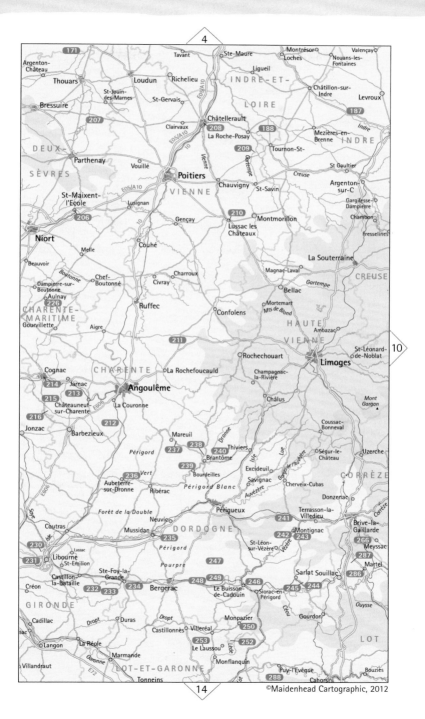

©Maidenhead Cartographic, 2012

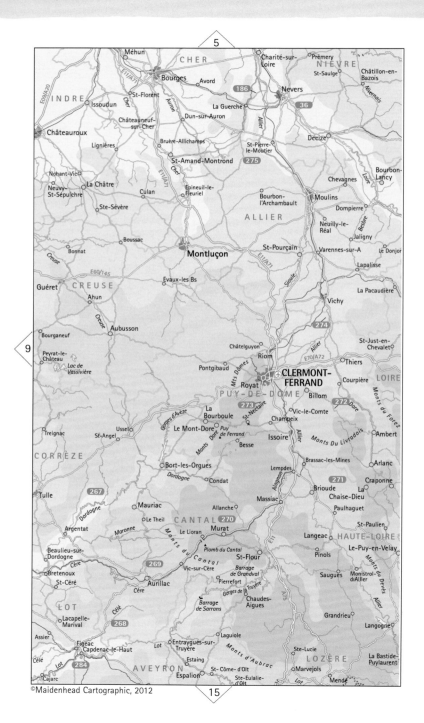

©Maidenhead Cartographic, 2012

Map 11

27

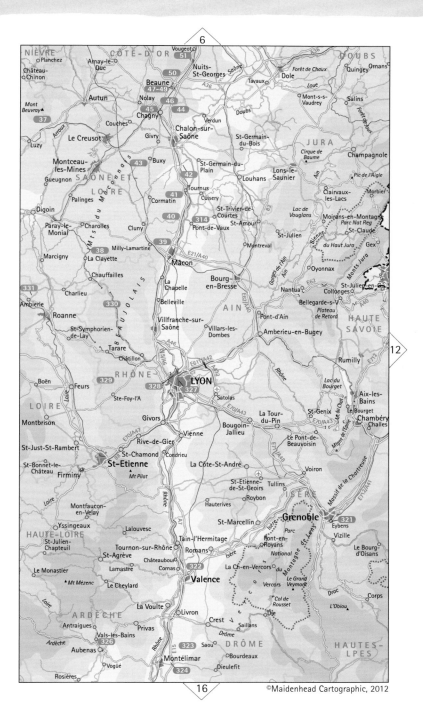

Map 13

29

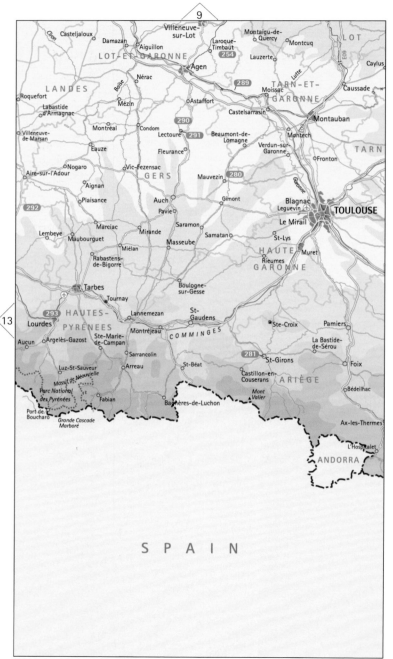

Map 15

31

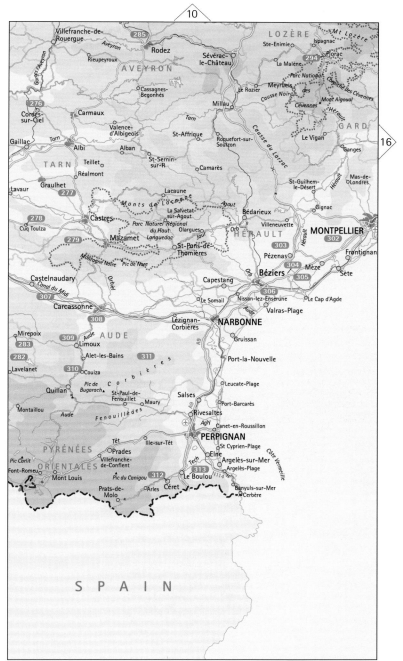

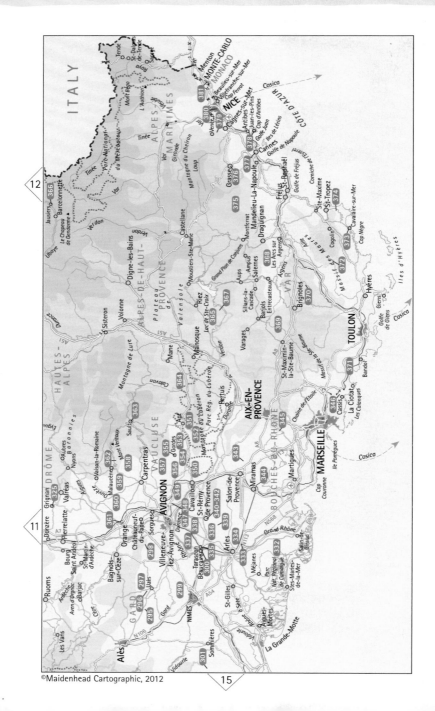

The North, Picardy & Champagne – Ardenne

Terrasses de l'Enclos – L'Enclos de l'Evêché

Up gracious steps you enter the 1850 mansion that almost rubs shoulders with Boulogne's basilica. All is polished parquet and hotel-like perfection, with the personal touch we so like. The charming young staff usher you up a cherry-red stairway to bedrooms above the restaurant or on the first floor of the main house. Each is big, airy, uncluttered and themed according to its name. 'Desvres', named after a porcelain town, is pretty and serene, with white painted furniture and blue toile de Jouy; 'Godefroy de Bouillon' (an 11th-century knight from Boulogne) sports rustic sand-blasted rafters and impeccable limewashed walls. Bathrooms are stocked with toiletries and towels, some have jacuzzis. The restaurant, Les Terrasses de l'Enclos, is a stylish backdrop to a gourmet menu that specialises in fish – and they plan jazz concerts for summer. The busy owners serve in the evening; breakfast is in a salon with immense 19th-century sideboards. There's a suntrapped courtyard, a day room for TV and a choice of tables for breakfast – be as convivial or as peaceful as you like.

Price	€75–€135.
Rooms	5: 2 doubles, 1 twin, 1 single, 1 family room for 4.
Meals	Lunch & dinner €17.20. Wine €20–€40. Restaurant closed Sunday eve & Monday. Book ahead.
Closed	Rarely.
Directions	Follow signs to 'Vieille Ville' & car park 'Enclos de l'Evêché'. House next to car park & cathedral.

Pascaline & Thierry Humez
6 rue de Pressy,
62200 Boulogne sur Mer, Pas-de-Calais

Tel	+33 (0)3 91 90 05 90
Email	contact@enclosdeleveche.com
Web	www.enclosdeleveche.com

Auberge d'Inxent

A sommelier in a restaurant in Lille, Jean-Marc won a Perrier contest on the luck of a draw. Off he tripped with his young wife and two children to a most emerald green valley and claimed a whitewashed, geranium-spilled, 18th-century country inn. Order a trout on the vine-covered terrace and back comes a live one in a bucket from their trout farm across the road by the river. Needless to say Jean-Marc's exceptional wine list and creative use of local produce should lead to a prolonged stay (and the nearby ramparts of Montreuil sur Mer are well worth a visit). Inside: wonky beams and low ceilings, a battery of copper pans behind the old zinc counter, deep green walls in the smaller dining room (our favourite), and all the cosiness of a modest country kitchen with open fires on chilly days. Bedrooms are snug, smallish and beamy, furnished with repro cherrywood antiques and refreshed with modern leather and wicker; bathrooms are spacious and airy. This may not be grand-chic but it's an endearing address: an uncommon treat to find such good food combined with such perfect service.

Price	€70–€76.
Rooms	5: 3 doubles, 2 twins.
Meals	Breakfast €9.50. Lunch & dinner €17–€29.50. Restaurant closes same dates as inn.
Closed	Tues & Wed (Tues only in July & August); 20 December to 30 January; 1st week in July.
Directions	From Boulogne N1 for Samer. After Samer at 5km for Bernieulles, Beussent, Inxent.

	Laurence & Jean-Marc Six 318 rue de la Vallée de la Course, 62170 Inxent, Pas-de-Calais
Tel	+33 (0)3 21 90 71 19
Email	auberge.inxent@wanadoo.fr

Le Manoir

Wrought-iron gates, a gravel drive, a spreading lime tree and afternoon tea on the terrace: heaven. Jennifer (English) and Helmut (German) run their 18th-century manor house with a sense of fun and a brilliant eye. There's space, too, in three reception rooms, big gracious bedrooms and 12 hectares of garden, orchard, potager and field; you can be as private or as jolly as you like. The salons exude an English country-house feel with their deep sofas and cream walls; the dining room, bathed in light from tall windows, furnished with small square tables, is a perfect place for perfect breakfast. As for the bedrooms, all are civilised spaces of subtle lighting and soft carpeting, gorgeous beds and dreamy colours, polished antiques and pretty porcelain. Throw open your elegant windows and the views – of manicured lawns, gravelled drives, dappled paths and countryside – will put a big smile on your face. No evening meals at Le Manoir but there's a wonderful restaurant on the edge of the village, and more in Montreuil. Beyond: beaches, riverside walks and birdwatching in abundance. Delicious in every way.

Price	€140-€150.
Rooms	4: 3 doubles, 1 twin.
Meals	Breakfast €10.
	Restaurants in village & Montreuil.
Closed	2 weeks in June; Christmas.
Directions	From A16 exit 25 for D939 Arras & Hesdin. Exit for Campagne les Hesdin. Look for Gouy St André; right at main x-roads; 1st iron gate on left.

Jennifer & Helmut Gorlich
34 rue Maresquel,
62870 Gouy Saint André,
Pas-de-Calais

Tel	+33 (0)3 21 90 47 22
Email	helmut.gorlich@wanadoo.fr
Web	www.lemanoir-france.com

Les Trois Fontaines

Here is a long, low, plain Scandinavian-style building dressed up to look like a French inn – and succeeding. It fits into the little market town (don't miss the Thursday morning market) as if it had always been there. Arnaud Descamps is friendly, eager to please and has acquired a new chef; we enjoyed an excellent dinner. Now, on warm days, you can have lunch in the garden 'under the apple trees', with an excellently priced 'menu fixe' and a special menu for children. A decked walkway runs along the front of the separate bedroom wings, with good garden furniture for each room. Ten are traditional, with candlewick bedcovers and new walk-in showers. Six are new and no-frills, light, airy, comfortable and decently clad with good-quality pine, good lighting and pristine bed linen. Most pleasing is the garden, especially the long walled and lawned strip, its central gravelled pathway smothered with flowers. This is a very typical small French hotel; peaceful, good value and well placed for cross-Channel visitors, as well as the great beaches of Le Touquet and Berck. A coastline worth discovering.

Price	€61–€74.
Rooms	16: 10 doubles, 6 twins.
Meals	Breakfast €8. Lunch & dinner €15–€37. Wine €15–€55.
Closed	20 December to 5 January.
Directions	Calais to Arras; after Montreuil, N39 for Hesdin. Follow signs to Marconne centre; hotel opp. the town hall.

Arnaud Descamps
16 rue d'Abbeville,
62140 Marconne Hesdin, Pas-de-Calais

Tel	+33 (0)3 21 86 81 65
Email	hotel.3fontaines@wanadoo.fr
Web	www.hotel-les3fontaines.com

La Cour de Rémi

A raved-about bistro, seven delicious suites in the grounds, a romantic treehouse, a fine and tranquil domaine – such are the ingredients for a very spoiling weekend. In the expert hands of Sébastien these terracotta-roofed farm buildings have become informally but fabulously chic. A manger skirts the old stables, a glassed-over brick well glows softly in the three-tier former tack room, floor-to-ceiling glass replaces high barn doors, grain storage attics have become vast beamed spaces with views to both sides, one suite has a jacuzzi, another has two baths side by side… but the cherry on top is surely the four-metre-high treehouse, wrapped spectacularly round a venerable sycamore, with a big decked balcony under the leaves. Breakfast can be delivered to your door as you consider your options: abbeys, châteaux, gardens, WWI sites, a bike ride, seal-spotting by the Somme. Whether you do all of these things or nothing at all, make sure you're back for Sébastien's 'râbles de lapin' (rabbit) or 'colvert rôti' (duck), served in the designer-chic, bistro-friendly dining room. La Cour de Rémi is sublime.

Price	€85–€100. Suites €140–€160. Treehouse €160.
Rooms	10: 6 doubles, 3 suites, 1 treehouse.
Meals	Breakfast €12.50. Dinner €30. Wine €15–€100.
Closed	Christmas.
Directions	From A16 exit 25, D303 dir. Montreuil for 4km; right onto D939 dir. Hesdin & St Pol sur Ternoise; 22km, left onto D98 to Bermicourt; right in village. Signed.

Sébastien de la Borde
1 rue Baillet,
62130 Bermicourt, Pas-de-Calais

Tel	+33 (0)3 21 03 33 33
Email	sebastien@lacourderemi.com
Web	www.lacourderemi.com

Maison de Plumes

Amid the agricultural fields of the Seven Valleys, this deeply rural address is quite urban in its way. In a mansion where General Douglas Haig once slept, wildly funky fabulous interiors now leap out at you – the handiwork of Vanessa who studied art and worked as a clothes designer. Fanning off from soft gold walls and glossy black woodwork, bedrooms – themed after birds and their plumage – are sensationally lavish. Ostrich feathers frame a four-poster in one, the air shimmers with turquoise in another, and 'Parokeet' is suave and handsome, perfect for decadent lie-ins. Each bathroom, luxurious with claw-foot tub and iridescent mosaics, harmonises perfectly with its room. Richard is the main wine and diner, serving breakfast eggs from their own hens on elegant white china and five-course gourmet meals most nights; enjoy a glass of bubbly before tucking into pan-fried duck breast with gratin dauphinois. Outside, a plain white wall awaits forthcoming film projections and a hot tub lies sunken in the ground. Country walks and fishing are nearby, battlefields and coast not much further.

Price	€99–€119.
Rooms	4: 3 doubles, 1 twin/double.
Meals	Breakfast included. Dinner €35 (not Sun,Tues,Thurs). Wine €12.
Closed	Rarely.
Directions	From Calais A26 for Paris exit 4; D351 for Aire sur la Lys 5km; right D94 for Heuchin. At village entrance, house set back from road on right.

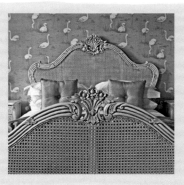

Richard & Vanessa Rhoades-Brown
73 rue d'Aire,
62134 Heuchin, Pas-de-Calais
Tel   +33 (0)3 21 41 47 85
Email   enquire@maisondeplumes.com
Web   www.maisondeplumes.com

Auberge du Bon Fermier

Forget your stilettos, the cobbles in the flowered courtyard continue into the deeply attractive bar and restaurant of this 16th-century island in a rebuilt town. It is a maze of passageways, burnished beams and tiny staircases. A copper washbasin greets you at the top of the stairs leading to the rooms. Looking down from a glassed-in corridor, you can almost hear the clatter of hooves arriving in the courtyard, now a quiet terrace for afternoon tea and snacks; the passengers jostling between Paris and Brussels were probably delighted to be delayed at this bustling staging inn. Bedrooms are all differently quirky, one with tapestried curtains and walls, another with red bricks and wooden struts, some not too well lit, all with baths and bathrobes. There are two larger, lighter ground-floor rooms with post-modern lamps and tables. Downstairs, where a suit of armour guards a wooden reception dais, the evenings sparkle when the main restaurant is lit by candles. Monsieur Beine takes great trouble devising new menus with his chef and most diners would raise a glass in his direction.

Price	€135-€140. Singles €110-€115.
Rooms	16: 14 doubles, 2 singles.
Meals	Breakfast €10.
	Lunch & dinner €26-€52.
Closed	24 December.
Directions	From Cambrai A2 for Brussels, exit Valenciennes centre. Do not leave autoroute before. Continue for Valenciennes centre; signed.

Monsieur Beine
64 rue de Famars,
59300 Valenciennes, Nord

Tel	+33 (0)3 27 46 68 25
Email	beinethierry@hotmail.com
Web	www.bonfermier.com

Château de Noyelles en Baie de Somme

Past ornate iron gates in the village of Noyelles, at the head of the Baie de Somme, a 19th-century château – a pretty gâteau of layered peach and white in splendid gardens. Beyond, a seven-acre landscaped park with box-hedged orchards, neat lawns, rose beds and a terrace scattered with smart parasols. Rooms, some with suite-style connecting doors, are spread spaciously over three floors, with terraces for those on the first. Snug tower rooms on the third flaunt jaunty angles. Pine floors provide funky bases for claw-foot baths. Whites, pearly greys, oyster greens, hazy blues and sand two-toned paintwork and panelling make for sober, sophisticated and TV-free spaces; Chinese antiques and objects d'art – an opium pipe here, a courtesan's fan there – provide delightful detail. Three airy reception rooms and two drawing rooms please the eye with their considered variety: a Starck chair slipped into the classic, plush décor; deep crimson oh-so-comfy sofas set before a handsome marble fireplace. Fabulous seafood and lots to do locally tops everything off perfectly; easy to ignore the rush-hour traffic.

Price	€95–€189. Suites €175–€269.
Rooms	8: 3 doubles, 3 twins/doubles, 2 suites (some interconnect).
Meals	Breakfast €14. Picnic available. Dinner €35, book ahead. Wine €16–€40.
Closed	Rarely.
Directions	From Calais A16 exit 24 for Saint Valéry sur Somme & Le Crotoy; at r'bout D1001 for Abbeville & Forest Montiers; in Nouvion, right onto D111, 5km to village. Château in centre behind high iron gates.

Jean Pierre Boutet
30 rue Maréchal Foch,
80860 Noyelles sur Mer, Somme

Tel   +33 (0)3 22 23 68 70
Email   info@chateaudenoyelles.com
Web   www.chateaudenoyelles.com

Château de Béhen

Donkeys to stroke, bicycles to hire and ponies to ride: horsey folk and families will be in clover. Surrounded by wooded parkland, the red-brick building with a limestone trim started life as a holiday house; later its ground floor was extended. In the 1950s the Cuveliers moved in, adding paddocks and a pond for swans, deeply traditional decoration with strong colours and some ornate oh-so-French flourishes. Today there are seven large bedrooms for guests, with solid oak floors and rugs, bedspreads plain or toile de Jouy, and furniture in Louis XV style. Two-tone panelling graces the first-floor rooms while those above have sloping ceilings and a beam or two. Bathrooms are hotel-perfect with double basins of mottled marble. Norbert-André, who managed stud pacers in Australia, has come home to cook and does a grand job, at one convivial table, or single tables if preferred. Cheeses are local, vegetables are just-picked, banquets can be arranged. Saddle up and enjoy a guided trek – for a day or even two. Lovely friendly people, perfect peace and 15 horses to ride.

Price	€119–€164.
	Suites & family rooms €171–€224.
Rooms	7: 2 doubles, 1 twin, 1 suite for 2,
	1 suite for 4, 2 family rooms for 4.
Meals	Dinner with wine, from €41;
	book 2 days ahead.
Closed	Rarely.
Directions	Calais A16 to Abbeville exit 23; A28 to
	Rouen. Exit 3 Monts Caubert to D928;
	800m, right to Béhen. Behind church,
	200m beyond, on right.

Cuvelier Family
8 rue du Château,
80870 Béhen, Somme

Tel	+33 (0)3 22 31 58 30
Email	norbert-andre@cuvelier.com
Web	www.chateau-de-behen.com

Le Macassar

Le Macassar is named after the rare ebony used in the drawing room panelling — one exquisite example of too many to mention! This gem of a 19th-century house was restyled in the Twenties and Thirties to please a pretty young wife — but it's more 'femme fatale' than blushing belle. Suave bathrooms, extra fine bed linen, feather duvets — only the best. The master suite is the epitome of Art Deco glamour, the ash and bird's-eye maple furniture set off by turquoise velvet walls, a carved stone fireplace and fine contemporary art. Under sloping beams, one wonderfully intimate and sophisticated room is decked in taupe, cocoa and pale blue, its exotic bathroom accessed through an ornate Moorish door. Downstairs are luxurious corners in which to lounge rakishly and admire the gorgeously varied art, the books and the glassware, the textures and the tones. Outside: a flowering Italianate courtyard, a splashing fountain, a haze of lavender. Splendid breakfasts and aperitifs are included in the price, the hosts are truly charming and Amiens is close. An oasis of elegance and calm and in the heart of bustling Corbie.

Price	€175. Suites €195-€250.
Rooms	6: 1 double, 1 twin, 4 suites.
Meals	Hosted dinner with wine, €50 (Sunday evenings only). Groups on request.
Closed	Rarely.
Directions	A16 exit 20 Amiens Nord; after toll, right at r'bout onto ring road (Rocade). Exit 36a Corbie; follow signs to Corbie 'centre ville'. On main square.

Miguel de Lemos
8 place de la République,
80800 Corbie, Somme

Tel	+33 (0)3 22 48 40 04
Email	info@lemacassar.com
Web	www.lemacassar.com

Entry 10   Map 5

Château d'Omiécourt

On a working estate, Omiécourt is a proudly grand 19th-century château and elegant family home (the Thézys have four children, mostly grown now), with tall slender windows and some really old trees. Friendly if formal, communicative and smiling, your hosts have worked hugely to restore their inheritance and create gracious French château guest rooms, each with an ornate fireplace and flooded with light. The 1900 room has a sweep of polished floor and a turn-of-the-century bed, the more modern Chambre des Ormieux sits brightly under the eaves in a separate 'maison'; near the two pools (one outdoor, one in), it comes with a super new blue and white tiled bathroom and a guest kitchen on the ground floor. Enjoy a buffet supper in your room one night – aperitifs, candlelight, champagne – and a Michelin-starred dinner in Roye the next. Breakfast is continental and something of a feast. There's table football and table tennis for the children, a boutique of pretty things and rambling green parkland to explore. A house of goodwill, deeply traditional, naturally hospitable.

Price	€105–€145. Extra bed €30.
Rooms	5: 3 doubles, 1 family room, 1 suite for 3.
Meals	Restaurants 12km.
Closed	Rarely.
Directions	From A1 south for Paris; exit 13 onto D1029 for St Quentin; in Villers Carbonnel right at lights D1017 for 9km to Omiécourt; right in village, château on right.

Dominique & Véronique de Thézy
80320 Omiécourt,
Somme

Tel	+33 (0)3 22 83 01 75
Email	contact@chateau-omiecourt.com
Web	www.chateau-omiecourt.com

Ferme de la Canardière

Forty kilometres north of Paris sits a long house of classic 18th-century stamp. Sabine, a smiling, generous professional cook, is proud of her immaculate guest house. Gleaming polished limestone floors lead to a light, airy sitting room with squashy leather sofas and huge stone fireplace. French windows gaze down the valley. Tucked privately in one corner of the house are two big bright bedrooms that lead directly onto a terrace, narrow lawn and pool. A traditional draped bedhead in pretty putty and white is partnered by splendid horsey curtains and posters of equestrian glories. The twin — rich blue bedcovers, antique cherrywood tables — is elegantly restrained and formal. The new room has its own wee terrace. Bathrooms tiled from top to bottom in blue and white are sybaritic. In the cook's kitchen, where Sabine produces her wonderful breakfasts, you may also book into a cookery master class. Her delightful down-to-earth husband tends the garden and the horses. You are deep in the heart of French racing country: who knows, you may get an insider tip for the French Derby at Chantilly.

Price	€140–€150. Extra bed €25.
Rooms	3: 2 doubles, 1 twin.
Meals	Breakfast included.
	Dinner, 4 courses with wine, €30.
	Restaurants 10-minute walk.
Closed	Rarely.
Directions	From Chantilly N16 for Creil. Leaving Chantilly, cross bridge, 1st left opp. 'Arc de Triomphe' on Rue Guilleminot to viaduct; straight on, house on right above road.

Sabine Choain
20 rue du Viaduc,
60500 Gouvieux Chantilly, Oise

Tel	+33 (0)3 44 62 00 96
Email	contact@fermecanardiere.com
Web	www.fermecanardiere.com

Auberge à la Bonne Idée

Deep in the forest, the ancient walled village is worth a visit and the Bonne Idée is where Parisians and Belgians come to escape from city madness, knowing they will find a sound welcome, country peace and superb food. The inn, a fabulous hulk of a building that was once a woodcutters' place, still has masses of its old timber and tiling. Start with a drink by the fire in the bar, move to an elegant table in the dining room where bread warms by the great hearth, and delve into a fine, gourmet meal. The emphasis is on food – and in summer there's a shaded terrace, flower-filled garden and space for children to play. The owners have renovated most of the bedrooms, four in the main house, the rest in the former stables, in a mixture of shabby-chic and brazen-contemporary with some striking surprises – low-hung art-deco crystal chandeliers in beaded glass serving as bedside lights; gold painted, wood-framed, purple-upholstered Louis XV chairs – and luxy design-conscious bathrooms. Ideal for walking, cycling, riding and relaxing; Compiègne and the great castle of Pierrefonds are close.

Price	€90–€100. Apartments €140–€165.
Rooms	23: 9 doubles, 9 twins, 5 suites.
Meals	Breakfast €14. Lunch & dinner €33–€79. Restaurant closes same dates as hotel.
Closed	Sundays evenings & Monday. January.
Directions	A1 exit 9 Verberie & Compiègne. Through Verberie, left on D332 for Compiègne for 5km; right on D85 for St Jean aux Bois.

Yves Giustiniani
3 rue des Meuniers,
60350 Saint Jean aux Bois, Oise

Tel	+33 (0)3 44 42 84 09
Email	a-la-bonne-idee.auberge@wanadoo.fr
Web	www.a-la-bonne-idee.fr

Domaine Le Parc

Down a tree-lined drive between tailored lawns you approach this 18th-century mansion built on castle foundations, now a family-run hotel. The river Oise slides gently by. There are ten lawned, tree'd and statued acres here and, at the back, a brick-walled belvedere terrace with soaring views over woodland, untamed countryside and river. Inside, wander at will between a gracefully decorated dining room, breakfast room and library, and a sitting room with gorgeous soft sofas. Up the spiral oak staircase are the bedrooms, classically and elegantly decorated, some with more of those views. Strong colours with floral fabrics stand out against striped or patterned fabric walls; luxurious bathrooms have jacuzzi baths; clusters of antique bottles on the window ledges and an antique hobby horse add whimsical touches to a formal décor. Dutch Jos has previously won Michelin stars for his cooking, Anne is a former maître d'hôtel, both are efficient, consummate, multi-lingual hosts, and you dine on the terrace in summer. Don't miss the fortified churches and great Gothic cathedrals. *No credit cards.*

Price	€75–€95.
Rooms	5: 3 doubles, 2 twins.
Meals	Dinner (set menu), with wine, €38.
Closed	20 December to 5 January.
Directions	Between Saint-Quentin and Laon; A26 exit 12; in Dainzy 2nd right.

	Jos & Anne Bergman
	Rue de Quesny,
	02800 Danizy, Aisne
Tel	+33 (0)3 23 56 55 23
Email	contact@domaineleparc.fr
Web	www.domaineleparc.com

La Villa Eugène

Surrounded by other 19th-century mansions, the former house of champagne magnate Eugène Mercier still feels remarkably like a family home. Indeed, the old family photos still line the staircase and the staff can tell you exactly which room belonged to whom. Then there's the décor, an enticing balance of traditional French with contemporary touches: walls the colour of whipped cream, furniture Louis XVI or 'colonial' (dark wood and wicker), soft yielding curtains, gracious parquet floors. There's modernity in flat-screens and WiFi, pampering in the bathrooms – all a good size – with fluffy towels and luxurious products by Damana; it earns the four stars of which the owner is so proud. The buffet breakfast is an array of homemade cakes, tarts, yogurts and breads, served in the light-filled conservatory – whose mosaic floor has been lovingly restored – or in the garden with its heated summer pool, colourful beds and resident lawn-hopping rabbits. Just 30 minutes from Reims and its mesmerising cathedral, a wonderful launch pad for the three major Routes de Champagne. Then return to the luxurious cocoon that is the bar.

Price	€129–€344. Extra bed €25.
Rooms	15 twins/doubles.
Meals	Breakfast €17. Restaurants 2km.
Closed	Never.
Directions	From Paris take A4 east, follow signs to Épernay.

Agnès Rafik
82-84 avenue de Champagne,
51200 Épernay, Marne

Tel	+33 (0)3 26 32 44 76
Email	info@villa-eugene.com
Web	www.villa-eugene.com

Château Les Aulnois

Among gracious chandeliers and panelled rooms you can just imagine the inhabitants of old in their 18th-century finery. Over 20 original – circa 1780 – château windows remain, gazing over topiary cones and preened gardens, gently sloping hills and acres of vines. Each bedroom has something special – extra space or central views, a private terrace, an alcove sofa; each has a motif that reaches meticulously across wallpaper, bedspreads and Marie-Antoinette chairs. All is enhanced by leather-topped bureaus, elaborate silver mirrors and dreamily opulent dressing-room bathrooms. Your refined hostess Madame Vollereaux adores cooking for her guests; idyllic breakfasts include omelettes of local eggs, homemade quiches, smoked salmon and organic coffee. Later, gather round the expansive table for mouthwatering dinners featuring her own herbs and vegetables and a different champagne for each course. Visit the vast 1700s grape press outside, venture to Épernay market or the wartime sites of Verdun and Amiens, and make the most of the sweeping landscapes: choose between leisurely walks and vineyard tours.

Price	€150-€340.
Rooms	5: 2 twins/doubles, 3 suites.
Meals	Breakfast included. Dinner €45. Gourmet dinner for 4, €125. Restaurant 10-minute walk.
Closed	Rarely.
Directions	Sent on booking.

Élisabeth Vollereaux
61 rue du Général de Gaulle,
51530 Pierry, Marne

Tel	+33 (0)3 26 54 27 23
Email	contact@chateau-les-aulnois.fr
Web	www.chateau-les-aulnois.fr

Château d'Étoges

Étoges, used as a stopover by French kings on journeys east, is a moated 17th-century château: through the wrought-iron gates then over the footbridge to a little island fortress, later transformed into a hotel by the family who have lived here for generations. The grounds are lovely, too, with their fountains, lawns and ponds. It is, indeed, fit for a king, from the fully French rooms with their delicious fabrics and linen to the elegant food with its home-grown veg. Opulent bedrooms glow with antiques and fresh flowers, some have four-posters and two have mezzanine beds over bathrooms; rooms in the orangery have less character. The handsome restaurant, also in the orangery, has a majestic fireplace and, fittingly, deep orange curtains. If you fancy breakfast in bed, smart staff will bring it to your lace-covered table: breads, croissants, jams, fruit. If you prefer to breakfast downstairs, take your pick from the buffet and drift onto the terrace. This intimate hotel is right in the middle of champagne-growing country; easy for cycling and fishing, too, with a well-stocked lake a ten-minute drive.

Price	€140–€200. Suites €300.
Rooms	28: 26 twins/doubles, 2 suites.
Meals	Breakfast €14. Lunch & dinner €35–€75. Wine €20–€200. Children's meals €18.
Closed	23 January to 9 February.
Directions	From Paris A4 exit 18 at Ferté sous Jouarre, follow signs for Chalons en Champagne. Château in centre of Étoges.

Anne Filliette-Neuville
4 rue Richebourg,
51270 Étoges, Marne
Tel   +33 (0)3 26 59 30 08
Email   contact@etoges.com
Web   www.etoges.com

La Maison de Rhodes

An exceptional place, this 16th-century mansion stands on Templar foundations. Thierry's breathtaking renovation has brought a clean contemporary finish to ancient bricks and mortar. Highlights include a courtyard of cobble and grass and heavy wooden doors under the coachman's porch onto the street. The house sits bang in the old quarter of Troyes, on the doorstep of the cathedral. Bedrooms are jaw-droppers – the best in minimalist luxury, huge beds are dressed in white linen, ancient beams straddling ceilings, walls of exposed rough stone, or smooth limestone, or a clever mix. Bathrooms, too, are outstanding, most of them enormous, and have terracotta floors, big bath tubs, fluffy robes. Views are to the courtyard or the formal gardens of the Museum of Modern Art opposite. A perfect blend of old and new, this is an exhilarating architectural landscape. Chef René makes meticulous use of organic and local ingredients – for 12 maximum. Troyes is full of wonders, though the bibulous may be tempted to venture beyond the city walls: the region is quite well known for its local tipple – champagne.

Price	€172-€218. Suites €235-€290.
Rooms	11: 7 doubles, 4 suites for 2-4.
Meals	Breakfast €18. Dinner €30-€50. Restaurant closed Sundays.
Closed	Never.
Directions	In centre of Troyes, at the foot of the cathedral, on the south side.

Thierry Carcassin
18 rue Linard-Gonthier,
10000 Troyes, Aube

Tel	+33 (0)3 25 43 11 11
Email	message@maisonderhodes.com
Web	www.maisonderhodes.com

Hôtel Champ des Oiseaux

Only the Museum of Modern Art stands between the cathedral and this amazingly pure group of 15th-century houses in the centre of lovely, unsung Troyes. The dazzling timbers, beams and rafters inside and out, the simplicity of the beautifully jointed stone paving, the wooden floors, the softly luminous natural materials, all will seduce you. The owners had their restoration done by craftsmen who knew the ancestral methods and made it look 'as good as 1460 new': Corridors twist round the creeper-climbed courtyard and the little internal garden, staircases change their minds, the place is alive with its centuries. Each bedroom has a personality, some soberly sandy and brown, others frivolously floral; they vary in size and status but all are warmly discreet in their luxury and good furniture. Bathrooms are perfect modern boudoirs. The unexpected salon, a long, white barrel vault of ancient stones, the original stonemason's craft lovingly revealed, was once a cellar, and the courtyard is delightful for breakfast. The Boisseau family can be justifiably proud of their contribution to medieval Troyes.

Price	€150–€190. Suites €240.
Rooms	12: 9 twins/doubles, 3 suites for 2-4.
Meals	Breakfast €17. Restaurants nearby.
Closed	Rarely.
Directions	In centre of Troyes, very close to cathedral.

Madame Boisseau
20 rue Linard Gonthier,
10000 Troyes, Aube

Tel	+33 (0)3 25 80 58 50
Email	message@champdesoiseaux.com
Web	www.champdesoiseaux.com

Domaine du Moulin d'Eguebaude

The secluded old buildings house two owner families, a restaurant, several guest rooms and 15 tons of ever-present live fish. Fishing folk gather on Sundays to catch trout in the spring water that feeds the ponds; groups come for speciality lunches. Meals may include trout terrine, home-reared salmon, a neighbour's potatoes, wild asparagus in buttery sauce, cinnamon custard. For breakfast round the big table there's brioche, baguette, croissants, yogurt, fruit salad, cereals, apple juice and their own jams and honey. Created in an old mill 40 years ago, the bedrooms under the eaves are mostly small-windowed, simply furnished and prettily decorated in rustic or 'grandmother' style. Other rooms are in the newly built half-timbered cottage across the drive. At one end of the shop – packed with cottage-industry goodies (charcuterie, honey, jams, wine and champagne) is a wide floor of thick glass under which immense fish can be seen swimming to and fro between the water tanks. A pony wanders freely in the grounds. Wonderful food and service – and good English spoken. *No credit cards.*

Price	€71–€76.
Rooms	6: 2 doubles, 1 twin, 1 triple, 2 family rooms.
Meals	Dinner with wine, €25. Guest kitchen.
Closed	Christmas, New Year & occasionally.
Directions	From Paris A5 exit 19 on N60 to Estissac; right Rue Pierre Brossolette; mill at end of lane, 1km.

Alexandre & Sandrine Mesley
36 rue Pierre Brossolette,
10190 Estissac, Aube
Tel   +33 (0)3 25 40 42 18
Email   eguebaude@aol.com
Web   www.moulineguebaude.fr

Ethical Collection: Food.
See page 429 for details

Lorraine & Alsace

Hostellerie du Château des Monthairons

If you seek peace and quiet in lovely large grounds, or a spot of fishing maybe – the river Meuse meanders through – this would be a good, utterly French, choice. Monthairons served as an American military hospital in the First World War and become a base for the Germans in the Second. It is now run by three offshoots of the Thouvenin family, who did a major refurbishment in the Eighties. One couple looks after the restaurant and food, the other two are in charge of the hotel and grounds. Because of this personal touch, there's a homely feel in spite of the proportions. Bedrooms are smart, classic French and come in all sizes, some with duplex suites ideal for families; we'd love a room facing the park. The restaurant is elegant and full of flowers, a place for a fancy dinner not a quick bite. You can swim and canoe here, too; a former owner diverted the river especially and the neighbouring meadow is now known as the 'old river'. Organised activities? They do several packages including introductions to fly-fishing, rides in a horse-drawn carriages, visits to Verdun. Return to be spoiled in the spa.

Price	€100–€165. Duplexes & suites €165–€210. Apts €260–€345.
Rooms	25: 12 doubles, 6 twins, 5 duplexes for 2-4, 2 apts for 2-4.
Meals	Breakfast €14–€15. Lunch €25, weekdays only. Dinner €40–€92. Wine €44–€96.
Closed	January to 11 February.
Directions	From Paris A4 exit 30 Voie Sacrée; for St Mihiel to Lemmes. At end of Lemmes, last road on left. Cont. to Ancemont; at last x-roads right to the château.

	Madame Pierrat
	26 route de Verdun,
	Le Petit Monthairon,
	55320 Les Monthairons, Meuse
Tel	+33 (0)3 29 87 78 55
Email	accueil@chateaudesmonthairons.fr
Web	www.chateaudesmonthairons.fr

Lorraine

Le Mas & La Lorraine

Not a luxurious address – as is reflected in the room prices – but a proud one, and solidly French. The hotel is a nostalgic reminder of a lost era – the great days of steam. Built in 1925, it stands across the square from the station; the Italian Express used to stop here. These days it is more of a restaurant with rooms, with the emphasis on the food. Owner chef Gérard Tisserant is a fine old gentleman, proud of a lifetime of catering in fine food, doing receptions, continuing culinary traditions, who still runs his kitchens and staff *à l'ancienne*... and his cheese board astonishes: 60 cheeses. Course after course flies at you: scallops, foie gras, fillet of veal, pineapple gratin with coconut cream, in a big room that is warmly inviting and where an open fire crackles in winter. Now and then live music nights are held and you dine to the accompaniment of classical guitar or jazz piano. Downstairs: off-white armchairs and huge bay windows in the sitting room; upstairs: old-style bedrooms that are clean and functional, suitable for a stopover. Belgium and Luxembourg are close – take the train!

Price	€65–€74.
Rooms	14: 5 doubles, 6 twins, 2 family rooms for 4, 1 triple.
Meals	Breakfast €10. Lunch & dinner €23–€72.
Closed	January.
Directions	From A4 exit 30 onto D603 then D618 to Longuyon. Hotel opp. railway station.

Gérard Tisserant
65 rue Augistrou,
54260 Longuyon, Meurthe-et-Moselle

Tel	+33 (0)3 82 26 50 07
Email	mas.lorraine@orange.fr
Web	www.lorraineetmas.com

L'Horizon

The house was only built in 1950 but its arcading anchors it and virginia creeper has snaked all over it, clothing its façade in lively warm character. Here is comfortable living in graceful surroundings, as in an elegant private house. A huge terrace envelops the ground floor; from here, from the restaurant (smart décor, excellent food) and from some of the balcony rooms on the first floor you have plunging views over Thionville and an astounding, glittering cityscape at night (the town is less pretty by day). Despite the surprising hall, with its marbled flooring and dramatic tented ceiling, the bedrooms are classic French chic (though carpets may be a little worn here and there and some rooms are smaller than others). Bathrooms border on the luxurious, some are positively glamorous. Above all, you will warm to your charming hosts; Madame is on hand with a happy welcome while Monsieur is in command of the kitchen. The area is steeped in Second World War history: this is Maginot Line country and Thionville is on the Liberty Road that is marked every kilometre from Cherbourg in Normandy to Bastogne in Belgium.

Price	€98–€145.
Rooms	12 doubles.
Meals	Breakfast €11.
	Lunch & dinner €39–€53.
	Restaurant closed Saturdays &
	Monday lunchtimes.
Closed	January.
Directions	From A31 exit 40 Thionville. Follow signs for Bel Air Hospital north of town. At hospital left up hill leaving town. Hotel 400m on left.

Jean-Pascal & Anne-Marie Speck
50 route du Crève-Cœur,
57100 Thionville, Moselle

Tel	+33 (0)3 82 88 53 65
Email	hotel@lhorizon.fr
Web	www.lhorizon.fr

Château d'Alteville

Within exploring distance of Strasbourg, Nancy and Metz, the château has more than a whiff of history. It was built for one of Napoleon's generals and the two paintings that hang in the Louis XVI salon were gifts from the Emperor. David's family has farmed here for five generations; now he and Agnieszka welcome guests with huge kindness and eco-awareness. Bedrooms are authentically French and solidly traditional, with carved armoires, Voltaire armchairs, perhaps a draped bedhead or a small chandelier. Parkland views float in through the windows and bathrooms have recently been updated. Downstairs is more stylish: a library/billiard room, a many-windowed salon hung with portraits, a majestic dining room where splendid candlelit dinners are served several nights a week in the company of your lively, interesting hosts (book ahead). Laze on the terrace at the back, admiring the château grounds, or pull on your hiking boots and follow your nose through the woods and round the ponds. Agnieszka fills the place with children and flowers. It's homely, well priced and definitely special. *No credit cards.*

Price	€68–€91.
Rooms	5: 4 doubles, 1 twin.
Meals	Breakfast included.
	Dinner €31–€38.50 by reservation.
	Wine €5–€15.
Closed	Mid-October to mid-April.
Directions	From Nancy N74 for Sarreguemines & Château Salins. At Burthecourt x-roads, D38 to Dieuze; D999 south 5km; left on D199F; right D199G to château.

Ethical Collection: Environment;
Community; Food. See page 429 for details

David & Agnieszka Barthélémy
Tarquimpol,
57260 Dieuze, Moselle
Tel +33 (0)3 87 05 46 63
Mobile +33 (0)6 72 07 56 05
Email chateau.alteville@free.fr

Entry 24 Map 7

Hotel

Hotel

Lorraine

Auberge de la Poulcière

Come in April and you'll find yourself in a sea of wild daffodils. The area is famous for them and Gerardmer's annual Fête des Jonquilles lures plenty of visitors. The auberge, a 1775 farmhouse, stands at 800m and has been simply and delightfully renovated, with a brand new façade. Friendly Madame, an English teacher, ensures that each of the suites has comfort and space; bright bedspreads and old painted wardrobes contrast with dark stone floors, bathrooms have Italian showers and a luxurious feel, and every suite has a kitchenette. Best of all, generous windows open to captivating views. You get your own outside sitting area, too – a wooden balcony or a generous slice of the decked terrace. This is skiing country and you can walk or ski straight from the house. As for Gérardmer, it buzzes with entertainments on and off the lake and prides in having the oldest tourist office in France. The famous Jardin de Berchigranges is nearby. Return at the end of a busy day for dinner: the restaurant is, by all accounts, excellent, and promises a rich 'menu gastronomique'.

Price	€90. €110 for 3. Half-board €75 p.p.
Rooms	6 suites: 5 for 2, 1 for 3, all with kitchenette.
Meals	Breakfast €9. Dinner €27-€39. Wine €12-€60.
Closed	20 October; 25 December.
Directions	From Gérardmer D486 dir. La Bresse. After Rochesson/La Bresse intersection stay on D486; left after 150m, then immediately right. Signed.

Jocelyne & Michel Bouguerne-Arnould
10 chemin du Bouchot,
88400 Gérardmer, Vosges

Tel	+33 (0)3 29 42 04 33
Email	contact@auberge-poulciere.com
Web	www.auberge-poulciere.com

Le Saint Barnabé – Hotel & Spa

At the top of its quiet valley, under the guidance of attentive and efficient owners, the whole hotel now has a modern, elegant feel: gone are the traditional Alsatian frills. Food is important here, and good. Éric is the chef. Trained with France's best and chef at Château d'Isenbourg for some years, he uses local, biodynamically-grown ingredients whenever he can. Clémence does the colourful garden and can also advise on what to do between the Vosges hills and the Alsace plain: there are typical villages and wine-growers to visit, excellent hiking, bike rides and good fishing places (they also have mini-golf on the spot, and a spa). The ferny woods are full of paths and burbling brooks and there's skiing in season. Rooms, quietly elegant and comfortable, are of two kinds: in the main house they are big with smashing bathrooms and the odd balcony; in the separate building behind, they are smaller, with a shower each – and cheaper! A great place for nature lovers and gourmets, the Saint Barnabé is fabulously quiet – bar the birdsong – and carefully eco-friendly. *Ask about wellness centre.*

Price	€98–€165.
Rooms	26 twins/doubles.
Meals	Lunch €16.80, Monday-Friday. Picnic on request. Dinner €29.80–€75. Restaurant closed 1 week in July.
Closed	3 days at Christmas; January.
Directions	From N83 (between Belfort & Colmar) D430 for Guebwiller & Lautenbach. D429 for Buhl then Murbach. Hotel on left.

Clémence & Éric Orban
53 rue de Murbach,
68530 Murbach, Haut-Rhin

Tel	+33 (0)3 89 62 14 14
Email	hostellerie.st.barnabe@wanadoo.fr
Web	www.le-stbarnabe.com

Hôtel à la Ferme – L'Aigle d'Or

In a simple, colourful Alsatian village, this typical old farm is framed by shrubs, roses, manicured hedges and a pretty brick terrace. The welcome from the family, who have been here for generations, is as gracious as the setting. Bedrooms, in the main house or converted outbuilding, are splendid: a good size and comfortable, they have polished floorboards, oriental rugs and fine beds, one carved in Alsatian style. In the new, exquisitely decorated stable suites you'll find timber balconies, wonderful fabrics and an even greater sense of luxury. Here, too, are the spanking new Aigle d'Or restaurant and the breakfast room, where Jean-Philippe's delicious brioches and pastries are served. His father mans the bar, his mother and grandmother help in the kitchen, Brigitte meets and greets, Jean-Philippe is master chef and the food is outstanding. Chalked up on the board are escargots, foie gras, asparagus in season, choucroute, tarte flambée, apfelstrudel. Then retire to the wainscotted guest salon, warmed by a fine ceramic stove. A superb place run by a family that is professional, enthusiastic, endearing.

Price	€84–€200. Suites €114–€118.
Rooms	12: 9 doubles, 3 suites.
Meals	Breakfast €14.50. Lunch & dinner €32–€78 (except Monday eve & Tuesdays). Wine €25.
Closed	Rarely.
Directions	From Strasbourg A35 south, exit N83 dir. Colmar; 14km exit Erstein. Immediately right; 2km; right onto D288 for Osthouse. Signed in village.

Jean-Philippe & Brigitte Hellmann
10 rue du Château,
67150 Osthouse, Bas-Rhin

Tel	+33 (0)3 90 29 92 50
Email	info@hotelalaferme.com
Web	www.hotelalaferme.com

Hôtel du Dragon

At the hub of old Strasbourg, looking over river and cathedral, the Dragon is solidly 17th century on the outside, temperately 20th century within. Built as a private mansion – Louis XIV stayed on his way to visit Marie-Antoinette in Austria – it became a hotel in the 1990s. The peaceful little courtyard received a classically pedimented porch and potted shrubs: a pretty place for an evening drink. They took a deeply contemporary approach inside – it is sober, minimalist-stylish and extraordinarily restful. Variegated grey and white are the basics: mushroom curtains on white walls, superb grey pinstripe carpeting, an arresting pattern of grey and white tiles in the bathrooms, muted mauve bedcovers for a dash of colour, and some good abstract paintings and sculptures here and there, displayed to great advantage. Some have river views and others see the cathedral's lovely spire. After 20 years as a mountain guide, Monsieur Zimmer returned to his native Strasbourg and has made the Dragon as welcoming as it is elegant. He is quiet and gentle and has a predilection for English-speaking guests.

Price	€79–€145. Apartments €174.
Rooms	32: 30 twins/doubles, 2 apartments for 4 (without kitchen).
Meals	Breakfast €12. Restaurants within walking distance.
Closed	Rarely.
Directions	Across river from Petite France, off Quai St Nicolas.

Jean Zimmer
2 rue de l'Ecarlate,
67000 Strasbourg, Bas-Rhin
Tel   +33 (0)3 88 35 79 80
Email   hotel@dragon.fr
Web   www.dragon.fr

Burgundy & Franche Comté

Auberge des Vieux Moulins Banaux

Take a 16th-century mill straddling a rushing stream (yet minutes from a motorway), new owners, revamped bedrooms and astonishingly good food: a recipe for success in an auberge in Burgundy. There's still carpeting on the corridor walls but the updating is almost done, so expect streamlined comfort and state-of-the-art bathrooms. The revamped bedrooms come with a corporate touch and contemporary baroque flourishes; most have showers, one has a double bath; all have proper hotelly extras. Chef-patron Christophe continues the auberge's tradition of great food, served in an impressive dining room dominated by beams and the old mill wheel. Tuck into fresh or grilled oysters, snails with parsley butter, stuffed rabbit with risotto, grilled veal kidney with béarnaise, poached quince and pineapple with spices – French country cooking at its best. Enjoy a summer breakfast on the great dining terrace overlooking the sprawling garden and river, then try your hand at boules – or walk off lunch on the trail nearby. You are near the chablis vineyards, and you can buy the wines here.

Price	€52–€72.
Rooms	14: 11 doubles, 3 suites.
Meals	Breakfast €9.50.
	Lunch & dinner €16–€42.
	Wine €25–€60. Restaurant closed Monday lunchtimes.
Closed	1 week at Christmas.
Directions	A5 exit 19 Villeneuve l'Archevêque; signed.

Priscila & Christophe de Clercq
18 route des Moulins Banaux,
89190 Villeneuve l'Archêveque, Yonne

Tel	+33 (0)3 86 86 72 55
Email	contact@bourgognehotels.fr
Web	www.bourgognehotels.fr

Château de la Resle

Built for a dignitary who lost his head in the French Revolution, this handsome house sits on an impeccable estate of landscaped gardens, neat, gravelled, lavender-lined paths, plus *orangerie*, pond and hornbeam maze. Johan and Pieter, your smiley, engaging, humorous hosts, came from Holland several years ago and have made everything elegant, modern and stylish. A fine stone staircase with a wrought-iron banister leads to spacious, minimally furnished rooms painted in muted hues of moss and deep-blue; views ponder over the gardens to hilly horizons, and fabulous modern art hangs on the walls. A further huge suite with a fine dressing area lies under dramatic roof carpentry in a cottage outside. Bathrooms are spotless white with state-of-the art showers, pale pebble floors, beautiful accessories and chunky towels. Tuck into breakfast in the vast dining room with its dark walls and limestone flags, then work it off in the first-floor fitness room. Or set off for the vineyards and the wine tastings, the pretty villages with their ancient half-timbered houses, the walks and the cycle rides. Fabulous in every way.

Price	€225–€350.
Rooms	4: 1 double, 1 twin/double, 1 suite for 2-4, 1 cottage suite for 2-4.
Meals	Breakfast included. Restaurant 2km.
Closed	Mid-November to mid-April.
Directions	A6 dir. Lyon exit 19 Auxerre; N77 dir. Pontigny to Montigny-la-Resle; right in centre opp. restaurant 'Le Soleil d'Or'; on for 2km.

	Johan Bouman & Pieter Franssens
	89230 Montigny la Resle, Yonne
Mobile	+33 (0)6 86 11 29 22
Email	info@chateaudelaresle.com
Web	www.chateaudelaresle.com

Château de Béru

Château life as you'd dream it: noble arches, exposed stonework and shuttered windows that survey glorious miles of vineyards. It's a place that transports you to another era, yet the well-worn choice antiques and tasselled tie-backs harmonise with modern backdrops of plum purple, flowery chintz and bold monochrome. Home to the Comtes de Béru since 1627, the history goes back to the 12th century and includes a working vineyard – a delectable extra as you can tour the cellars. You can also wander the château, where the legacy of lost years is tangible: Joan of Arc once passed through the foothills and Louis XIV's great-grandson stayed here. There's an exquisite contemporary simplicity to the guest bedrooms, with their raw brickwork and pretty fabrics, fresh linens, generous beds and chic bathrooms; we loved 'Havane'. Have breakfast in the sitting-dining room, by the pool, or in bed; you'll like Madame Béru's homemade jams. You are in one of Chablis' prettiest valleys where there are heaps of abbeys to visit and shops to plunder… but you'll most probably stay put, it's such an enchanting spot.

Price	€130-€150.
Rooms	4: 3 doubles, 1 suite for 3-4.
Meals	Dinner €30. Wine €12-€22. Restaurant 7km.
Closed	Rarely.
Directions	Sent on booking.

Laurence de Béru
32 Grande Rue, 89700 Béru, Yonne
Tel   +33 (0)3 86 75 90 43
Email   contact@chateaudeberu.com
Web   www.chateaudeberu.com

Hôtel de la Beursaudière

Monsieur Lenoble's attention to detail is staggering. Not content with creating a buzzing, cheerful restaurant he has lovingly transformed a priory and farm buildings – stables, dovecotes, stone structures on varied levels, wooden verandas topped with red-patterned Burgundian roof tiles – into a very seductive hotel. Each bedroom has a trade for a theme: a typewriter and old books for the 'writer'; antique irons for the 'laundress'; horse and ox collars for the 'ploughman'; vine-decorated wooden panels for the 'wine-grower'. The walls have been lightly skimmed in plaster in natural shades of ochre, pigeon-egg grey or light yellow. Floors are terracotta or flagstone, stone walls are painted, rafters exposed and windows round or cottage square with curtains of vintage linens and lace. Beds are king-size, mattresses are excellent and TVs are hidden in antique cabinets. Most bathrooms are open plan so as not to detract from the beams and volumes. There is even a sheltered sun lounge on the terrace only overlooked by sparrows. A nice place to sit and sample your chilled choice picked up in Chablis.

Price	€80–€120.
Rooms	11: 6 doubles, 5 twins.
Meals	Breakfast €10.
	Lunch & dinner €20.50–€43.50.
	Wine €15–€100.
Closed	Last 3 weeks January.
Directions	A6 exit 21 Nitry; right to Nitry for 500m. Left at church to Vermenton for 200m. Signed.

Monsieur & Madame Lenoble
5-7 rue Hyacinthe Gautherin,
89310 Nitry, Yonne

Tel	+33 (0)3 86 33 69 70
Email	message@beursaudiere.com
Web	www.beursaudiere.com

Petit Manoir des Bruyères

Fruit trees, roses galore, aviaries of canaries and rare pheasant breeds: the gardens heave with floral splendour. As for the manoir, it is a rococo place unlike anything you've seen. Behind the creeper-clad façade with only the Burgundian roof as a clue is eye-boggling glamour: a vast beamed living room, an endless polished dining table, rows of tapestried chairs, many shiny ornaments. Upstairs, step out of the loo — once you've found the door in the trompe l'œil walls — to cupids, carvings, gildings, satyrs, velvet walls and clouds on the ceilings. There's a many-mirrored bathroom reflecting multiple magical images of you, marble pillars and gold-cushioned bath; a Louis XIV room whose red/gold bathroom has gold/ivory taps; an antique wooden throne with bell-chime flush… and the biscuit goes to the deeply, heavily pink suite with its carved fireplace, painted ceilings and corner columns — wild! But such is Monique's attentiveness, the peace of the house and garden, the quality of comfort, food and wine, that we feel it's perfect for lovers of French extravaganza. Theatrical and delightful.

Price	€150–€220. Suites €150–€170. Cottage €1,000 per week.
Rooms	5 + 1: 3 doubles, 2 suites: 1 for 2, 1 for 2-3. Cottage for 2-4.
Meals	Breakfast included. Hosted dinner €46; book ahead.
Closed	Never.
Directions	From Auxerre D965 to Villefargeau; right on C3 to Les Bruyères.

Monique Joullié
89240 Villefargeau, Yonne

Tel	+33 (0)3 86 41 32 82
Email	jchambord@aol.com
Web	www.petit-manoir-bruyeres.com

Château de Saint Fargeau

With a 1,000-year-old history, this handsome, moated, pentagonal château, embraced by a swan-flecked lake and 240 acres of rolling woodland, is deeply impressive: not just its history but the scale of its renovation. Four flanking towers enclose a courtyard with its own museum, while five metre-high ceilinged rooms, more authentic than immaculate, whisk you back in time with wood panelling, leather riding-boot lined passages, buffed Versailles parquet, a damask draped four-poster, 18th-century printed wallpaper, a red velvet chaise longue… and soaring views. Breakfast regally in the intimate, circular, pale grey panelled boudoir (porcelain tucked into a fitted cupboard) and a quiet corner to read or write. Free to explore, roam the grounds, the panelled library, the sword-and-trophy decked armour room, and passionate owner Michel's incredible collections (art, porcelain, antiques, steam engines); discover your inner knight or damsel. Cordial co-host Noémi gives guided tours – and the weekly summer son-et-lumières, with a cast of hundreds, are not to be missed. Wonderfully preserved, very special.

Price	€200. Child €35. Extra person €50.
Rooms	1 suite for 2-4.
Meals	Restaurants 12km.
Closed	October to mid-April.
Directions	Sent on booking.

Noémi Brunet & Michel Guyot
89170 Saint Fargeau, Yonne

Tel	+33 (0)3 86 74 05 67
Mobile	+33 (0)6 32 37 05 73
Email	saintfargeau@chateaudesaintfargeau.com
Web	www.chateau-de-st-fargeau.com

Le Coq Hardi

Anyone who loves France and what it stands for will coq-a-doodle-do. This small, modest hotel was built in the 30s to cater for the ever-growing motoring tribe – from Paris to the Riviera. It experienced its heyday in the late 50s and 60s when the rich and famous would stop over for a night or two to wine and dine before heading down to St Tropez. These hotels and restaurants are now undergoing a revival, a reminder of when the pace of life was slower and food a priority. Here, summer meals are served on a pretty lime-tree-shaded trellised terrace overlooking the Loire. Chef-patron Dominique Fonseca comes from the kitchens of the Ritz in Paris and has the talent and ambition to continue this respected restaurant's standards. Under the Fonsecas' ownership, bedrooms, some large, some small, some with balconies, have been refreshed and improved, with white bedcovers and plain pale colours; bathrooms still sport the colours of the 70s. Outside, expanses of mown grass slope down to river's edge and rose beds are neatly pruned and trimmed. It's a pretty setting for summer dining.

Price	€78.
Rooms	9: 8 doubles, 1 suite.
Meals	Breakfast €11. Lunch & dinner €24–€59. Restaurant closed Sunday eve & Mondays October–April.
Closed	Mid to late December. Mid-February to late March.
Directions	From A77 exit 25 & cont. thro' Pouilly sur Loire. Hotel opposite Cave Cooperative.

	Françoise & Dominique Fonseca
	42 avenue de la Tuilerie,
	58150 Pouilly sur Loire, Nièvre
Tel	+33 (0)3 86 39 12 99
Email	lecoqhardi@orange.fr
Web	www.lecoqhardi.fr

Château de Prye

The Queen of Poland, Marie-Casimire, lived here at the tail end of the 17th century – in this château extraordinaire, this architectural curiosity. The rooms are vast, the marble stables are palatial and the corridors heave with antlers and stag heads from previous ancestors; the history is intriguing. The young Marquis and Marquise, recently installed, have joyfully taken up the challenge of running both château and estate (they breed Charolais cattle) and host their national and international guests with grace and ease. Each cavernous bedroom is furnished with antiques – a triple-mirrored wardrobe from the Thirties, a Breton carved bedstead, a vintage oil-fuelled heater; bathrooms are en suite. Take a peek at the château kitchen with its wonderful old range and copper saucepans... from here breakfast is dispatched to a boudoir-like room with pretty white wainscotting. This rambling, asymmetrical, turreted château, its woodlands, gentle river and age-old trees of exotic and distant origins are contained within seven kilometres of walls... relish the fairy tale.

Price	€110–€185.
Rooms	4: 2 doubles, 2 suites for 2-4.
Meals	Dinner €35, book ahead. Wine €8–€105.
Closed	Mid-October to mid-April.
Directions	Nevers-Château-Chinon exit 36; D18 thro' Sauvigny les Bois. Gates between 2 pavilions open & close manually.

Magdalena & Antoine-Emmanuel du Bourg de Bozas
58160 La Fermeté, Nièvre

Tel	+33 (0)3 86 58 42 64
Email	info@chateaudeprye.com
Web	www.chateaudeprye.com

Château de Villette

Coen and Catherine – he's Dutch, she's Belgian – fell in love with this little château in 2002, did it up together, then had their wedding here and now have two children: they love their adopted country. They've opened just five rooms to guests so they can spoil you properly. And get to know you over dinner. (Though, should you prefer a romantic dinner for two, they'll understand.) Deep in the Parc du Morvan, the château was built in 1782 as a summer retreat. Bedrooms, charmingly decorated by Catherine, are large, light and airy, with warm colours and polished floors. They are dressed in château-style finery with canopied four-poster or draped bedheads, except for the sleigh bed in one of the two-bedded family rooms. Bathrooms are as they should be – new claw-foot baths carry exquisite antique taps – and views sail out of great windows to meadows and woodland beyond. Your five-course dinner is served in a candlelit dining room or outside. The grounds are perfect for duck and pheasant shoots. Families would love it here; Beaune and the vineyards lie temptingly close.

Price	€165–€250. Suites €300–€460.
Rooms	5: 2 doubles, 3 family suites for 5.
Meals	Dinner €60, book ahead. Wine €18–€100.
Closed	Rarely.
Directions	From N6 exit Beaune for Autun. N81 for Moulins for 18km, right to Poil. Thro' village, 2nd left. Signed.

Catherine & Coen Stork
58170 Poil, Nièvre

Tel	+33 (0)3 86 30 09 13
Email	catherinestork@chateaudevillette.eu
Web	www.chateaudevillette.eu

Château de Vaulx

Described in 1886 as "well-proportioned and elegant in its simplicity," Vaulx is as lovely now as then, and in the most beautiful position, in deep country, high on a hill with views that stretch to distant purple mountains. Marty, your charming, amusing host, and the animals (Nema the Jack Russell, Urga the filly, Otto the donkey... plus hens, sheep and beehives) welcome you to this generous estate. There's a fully panelled drawing room with chandeliers, a huge dining room with fresh flowers, curiosities, fashionable strong, exciting colours in big bedrooms. Sleep peacefully: not a hint of traffic rumble. The gardens are beautifully maintained, the lawns manicured, the box balls tightly topiaried; stroll down the romantic avenues in dappled sunlight. The fabulous vegetable garden provides food for delicious table d'hôtes, the birds twitter, there's countryside all around and plenty of places to visit, including a 13th-century bell tower in the village. And moreover... Bernard Dufoux, one of the best chocolate makers in France, is in La Clayette and Saint Christophe has a weekly cattle market.

Price	€95–€115. Suites €139. Apartment €190.
Rooms	5: 2 doubles, 2 family suites for 4, 1 apartment for 5.
Meals	Dinner €30. Wine €18. Restaurant 3km.
Closed	Rarely.
Directions	From Charolles, D985 for Clayette 8km. Cross r'way, 1km, 2nd road signed Vaulx. Up to top of hill, right at junc. Bell on iron gate.

Marty Freriksen
71800 Saint Julien de Civry,
Saône-et-Loire

Tel	+33 (0)3 85 70 64 03
Email	marty@chateaudevaulx.com
Web	www.chateaudevaulx.com

Entry 38   Map 11

Château des Poccards

It is all most comforting, this Tuscan-style villa built in 1805 to woo a Burgundy-based Italian beauty. Now with new owners and a charming manager, the cream and ochre villa is a good place to stay. After sampling the great restaurants of the Lyon-Mâcon corridor, exploring the wine routes of Beaune or the shops of Geneva, what could be nicer than to return to a big retro tub in a bathroom that glows with uplighters and oozes warm towels? Bedrooms are generously big, different and informally country-house, with pale-papered walls, elegant furnishings and *tout confort*. Some have windows to all sides so you feel you're in the tree tops – bliss when the sun streams in. In the mature park, a serene pool with wooden loungers and vineyard views. Families would be happy here, as would romancers. The fabulous parquet & ornate original white & gold panelling in the sitting room embrace a grand piano and a contemporary finish. Hearty Belgian breakfasts happen in the ochre-walled breakfast room with its wraparound wainscotting and pale grey floor-to-ceiling fireplace. Good value. *No credit cards.*

Price	€107–€147.
Rooms	5 doubles. Some rooms interconnect.
Meals	Restaurants 10-minute drive.
Closed	December to February.
Directions	A6 exit 28 to Sennecé les Mâcon. Left to Laizé & Blagny. At stop, 1st left to Hurigny; 1st right Rue de la Brasse; château 100m on left.

Erik & Erika Bruyneel
120 route des Poccards,
71870 Hurigny, Saône-et-Loire
Tel   +33 (0)3 85 32 08 27
Email   chateau.des.poccards@wanadoo.fr
Web   www.chateau-des-poccards.com

Relais de Montmartre

The 17th-century façade of this limestone country inn – once a staging post in the heart of the village – conceals not a few surprises. Behind the muted peacock shutters lies a flashy, fun, excitingly unexpected lair of Designers Guild chic, and each of the ten bedrooms – from good-sized to palatial – is different. There's one in bright turquoise, another deep pink, a third with walls papered baroque-style in gold on white. Mattresses are divine, duvets plump, and one black-lacquer bed is lit from underneath. Bathrooms are suitably style-conscious, too – luxuriously functional, with sparkling tiles, some claw-foot tubs, good-quality smellies and cosseting towels. There's scant outside space but how far do you wish to venture, with the Relais' restaurant so enticing? Perfectionist owner-chef Frédéric Carrion and his wife Marie only opened in 2009 and have already netted a Michelin star. Specialities include frogs' legs, Loctudy lobster and Grand Marnier soufflé… and gourmet picnics, accompanied by fine Viré-Clessée wine, can be arranged to take on walks amid the nearby vines. Bon appétit!

Price	€140–€320.
Rooms	10: 7 doubles, 3 twins.
Meals	Breakfast €16. Dinner €38–€52. Wine €20–€400.
Closed	January.
Directions	Sent on booking.

Frédéric Carrion
Place André Lagrange,
71260 Vire, Saône-et-Loire

Tel	+33 (0)3 85 33 10 72
Email	contact@relais-de-montmartre.fr
Web	www.relais-de-montmartre.fr

Château de Messey

One of the dreamiest spots ever, for families or couples. An impressive bull keeps his eye on his harem and shares the buttercup meadows with an 16th-century château — surrounded by woodlands with wandering paths, duck-filled ponds, a dovecote and vines. Delphine and her German husband Markus have taken over from her parents and live in one of the beautifully rustic vine workers' cottages with their family. With charming efficiency they manage three B&B rooms — under the eaves but light and spacious. Expect flagstone floors and huge stone fireplaces, heavy oak beams and pale limestone walls, wooden beds and splashes of colour. The grandest rooms are in the château itself, on the first floor with lovely high ceilings and big windows. Surrounding a grassed courtyard shaded by a weeping willow, with benches for watching water and ducks, are three pretty gîtes, the largest with their own terraces. Seventeen hectares of chardonnay and gamay vines are grown here, within the tiny appellation of Mâcon-Cruzille. A most welcoming if sometimes very busy place, and you can experience delightful table d'hôtes if you book ahead.

Price	€107–€130.
	Cottages €445–€870 per week.
Rooms	5 + 3: 2 twins/doubles, 2 twins,
	1 triple. 3 cottages for 2–6.
Meals	Dinner €30. Wine €10–€15.
	Restaurant 2km.
Closed	Occasionally.
Directions	A6 exit Tournus; in centre, right D14.
	Château on left of D14 between
	Ozenay & Martailly, 9km from
	Tournus.

Delphine & Markus Schaefer
71700 Ozenay,
Saône-et-Loire

Tel	+33 (0)3 85 51 16 11
Email	info@messey.fr
Web	www.messey.fr

Maison Nièpce

All the modern necessities, of course, but otherwise little has changed since the old inn was turned into a family mansion by the uncle of Joseph Nicéphore Nièpce, inventor of photography. It's a bit like staying in a charming museum – a place of candlelight, atmosphere and 18th-century elegance, plus a dash of antique grime. The owners and their golden retriever live in one great wing and guests in the other, while two odoriferous cats roam freely. First-floor passageways run hither and thither to graceful rooms with good beds and bathrooms, fine antiques and oriental rugs. On the sloping-ceilinged second floor, La Chambre Nièpce can link up to form a three-room apartment with bathroom. A display of arms in one bedroom and an oven for baking bullets in another recall the Revolution; a third, less bellicose, holds serried ranks of books. Plump for a room at the back, quieter than those over the street, and gaze down on the big and enchanting walled garden. Breakfast and dinner (usually table d'hôtes) are in the fascinating dining room, aglow with copper pans.

Price	€50–€130. Apartment €500 per week.
Rooms	5 + 1: 1 double, 4 twins. Apartment for 4.
Meals	Breakfast €8. Dinner €25, book ahead.
Closed	Rarely.
Directions	20km south of Chalon sur Saone, N6 for Mâcon; left on leaving village.

Huguette & Jehan Moreau de Melen
8 avenue du 4 Septembre,
71240 Sennecy le Grand,
Saône-et-Loire

Tel	+33 (0)3 85 44 76 44
Email	moreau.jehan@wanadoo.fr
Web	www.maisonniepce.com

L'Orangerie

Ring the bell on the gate and enter gardens that are secluded, charming, full of colour and the babble of the brook. Being in the heart of burgundy country you are immersed in the silence of a valley of vines. Light spills into the sitting room through arched vine-clad windows while cream walls and Indian rugs add to the simple elegance of this *maison de maître*. Antiques and travel are the owners' passion, and David's gentle Irish brogue is enchanting (no surprise to hear he has interviewed European royalty for a prestigious magazine). The grand staircase in the centre of this gracious house would not be out of place on a 1930s luxury cruise liner, while interesting paintings and handsome oriental fabrics add up to a mix of styles that work beautifully together. Bedrooms vary in size and have lovely seersucker linen and antique prints; bathrooms are classically tasteful. Terraced lawns lead down to the heated pool, the meadows and trees, breakfasts are superb, and the wonderful Voie Verte cycle route, along the former railway, runs nearby. *Cash or French cheque only. Minimum stay two nights.*

Price	€80–€110.
Rooms	5 twins/doubles.
Meals	Hosted dinner with wine, €25–€40, on request. Restaurants 4km.
Closed	Mid-November to mid-March.
Directions	From A6 exit Chalon Sud on N80 for Le Creusot; exit Moroges. Signed from village centre.

David Eades & Niels Lierow
20 rue des Lavoirs, Vingelles,
71390 Moroges, Saône-et-Loire

Tel +33 (0)3 85 47 91 94
Email info@orangerie-moroges.com
Web www.orangerie-moroges.com

La Dominotte

On the edge of an old Burgundian village is a mellow farmhouse where grapes were gathered, pressed and stored; you can see the barrel marks on the breakfast room wall. They are less visible in the evening with low lighting, candles and a board announcing the day's specials (dinners are twice-weekly). This room — stylishly simple in that perfect Dutch way — leads to the garden where it's bliss to lie by the discreetly hedged pool. You are surrounded by vineyards and vast sloping hills; the owners arrange tastings and sales of local wines in their vaulted cellars. Dutch, multi-lingual and hugely helpful, Mart and Marÿ have been here for over a decade and are a fount of knowledge on all things Burgundian, gastronomy in particular. The famous villages of Montrachet, Meursault and Pommard are a ten-minute drive, Beaune is a short cycle ride away (borrow the bikes). Rooms are functional and restful, the smallish doubles on the ground floor of the old barn given much character by their exposed rafters and slit windows. The views of garden and pool are from the big airy room upstairs, with extra long beds.

Price	€95–€136. Suite €160.
Rooms	11: 10 doubles, 1 suite (with kitchen).
Meals	Late afternoon snacks. Hosted dinner €22–€25, twice weekly. Restaurant 400m.
Closed	22 November to 1 April.
Directions	A6 Dijon & Beaune exit 24.1 to Bligny lès Beaune onto D113, then to Demigny D18. Left at T-junc. after Casino; 3rd left to end of village; last house on right.

Martin & Marÿ Franssen
42 rue de Jasoupe le Bas,
71150 Demigny, Saône-et-Loire

Tel	+33 (0)3 85 49 43 56
Mobile	+31 (0)6 30 49 66 55
Email	info@la-dominotte.com
Web	www.la-dominotte.com

Château de Chassagne-Montrachet

You are in top wine country and the drive to this businesslike château passes through a small vineyard. The winery is in the middle, the chambres d'hôtes to the right. Its stark 19th-century exterior does not prepare you for the modernism inside: sweeping wooden staircase, pink-marble and slate floor, stunning leather furniture, billiard room with bamboo decoration and underfloor lighting. This refreshing irreverence continues upstairs; you might spot a Jacobsen egg chair, feast on the richness of purple walls and oak floor or enter a room of zen-like calm. Windows show the vineyards floating away to the hills of the Massif Central or the Saône valley; on a good day you can see the Alps. Bathrooms are ravishingly contemporary; most have tubs surrounded by wooden decking, one has a double basin of rough-cast bronze mounted on rock – half basin, half art. You breakfast at two large steel tables seated on sculpted chairs by a wonderful fireplace and floor-to-ceiling doors. The village restaurant is 300 metres away and there's excellent walking in the hills. *Wine tour included, by arrangement.*

Price	€250.
Rooms	5 doubles.
Meals	Lunch €40–€50, with fine wines for tasting. Restaurant 300m
Closed	Never.
Directions	From Beaune, D974 exit Chassagne-Montrachet; château signed at village entrance.

Francine Picard
5 rue du Château,
21190 Chassagne Montrachet,
Côte-d'Or

Tel	+33 (0)3 80 21 98 57
Email	contact@michelpicard.com
Web	www.michelpicard.com

Le Clos

A rustic-style hotel where you can have breakfast on the terrace overlooking the manicured *jardin de curé*. Then choose your suntrap in the garden – it's full of hidden corners; or wander, shaded by generous trees, among the quaint agricultural machinery that sculpturally dots the lawns. This white-shuttered farmhouse, in a peaceful semi-rural area, has been renovated to reveal exposed limestone walls and massive rafters; note the charming country breakfast room and the light and lofty sitting room whose ancient tiles have been garnished with oriental rugs and sofas. Big, neat, carpeted bedrooms have matching floral bed linen and curtains, some fine antique bedsteads and the odd exotic touch. Bathrooms are spotless and there are no half measures: big tubs, walk-in showers, an abundance of towels. There's no restaurant here, though there is a bar; the pretty village is just down the road. Montagny lès Beaune is deep in wine country – and when you've had your fill of burgundies and beaunes, there are mustards to try in a nearby village. Beaune is conveniently close.

Price	€85-€125. Duplex suites €140-€200.
Rooms	24: 19 twins/doubles, 5 duplex suites.
Meals	Breakfast €13. Restaurants 100m & 3km.
Closed	December to January.
Directions	From Lyon A6 exit 24.1 towards Beaune Centre; 300m r'bout to Montagny lès Beaune on D113. Signed.

Monsieur & Madame Oudot
22 rue Gravières,
21200 Montagny lès Beaune,
Côte-d'Or

Tel	+33 (0)3 80 25 97 98
Email	hotelleclos@wanadoo.fr
Web	www.hotelleclos.com

La Terre d'Or

The night view of twinkling Beaune, five minutes down the hill, is glorious. Jean-Louis loves sharing 'his' Burgundy: the making of the elegant vintages, the best Burgundian chefs, great Romanesque art. All this by bike, horseback, jeep or hot-air balloon. The Martin family – Jean-Louis and Christine now joined by son Vincent – run three wonderful houses, each surrounded by mature trees and a terraced garden enlivened by Vincent's wife Jurga's sculpted figures. The modern, multi-levelled main house has five large and lovely bedrooms while the stone cottage, for B&B or self-catering, is traditional, the third house being more independent. The noble old beams and rosy tomette floors frame a fine new, pale, contemporary look warmed with stylish lighting, crisp linen and polished country pieces (including wine-growers' chairs). The honeymoon suite has a private piece of garden. It's bliss to relax on the main terrace and gaze across vineyards to the ramparts of old Beaune. Down a wildflower path is a family-run restaurant. Stay three nights or more.
Themed stays for groups (wine, cookery, culture).

Price	€125-€205. Cottages €340-€390.
Rooms	5 + 2: 1 twin, 4 suites. 1 cottage for 4-6, 1 cottage for 4.
Meals	Breakfast €13. Picnic available. Restaurant 400m.
Closed	Rarely.
Directions	From Beaune, D970 for Auxerre & Bouze lès Beaune. After 2km, right to La Montagne; signed.

Vincent, Christine & Jean-Louis Martin
Rue Izembart La Montagne,
21200 Beaune, Côte-d'Or

Tel	+33 (0)3 80 25 90 90
Email	jlmartin@laterredor.com
Web	www.laterredor.com

Les Jardins de Loïs

This 200-year-old house once belonged to a wine broker. Now, under the connoisseurship of its charming, attentive owners, Philippe and Anne-Marie, it has returned to its roots; they are both wine buffs and their pride and joy is their cellar, open to guests. Details delight throughout. Bedrooms, reached by a splendid exterior staircase, are lavish, trad/modern, and beautiful: lilacs and suave creams offset polished limestone and black cabochon; antique armoires flatter oriental rugs; bathrooms (and a pretty steam room) are immaculate in russet-ochre marble with Italianate monsoon showers. The garden suite, Clos des Renards, is the most private, in its own outbuilding with a sitting room and huge bath. Enjoy a generous breakfast with homemade jams in the elegant, airy dining room, stroll Beaune's ancient cobbles, visit the famous Hospices, drink the fruits of the region's wine capital. Then retire with a bottle of their own fine burgundy to the gem of a garden – half a hectare, walled, teak-furnished, with neat beds, roses, shady magnolias and fruit trees – a stunning surprise in this city-central position.

Price	€140. Suites €160-€180.
Rooms	5: 3 doubles, 2 suites.
Meals	Restaurant 150m.
Closed	1 to 15 February.
Directions	Sent on booking.

Anne-Marie & Philippe Dufouleur
21200 Beaune,
Côte-d'Or

Tel   +33 (0)3 80 22 41 97
Mobile   +33 (0)6 73 85 11 47
Email   contact@jardinsdelois.com
Web   www.jardinsdelois.com

Chez Les Fatien

Lavish luxury in beautiful Beaune. This is a 300-year-old vine workers' house with stables, set round an inner courtyard, beautifully revived with no expense spared. Smart cobbles are topped with clipped potted shrubs, seats are modern wicker and you enter via a lofty porch. On the ground floor: a salon on the right (ancient limestone flags, chocolate leather sofas) and a bedroom suite with an Asian twist. Up the outside stair, sheltered by that glass awning, three more lavish rooms – one on two levels, another with a 17th-century fireplace and a glory of beams. Hand basins are antique, showers are gorgeous, linen is snow white, walls are dressed with handsome prints and oils. Discover Beaune, its cheese shops and pâtisseries behind striped awnings, its white-napped restaurants, its delicious food, its café-lined squares and, above all, its famous 'caves', those medieval passageways beneath the cobbles lined with thousands of wines. Your hostess Karine looks after you well so return to a glass of brandy by the open wood fire before retiring to fluffy bathrobes and fine oils from Clarins.

Price	€220–€350.
Rooms	4 suites.
Meals	Restaurants within walking distance.
Closed	Rarely.
Directions	Sent on booking.

Monsieur Fatien
17 rue Sainte Marguerite,
21200 Beaune,
Côte-d'Or

Tel	+33 (0)3 80 22 82 84
Email	reservation@chezlesfatien.com
Web	www.maisonfatien.com

Château de Chorey

Typically Burgundian, this robust, sturdy collection of buildings under high slate roofs dates from the 13th and 17th centuries. Complete with towers, ancient yews and dovecotes, flanked on both sides by a 34-acre vineyard producing prestigious premier cru wines, it has views that sail over a noble moated domaine. Interiors are handsome, formal and absolutely French with rich reds and rusts, mustards, golds and raspberry pinks; suave sobriety presides over period furniture, ornate wallpapering, polished wooden floors, high windows heavily draped and regal beds swathed in canopies matched to quilted spreads. Bathrooms are immaculate. Landings with Venetian mosaic floors lead to venerable stone stairs and down through doorways with ornately carved lintels (one sporting the family crest) and perfectly tailored arched panelling. A sitting room impresses with a monumental fireplace; the dining room, with high overhead beams, is where wholesome breakfasts are set before wide arched windows, overlooking the vines and interior courtyard. Wine tours and tastings are a must; Beaune oozes gastronomic delights.

Price	€175–€195. Suites €220–€260. Triple €225. Extra bed €30.
Rooms	5: 2 doubles, 2 suites for 2-4, 1 triple.
Meals	Restaurant 1km.
Closed	End October to Easter.
Directions	From A6 south dir. Lyon exit 24 (Beaune St Nicolas); at r'bout, 1st right; right at next r'bout onto D974 dir. Dijon. 1st right to Chorey les Beaune. Château 1st on left after x-roads at village entrance.

François Germain
2 rue Jacques Germain,
21200 Chorey les Beaune, Côte-d'Or

Tel	+33 (0)3 80 22 06 05
Mobile	+33 (0)6 10 84 34 34
Email	contact@chateau-de-chorey-les-beaune.fr
Web	www.chateau-de-chorey-les-beaune.fr

Hôtel de Vougeot

Rows of vines sweep down an incline, surround the regal Château de Clos de Vougeot, and come to an abrupt halt at the back doorstep of this modest converted townhouse; ask for a room with views of château and vines. For centuries, Clos de Vougeot was considered the finest of all burgundies; the Cistercian monks planted some of the vines in the 12th century and the cloister, cellar and vast presses are among the most interesting examples of architecture in Burgundy; come for the autumn grape harvest. Alain speaks excellent English and is charming, but you are mostly on your own here, with a key to come and go as you please. The staircase could be awkward for the very young or very old, and there's no lounge; the terrace has the most marvellous views. Inside, everything has been kept simple and clean, the rough outlines of dark timbers contrasting with white walls, light coloured bedspreads, parquet floors and teak furniture. The buffet breakfasts and the cold supper platters are delicious – or splash out on a Michelin-starred table in the next village, the perfect end to a great day.

Price	€62-€115.
Rooms	16: 12 doubles, 1 triple, 2 quadruples, 1 room for 5.
Meals	Buffet breakfast €10. Cold platter €20. Wine from €15.
Closed	20 December to 20 January.
Directions	A31 exit 1 Nuits St Georges, D974 towards Vougeot. Hotel in village.

Alain Senterre
18 rue du Vieux Château,
21640 Vougeot, Côte-d'Or

Tel	+33 (0)3 80 62 01 15
Email	contact@hotel-vougeot.com
Web	www.hotel-vougeot.com

Castel de Très Girard

Nuits Saint Georges, Gevrey Chambertin, Clos de Vougeot, Vosne Romanée – all tongue-twisters in the best sense of the word and all strewn in your path as you travel down the main road from Dijon. Why not stop here and be greeted by this friendly team who handle everything in the nicest manner? The warmth comes not only from the embers in the fireplace by the leather club chairs but from the whole atmosphere of this renovated wine press and 18th-century Burgundian manor. There are confident touches of burgundy reds (naturally) in the carpeted bedrooms, plus padded leather headboards, cream walls and just enough golden stone and beam exposed to give the large hotelly bedrooms character; small vestibules ensure ultimate peace. Even the gleaming white bathrooms have views over the rooftops or to the Côtes de Nuits vineyards. Outside is a grassed and swimming-pool'd garden, sheltered from the car park by immaculate hedging. Plans are afoot for the restaurant to expand. Food has always played a major role at the Castel de Très Girard, and is matched by wines from the region's best producers.

Price	€130–€180. Suites €240–€250.
Rooms	9: 3 doubles, 2 suites, 4 triples.
Meals	Breakfast €12. Lunch €21–€39. Dinner €37–€60. Wine €30–€150. Restaurant closed Mon & Sun in winter.
Closed	Mid-February to mid-March.
Directions	20km from Dijon; A31 exit Dijon Sud for Nuits St Georges on N74, then right to Morey St Denis. Signed.

Didier Petitcolas
7 rue Très Girard,
21220 Morey Saint Denis, Côte-d'Or

Tel	+33 (0)3 80 34 33 09
Email	info@castel-tres-girard.com
Web	www.castel-tres-girard.com

Château de Flammerans

All is fresh, charming, relaxing – and Guy has the perfect pinch of passion for Burgundian cuisine – even though he hails from Cantal. Ask to see the 18th-century kitchen with its original painted ceiling where he teaches the secrets of 'jambon persillé' and 'fricassée d'escargot'. The billiard room and the library are just off the entrance hall with its handsome iron banister leading upstairs. Breakfast on the large balcony overlooking the park, in the sitting room – creamy walls, oriental rugs, green and gold upholstered easy chairs – or in the elegant dining room. Bedrooms are big and uncluttered with working fireplaces and mineral water on the side tables. Find robes in gorgeous bathrooms along with weathered marbled floors from the south of France. If you're lucky, you'll catch one of the concerts, baroque or jazz, that Guy and Catherine organise. Sit and dream on a bench in a shady glen in the large grounds, discover the old ponds (one was used to clean the carriage wheels), work out in the gym, steam away in the super little spa. Kids will love the waggy dog and the donkey.

Price	€88–€178. Suites €158–€198.
Rooms	6: 3 doubles, 1 twin, 2 suites.
Meals	Light lunches available. Hosted dinner with drinks, €45; book ahead.
Closed	Never.
Directions	A39 exit 5 to Auxonne; D20 for 6km to Flammerans. Signed.

Guy & Catherine Barrier
21130 Flammerans,
Côte-d'Or

Tel	+33 (0)3 80 27 05 70
Email	info@chateaudeflammerans.com
Web	www.chateaudeflammerans.com

Le Château de Courban

This ambitiously renovated 19th-century mansion – a 17th-century dovecote in the courtyard bears witness to an even older heritage – was transformed into its present incarnation by Jérôme's father, perfectionist Pierre Vandendriessche. Most of the 24 rooms are in the original mansion and flaunt a wide variety of styles, from the bold and bright to the floral and cosy, all tastefully harmonised and generously comfortable: recessed bedheads, draped four-posters, crisp colour schemes and carefully chosen prints. Newer outbuildings vaunt more contemporary design, and have their own verandas. Bathrooms feature claw-foot tubs in some, walk-in showers with monsoon heads in others. Meals – excellent, reliable, robust Burgundian cuisine – can be taken in the expansive restaurant, the orangery or on the veranda; breakfast should be enjoyed in bed with the shutters wide open. An ivy-smothered wooden cottage conceals a delightful suite. Behind the house, a broad terrace precedes two pools – one slender and black, stretching across the garden – and a spa where you can burn your lunch off. Failing that there's an abutting bar.

Price	€130–€160. Suites €260–€320.	
Rooms	24: 14 twins/doubles, 10 suites for 2.	
Meals	Breakfast €16. Dinner €42–€78. Wine €22–€235.	
Closed	Christmas.	
Directions	A26 to A5, exit 23 to D396 for 14km to Gevrolles; D996 thro' Montigny sur Aube, D995 to Courban; follow signs in village, entrance on left.	

	Jérôme Vandendriessche
	7 rue du Lavoir Courban,
	21520 Courban, Côte-d'Or
Tel	+33 (0)3 80 93 78 69
Email	contact@chateaudecourban.com
Web	www.chateaudecourban.com

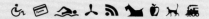

Château d'Epenoux

The dear little 18th-century château and its baroque chapel are set back from the quiet village road. Susanne and Eva, Swiss-born, energetic and delightful, have given both the facelift they deserved – windows sparkle and floorboards gleam. They first opened five airy bedrooms in the château, all generously big and different, then an apartment in the chapel and two above the *orangerie*. Most recent are four apartments in the manor house. The château suite, prettily papered in blue, its beds draped with soft white duvets, overlooks majestic trees, copses and lawns; the large double is panelled in French green; fresh, feminine Mona Lisa is all deep pink walls and cream sofa. White bathrooms sparkle. In the blue-carpeted salon, sink into the wildly floral armchairs for a pre-dinner drink, drift into the grand dining room with its glass chandelier for dinner: maybe perfectly roasted duck and a well-chosen wine. Next morning, stroll through the ancient chestnut trees to the sun-lapped pool, or visit charming Vesoul, notable for its lake and recreational park, and intriguing Gothic façades in the old quarter.

Price	€103–€123. Apartment €85–€140. All prices per night.
Rooms	5 + 7: 4 doubles, 1 suite; 7 apartments for 2-4.
Meals	Dinner (weekends only) €29. Wine €12–€38.
Closed	Rarely.
Directions	From Chaumont, N19 to Vesoul; D10 for approx. 4km. Château on left at entrance to village of Épenoux. Ring bell on gate.

Eva Holz & Susanne Hubbuch
70000 Pusy et Épenoux,
Haute-Saône

Tel	+33 (0)3 84 75 19 60
Email	chateau.epenoux@orange.fr
Web	www.chateau-epenoux.com

Paris – Île de France

Hôtel Opéra Richepanse

On a little street off Rue Saint Honoré, a short walk from the Louvre, the Champs Elysées, the Tuileries, is this gem. The marquetry, the panelling, the smooth leather furniture and the mouldings of the lobby-salon were all custom-designed: expect a cool 1930s look and a courteous welcome. There's a minor concession to things 21st century in the atmospheric stone vault, where a sumptuous breakfast buffet is served: sausages and scrambled eggs, cold cuts, six different breads. A small lift transports you to bedrooms that are a fair size (though some are enormous, with floor-to-ceiling windows – a treat in Paris); ask for one of the quietest. There are new carpets, firm mattresses, clean-limbed Deco furniture and thick-textured fabrics for perfectly fitted bedcovers – no swags, no frills, no fuss. This gives space to appreciate the art that draws the eye and – in the magnificent great suites – original paintings. Bathrooms are excellent and trumpet the latest in basin design and triple bevelled mirrors. All feels clean-cut and rich, polished and pristine, and the service is attentive and generous.

Price	€280–€550. Suites €490–€620.
Rooms	38: 35 twins/doubles, 3 suites.
Meals	Breakfast €13–€19. Restaurants nearby.
Closed	Rarely.
Directions	Metro: Madeleine (8, 12, 14), Concorde (1, 12). RER & Roissybus: Auber, Opéra. Buses: 42, 52, 84, 94. Parking: Madeleine.

Édith Vidalenc
14 rue du Chevalier de Saint George, 75001 Paris

Tel	+33 (0)1 42 60 36 00
Email	hotel@richepanse.com
Web	www.richepanse.com

Hôtel Le Relais Saint Honoré

Unique, the Rue Saint Honoré is a delight: once past the gardens of the Presidential Palace it becomes human-sized and unpasteurised, meanders along the Tuileries, crosses Place Colette and charges into an area of higgledy-piggledy streets and iconoclastic shops. The Relais, once a brasserie frequented by Jean Cocteau, dates from 1650 and has the gnarled beams to prove it – now painted lapis lazuli blue, bamboo green or cranberry red to pick up nuances from exquisitely patterned fabrics on curtains and bedheads. To each floor, a different colour theme and set of pictures (horse riding, African dancing); rooms are small but perfect, with huge mirrors and olive oil-based soaps and lotions. The large suite is clothed in soft blue with a sofabed; the sunny yellow junior suite has a child's bed squeezed on a tiny mezzanine. Breakfast, classic French or with cereals, arrives at your door in the morning – and if you need a break from sightseeing, plump down on squishy sofas in the soft yellow reception area and watch the whole of Paris march past the door. No ostentation, no frills, just comfort and caring staff.

Price	€219. Suites €280–€390.
Rooms	15: 13 twins/doubles, 2 suites.
Meals	Breakfast €13 (served in bedroom only). Restaurants nearby.
Closed	Never.
Directions	Metro: Tuileries (1), Pyramides (7, 14). RER: Musée d'Orsay, Châtelet-les Halles. Buses: 68, 72. Parking: Place du Marché Saint Honoré.

Marie-Pierre Peron
308 rue Saint Honoré,
75001 Paris

Tel	+33 (0)1 42 96 06 06
Email	contact@relaissainthonore.com
Web	www.relaissainthonore.com

Le Relais du Louvre

Look down the throats of gargoyles, soak up the history. The Revolutionaries printed their newsletter in the cellar; the place inspired Puccini's Café Momus in *Bohême*. It is utterly delightful and so are the charming young managers who greet you from the antique desk. Everywhere, antiques and oriental rugs complement the modernity of firm beds and perfect bathrooms. Front rooms look onto the church's Gothic flights of fancy and along to the austerely neo-classical Louvre; others give onto a light-filled patio. Top-floor junior suites have space for a sofabed, pastel walls, exuberant upholstery and heaps of light from mansard windows. The apartment is big and beautiful with fireplace, books, music, old engravings and a superb veranda kitchen. Smaller rooms are luminous, fresh and restful – yellow, a favourite colour, brings sunny moods into small spaces. You feel softly secluded and coddled everywhere. The sense of service is highly developed and, as there is no dining room, breakfast comes to you. *On each floor: 2 rooms interconnect to make a family suite.*

Price	€155–€255. Singles €135–€175. Suites €235–€340. Apartment €415–€475. All prices per night.
Rooms	20 + 1: 13 twins/doubles, 5 singles, 2 suites. 1 apt for 5.
Meals	Breakfast €13 (until 2pm). Dinner €10–€30 (6pm-3am). Wine €7. All meals: room service only.
Closed	Never.
Directions	Metro: Louvre-Rivoli (1), Pont Neuf (7). RER: Châtelet-Les Halles. Buses: 67, 69, 72, 74, 85. Parking: Private car park on request, €26.

Sophie Aulnette
19 rue des Prêtres St Germain l'Auxerrois, 75001 Paris

Tel	+33 (0)1 40 41 96 42
Email	contact@relaisdulouvre.com
Web	www.relaisdulouvre.com

Entry 58   Map 5

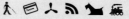

Hôtel Molière

This is an enchantingly French hotel with a sensitive mixture of urban and country comforts. The big lobby/salon is smart and rather grand with its faux-marbre columns, potted palms and beige bucket chairs, and the staff at reception are very competent, very friendly; the young owners infuse the place with their intelligent enthusiasm. The breakfast room is a delight, and red and white striped blinds frame the leafy, cobbled courtyard. There's also a small, deep-chaired salon round the corner for your quiet moments. Bedrooms are just as pretty with judicious use of nostalgic Jouy prints on walls and coordinated checks on quilts – or vice versa, or stripes, or sprigs… The Jouy colours go perfectly with the occasional antique: red and yellow, grey and green, blue and ivory, a little old writing desk, an unusual chair. Bathrooms, some vast, some snug, are modern; those in the suites dazzle with rectangular double sinks, huge tubs and swish Italian showers. Interesting paintings and ornaments give the hotel a well-cared-for feel. Everyone loves the Molière.

Price	€170–€190. Singles €145–€170. Suites €220–€300. Triples €220.
Rooms	32: 14 doubles, 8 twins, 5 singles, 3 suites for 4, 2 triples.
Meals	Breakfast €14. Restaurants nearby.
Closed	Never.
Directions	Metro: Palais Royal-Musée du Louvre (1, 7), Pyramides (7, 14). RER & Roissybus: Auber, Opéra. Buses: 21, 24, 27, 29, 39, 48, 72, 81, 95. Parking: Pyramides.

Patricia & Rémy Perraud
21 rue Molière,
75001 Paris

Tel	+33 (0)1 42 96 22 01
Email	info@hotel-moliere.fr
Web	www.hotel-moliere.fr

Hôtel du Jeu de Paume

The Île Saint Louis is the most exclusive 17th-century village in Paris and this renovated 'tennis court' – three storeys soar to the roof timbers – is one of its most exceptional sights. Add genuine care from family owners, fresh flowers, time for everyone and super staff. Regulars will be stunned – and delighted – by the recent revamp, which sees sleek designer furniture set under ancient beams, bright colours flung across stone walls, new large built-in cupboards and funky lighting to show off contemporary art. Some rooms feature beautiful beams, one gives onto a little garden; number 109's bed perches on a high platform. We love it – for its sense of history, eccentricities, aesthetic ironies, peaceful humour and feel of home; and for its unconventional attitudes and relaxed yet thoroughly efficient staff. The serene, spacious lounge has low armchairs in chocolate and red, modern art and Scoop the soft gold dog; breakfast is beneath magnificent timbers by faux Greek columns; work out or take a sauna in a new spa in the vaulted cellars. *Let Madame Heckel know if your stay spans a birthday or anniversary.*

Price	€285-€360. Singles €185-€255. Suites €560. Apartments €600-€900. All prices per night.
Rooms	30 + 2: 20 twins/doubles, 7 singles, 3 suites. 2 apartments for 4-6.
Meals	Breakfast €20. Restaurants nearby.
Closed	15 June to 1 September.
Directions	Metro: Pont Marie (7), Cité (4), St Paul (1). RER: St Michel-Notre Dame. Bus: 67. Parking: Pont Marie.

Nathalie Heckel
54 rue St Louis en l'Île,
75004 Paris

Tel	+33 (0)1 43 26 14 18
Email	info@jeudepaumehotel.com
Web	www.jeudepaumehotel.com

Hôtel du 7è Art

The 'Seventh Art' is French for cinema. The director's chair is yours where black and white images of film are lovingly tended, as eternally youthful as the stars of yesteryear. Besides a pleasingly quirky little hotel, there is a lively bar where log fires burn in winter. The charming young owners have thought of everything, including a laundry room and a trio of fitness machines to maintain your Hollywood muscles in decadent Paris. Black and white is the theme – viz. that checked floor in the bar/breakfast room – and old film posters decorate the walls. Up the black carpeted stairs, the bedrooms are small and un-showily decorated – some hessian walls, some pine slatting, brown carpets – and have… white and black bathrooms with the occasional star-studded shower curtain! Some rooms are tiny – the largest are on the top floor – and some have ceiling fans. The atmosphere is peaceful (the bar closes at midnight), the street is full of antique shops and the oldest part of Paris is all around you. Nowhere in Paris does funky modern so well. *No lift. Free WiFi.*

Price	€100–€160. Single €75.
Rooms	23: 15 doubles, 7 twins, 1 single. Extra beds available.
Meals	Continental-plus breakfast €8. Restaurants nearby.
Closed	Rarely.
Directions	Metro: St Paul (1), Pont Marie (7), Sully Morland (7). RER: Châtelet-Les Halles. Buses: 69, 96. Parking: Pont Marie, Rue Saint Antoine.

	Michel & Yolène Kenig
	20 rue Saint Paul,
	75004 Paris
Tel	+33 (0)1 44 54 85 00
Email	hotel7art@wanadoo.fr
Web	www.paris-hotel-7art.com

Hôtel du Collège de France

This sweet hotel has an atmosphere of well-established family comfort: exposed stones, lots of wood, soft armchairs by the fireplace in the red salon, good lighting. You will be greeted by the delightful young manager and by a less animated and considerably older Joan of Arc. The breakfast room, off the lobby, is warmly, elegantly red; find old Parisian prints and a Madonna. Bedrooms are mostly not very big but each has a full-length mirror, a practical desk unit, a super-duper shower. If you want a feeling of space, ask for one with French windows opening to a small balcony. The décor is colourful in places with coordinated botanical fabrics, and soft quilts – it is careful and restful, and beds are most comfortable. The staircase is worth visiting just for its round timbers and windows encrusted with autumn leaves; rooms at the top are worth the walk up from the fifth floor. Above all, a genuinely friendly reception is assured. Generous breakfasts and good value on a quiet street away from the bustle of the main student drags – and you may receive useful intellectual vibrations from the Collège as a bonus.

Price	€90–€145.
Rooms	29: 23 doubles, 6 twins.
Meals	Buffet breakfast €10.
	Restaurants nearby.
Closed	Never.
Directions	Metro: St Michel (4),
	Maubert Mutualité (10).
	RER: St Michel-Notre Dame.
	Buses: 21, 24, 27, 38, 63, 85, 86, 87.
	Parking: Maubert Mutualité.

Jean Marc
7 rue Thénard,
75005 Paris
Tel   +33 (0)1 43 26 78 36
Email   info@hotelcdf.com
Web   www.hotel-collegedefrance.com

Hôtel Agora Saint Germain

Deep in the heart of the Latin Quarter – one of the oldest centres of learning in Europe –
is a quiet place to stay a few steps from the animation of St Germain, the student buzz of
St Michel and the rafts of history that carry Notre Dame beyond. Enter reception, très
moderne, with crisp lighting and modish wallpaper on one wall, opening to a pretty
glassed-in planted patio – greeting enough. Then you'll be welcomed by the charming
receptionist or Madame Sahuc herself, youthful and bright. She has recently renovated
with style: a gold and beige wallpaper in the corridors, solid blond wood doors, muted
bronze curtains with bedcovers to match, sparkling chrome trimmed bathrooms
with floating basins. There is an atmosphere of relaxed, feminine attention to detail.
The old-stone basement breakfast room is comfortable with high-backed leather chairs and
orange table dressings – and heavenly croissants and raisin rolls from Kayser, one of the
master bakers of Paris. Next door, a lively outdoor market is a morning's entertainment
on Tuesday, Thursday and Saturday. A good reliable address.

Price	€189–€195. Singles €149. Family room €210.
Rooms	39: 2 doubles, 9 twins, 27 singles, 1 family room for 3.
Meals	Continental buffet breakfast €11. Restaurants nearby.
Closed	Never.
Directions	Metro: Maubert Mutualité (10). RER: St Michel-Notre Dame. Buses: 47, 63, 86, 87, 24. Parking: St Germain.

	Pascale Sahuc
	42 rue des Bernardins,
	75005 Paris
Tel	+33 (0)1 46 34 13 00
Email	resa@agora-paris-hotel.com
Web	www.hotelagorasaintgermain.com

Hôtel Abbatial Saint Germain

Relaxed and affable, Michel Sahuc is an enthusiast and his style informs his hotel: the receptionist may choose the music playing over the desk and nearby sitting area but the salon with its long caramel coloured leather sofas is quiet. Rooms are mostly a decent size, some special ones are on a corner, and almost all have two windows. They have just been redecorated: a brown and white swirly patterned carpet sets the colour theme with half-moon wooden headboards or long panelling behind the beds, new quilted coverlets and thick taffeta-like curtains in muted bronze. It's all spic and span and the new lighting arrangements are more than considerate of the nocturnal reader; some bathrooms have sliding doors and rain-head showers. A few rooms at the top have fabulous views swinging round from the colonnade of the Pantheon on its hill to the north rose of Notre Dame on her island, all within a few minutes' walk. The lush foliage on the trees fronting the hotel and a scattering of small neighbourhood bistros are a plus. A friendly and unpretentious place.

Price	€160–€195. Singles €140. Triples €220.
Rooms	43: 22 doubles, 13 twins, 5 singles, 3 triples.
Meals	Continental buffet breakfast €12. Restaurants nearby.
Closed	Never.
Directions	Metro: Maubert Mutualité (10). RER: St Michel-Notre Dame. Buses: 47, 63, 86, 87. Parking: St Germain.

	Michel Sahuc
	46 boulevard Saint Germain, 75005 Paris
Tel	+33 (0)1 46 34 02 12
Email	resa@abbatial-paris-hotel.com
Web	www.abbatial.com

Hôtel des 3 Collèges

No-one can push the walls back to make the rooms bigger but Jonathan is eager to please where he can. He has whipped up an easy-to-use bus guide (a far more pleasurable way of getting around Paris than the metro), a list of neighbourhood restaurants and can arrange tickets for the Orsay and Luxembourg museums. Breakfast comes in two formats with two prices: a quick bite for those on the run, a more elaborate affair for those who want a slow start – watching the world rush past the big windows of the open-sided ground floor. The walls are hung with ancient maps showing the Latin Quarter through the ages: the building's foundations were probably laid when Lutetia was capital of Roman Gaul and a 22-metre well still holds water. Bedrooms are spotless and simple, with white furniture and pastel-hued piqué bedcovers; there are splashes of colours in the curtains and each snug, functional bathroom has a clothes line. It's a pleasant place to stay, beneath the looming wall of the Sorbonne where tomorrow's leaders are as yet learning their future trades. Good service, good value, great spot.

Price	€106–€150. Singles €85. Triples €150–€170.
Rooms	44: 27 doubles, 5 twins, 10 singles, 2 triples.
Meals	Breakfast €5–€9. Restaurants nearby.
Closed	Rarely.
Directions	Metro: Cluny La Sorbonne (10), St Michel (4). RER: Luxembourg, St Michel-Notre Dame. Buses: 21, 27, 38, 63, 82, 84, 86, 87. Parking: Rue Soufflot.

	Jonathan Wyplosz 16 rue Cujas, 75005 Paris
Tel	+33 (0)1 43 54 67 30
Email	hotel@3colleges.com
Web	www.3colleges.com

Hôtel Les Jardins du Luxembourg

Freud once trampled this still peaceful cul-de-sac when he stayed in 1885 – and we know that the curtains round his bed were yellow: his disciple Ernest Jones relates that he applied chemical tests to make sure they did not contain arsenic. Now there are curtains at the windows only, some falling nicely to the floor; original beams are still on view on the top floor. Rooms are small, balconies minute, furnishings immaculate. We can imagine Freud sitting with a coffee in the tiny salon; Art Deco chairs and brass lights over paintings give it an intimate feel, and daily papers come free. The reception area, by contrast, is a big open space, with a handsome mahogany desk that doubles as a bar. Facing it is a long wrought-iron park bench with colourful cushions to remind us that the Luxembourg Gardens – one of Paris' largest, loveliest green spaces – are just across the street. Keep your eye out for the delightful ochre and orange checkerboard tiles in the downstairs breakfast room and joyful trompe l'œil lizards and vine wreaths in the bathrooms, some of which have free-standing basins and four-legged tubs.

Price	€169–€179.
Rooms	26: 18 doubles, 7 twins, 1 single.
Meals	Breakfast €11. Restaurants nearby.
Closed	Rarely.
Directions	Metro: Cluny la Sorbonne (10). RER: Luxembourg. Buses: 21, 27, 38, 82, 84, 85, 89. Parking: Public parking available.

Les Jardins du Luxembourg
5 Impasse Royer Collard,
75005 Paris,

Tel	+33 (0)1 40 46 08 88
Email	jardinslux@wanadoo.fr
Web	www.les-jardins-du-luxembourg.com

Grand Hôtel des Balcons

Les Balcons has the lot: an idea of service that produces tea on winter afternoons, a clothesline over the bath, and a daily feast of a breakfast (cooked specials, organic yogurt, fruit salad, espresso), that's free on your birthday. Owners and staff appear to work with lightness and pleasure. Having decorated her Art Nouveau hotel by taking inspiration from the floral 1890s staircase windows, Denise Corroyer now teaches ikebana and flowers the house – brilliantly – while her son Jean-François and his wife Sabine charmingly manage. Rooms are simple yet pleasing. The five big family rooms have smart décor and pretty modern lamps, parquet floors and two windows, decent bathrooms (two basins, pretty tiles); singles have new walk-in showers. Some rooms are tiny but purpose-made table units use the space judiciously, amusing prints decorate the walls and front rooms have balconies with planted window boxes. At the back, you may be woken by the birds. An eagle eye is kept on maintenance, beds are firm, colours and fabrics simple and bright. Remarkable value, super people, and bang in the heart of the Latin Quarter.

Price	€112–€175. Singles €92–€175. Family rooms €210.
Rooms	50: 17 doubles, 13 twins, 15 singles, 5 family rooms for 4.
Meals	Breakfast €12. Restaurants nearby.
Closed	Rarely.
Directions	Metro: Odéon (4, 10). RER: Luxembourg. Buses: 21, 24, 27, 58, 63, 86, 87, 95, 96. Parking: École de Médecine.

Jean-François & Sabine André
3 rue Casimir Delavigne,
75006 Paris,

Tel	+33 (0)1 46 34 78 50
Email	grandhoteldesbalcons@orange.fr
Web	www.balcons.com

Hôtel de Buci

On one of the little streets in the heart of St Germain, where tempting galleries, restaurants, antique shops, fashion houses, cafés and bars are encroaching on the much-loved market, stands the Buci, full of refined comfort and hospitality. From the chandeliered salon (with honesty bar and posh tea selection), descend a curling wooden staircase to the light, bright breakfast room: its plump black sofas, sky-blue screens and background music form a fitting stage for a generous buffet. Rooms are newly decorated in – if you can imagine this – 18th-century boudoir style, with bleu celeste a recurring theme and period furniture posing before heavy draped curtains and flamboyant patterned walls. They vary wildly in peacefulness and size (if you wish to keep windows open, choose a room at the back) and are reached via a lift and narrow sloping corridors whose fabric-covered walls are a map of ancient Paris. Come evening, the morning's classical music turns to jazz and the espresso machine is in demand. This is a reliable place to stay on one of the most fabulous streets in St Germain — with thoroughly helpful staff.

Price	€195-€335. Suites €330-€550.
Rooms	24: 12 doubles, 8 twins, 4 suites for 3-4.
Meals	Breakfast €17-€22. Restaurants nearby.
Closed	Never.
Directions	Metro: St Germain des Prés (4), Mabillon (10), Odéon (4,10). RER: St Michel-Notre Dame. Buses: 58, 63, 70, 86, 87, 96. Parking: St Germain des Prés..

Romain Binet
22 rue Buci, 75006 Paris
Tel   +33 (0)1 55 42 74 74
Email   reservations@buci-hotel.com
Web   www.buci-hotel.com

Artus Hôtel

Attitude and plenty of it. The Artus already had a young, trendy art crowd who would stay at no other place, so the owner – a collector – could afford to be bold. A sweep of an entrance, bare except for large windows and the name of the hotel boldly embossed in mosaic, leads you past the slim crescent of a reception desk to a gleaming honesty bar with espresso machine and a cluster of bright bucket chairs. Downstairs, find a breakfast room decked out in fire engine red, dotted with neat white square tables. It is all rather breathless and new, and the rotating art exhibitions showcase some exhilarating works by Paris's up-and-coming talents. The challenge here is space; rooms were never big, so expect functionality mixed with style, a minimum of colour and top-class textiles. Leather trims, red silk curtains, Murano basins, open bathrooms with smoked green glass, tweed curtains: it's refreshing and new. Each room has an artistic detail – an antique door, perhaps, or modern doll sculpture on the wall. A lot has changed – except for the imperturbable Sangay, irreproachably manning the desk.

Price	€195–€305.
	Duplex & suite €395–€415.
Rooms	27: 20 doubles, 5 twins, 1 duplex, 1 suite for 2.
Meals	Buffet breakfast included. Restaurants nearby.
Closed	Never.
Directions	Metro: St Germain des Prés (4), Mabillon (10), Odéon (4,10). RER: St Michel-Notre Dame. Buses: 58, 63, 70, 86, 87, 96. Parking: St Germain des Prés.

Romain Binet
34 rue de Buci, 75006 Paris

Tel	+33 (0)1 43 29 07 20
Email	info@artushotel.com
Web	www.artushotel.com

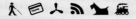

Hôtel Relais Saint Sulpice

Smack on the back doorstep of Saint Sulpice church, tucked into one of those tiny magic streets untouched by time, this is the perfect hideaway for sleuthing around for Da Vinci Code clues or spotting the literati of Saint Germain des Prés. You might miss the entrance if you are not careful; it's more an entryway into an aristocratic 18th-century home than a door to a hotel. The womb-like salon continues the lived-in feeling with deep red papered walls, screened mahogany bookcases, a white faïence stove, Chinese jars and some bottles of French liqueur tempting guests to an evening aperitif; in the lobby, find trompe l'œil bookshelves and a vast oriental frieze reflected in tall mirrors. No reception desk to speak of here, just a friendly spirit behind the table to hand out keys to your small but cosy room. The attention to detail is impressive: you may spot a fringe-like frieze along the walls or an elegant wrought-iron bed and bistro table; most bathrooms have colourful floor tiles. A huge glass roof and a bounty of greenery give the downstairs breakfast room a winter garden feel. An exceptional address.

Price	€213–€260.
Rooms	26: 19 doubles, 7 twins.
	Triple available on request.
Meals	Breakfast €12. Restaurants nearby.
Closed	Never.
Directions	Metro: Odéon (4, 10), Mabillon (10).
	RER: St Michel-Notre Dame,
	Luxembourg.
	Buses: 58, 63, 70, 84, 86, 87, 96.
	Parking: Place Saint Sulpice, Marché
	Saint-Germain.

	Relais Saint Sulpice
	3 rue Garancière,
	75006 Paris
Tel	+33 (0)1 46 33 99 00
Email	relaisstsulpice@wanadoo.fr
Web	www.relais-saint-sulpice.com

Hôtel Saint Paul Rive Gauche

An exceptionally welcoming place with a flickering fire in the sitting room, a day-lit interior patio and Skype the sleeping cat. With the Luxembourg Gardens a stroll away, bustling Saint Germain at the end of the street, and exceptional service and attention to detail (like organic croissants at breakfast), it's the favourite of many guests. Expect crisp white duvets with a mohair throw for a splash of colour, a thick tiger-stripe carpet underfoot, spotless bathrooms with real shower heads, Roger & Gallet soaps and towel heaters. Bedrooms come in different sizes and that includes small – as with most Paris hotels. Those in the back have handsome views onto the prestigious Lycée St Louis with its classical façade, those in front look onto the ever fascinating Rue Monsieur le Prince. There are beamed ceilings, sleigh beds, faux ostrich bedheads, clever corner armoires, family antiques, even two baldaquin beds on the lower floors with the high ceilings. The fourth generation of a Franco-British family has made the Saint Paul a welcoming marriage of French elegance and English comfort. *Babysitting can be arranged.*

Price	€178-€248. Family rooms €288-€358.
Rooms	31: 21 doubles, 7 twins/doubles, 3 family rooms for 3-4. Some rooms interconnect.
Meals	Buffet breakfast €13. Restaurants nearby.
Closed	Never.
Directions	Metro: Odéon (4,10). RER: Luxembourg. Buses: 21, 27, 38, 58, 63, 82, 84, 85, 86, 87, 89, 96. Parking: École de Médecine, St Sulpice.

Marianne Oberlin
43 rue Monsieur le Prince,
75006 Paris

Tel	+33 (0)1 43 26 98 64
Email	contact@hotelsaintpaulparis.com
Web	www.hotelsaintpaulparis.com

Entry 71   Map 5

Hôtel Le Clos Médicis

You can see right into the lobby through what was a shop window; slip in from the excitable Boulevard St Michel and you hear muted jazz, feel soft air. In this place of quiet contemporary class, the attractive countersunk salon has a welcoming fire, deep brown armchairs, jungle pictures and a fine stone pillar; beyond it are a sunny Tuscan patio and a delightful young team at reception. To ground its very Parisian personality, the Hôtel Le Clos Médicis has opted for roots in provincial soil: a *clos* is a vineyard, and each room is named after a famous wine. Bedrooms have been redesigned by fashionable names in strong silent colours – rich red and blue, white, ginger and brown – real fabrics with wide contrasting borders, deep-framed mirrors and sophisticated wildlife prints. One room has a private terrace, another is a nicely arranged duplex; all are soundproofed and, if not always very big, are most comfortable. Bathrooms are still impeccable. The details have all been thought through. Add that lively sense of hospitality, and it's all you could hope for, and possibly more.

Price	€225–€310. Singles from €185. Duplex & family room €510.
Rooms	38: 16 doubles, 20 twins/doubles, 1 duplex, 1 family room for 3.
Meals	Buffet breakfast €13. Restaurants nearby.
Closed	Never.
Directions	Metro: Odéon (4,10). RER: Luxembourg. Buses: 21, 27, 38, 58, 63, 82, 84, 85, 86, 87, 89, 96. Parking: École de Médecine, St Sulpice.

Olivier Méallet
56 rue Monsieur le Prince,
75006 Paris

Tel	+33 (0)1 43 29 10 80
Email	message@hotelclosmedicisparis.com
Web	www.hotelclosmedicisparis.com

Hotel

Paris – Île de France

Hôtel Sainte Beuve

This beautifully decorated hotel, well-known and loved during the wilder days of Montparnasse, exudes an atmosphere of unstuffy designer luxury – quiet good taste in gentle tones and thick fabrics. The harmoniously hued lobby/salon, which doubles as a breakfast room, has superb silk curtains, a winter fire in the marble fireplace, modern paintings and old prints. It is all small and intimate and the attentive, efficient staff are a vital element in your sense of well-being. Bedrooms come in ancient and modern finery: lots of pale walls, soft colours and textured fabrics, colourful chintzes and paisleys, at least one antique per room – a leather-topped desk, a walnut dressing-table, a polished armoire – and 18th/19th-century pictures in rich old frames. The Sainte Beuve room is the largest and it's dazzling. Bathrooms are superbly modern with bathrobes and fine toiletries. Start the day with a feast of croissants and brioches… then you can run it off in the Luxembourg Gardens. End the day with très tasty food at teensy Le Timbre, in the same street.

Price	€187-€287. Suite €315-€365.
Rooms	22: 11 doubles, 10 twins, 1 suite for 3.
Meals	Breakfast €15. Restaurants nearby.
Closed	Never.
Directions	Metro: Notre Dame des Champs (12), Vavin (4). RER: Port-Royal. Parking: Montparnasse.

Monsieur & Madame Inchauspé
9 rue Sainte Beuve,
75006 Paris

Tel   +33 (0)1 45 48 20 07
Email reservation@hotelsaintebeuve.com
Web   www.hotelsaintebeuve.com

Hôtel Madison

Bang opposite the Saint Germain des Prés church and vastly celebrated Deux Magots café, the Madison's Art Deco façade is as supremely Parisian as the artful blend of contemporary and classic that greets you through the glass sliding doors. Adventurous imagination guides the rich choice of colours and textures inside: shocking pink, mint green, smooth grey fabric-clothed walls, heaps of heavy velour and velvet. Bathrooms have stunning Italian tiling and chunky ceramic basins in blue, red or yellow; funky modern lighting glows. Set your iPod in the dock and sink back on super-soft beds. All rooms are different, bursting with personality; the top-floor suite is a triumph of space and wraparound views over Saint Germain – priceless. Downstairs, a gleaming salon of curves, crescents and heavily patterned black-and-white chairs transforms into a breakfast room, with a generous buffet appearing like magic from behind the most extraordinary buddha screen. Young staff have just the right mix of polite class and friendly cheerfulness. A reflection of Paris, in many ways: vital, provocative, alive.

Price	€235–€395. Singles €175–€195. Suites €415–€435.
Rooms	52: 46 twins/doubles, 3 singles, 3 suites.
Meals	Restaurants nearby.
Closed	Never.
Directions	Metro: St Germain des Prés. RER: Saint Michel.

Caroline Demon
143 boulevard Saint Germain,
75006 Paris

Tel   +33 (0)1 40 51 60 00
Email   resa@hotel-madison.com
Web   www.hotel-madison.com

Entry 74   Map 5

Millésime Hôtel

"Our room had an impossible peacefulness – all we could hear was birdsong," writes a guest. Behind its imposing old doors, the Millésime is intimate, pretty, peaceful and welcoming – as are sparkling, multi-lingual Inga and her young, bright team. The reception is warmly Mediterranean, with soft ochre sponging in the lobby, deep sofas set on glowing parquet and a charming little patio with mosaic-topped tables; three rooms open from the patio itself. The Mediterranean theme continues in smartly carpeted bedrooms, which vary in size but are never too tiny (a rarity in Paris): ancient-looking cast-iron lamps contrast with sunny yellow walls and splashes of bright blue; warm, earthy colours embrace beds. The top-floor suite has brilliant high-peaked ceilings and tall windows overlooking historic towers and domes. Reach it via the lift or the 17th-century wooden staircase, a genuine piece of French heritage. The vaulted breakfast room is as charming as all the rest, and the Left Bank position is unsurpassed. One of our favourite city hotels, and good value for Saint Germain.

Price	€140–€285. Suite €290–€445.
Rooms	21: 20 twins/doubles, 1 suite.
Meals	Breakfast €13. Buffet €16. Restaurants nearby.
Closed	Rarely.
Directions	Metro: St Germain des Prés. RER: St Michel-Notre Dame. Buses: 39, 48, 63, 86, 95. Parking: St Germain des Prés.

Inga Holzinger
15 rue Jacob,
75006 Paris

Tel	+33 (0)1 44 07 97 97
Email	reservation@millesimehotel.com
Web	www.millesimehotel.com

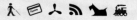

Hôtel des Marronniers

Another of the family's private mansion hotels, it stands between quiet courtyard and real garden. The almost dramatically Second Empire salon, all ruches and gilt, leads to a delectable old-style conservatory where red-cushioned iron chairs and marble-topped tables await you under the fruity 'chandeliers', reflecting the big shrubby garden – privilege indeed. Rooms vary: mostly smallish, they give onto the garden or the front courtyard – no need for double glazing. From the top floor you see higgledy-piggledy rooftops or the church tower; from all rooms you hear the chimes. The décor is based on coordinated fabrics (walls, curtains, canopies, beds), bright floral prints or Regency stripes serving as backdrop to an antique desk, a carved armoire or a pair of lemon-tree spray lights... lots of character here. Renovated bathrooms are most attractive, be they grey and ginger marble or white tiles with an original tropical island 'picture'. After so much light, the basement breakfast room is in soft, dark contrast for cool winter mornings. Or hie ye to the conservatory.

Price	€190–€200. Singles €139. Triple €240.
Rooms	37: 24 doubles, 8 twins, 3 singles, 2 triples.
Meals	Breakfast €12–€14. Restaurants nearby.
Closed	Never.
Directions	Metro: St Germain des Prés. RER: St Michel-Notre Dame. Buses: 39, 48, 63, 86, 95. Parking: St Germain des Prés.

Perrine Henneveux
21 rue Jacob, 75006 Paris

Tel	+33 (0)1 43 25 30 60
Email	hotel-des-marronniers@wanadoo.fr
Web	www.hoteldesmarronniers.com

Hôtel des Deux Continents

The hotel and its three ancient listed buildings sink discreetly into the background among the decorating and antique shops. Its public rooms are atmospheric with fresh flowers, beams, gilt frames, draperies and dark furniture, lightened at the front by the big street window and at the back by a little patio. Venus stands shyly among the greenery and tables are laid with fine white cloths and bright china against a green and gold backdrop. The geography is intriguing: two buildings look onto quiet inner courtyards, the larger, noisier rooms are at the front; choose the quadrangle side. All are done in contemporary-classic style with yards of fabric – walls, bedheads, covers, curtains, pelmets, the odd canopy – in occasionally surprising mixtures of colours and patterns; but it all 'works', as do the bronze lights and pretty old mirrors. In the last building (two storeys, no lift), the very smallest rooms are peaceful, charming and air-conditioned (the rest have fans). The whole place has masses of personality, the staff are young and welcoming and St Germain des Prés hums. Good value.

Price	€189. Singles €160. Triples €230.
Rooms	41: 19 doubles, 10 twins, 8 singles, 4 triples.
Meals	Breakfast €11–€12. Restaurants nearby.
Closed	Never.
Directions	Metro: St Germain des Prés. RER: St Michel-Notre Dame. Buses: 39, 48, 63, 86, 95. Parking: St Germain des Prés.

Perrine Henneveux
25 rue Jacob, 75006 Paris

Tel	+33 (0)1 43 26 72 46
Email	continents.hotel@wanadoo.fr
Web	www.hoteldes2continents.com

La Villa Saint Germain

A showcase of contemporary French design that screams trendy Saint Germain. Step in to soberly studied forms and colours: a blocky black desk, soft silky chestnut curtains, a curvy steel stair rail, ochre-flecked stone floor slabs; gentle music too, and grey and café latte chairs on a teak floor by the bar. Staff are appropriately young, bright, attentive. Bedrooms reflect Saint Germain's split personality: the drama of wine red, brown, white; the gentleness of ivory, beige. Materials are rich and yielding – thick burgundy curtains folded back on silk linings, 'crocodile-skin' bedheads, fluffy white duvets against scarlet walls. (If you like your room with extra personality, ask for a newly redesigned one on the fourth floor, where shelves groan with modern white objets and funky lighting gleams on half-moon tables.) And the details: room numbers light-projected by the door, monogrammed linen, superb designer bathrooms in chrome and ground glass. The bar is peaceful, the lift speedy, and breakfast is down the 1930s-look stairs in a stylish rich red space. It all feels so good and the cool Left Bank laps at your feet.

Price	€210-€400. Suites €350-€500.
Rooms	31: 17 doubles, 10 twins, 4 suites.
Meals	Buffet breakfast €22; continental €16. Restaurants nearby.
Closed	Never.
Directions	Metro: St Germain des Prés. RER: St Michel-Notre Dame. Buses: 39, 48, 63, 86, 95. Parking: St Germain des Prés.

Christine Horbette
29 rue Jacob, 75006 Paris

Tel	+33 (0)1 43 26 60 00
Email	hotel@villa-saintgermain.com
Web	www.villa-saintgermain.com

Hôtel Prince de Condé

In one of the smallest, most intimate hotels in Paris, in one of the most sauntering streets – named after the great river to which it leads – you'll meet delightful staff and real attention to detail. The city is full of vaulted cellars converted into breakfast rooms, though here it's a breakfast salon: a red carpet warms exposed stone, low round tables invite intimacy, sofas tell of relaxation and low armchairs in broad stripes are a lesson in cosiness (you'll forgive the slight whiff of damp after rain). There's also a little sitting room with an intriguing *cabinet de curiosités*. Upstairs are bright bedrooms with Jouy fabric on walls, double-glazed windows and just the right designer chair or Napoleon III desk to personalise a room – a pleasing partnership of classic and modern. The top floor suite gets a royal bathroom: jacuzzi tub, double basins, swish Italian taps. It's big enough to wear red-green medallion wallpaper, sit two armchairs and still have room for a green sofa and red-trimmed cushions. Lots of galleries for gazing and people for watching in the little streets outside. Just lovely.

Price	€234. Suite €336.
Rooms	11: 10 twins/doubles, 1 suite for 2.
Meals	Breakfast €13. Restaurants nearby.
Closed	Rarely.
Directions	Metro: St Germain des Prés (4), Mabillon (10), Odéon (4, 10). RER: St Michel-Notre Dame. Buses: 39, 48, 58, 63, 70, 86, 87, 95. Parking: Rue Mazarine.

	Prince de Condé
	39 rue de Seine, 75006 Paris
Tel	+33 (0)1 43 26 71 56
Email	princedeconde@wanadoo.fr
Web	www.prince-de-conde.com

Hôtel de Seine

Underneath the arches, through the big doors: it still feels like the private mansion it was. The welcome adds to this impression. There are two really French salons off the hall, fresh flowers, space, deep quiet. The breakfast room, supervised by a fine little Pan, aims to please all sorts with a large table for the sociable and several small tables for the less so; walls are clothed in Florentine-style fabric, chairs are blue and studded, antique corner cupboards glow, swags and tassels bobble, but it's not cluttered. Bedrooms have class too, with their strong colour schemes, furniture that is gently painted Louis XVI or highly polished, cane-seated Directoire and, again, that sense of being in a home not an anonymous hotel. One room displays rather daring black paint and gilt edging in honour of the 1850s craze for all things Far Eastern; others have quirky layouts dictated by the old architecture. Elegant bathrooms are much mirrored and the higher floors naturally carry 18th-century timbers and the occasional balcony for rooftop views or bird's-eye vistas of Parisian façades. A most welcoming place to stay.

Price	€215–€220. Singles €185. Triples €245.
Rooms	30: 14 doubles, 8 twins, 4 singles, 4 triples.
Meals	Breakfast €12–€13. Restaurants nearby.
Closed	Never.
Directions	Metro: St Germain des Prés (4), Mabillon (10), Odéon (4, 10). RER: St Michel-Notre Dame. Buses: 39, 48, 58, 63, 70, 86, 87, 95. Parking: Rue Mazarine.

Perrine Henneveux
52 rue de Seine, 75006 Paris

Tel	+33 (0)1 46 34 22 80
Email	hotel-de-seine@wanadoo.fr
Web	www.hoteldeseine.com

Welcome Hôtel

A small affordable hotel on one of the coolest crossroads of Paris, where the cute shopping streets and the legendary cafés of St Germain des Prés meet. The Welcome has an easy, friendly atmosphere and an unpretentious style. The ground-floor reception is tiny but the space grows as you move up; on the first floor is the small, timbered and tapestried Louis XIII salon from where you can look down from your breakfast table onto the bustle below. Most of the bedrooms are smallish, too. Corner rooms have the best views, but all overlook one or other of the streets – be prepared to hear trucks unloading. Among all sorts of angles and juttings-out, the variegated décor has in some rooms been revived with floral fabrics and bottle-green carpeting; furniture is functional wood, bathrooms are clean. On the top floor are sloping ceilings and beams, and one bedroom is reached through its half-timbered bathroom. It's quirky, night-noisy and absolutely in the thick of things. Breakfast is a communal affair in the hall and you can walk to almost everything, including the Louvre.

Price	€129-€149. Single €99.
Rooms	29: 14 doubles, 9 twins, 4 singles, 2 family rooms.
Meals	Breakfast €11. Restaurants nearby.
Closed	Never.
Directions	Metro: St Germain des Prés (4), Mabillon (10), Odéon (4, 10). RER: St Michel-Notre Dame. Buses: 39, 48, 58, 63, 70, 86, 87, 95. Parking: Rue Mazarine.

	Perrine Henneveux
	66 rue de Seine, 75006 Paris
Tel	+33 (0)1 46 34 24 80
Email	welcome-hotel@wanadoo.fr
Web	www.welcomehotel-paris.com

Hôtel Mayet

The dynamic and welcoming new owner of the Mayet brings enjoyment of people and his taste for conviviality from his previous life as a doctor. He and his son have created a more service-based hotel – 24-hour bar, modern media, air conditioning, a sitting/meeting room in the vaulted basement – yet, with the breakfast and sitting area now on the ground floor, it feels more relaxed and open. The well-loved colourful, drippy murals still brighten the space, the meats and cheeses buffet is fabulous value, you can boil your own egg, the croissants and baguettes are tasty and fresh from the local bakery. Here, too, guests can sit in comfort and enjoy a leisurely coffee or drink at any time of day. Some rooms are compact and fun in grey, white and dark red, with 'office' furniture. The newest are just as snug, in white with flashes of orange and an 'oriental' touch – an exotic photograph, excellent new bedding and super Italian-style walk-in showers. In a quietish street in a great neighbourhood, this is a place for living in and getting to know Paris, not just passing through.

Price	€150–€160. Triple €190.
Rooms	23: 4 twins/doubles, 17 doubles, 1 single, 1 triple. Children under 3 free.
Meals	Buffet breakfast €10. Restaurants nearby.
Closed	Rarely.
Directions	Metro: Duroc (10, 13), Vaneau (10). RER: Invalides, St Michel-Notre Dame. Buses: 28, 39, 70, 82, 87, 89, 92. Parking: Bon Marché.

Philippe & Timothée Leverbe
3 rue Mayet, 75006 Paris

Tel	+33 (0)1 47 83 21 35
Email	hotel@mayet.com
Web	www.mayet.com

Hôtel d'Aubusson

Through the superb old doors into the flagstoned hall – touch the space, hear the quiet piano in the bar, see the promise of moulded, fountained magnificence through the patio doors, and unwind. It is an absolutely beautiful stone building, serene and elegant in its golden 17th-century proportions, properly modern in its renovation. Take an aperitif out to the lovely summer patio, read by the great fireplace in the antique-furnished salon or feast on a full English breakfast under an original 17th-century Aubusson tapestry. You are cocooned in pure French style: a forest of beams above your head, tall slim windows, superb parquet floors, monogrammed china. There is a luxurious bar, jazz concerts, piano entertainment, and a Louis XV internet point in a quiet corner. Bedrooms are large, some with wonderful beams, all richly, unfussily furnished in custom-made mahogany, thick fabrics, gleaming granite bathrooms. You are a short walk from Pont Neuf, the Louvre, Luxembourg Gardens, everything... in a grand house where guests are nurtured by the gentle, impeccable Monsieur Spove and his team of faultless staff. Magnificent.

Price	€250–€475. Duplexes €515. Suites €625.
Rooms	49: 39 doubles, 3 duplexes, 7 suites.
Meals	Breakfast €7–€25.
Closed	Rarely.
Directions	Metro: Odéon. RER: St Michel-Notre Dame, Pont-Neuf. Buses: 56, 63, 70, 86, 87, 96. Parking: At hotel.

Andreas Spove
33 rue Dauphine, 75006 Paris

Tel	+33 (0)1 43 29 43 43
Email	reservations@hoteldaubusson.com
Web	www.hoteldaubusson.com

Hôtel Le Clément

This cute little hotel has been in the same family for 100 years and Madame Charrade, should you be lucky enough to meet her, is the gentlest hotelier you could hope to meet. More cosy living room than lobby is the inviting sitting area off the new breakfast room, with fireplace, gleaming wood panelling and bookshelves. From the higher floors, the view across the St Germain marketplace to the towers of St Sulpice church is super. These rooms at the top have loads of character with their sloping ceilings, though little space, and access is by narrow stairwell or even narrower lift! Back rooms have no view, of course, except over the pretty planting at the bottom of one of the lightwells (the hotel occupies two connecting buildings), but peace is guaranteed. Madame's decorative style is southern cottage: small spriggy or floral prints, harmonious fabrics, good colour combinations – midnight-blue and ivory, Provençal red and orange – and crisp, white piqué bedcovers; bathrooms are often tiled in colourful mosaic. A hotel of good value – from which reaching all the sights is a breeze.

Price	€145–€156.
	Family rooms & triples €175.
Rooms	28: 12 doubles, 6 twins,
	5 family rooms for 3, 5 triples.
Meals	Buffet breakfast €12.
	Restaurants nearby.
Closed	Never.
Directions	Metro: St Germain des Prés (4),
	Mabillon (10).
	RER: Luxembourg.
	Buses: 63, 70, 85, 86, 95, 96.
	Parking: Opposite hotel.

Madame Charrade
6 rue Clément, 75006 Paris

Tel	+33 (0)1 43 26 53 60
Email	info@hotel-clement.fr
Web	www.hotel-clement.fr

Pension Les Marronniers

It's an honest-to-goodness pension de famille, one of the very last, so if you're young and penniless or old and nostalgic, head for Marie's quintessentially French family place overlooking the Luxembourg Gardens. It's been in her family since the 1930s and is as personal and cluttered as anything in Balzac. There are countless pictures, portraits and photographs, statues and plants galore, notices from inmates on flower pots and mantelpieces, a cuckoo clock that was silenced 20 years ago and a superbly carved, grass-green armoire topped with candlesticks – plus a motley crew of friendly dogs. Marie coddles her guests (some return year after year) and loves cooking for them: she clearly enjoys food herself, especially vegetarian, and makes sure others do too. She is also down-to-earth, compassionate, perceptive and hard-working – a remarkable woman. The bedrooms for short-stayers have less personality than the dining and drawing room, rather as if they have been furnished with what was left over, and some share washing facilities. But what counts is the wonderful welcome, the tradition and the food.

Price	Half-board €47-€70 p.p. Weekly & monthly rentals.
Rooms	11: 6 twins/doubles; 5 twins/doubles sharing bath.
Meals	Half-board only, except Saturdays & Sundays (brunch on Saturdays included).
Closed	Rarely.
Directions	Metro: Vavin (4), Notre Dame des Champs (12). RER: Luxembourg. Buses: 58, 82, 83. Parking: Rue Auguste Comte.

Marie Poirier
78 rue d'Assas, 75006 Paris

Tel	+33 (0)1 43 26 37 71
Email	infos@pension-marronniers.com
Web	www.pension-marronniers.com

Grand Hôtel de l'Univers

The giant Boulevard St Germain slices this little one-way street in half; the lower bit, more a pavement than a street, is only ten steps long and finishes on trendy Rue de Buci. As you've guessed, you are in an old part of town and the 15th-century effigy of a man leaning on his truncheon, found above the door, remains a mystery. Even seen through large windows on the street the big airy salon is a surprise with the theatricality of its 18th-century sofa, armchairs and antique dresser set against a huge wall of honey-coloured stone; the bar behind the reception is a much cosier affair. Rooms are delightful, quiet, and decorated with real French flair; bathrooms are recent in marble and chrome. If size is important, opt for the deluxe rooms. Breakfast in the stone-vaulted cellar is a real treat, with eggs, sausages, fresh orange juice and delicious breads. Extra atmosphere comes from the backlit medieval sconces. What's more, the two stunning contemporary executive rooms bear the signature of Pierre-Yves Rochon, they are prototypes for the Hôtel Keppler at two thirds of the price.

Price	€150–€280. Singles €130–€185.
Rooms	33 twins/doubles.
Meals	Buffet breakfast €10.
	Restaurants nearby.
Closed	Never.
Directions	Metro: Odéon (4,10).
	RER: St Michel-Notre Dame.
	Buses: 58, 63, 70, 86, 96.
	Parking: Rue Mazarine,
	St Germain des Prés.

Éric Desfaudais
6 rue Grégoire de Tours,
75006 Paris

Tel	+33 (0)1 43 29 37 00
Email	grandhotelunivers@wanadoo.fr
Web	www.hotel-paris-univers.com

Trianon Rive Gauche

Cosy, functional, on the Left Bank and near everything – three steps from the Sorbonne, three minutes from the Jardin du Luxembourg. A pair of buildings (one built in 1860, one Art Deco) run up eight storeys linked by a staircase that wraps its graceful self around the old-world cage-style lift... and the rooms on the top floor get the great views over Parisian rooftops to the Eiffel Tower and the Sacré Coeur. Inside, all has been refurbished. Step into a flashy black, white and silver reception lobby, manned by delightful staff, with sofas upholstered in neo-baroque prints and a fabulous round mirror overseeing the space. There's an airy beige-tiled breakfast room for a buffet start to the day (or you can have continental in your room) and, on the way to breakfast, a big basement bar. Comfortable bedrooms, not huge but a fair size for Paris, have fabric-covered walls in dark orange and mustard, heavy coordinated curtains, wall-to-wall carpeting in thin stripes and new duvets. Reproduction old masters hang on the walls; bathrooms, though tiny, are sparklier. Paris lies at your feet.

Price	€188-€269. Singles €129-€165. Triples €239-€309.	
Rooms	110: 10 twins/doubles, 51 doubles, 33 twins, 5 singles, 11 triples.	
Meals	Breakfast €14. Choice of restaurants 50m and beyond.	
Closed	Never.	
Directions	Metro: Cluny, Odéon (10), St Michel (4). RER: Luxembourg (B). Buses: 21, 27, 38, 82. Parking: Rue de l'École de Médecine, Rue Soufflot.	

Perrine Henneveux
1 bis & 3 rue de Vaugirard,
75006 Paris

Tel	+33 (0)1 43 29 88 10
Email	trianon.rg@wanadoo.fr
Web	www.hoteltrianonrivegauche.com

Hôtel Odéon Saint-Germain

Once across the threshold of this small hotel you will be swept away by the understated luxury, Parisian elegance and generous envelope of well-being. There is an honesty bar in the lobby along with black and white striped armchairs with red satin backs and a comfy toffee-coloured sofa facing an ancient stone fireplace and an open stone wall. A tiny lift brings you to the smallish rooms (this is St Germain, after all), some with high ceilings and silk canopies, others with chaises longues for lounging, or a luscious panel of flowered silk hung behind the leather headboards. Most have beams, painted eggshell or off-white. Sounds are muffled, even the doors to the rooms have been padded for everyone's comfort. Attention to detail is evident, from the chocolates popped on the pillow at night to the lovely soaps in the bathrooms; the staff are a delight. The owners were previously in the restaurant business so breakfast is a feast with homemade fruit compotes and cakes, prunes plumped in a cinnamon syrup and the best pastries that Paris can offer. Ask for one of the larger rooms, and book ahead.

Price	€145–€370.
Rooms	27: 15 doubles, 6 twins, 2 singles, 4 triples.
Meals	Breakfast €14. Restaurants nearby.
Closed	Never.
Directions	Metro: Odéon. RER: St Michel-Notre Dame.

Monsieur & Madame Triadou
13 rue Saint Sulpice, 75006 Paris

Tel	+33 (0)1 43 25 70 11
Email	mail@hotelosg.com
Web	www.hotelosg.com

Hôtel Saint Germain des Prés

There are two spirits afloat in Saint Germain. And because it sometimes feels that the bright-and-blinky has the upper hand, one flees to quiet reminders of another time, like the Place de Furstenberg with the Delacroix museum, or the tiny, almost hidden garden next to the church. Or take a room here, where the time button has hit pause. When we visited, there was an elegantly bejewelled matron – a regular guest – dressed in a stylish white beret chatting with the delightful manager, Éric Desfaudais. Perched on one of the high-backed chairs, she matched the décor to perfection. Be seduced by the pale translucent beauty of the Murano chandelier over the reception desk and the antique tapestry on the wall. The salon, which doubles as the breakfast room, is lit by a glass wall, with a winter garden and a painted mural; the red velvets and smart fabrics of the padded armchairs sit nicely against exposed stone walls. The lift is tiny, and so are the rooms, with a boudoir feel and beams galore. (If you're staying in midsummer, ask for one with wall-mounted air con.) But bathrooms are proper 21st century.

Price	€170-€290. Single €130. Suites €350.
Rooms	30: 27 twins/doubles, 1 single, 2 suites for 2.
Meals	Buffet breakfast €10. Restaurants nearby.
Closed	Never.
Directions	Metro: St Germain des Prés (4). RER: St Michel-Notre Dame. Buses: 39, 48, 63, 86, 87, 95. Parking: 169 boulevard St Germain.

	Éric Desfaudais
	36 rue Bonaparte, 75006 Paris
Tel	+33 (0)1 43 26 00 19
Email	hotel-saint-germain-des-pres@wanadoo.fr
Web	www.hotel-paris-saint-germain.com

Hôtel Prince de Conti

The narrow, peaceful Rue Guénégaud, just off the riverside, is one to savour slowly. Thankfully, most of the galleries and one-of-a-kind shops have been there almost as long as La Monnaie, the French Mint, now revamped with interesting exhibitions and gift shop. The Prince de Conti – the Princess lived here in 1670 – feels just as authentic the moment your feet hit the lobby's parquet floor. The choice is eclectic but it works: a little sofa fits perfectly in the bay window, a faïence stove sits next to a chinoiserie bamboo chair, a lovely bronze figure in movement watches all from its three-legged pedestal. If you are splurging and want a view, ask for the suite on the top floor with its antique desk and double-sinked bathroom; or take a ground-level room opening to the inner courtyard. All rooms bear evidence of recent redecoration and Madame Touber's eclectic sense of style. In the morning, over fresh croissants and eggs, check your reflection in the mirrors which line the lovely stone-walled breakfast room with its wooden tables and wicker chairs.

Price	€185–€340.
Rooms	24: 6 doubles, 14 doubles/twins, 2 suites for 4, 2 duplexes. Triple room available on request.
Meals	Breakfast €13. Restaurants nearby.
Closed	Never.
Directions	Metro: St Germain des Prés (4), Odéon (4,10), Pont Neuf (7). RER: St Michel-Notre Dame. Buses: 58, 70. Parking: Rue Mazarine.

	Prince de Conti 8 rue Guénégaud, 75006 Paris
Tel	+33 (0)1 44 07 30 40
Email	princedeconti@wanadoo.fr
Web	www.prince-de-conti.com

Hôtel Bourgogne & Montana

Luxury of the four-star variety has now taken over the whole of this marvellous hotel where the quiet, sober atmosphere may reflect serious work being done in the nearby National Assembly – note the bountiful gendarmes! (An excellent area, convenient for Place de la Concorde, Tuileries, Louvre, Musée d'Orsay.) The owner's grandfather, a bored MP in the 1890s, drew those wicked caricatures of his solemn colleagues; his antiques and pictures are placed for your pleasure in the famous raspberry rotunda, primrose salon and deeply tempting breakfast room that is full of light and the most sinful buffet (included in the price). This combination of wit and creature comforts is peculiarly French and civilised – as is the quaint little 'birdcage' lift. Abandon yourself to the caress of fine damask and deep velvet, smart designer fabrics and oh-so-French traditional Jouy prints. The bigger rooms and suites have antiques, quilted upholstery and extraordinary Italian tiled bathrooms; if you like a little more snazz, ask for a newly renovated room on the top floor with funky dimmer lights and views over the rooftops of Paris.

Price	€230-410. Singles €230-€260. Suites €395-€410.
Rooms	32: 23 twins/doubles, 3 singles, 6 suites.
Meals	Restaurants nearby.
Closed	Never.
Directions	Metro: Assemblée Nationale (12), Invalides (8,13). RER & Air France bus: Invalides. Buses: 63, 83, 93. Parking: Invalides.

	Emilie Arabyan
	3 rue de Bourgogne, 75007 Paris
Tel	+33 (0)1 45 51 20 22
Email	bmontana@bourgogne-montana.com
Web	www.bourgogne-montana.com

Hôtel de Varenne

Step into the little green cul-de-sac with its ivy covered walls, hidden fountain and exquisite canopy over the entrance door and you will feel like Alice in Wonderland; you have tumbled into an oasis of peace and calm, far from the hustle bustle of the city streets. The front doors slide open, the reception desk is a friendly antique writing table, two bronze statues grace antique chests of drawers and a handsome gilt-studded balustrade leads you upstairs. There's a country air to the bedrooms as most of them (the quietest) look onto the courtyard where breakfast or an evening drink is a delight. Most are a reasonable size for Paris and all have a desk and a chair. Monsieur Pommier is a man of detail and classic taste: green, gold, blue or wine red are the classic figured bedspreads while the striped curtains repeat the colour schemes. There are framed prints of Parisian monuments and well-kept bathrooms with smooth moulded basins and plenty of shelf space. Four bigger rooms give onto the street; slightly less quiet than the rest. The charming staff will always go out of their way to make your stay special.

Price	€139–€209.
Rooms	25: 15 doubles, 10 twins.
Meals	Breakfast €11. Restaurants nearby.
Closed	Rarely.
Directions	Metro: Varenne (13), Invalides (8, 13). RER & Air France bus: Invalides. Bus: 69. Parking: Invalides.

	Jean-Marc Pommier
	44 rue de Bourgogne, 75007 Paris
Tel	+33 (0)1 45 51 45 55
Email	info@hoteldevarenne.com
Web	www.hoteldevarenne.com

Duc de Saint Simon

If Lauren Bacall chose this jewel over the Ritz, there must be a good reason: perhaps it was the hideaway feel. Terrifically peaceful on a tiny street, it opens with a discreet archway that would go unnoticed were it not for the lanterns and wisteria over the cobblestone terrace. Or perhaps it is the elegant cosiness of the salon, enveloped in an extraordinary pleated yellow and red fabric with swagged garlands, with a slinky moss green sofa and maroon-trimmed chairs. The Bacall 'suite' is big enough for its strong golds and browns and dripping chandeliers. The other rooms, four with terraces, are not large but just as appealing in their décor, fabrics, the careful choice of antique desk or objet. Street-side rooms (just as peaceful) have air con, the rest have fans. Service is responsive and charming, the stone-vaulted breakfast room has a giant trompe l'oeil painting, you can walk to the Louvre and Notre Dame, and if you arrive early, enjoy a leisurely drink in the cute cubbyhole of a bar or at one of the patio tables serenaded by birdsong. Once you stay here you may never want to try anywhere else…

Price	€265–€305. Suites €410.
Rooms	34: 29 twins/doubles, 5 suites for 2.
Meals	Breakfast €15. Restaurants nearby.
Closed	Never.
Directions	Metro: Rue du Bac (12).
	RER: St Michel-Notre Dame.
	Buses: 63, 68, 69, 83, 84, 94.
	Parking: Private parking available.

	Gisela Siggelko
	14 rue de Saint Simon, 75007 Paris
Tel	+33 (0)1 44 39 20 20
Email	duc.de.saint.simon@wanadoo.fr
Web	www.hotelducdesaintsimon.com

Hôtel La Sanguine

Through a little lobby and up one flight to a house of flowers and easy friendliness. You will be welcomed by delightful, energetic people – family or long-standing staff – and Tokyo, the sausage dog. The atmosphere is one of quiet country-style comfort; find a desk and a couple of classical statues overlooking the floral breakfast tables and wander through to a little green patio. Carpets are thick, rooms are fresh and bright with good designer fabrics, upholstered chairs to complement colourful bedcovers, discreet personality, well-equipped marble bathrooms and umpteen red-chalk drawings to lend gentle interest; the little singles take one back to childhood and Beatrix Potter. Service here is infinitely human and attentive: in season, the owners make your breakfast jam with fruit from their orchard; Monsieur bakes your breakfast croissant then irons your monogrammed towels; Madame is full of good advice on what to see and do. Hard to believe that the powers of this world – ministers, fashion gurus, ambassadors – live just around the corner. *Wines & champagne for private consumption. No lift, 4 floors.*

Price	€125-€150. Singles €100. Family room €150-€300.
Rooms	31: 17 doubles, 5 twins, 8 singles, 1 family room for 3.
Meals	Breakfast €10-€13. Restaurants nearby.
Closed	Rarely.
Directions	Metro: Madeleine (8, 12, 14), Concorde (1, 8, 12), Opéra (3,7), Auber (8). RER & Roissybus: Auber, Opéra. Buses: 42, 52, 84, 94. Parking: Madeleine, Concorde.

	Monsieur & Madame Plumerand
	6 rue de Surène, 75008 Paris
Tel	+33 (0)1 42 65 71 61
Email	info@hotel-la-sanguine.com
Web	www.hotel-la-sanguine.com

New Orient Hôtel

Pretty, original and fun, the New Orient is close to lute-maker land – and the Batignolles
Organic Food Market. Behind a superb bottle-green frontage flanked by carriage lamps
with ivy geraniums pouring off the windowsills, Catherine and Sepp display their love of
trawling country-house sales for furniture, pictures and mirrors and the mixed styles are
sheer delight – Louis XVI, 1900s, Art Deco… Bedrooms have brass beds, carved beds,
perhaps a marble washstand, a pretty table, everywhere oriental or Mediterranean fabrics;
newly redecorated rooms have smooth parquet floors and modern bathrooms in calm,
sober colours. The ground floor houses a painted telephone box, a carved dresser and a set
of light country watercolours while a fine grandfather clock supervises the breakfast area
with its large street-side windows and bamboo chairs (don't miss out on the homemade
hot chocolate!). All the balconies are lit (day and night) to display colourful box displays of
seasonal flowers. Given the pervasive opulence of the 8th arrondissement, this is a
wonderfully unassuming place with the nicest possible owners – and staff.

Price	€125–€165. Singles €105.
Rooms	30: 12 doubles, 8 twins, 10 singles.
Meals	Buffet breakfast €12; continental €8. Restaurants nearby.
Closed	Never.
Directions	Metro: Villiers (2, 3), Europe (3). RER & Roissybus: Auber, Opéra. Buses: 30, 53. Parking: Europe.

	Catherine & Sepp Wehrlé
	16 rue de Constantinople, 75008 Paris,
Tel	+33 (0)1 45 22 21 64
Email	new.orient.hotel@wanadoo.fr
Web	www.hotelneworient.com

Hôtel François 1er

The François 1er is a house of taste and luxury whose attentive owners, along with decorator Pierre-Yves Rochon, chose period furniture, lamps and pictures in a brilliant mix of classic, baroque and contemporary. The salon and bar areas are intimate and warmly panelled; a glassed-in patio with year-round greenery, moulded ceilings, a Turkish rug on parquet, real books on coffee tables and faux books around the bar summon you to comfort and ease. Even though a portrait of François 1er greets you in the lobby, you'll quickly discover that Alain Lagarrigue is the real spirit of the house and seems to be everywhere at once. He prides himself on the well-kept rooms and rich varied fabrics; those stretched on the walls match the patterns on the fine beds to offset the average-sized rooms. Some are incredible jewel boxes of intense poppy reds or elegant pale yellows. If other stimuli besides hot liquid can help you get the right start in the morning, the breakfast room is for you: a tropical theme of flowers and vines, fruits and frills all in reds and yellows, it is a joy. Porcelain patterns join in the fun.

Price	€270–€490. Suites €600–€1,000.
Rooms	40: 38 twins/doubles, 2 suites.
Meals	Breakfast €22. Restaurants nearby.
Closed	Rarely.
Directions	Metro: George V (1). RER & Air France bus: Charles de Gaulle-Étoile. Buses: 22, 32, 73, 92. Parking: George V.

Alain Lagarrigue
7 rue Magellan,
75008 Paris

Tel	+33 (0)1 47 23 44 04
Email	hotel@hotel-francois1er.fr
Web	www.the-paris-hotel.com

Entry 96   Map 5

Le Relais Madeleine

If you are wondering where in Paris you can you sink into a warm bubbly bath *and* watch all the channels at the same time, come to the Relais Madeleine. There's a delightful patio for breakfast on summery days, a brick cellar with a vaulted ceiling for cooler ones, and four bedrooms on every floor – two overlooking the central patio, two facing the rue Godot de Mauroy. And a marvellous suite with its own sauna and terrace spread across the entire sixth floor. (There's a lift, too.) The hotel is on a charming little street lined with small ethnic restaurants, midway between the business district and the smart shopping areas around the Opéra and the Madeleine. The theatre where the 70s stars performed is right around the corner, so it's only right that nostalgia be on display, and down in the breakfast room they're all there: Chuck Berry, Jimi Hendrix, Georgie Fame, Marianne Faithfull. A decent size by Parisian standards, rooms are carefully decorated in warm florals, with classic pieces of furniture, top mattresses, soft linens. The very friendly, professional service is the final treat.

Price	€189–€280. Suite with sauna €495.
Rooms	23: 21 doubles/twin, 1 single, 1 suite for 4.
Meals	Breakfast €13. Restaurants nearby.
Closed	Never.
Directions	Metro: Madeleine. RER & Roissybus: Auber.

	Bernadette Keller 11 bis rue Godot de Mauroy, 75009 Paris
Tel	+33 (0)1 47 42 22 40
Email	contact@relaismadeleine.fr
Web	www.relaismadeleine.fr

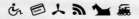

Hôtel Résidence Les Gobelins

All here is quiet, attentive and unassuming – street, hotel, owners. And the patio is a treat. Workers in the great Gobelins tapestry shops lived in this area and it was never very smart, but nearby is the entertaining, slightly bohemian rue Mouffetard – little eating houses, big mosque (try the hammam!), lively market, left-wing culture. The reception area, with country-cushioned wicker furniture, and the bright yellow airy breakfast room decorated with much-loved black and white photographs of Paris and Parisians, lie round that honeysuckle-hung inner courtyard where guests can sit in peace amid a profusion of colourful flowers. Bedrooms and bathrooms are simple, cosy and well-equipped – a writing table and chair, a decent cupboard, an excellent shower – and the green and dark red rattan furniture is ageing with grace. All rooms are quiet and light, and some interconnect – perfect for families or two couples travelling together. All is restful and harmonious. The Poiriers' gentle unobtrusive friendliness reminds us that the family used to keep a pension de famille.

Price	€98–€115 Singles €75–€85. Triples €130.
Rooms	32: 14 doubles, 4 twins, 10 singles, 4 triples. Some rooms interconnect.
Meals	Breakfast €9. Restaurant 100m.
Closed	Rarely.
Directions	Metro: Gobelins (7). RER: Port Royal. Buses: 27, 47, 83, 91. Parking: Place d'Italie.

Jennifer & Philippe Poirier
9 rue des Gobelins,
75013 Paris

Tel	+33 (0)1 47 07 26 90
Email	hotelgobelins@noos.fr
Web	www.hotelgobelins.com

Hôtel Raspail Montparnasse

Below the satisfyingly genuine 1924 frontage, the old doors spring towards you as you approach – 20th-century magic. There's old-style generosity in the high Art Deco lobby with its ceiling fans, leather chairs and play of squares and curves. The intimate hideaway bar with its leopard skin stools is a reminder of all night conversations about art and love, or the art of love… enjoy a coffee over the international papers. In street-side bedrooms, gauze curtains soften the daylight and elegant side tables match the handsome two-toned wooden headboards and desks. Fine fabric curtains and unfussy quilts add to the sober style. To each floor a colour: quiet grey, sunny ochre, powder-puff blue; to each landing a stained-glass window. Obviously, the higher the price, the bigger the room, but even the 'standards' have a decent desk and an armchair; some have the added perk of a glittering Eiffel Tower view at night. Montparnasse still bustles crazily down below and owner Christiane has heaps of ideas on where to shop and dine. A friendly and efficient welcome is the first and final flourish.

Price	€129-€220. Singles €109-€150. Suites €225-€280.
Rooms	38: 31 twins/doubles, 5 singles, 2 suites.
Meals	Breakfast €12. Restaurants nearby.
Closed	Rarely.
Directions	Metro: Vavin (4), Raspail (4, 6). RER: Port Royal. Buses: 58, 68, 82, 91. Parking: Boulevard du Montparnasse.

Christiane Martinent
203 boulevard Raspail,
75014 Paris

Tel	+33 (0)1 43 20 62 86
Email	raspailm@wanadoo.fr
Web	www.hotelraspailmontparnasse.com

Hôtel Passy Eiffel

The first owner was a passionate bee-keeper so he perhaps picked a place with a bit of nature as a centrepiece. When you step off the smart shopping street you can certainly believe that Passy was just a little country village a hundred years ago. Breathe deeply in this calm atmosphere, a restful mix of old-fashioned and contemporary styles where nothing is overdone. Lounge in the glassed-in veranda where you can see a darling gardener's cottage across the tiny cobbled yard. There is a comfortable salon and a an inviting breakfast room off the panelled hall which give onto the street through arching windows. Rooms are decorated in firm but unaggressive colours with floral quilts and curtains. The family rooms have large windows, some of which provide an excellent view of the Eiffel Tower. Beams and timbers frame the upper floors; furniture is cane and wood; storage space behind mirrored folding doors is good. On the courtyard side, you look down onto the hotel's green patio and the next-door neighbour's very well-kept garden. Lovely staff, too.

Price	€160–€185. Suites & family rooms €210–€250.
Rooms	49: 46 twins/doubles, 3 family rooms for 3.
Meals	Breakfast €14. Restaurants nearby.
Closed	Never.
Directions	Metro: Passy (6). RER: Boulainvilliers. Buses: 22, 32. Parking: 19 rue de Passy.

Christine Horbette
10 rue de Passy, 75016 Paris

Tel	+33 (0)1 45 25 55 66
Email	contact@passyeiffel.com
Web	www.passyeiffel.com

Hôtel Gavarni

The neat little Gavarni astonishes, heaving itself up into the miniature luxury class on ropes of rich draperies, heavenly bathrooms and superb finishes – and growing more eco-friendly by the year. A delight from its ground floor of deep raspberry and yellow richness up. The suites and doubles at the top are big and stunning with their jacuzzi and massage shower panels, fine canopies and beautiful furniture – supremely French with Eiffel Tower views – yet never overdone. The first-floor rooms are less luxurious but the quality is the same: thick lovely carpets, finely stitched quilts, heavy curtains and good little pieces of furniture. The triumph is those little bathrooms which have gained so much space with their utterly ingenious made-to-measure red 'granite' basin, shower and loo. Xavier, the dynamic young manager, is dedicated to making the Gavarni as 'green' as possible and a terrific organic, fairtrade breakfast is served in the conservatory; energy is renewable and all cleaning is done with eco-friendly ingredients. This is a superb combination of rich, strong modern style and pure traditional comfort.

Price	€160–€200. Singles €110–€170. Suites & family rooms €240–€500.
Rooms	25: 10 doubles, 6 twins, 4 suites, 5 family rooms for 3-4.
Meals	Breakfast €15. Restaurants nearby.
Closed	Never.
Directions	Metro: Passy (6), Trocadéro (6, 9). RER: Boulainvilliers. Buses: 22, 32. Parking: Garage Moderne, Rue de Passy.

Xavier Moraga
5 rue Gavarni, 75116 Paris
Tel   +33 (0)1 45 24 52 82
Email   reservation@gavarni.com
Web   www.gavarni.com

Ethical Collection: Environment.
See page 429 for details

Hôtel Pergolèse

Once past the doors you exchange the trumpeting sculptures of nearby Arc de Triomphe for a festival of modern design where light and natural materials, custom-made furniture and minute details all add up. Édith Vidalenc worked with renowned designer Rena Dumas, creator of Hermès boutiques worldwide, to keep a sleek but warmly curvaceously human hotel. Her sense of hospitality informs it all: the faithful team at reception are leagues away from the frostiness that can pass for four-star treatment. Pastel tones are mutedly smart so the multi-coloured breakfast room is a slightly humorous wake-up nudge, the linen mats and fine silver a bow to tradition: not taking oneself too seriously while being professional is the keynote. Rooms, not vast but with good storage, are fresh and furnished in pale wood and leather, thick curtains and soft white duvets: no distracting patterns, just coloured plush cushions to soften. The star Pergolèse room is a small masterpiece in palest apricot with a few spots of colour and a superb open bathroom. Édith's charming daughter-in-law Julia and her staff take good care of you.

Price	€175–€300. Suite €270–€400.
Rooms	40: 36 doubles (some interconnect), 3 singles, 1 suite.
Meals	Breakfast €12–€17. Restaurants nearby.
Closed	Rarely.
Directions	Metro: Argentine (1). RER A: Charles de Gaulle-Etoile; RER C: Porte Maillot. Air France bus: Porte Maillot. Parking: Avenue Foch/Porte Maillot.

Edith & Julia Vidalenc
3 rue Pergolèse, 75116 Paris

Tel	+33 (0)1 53 64 04 04
Email	hotel@pergolese.com
Web	www.pergolese.com

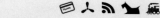

Hôtel Keppler

Get ready for lift-off with this stunning luxury creation from the Nouvel family and decorator Pierre-Yves Rochon. It's a top-class hotel with all the bells and whistles in one of the ritziest parts of Paris, nicely near the Champs-Elysées yet far enough away to hear your own footsteps on the small side street. The bedrooms are small but outstanding. Rochon has expanded on the moulded ceiling and exaggerated a crenellated pattern around the rooms to soften the overhead lighting. The sleek black and white theme is splashed with a touch or two of mauve, Chinese red or sun yellow as counterpoints. Thick white damask curtains contrast sharply with dark leather headboards and plaid bedcovers. An astonishing waterproof toile de Jouy, also in black and white, muffles the shine of marble tiles and basins in the bathrooms. There is a glass canopied salon, an flamboyant lounge bar, a sauna and small fitness room in the cellar and an architectural feat of daylight and garden in the swish open-sided breakfast space downstairs. Staff are fittingly young, bright and professional. *Room service is available from 12pm – 2am*

Price	€300–€500. Suites €600–€1,200.
Rooms	39: 34 twins/doubles, 5 suites.
Meals	Buffet breakfast €22. Restaurants nearby.
Closed	Never.
Directions	Metro: Charles de Gaulle-Étoile. RER & Air France bus: Charles de Gaulle-Étoile. Buses: 22, 32, 73, 92. Parking: Avenue Marceau.

François Gelly
10 rue Keppler, 75116 Paris

Tel   +33 (0)1 47 20 65 05
Email   hotel@keppler.fr
Web   www.keppler.fr

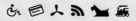

Hôtel Eiffel Trocadéro

Paris's latest eco-hotel, sister to the Gavarni, is a gem with Eiffel Tower views, beautiful new rooms and impressive water, energy and materials-saving credentials. Under Xavier Moraga's committed baton, there is inventive use of led lighting, intelligent fittings in small spaces and a fun choice of décor. Landing walls, done in metallised limewash, glow softly under hand and eye. Choose a soberly chic modern-classic room in quiet grey, brown or caramel stripes with a sensuously padded wall behind the bed, or a joyous, hand-painted backdrop of giant flowers – turquoise, fuchsia, mimosa – matching velvet curtains and floor-level lighting, or one of the older rooms, less rejuvenated, more affordable, just as cosy. The Eiffel suite is a hymn of joy to its namesake. Many are connected to the latest in eco-friendly air treatment and have recycling showers or jacuzzi baths in their excellent (unchanged) marble bathrooms. Organic breakfast is in the jaunty black and white basement, fine French food with oriental tinges is in the stunning ground-floor restaurant with its variegated seating and living walls. A delight.

Price	€169-€309. Suite €500-€600. Family apartment €399-€449.
Rooms	17: 8 doubles, 8 twins/doubles, 1 suite for 4. Family apartments available.
Meals	Breakfast: 3 types €8-€18. Snacks, lunch from €23; dinner à la carte. Wines €20-€200.
Closed	Never.
Directions	Sent on booking.

Xavier Moraga
35 rue Benjamin Franklin, 75116 Paris,
Tel   +33 (0)1 53 70 17 70
Email   reservation@hoteleiffeltrocadero.com
Web   www.hoteleiffeltrocadero.com

Hôtel le Relais Montmartre

There are good reasons why artists still live in this village, tucked in behind the Sacré Coeur, that giant marshmallow of a church. It could be the views over the rooftops of Paris, or the meandering little streets, or Montmartre's transformation at dusk as bistro, bar and club come into their own. It deserves much more than an afternoon visit so book into this little jewel and the secrets of this 'rediscovered' neighbourhood will be revealed. Just up from Amélie's celebrated café, tucked into a sweet side street, the entrance is discreet. Elegance and intimacy blend in the lobby with fireplace and antique desk; the sofa, the period chairs and the curtains are an extraordinary mix of rich fabrics; the small trellised patio set with sunny yellow garden furniture is the cherry on the cake. It feels like someone's home and anglophone Vincent knows every café and gallery by heart. In the rooms, find deep armchairs, quilted headboards and curtains in quiet pastels or reds, pinks and greens, mixed and matched with care. The mattresses are dreamy, the staff are delightful; this is simple luxury at its best.

Price	€185–€240.
Rooms	26 doubles.
Meals	Breakfast €13. Restaurants nearby.
Closed	Never.
Directions	Metro: Blanche (2), Place de Clichy (13, 2), Abbesses (12). RER: Gare du Nord. Buses: 30, 54, 80, 95. Parking: private parking, enquire at hotel.

Samia Mobarek
6 rue Constance, 75018 Paris

Tel	+33 (0)1 70 64 25 25
Email	contact@relaismontmartre.fr
Web	www.relaismontmartre.fr

Terrass Hôtel

The Terrass is the biggest (and highest) hotel in this book but its owner has so proper an idea of receiving guests that the atmosphere is as genuinely warm as at his smaller hotels. Antiques and tapestries, bronzes and old prints remove any sense of cold grandeur, a pianist plays in the club-like bar every evening, the breakfast buffet is a masterpiece in a room flooded with the light that pours up the hill, the chef has an excellent reputation and you may have the fine-weather privilege of eating on the seventh-floor terrace looking across the whole city – four-star class indeed. The suites are superb (one has a private terrace): big and light with windows that fling you across the greenery of Montmartre cemetery, pale modern furniture and lovely matchings of green, blue, raspberry, beige, and yellow textured fabrics. Other rooms have a more classic Louis XVI cane style and, of course, less space but all have delectable colours, different pictures and that rich, soft welcome of real taste and attention to detail. Buses, just across the street, sweep you down to Saint Germain des Prés or to the Opéra.

Price	€280-€330. Suites €380-€410.
Rooms	98: 83 twins/doubles, 15 suites.
Meals	Breakfast €17.
Closed	Never.
Directions	Metro: St Lazare, Gare du Nord. Buses: 80, 95.

Marie Jamet & Stéphanie Chevrier
12-14 rue Joseph de Maistre,
75018 Paris

Tel	+33 (0)1 46 06 72 85
Email	reservation@terrass-hotel.com
Web	www.terrass-hotel.com

Hostellerie du Prieuré

Medieval Saint Prix, on the edge of the forest, feels delightfully rural. But from the village church you can see the Sacré Coeur: Paris is 15 minutes by train. This is an immaculate small hotel in a beautiful village, with bedrooms that are really quite something. Decorated with a flourish and a theme, from boudoir chic to eastern exotica, all have Middle Eastern carpets, gorgeous textiles, crisp sheets. There's purple-walled Aladdin with an octagonal Syrian table and a silver hand basin and mirror, and lovely Coloniale, with a bamboo four-poster and magnificent long views – to Paris, of course. Bathrooms are worth a wallow, thanks to scented oils and fine soaps. Yves and Frédérique are a warmly professional couple and breakfast is worth getting up for, served in the creamy-walled Café de la Côte with a long velvet banquette and 1900s-style bar. Reservations for dinner are essential as there are only a handful of tables. You will find gourmet dishes and an organic wine list is as long as your arm plus a choice of nine champagnes. All this on the edge of fine forest; take the bikes and explore.

Price	€115–€185.
Rooms	8: 2 doubles, 1 twin, 4 suites, 1 family room.
Meals	Breakfast €13. Dinner €35–€50. Wine €22–€50. Restaurant closed Sundays.
Closed	3 weeks mid-August.
Directions	From Paris A15 for Cergy Pontoise, exit 115 dir. Taverny; exit St Leu La Forêt, St Prix on D139; 2nd street on right at r'bout; St Prix Village D144; left at lights dir. Chauvry D193.

Frédérique & Yves Farouze
74 rue Auguste Rey,
95390 Saint Prix, Val-d'Oise

Tel	+33 (0)1 34 27 51 51
Email	contact@hostelduprieure.com
Web	www.hostelduprieure.com

Entry 107 Map 5

Cazaudehore – La Forestière

The rose-strewn 'English' garden is like an island in the great forest of St Germain and it's hard to believe the buzzing metropolis is just a short train journey away. The first Cazaudehore built the restaurant in 1928, the second built the hotel in 1973, the third generation apply their imaginations to improving both and receiving their guests with classic French charm. The buildings are camouflaged among the greenery of the garden, summer eating is deliciously shaded under rose-red parasols; hotel guests have the elegant, beamed dining room with its veranda to themselves (there are several seminar and reception rooms). Food and wine are the main focus – the wine-tasting dinners are renowned and the chef's seasonal menus are a delight, skilfully mixing tradition and invention; you will eat supremely well here. Bedrooms have been renovated in refined but unostentatious style with good fabrics, original gentle colour schemes – saffron, blue and green, for example – period furniture and prints, modern gadgets and masses of character. The perfect treat for a grown-up occasion. *Winter jazz dinners.*

Price	€205–€220. Suites €265–€295.
Rooms	30: 13 doubles, 12 twins, 5 suites.
Meals	Breakfast €20.
	Lunch & dinner €55–€70.
	Children's meals €23.
	Restaurant closed Mon & Sun eve Nov–Mar.
Closed	Rarely.
Directions	A13 for Rouen exit 6 for St Germain en Laye on N186. N184 for Pontoise. Hotel on left 2.5km after château. RER A from Paris, then 5 mins by taxi.

Philippe Cazaudehore
1 avenue Kennedy,
78100 Saint Germain en Laye, Yvelines

Tel	+33 (0)1 39 10 38 38
Email	cazaudehore@relaischateaux.com
Web	www.cazaudehore.fr

Pavillon Henri IV

The historic and artistic credentials are impeccable. Louis XIV was born here, Dumas, Offenbach and Georges Sand stayed here. There's a fascinating mix of styles, too – Renaissance domed roof, Art Nouveau porch – and materials – ivory limestone, rosy brick. As for the views, the panorama sweeps across the valley of the Seine to Paris and La Défense; the city centre is 20 minutes away. Relish them from the rooms, the restaurant, the terrace: feel on top of the world. Since the hotel changed ownership some years ago the bedrooms have been undergoing a gradual and welcome transformation, from classic sobriety to luxurious charm, while reception rooms are big and beautiful – white walls, shining parquet and mellow rugs, gilded antiques, moulded cornices, marble busts, sumptuous chandeliers and striking flowers; there's even a self-playing piano. The dining is unquestionably lavish, and should you wish to walk off your indulgence afterwards, a wrought-iron gateway allows you into the vast walled and terraced gardens of Château de St Germain en Laye next door. Supremely enjoyable, wonderfully French.

Price	€139–€299. Suites €390.
Rooms	42: 40 twins/doubles, 2 suites.
Meals	Breakfast €19. Lunch €49. Dinner à la carte, approx. €90.
Closed	Rarely.
Directions	A13 Paris-Rouen; exit St Germain en Laye on N186 to St Germain centre via Ave Général Leclerc. Over r'bout to Ave Gambetta; right at end to Rue Thiers. On left.

	Charles Eric Hoffmann
	19-21 rue Thiers,
	78100 Saint Germain en Laye, Yvelines
Tel	+33 (0)1 39 10 15 15
Email	reservation@pavillonhenri4.fr
Web	www.pavillonhenri4.fr

Saint Laurent

Cobbled, exceptionally pretty Monfort L'Amaury is home to some remarkable Renaissance stained-glass windows, a Ravel festival in October and this venerable private mansion. Built in the early 1600s, it later became a town hall; now it is an excellent hotel. The renovation is recent and thorough – lift, soundproofing, fine panelling – and in good taste. Old rafters reign in some bedrooms, the beams in the breakfast are splendid, and skilful carpentry shows in headboards and cupboards of new oak. There are pure white walls and simple, elegant bedspreads, and ground-floor rooms with private terraces looking over the lawn where, under the big old linden trees, staff lay out chairs in summer. Each sedate bedroom bears the name of a plant or a tree from the Rambouillet forest. Fifty yards away, in a second townhouse, are three bedrooms, large and luxurious, with white-painted beams, marble bathrooms and comfy armchairs. Breakfasts are generous and include cooked ham and cheese. A peaceful stopover on the way to Paris – and Versailles, just 20 kilometres away.

Price	€105–€199.
Rooms	15: 12 doubles, 3 twins.
Meals	Breakfast €14. Restaurants within walking distance.
Closed	1-23 August.
Directions	From Paris A13; A12; N12 to Dreux then Monfort L'Amaury. In Monfort, through gates for car park.

Christiane Delabarre
2 place Lebreton,
78490 Monfort l'Amaury, Yvelines

Tel	+33 (0)1 34 57 06 66
Email	reception@hotelsaint-laurent.com
Web	www.hotelsaint-laurent.com

Hôtel de Londres

Gaze on the Château de Fontainebleau, one of France's loveliest buildings, from your room in this 18th-century hostelry; it lies opposite. The hotel has been in the family for three generations; Philippe runs it quietly and considerately, with occasional help from his brother. The sitting room has an 18th-century classical look, also rich colours, comfy armchairs, plump cushions, grand flowers. The breakfast room – for simple breakfasts – has the feel of a small brasserie; both rooms have views to Fontainebleau. Bedrooms, on the upper floors, are similarly classical in style – smart, spotless and traditional; colours are bold, fabrics floral. A sense of timelessness pervades this peaceful place. You are also brilliantly placed for exploring the Forest of Fontainebleau, the hunting grounds of kings. As for the château, it was built around the keep of a smaller medieval building, completed in 1550 and has been added to over the years; the gallery of François I is considered one of the finest in Europe. You can visit free on Sundays and it's magnificently floodlit at night.

Price	€120–€180. Single €90–€160. Suites €150–€200. Triples €200.
Rooms	16: 5 doubles, 1 single, 8 suites, 2 triples.
Meals	Breakfast €14. Restaurants within walking distance.
Closed	12 to 18 August; 23 December to 9 January.
Directions	A6 exit Fontainebleau for château. Hotel opposite château.

Philippe Colombier
1 place du Général de Gaulle,
77300 Fontainebleau, Seine-et-Marne

Tel	+33 (0)1 64 22 20 21
Email	hdelondres1850@aol.com
Web	www.hoteldelondres.com

Château de Bourron

Surrounded by perfectly clipped yew and box topiary, the early 17th-century château built on fortress foundations is hugely warm and inviting. Louis XV and his regal in-laws once met here; now it is owned by a charming young family. Inside is a feast of original Versailles parquet, oriental rugs and period pieces, exquisite fabrics and elegant tapestries. Breakfast tables are laid in a fine big ground-floor room that leads to the cosy guest sitting room. Upstairs, bedrooms in perfectly chosen bold colours display pale marble bathrooms – some with draped free-standing tubs – handsome fabrics and fitting period-style furniture: five-star stylishness in a château setting. On the first floor is the library, with panelled walls and shelves laden with leather-bound tomes. Outside, there are more treasures to uncover. The 80 acres of walled gardens and woodland are extraordinary... statues of Ceres and St Joseph, a chapel in one of two small pavilions, and the St Sévère spring supplying moat, canal and village wash-house. Your friendly hosts will tell the stories. Beyond lie the pretty village and the great forest.

Price	€180–€500.
Rooms	8 twins/doubles.
Meals	Breakfast €15. Dinner €33.
Closed	25 & 31 December.
Directions	Paris-Lyon A6 exit Fontainebleau. At 'obelisk' r'bout N7 Nemours-Montargis; 8 km. Right for Villiers-sous-Grez, follow Bourron Marlotte Centre. Ring interphone at wooden gates in 2nd courtyard.

Comte & Comtesse Guy de Cordon
14 bis rue du Maréchal Foch,
77780 Bourron Marlotte,
Seine-et-Marne

Tel	+33 (0)1 64 78 39 39
Email	bourron@bourron.fr
Web	www.bourron.fr

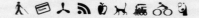

Château des Moyeux

Imagine a tree-lined approach and a circular drive, formal gardens and opulent topiary: perfect French elegance in deep country. Built in the thick Fontainebleau woodland, this manicured estate's pedigree includes General Lafayette's daughter and the mistress of Napoleon III. History defines the place, from the wainscotted dining room to the handsome library; but best of all is the genteel music room whose original mountain fresco and 17th-century furniture are sheer delight. The fine setting is matched by sober well-proportioned bedrooms with indulgent bath tubs, excellent mattresses and antique touches. There's an indoor pool and a circular salon with immense sofas, and the grounds are unquestionably handsome: neatly clipped foliage, no flowers(!), concentric formal gardens, a romantic chapel. Your hosts gladly share anecdotes (Madame was raised locally, Monsieur adores history), recommend restaurants and lend bikes to help you discover this rich region – do not miss medieval Provins. The gracious surroundings will impress you but the joy lies in calling it home, so stay as long as you can.

Price	€130–€150. Extra bed €30.
Rooms	4: 1 double, 2 family rooms for 3, 1 suite for 5.
Meals	Breakfast included. Restaurant 5km.
Closed	Rarely.
Directions	Sent on booking.

Nicolas Galazommatis
Epidaure,
77370 La Chapelle Rablais,
Seine-et-Marne

Tel	+33 (0)1 64 08 49 51
Email	n.g@alphacomgroup.com
Web	www.chateau-des-moyeux.com

Entry 113 Map 5

Auberge de la Source

An auberge since 1763, this charming village restaurant-hotel was, in the late 1800s, a favourite haunt of Monmartre artists drawn to sublime Champagne countryside an hour from Paris. Today the auberge is intimate, classy, special. Outside, a wisteria-smothered terrace for al fresco dining. Over the lane, a heated pool with loungers and lavender, romantic sit-outs beneath a vast chestnut tree, a small bar, a summer sitting room. Inside, an excitingly red entrance hall and a handsome restaurant lit by tall French windows. There are swathes of tiny tinkling fairy lights, light oak tables, armchairs upholstered in black, anthracite floors, teak cross beams, stainless steel cabochons and refined bistro food with exotic touches. Bedrooms, comfortable, comforting, are the biggest treat: tones of chocolate, tobacco, cream and white, and furnishings in decorative neo-classical style, wavy-fronted chests of drawers, wood-framed sofas in 'distressed' patina. After a hard day's champagne tasting, return to soft carpeting to pamper the feet and a jacuzzi bath to soothe the limbs. Oh, and the staff are delightful.

Price	€85–€148. Suites €145–€153.
Rooms	8: 4 doubles, 4 suites.
Meals	Breakfast €12. Dinner €29–€39.
Closed	Late January to late February.
Directions	From Paris A4 dir. Metz, exit 18 thro' La Ferté sous Jarre to D407 dir. Monmirail for 6km. Right onto D68 to Saint Ouen sur Morin. Auberge in centre.

Laurent & Françoise Tizio-Cassou
8 place Saint Barthélémy,
77750 Saint Ouen sur Morin,
Seine-et-Marne

Tel	+33 (0)1 60 24 80 61
Email	contact@aubergedelasource.fr
Web	www.aubergedelasource.fr

Normandy

Château de Pont Rilly

The Roucherays' passion, talent, attention to detail and good dose of patience have wrought a miracle of beauty and harmony. They have only been here 25 years (ten of which were spent with workers in their midst) but when a cubic metre of archives from the 18th century turned up giving itemised details on colour, paintwork, fabric… there was only one choice. It helps to be a restorer like Jean-Jacques who mixes his own paints, and a decorator like Annick who creates the bedspreads, curtains and cushions. Breakfast is served in the old kitchen with its monumental fireplace and original spit mechanism. The beds in the rooms above sit on rare Marie Antoinette parquet, tall windows are draped in white voile; one overlooks the front moat, paddocks and long drive, and a stone staircase leads up to the suite. Bath tubs are panelled, basins are set in stone surrounds. There are trout and eel in the stream, donkeys, sheep and goats in the paddocks and Léonne, a friendly peacock, shows up for the welcome. *Minimum three nights November-March in cottages.*

Price	€150. Suite €200. Cottages €750-€1,500 per week.
Rooms	4 + 3: 3 doubles, 1 suite for 5. 3 cottages: 1 for 4, 1 for 6, 1 for 6-8.
Meals	Restaurants 3km.
Closed	Never.
Directions	From Cherbourg RN13 south. Approaching Valonges, exit 'Zone d'Armanville'. D62 to Sottevast. 5km to château, entrance on right.

Annick & Jean-Jacques Roucheray
50260 Négreville, Manche

Tel	+33 (0)2 33 40 47 50
Email	chateau.pont.rilly@gmail.com
Web	www.chateau-pont-rilly.com

Château de Saint Blaise

You will be staying in the coach house, not the château, and all will be perfect, right down to the bathroom's flowers. When Ernst bought the coach house a few years back nothing remained of the building but the walls, so he rescued two staircases, one stone, one spiral, and a balustrade from another place. There are just two suites here, and an old-fashioned, peaceful luxury. The Grande Suite is a rich shade of dark blue, with a Napoleon III bed and draped curtains; one tall window overlooks the courtyard, with its pond of pink lilies and fish, the other looks onto fields. The Petite Suite is in blue and beige, with the same views and a narrow but elegant bed. You are served breakfast in a small, pretty room with flowers on the table, as late as you like, and the staff will be happy to light the fire in winter. There's fresh orange juice, coffee or tea and eggs just as you like them. The grounds, with their walled garden, are stunning, and you can walk to Briquebec, nice little market town – it's five minutes away. Return to a deep blue and burgundy salon with gleaming leather chesterfield and chairs.

Price	€220–€250.
Rooms	2 suites.
Meals	Restaurant 3km.
Closed	November to March.
Directions	N13 Cherbourg-Valognes, exit Bricquebec. D902 for 10km then right on route Les Gromonts. Château entrance 100m on left.

Ernst Roost
50260 Bricquebec, Manche
Tel +33 (0)2 33 87 52 60
Email info@chateaudesaintblaise.com
Web www.chateaudesaintblaise.com

Manoir de Coutainville

Secluded rooms with views over rooftops and sparkling seas are a traveller's joy. Add a cultured hostess, delectable dining and a 15th-century manoir and you have a dash of French magic. Through pale stone arches serenity awaits, genteel aperitifs ushering in five-course dinners that showcase local lobster, sea bass or oysters. Madame Véron provides spare wellies and captivating conversation, her fashion career informing her calm interiors while history resonates through every sea-view room. Try 'Sénéchal's' Japanese zinc shower or linger in the roll-top bath of the three-bedroom'd 'Seigneurie'; then snuggle into fluffy robes and watch the waves. 'Mahogany's' bedroom is white tranquillity and links with sweet 'Prairie', the twin, but note that, when taken separately, the latter is reached via a steep ladder stair from its private shower on the ground floor. Downstairs in the annexe, library armchairs and a scullery kitchen offer rest and refreshment. Stroll to Coutainville, watch the sailing boats, return to the tick-tock of the manoir's grandfather clock and see night creep over the skyline.

Price	€160–€250.
Rooms	5: 1 double, 1 suite for 2-5. Courtyard annexe: 1 double, 1 suite for 2-4; 1 twin with separate shower.
Meals	Breakfast included. Dinner with wine, €48.
Closed	January.
Directions	From A84 exit 37 for Gavray then Coutances; D57, D44 to Agon Coutainville; right after Agon church, follow signs Blainville sur Mer. Manoir on corner.

Sophie Véron
2 rue de la Maugerie,
50230 Agon Coutainville, Manche
Tel   +33 (0)2 33 47 05 90
Mobile +33 (0)6 07 55 29 77
Email sophie-veron@manoir-de-coutainville.com
Web   www.manoir-de-coutainville.com

Le Castel

A classic Napoleon III château, Le Castel is large but not palatial, grand but not ornate, the haven that families dream of in summer (supervised playtime in July and August), a superior B&B the rest of the year. Château suites and cottages include one double and one twin room (the latter filled with toys and oversized teddy bears, giraffes, tigers), bedtime storybooks and games, and a small kitchen. Outside: sandpit, swings, toys and a woodland den, a wet weather marquee, big trampolines and an above-ground pool. They do high tea for the young, supper for adults and gourmet dinners on Fridays – all included. Space aplenty inside, too: two salons scattered with French and oriental furniture, a white baby grand, paintings, wall hangings and tapestries throughout. French windows open to the terrace; eat out here or at the big friendly walnut table amid porcelain, cut glass and candles. Classic country-house bedrooms have striped or silk wallpaper, polished French beds, an escritoire. A charming host, cosy Burmese cats... bring the family, or book it all for a special occasion. *Min. stay one week Easter to mid-Sept.*

Price	B&B €140–€290 for 2–4. €1,980–€2,860 for 4 per week July/Aug (incl. dinner, drinks & play sessions). Cottages €550–€990 per week.
Rooms	3 + 3: 3 family suites for 2–4. 3 cottages for 4.
Meals	Dinner, 5 courses with coffee, €45. Wine €16.
Closed	Rarely. B&B closed July & August.
Directions	From Montpinchon, D102 to Pavage. Right at junc., immediately left onto D252. Le Castel 2 minutes on left. Entrance 2nd white gate.

Jon Barnsley
50210 Montpinchon,
Manche

Tel	+33 (0)2 33 17 00 45
Email	enquiries@le-castel-normandy.com
Web	www.le-castel-normandy.com

La Verte Campagne

From time to time, celebrities and politicians have escaped to this 300-year-old inn to relish the food and the deep peace. André is maitre d'hôtel, Lynne, an excellent chef, is responsible for the restaurant and the fresh-from-the-oven pastries at breakfast. They know how to make guests feel welcome. Bedrooms are comfortable, some might say quaint, and there are a couple of 1960s bathrooms that could be collectors' items. The place is utterly rural, surrounded by pastures and orchards, fronted by a festival of red, white and blue roses and clematis, with a rambling walled garden. The cosy sitting room has tapestry wall hangings, pictures of the area and a monumental stone fireplace with a wood-burning stove; off here, a tartan-walled, low-ceilinged bar and a tempting selection of fine whiskies. Oriental rugs add a stylish touch. In the romantic restaurant with its great stone fireplace and log fire, specialities include preserved duck with honey, fresh fish from Granville and lamb from Mont St Michel. Most come to eat well, make merry and tuck into bed! A true country auberge.

Price	€50–€78. Half-board €58–€65 p.p.
Rooms	5: 3 doubles, 2 family rooms.
Meals	Breakfast €8. Lunch €19.50–€45. Dinner €24–€55. Wine €15–€65. Restaurant closed Wednesdays.
Closed	Mid-November to mid-December.
Directions	From Caen, A84 for Rennes, exit 37; 6km to Gavray. A7 junc. right, for Coutances on D7 for 9km. D49 for Montmartin sur Mer to Trelly; signed in village.

André & Lynne Tamba
Le Hameau Chevalier,
50660 Trelly, Manche

Tel	+33 (0)2 33 47 65 33
Email	lavertecampagne@wanadoo.fr
Web	www.lavertecampagne.com

Le Manoir de l'Acherie

A short way from the motorway is this hotel, deep in the Norman countryside, a lovely, ever-so-French discovery: an old granite house with immaculately tended gardens and an ancient granite cider press sunk into the lawn brimming over with red roses. At one side is a chapel, now bedrooms; on the other is an extension providing a sort of *cour d'honneur* entrance. Some of the furniture is authentically old though most is solid quality repro in the rustic Norman style; rooms are carpeted, bed covers are patterned, curtains are frilly. Mother and daughter Cécile handle the hotel and restaurant service, Stéphane runs the kitchen and continues to win prizes for his robust cuisine. Charcuterie is homemade, cider and calvados comes from the locality. The tables are dressed in prim, cream tablecloths; dark wooden beams, well worn floor tiles and a giant stone fireplace create a pleasant, cosy feel. The small number of people running this establishment and the quiet unstressed, unhurried but efficient way they do so, is admirable. Note that last orders in the restaurant are at 8.30pm.

Price	€60–€115. Suites €115.
Rooms	18: 10 doubles, 4 twins, 4 suites.
Meals	Breakfast €9. Lunch & dinner €18–€41. Restaurant closed Mon Sept–June; Sun eve mid-Oct to week before Easter.
Closed	3 weeks in November; 2 weeks in February.
Directions	See owner website.

Stéphane & Cécile Poignavant
37 rue Michel de l'Epinay,
50800 Sainte Cécile, Manche

Tel	+33 (0)2 33 51 13 87
Email	manoir@manoir-acherie.fr
Web	www.manoir-acherie.fr

Ethical Collection: Environment; Food.
See page 429 for details.

La Ramade

La Ramade, half a century old, was built in golden granite by a livestock merchant who made his fortune. Véronique took it on in 2001 and transformed it from B&B into charming hotel, fulfilling a long-held dream. Her individual interiors are a pleasing mix of modern and brocante finds – with her own Breton cradle sweetly displayed on the second floor. Bedrooms feel feminine and are named after flowers. Green-carpeted 'Laurier' has white-painted furniture and steps to a bathroom with a sunken bath, 'Coquelicot' has a poppy theme and matching yellow curtains and towels. Pretty 'Eglantine' has a canopied bed and afternoon sun streaming through large windows, 'Amaryllis' – tailor-made for wheelchairs – a superb hydromassage shower. The grounds are filled with mature trees that give privacy from the road, and you are near Mont St Michel and the sea – a great spot for children who will love the guided tour across the great bay at low tide. Véronique has added a lovely glassed-in conservatory for breakfast, and a tea room and a bar for samplings of the local pommeau – or a calvados before tucking into bed. *Monthly musical soirées.*

Price	€78-€140. Suite €160-€200. Extra bed €20.
Rooms	12: 9 twins/doubles, 2 doubles, 1 suite for 2-5.
Meals	Breakfast €11. Restaurants nearby.
Closed	January to 4 February; 20 to 30 November.
Directions	From Avranches D973 for Granville; over river, then left on D911 for Jullouville; immediately on right.

Véronique Morvan Gilbert
2 rue de la Côte, Marcey les Grèves,
50300 Avranches, Manche

Tel	+33 (0)2 33 58 27 40
Email	hotel@laramade.fr
Web	www.laramade.fr

Château de Colombières

When the marshes were tidal, the château was an island fortress. Towers, turrets, 2.8m-thick walls, arrow slits, arches, moat: history jumps out at you. A long curving drive, a breathtaking first view, a bridge to a courtyard and there is Monsieur (senior) – charming, witty, dapper. The château has been in his wife's family for 300 years and he knows every inch by heart. Enter the grand 18th-century dining room, where breakfasts are served at a table under the gaze of an ancestress, rescuer of Colombières after the Revolution. The suites are three centuries older. One is reached via a rare circular elm-tread stair; its salon, vast, carpeted and inviting, has a monumental stone fireplace and a red and cream striped sofa; duck through the stone archway to the bedroom in the tower with the floral balaquined bed. The Louis XVI room is as lofty, as sumptuous, its fabrics pink, bold and coordinated, its bathroom with new green tiles and medieval tomettes. Garden arbours are equipped with chairs… wander at will, fish in the moat. It is a privilege to stay here – with Monsieur *tout compris*!

Price	€150–€200.
Rooms	3: 1 double, 2 suites for 4.
Meals	Breakfast €10 (children €5). Restaurant 10km.
Closed	Mid-October to mid-April.
Directions	From Bayeux D5 to Colombières, right on D29, left on D29A; signed.

Charles & Claire de Maupeou d'Ableiges
14710 Colombières, Calvados

Tel	+33 (0)2 31 22 51 65
Email	colombieresaccueil@aliceadsl.fr
Web	www.chateaudecolombieres.com

Hôtel Tardif

A mid 18th-century house in the centre of Bayeux, this is an architectural jewel. It was built for a botanist who worked at Versailles and specimen trees still stand in the grounds. In those days, carriages would rumble through the archway and enter the central 'cour d'honneur'; still cobbled, the yard is an exquisite spot from which to glimpse a fascinating range of building styles. Delighted to share all he knows about this house and its history, Anthony, with impeccable English, is an exceptionally generous young host. Inside are white walls, parquet étoile floors and a curved and suspended staircase, one of only two in France. And such beautiful things: antiques and tapestries, brocade chairs and gilt-framed mirrors, a grand piano and a chandelier from Compiègne where the Empress Josephine lived. Bedrooms are elegant, spacious and sober, in keeping with the history. One bedroom, on the first floor, is a listed 'monument historique', its panelling immaculately revived in regulation browns and golds. Other rooms have pale stone walls; all are uncluttered and serene. What value!

Price	€50–€160. Suite €150–€200. Extra bed €20.
Rooms	7: 6 doubles, 1 suite for 4.
Meals	Breakfast €10. Restaurants walking distance.
Closed	Christmas.
Directions	From RN13, exit 36 for Bayeux, follow signs to 'centre ville'; left at 1st r'bout, right at 2nd r'bout. Large green gate 300m on right. (Car access 57 rue Larcher.)

Anthony Voidie
16 rue de Nesmond,
14400 Bayeux, Calvados

Tel	+33 (0)2 31 92 67 72
Email	hoteltardif@orange.fr
Web	www.hoteltardif.com

Manoir de Mathan

A perfect size is this elegant manor house, introduced by a lovely crunching sound on the driveway and a 17th-century baroque arch. Finding this sober elegance in a typical Bessin farm, with its large courtyard and outbuildings, makes you wonder if all the farmers around here weren't aristocrats. Stay awhile and relax in the lounging chairs on the lawned grounds under the branches of mature trees. It's evident that the renovation was done with much loving thought and care; revealed and enhanced are the lovely beams and timbers, exposed stone walls, original fireplaces and spiral staircase. The large bedrooms were given proper space and light, bathrooms well integrated; it is classy but never overdone. The beds are big, the furniture regional, the windows large with over-the-field views. Some suites have canopied beds; some rooms are on the ground floor for easy access. Meals are a ten-minute stroll to the sister hotel up the road (La Rançonnière). Perfectly placed for Bayeux *and* near the landing beaches: you'll need two or three days to enjoy it all. *Check-in/out at sister hotel La Rançonnière.*

Price	€110–€130. Suites €160–€260.
Rooms	21: 18 doubles, 3 suites.
Meals	Breakfast €12. Lunch & dinner at Ferme de la Rançonnière, €24–€48. Wine €15–€40.
Closed	Rarely.
Directions	From Caen exit 7 to Creully on D22 for 19km. Right at church for Arromanches on D65. In Crépon, 1st on right.

Isabelle & Koen Sileghem
14480 Crépon,
Calvados

Tel	+33 (0)2 31 22 21 73
Email	manoir.mathan@gmail.com
Web	www.normandie-hotel.org

Ferme de la Rançonnière

Drive through the narrow arch into the vast courtyard and history leaps out and grabs you. This was originally a fortified stronghold – the tower is dated 13th century – to protect against English reprisals after Duke William of Normandy conquered England. Inside, exposed timbers and limestone walls and floors announce the Norman heritage. The amazing family suite has stone steps down into a double bedroom then up a spiral staircase to a children's bedroom in a tower with tiny windows. Some very handsome, solid furniture, too. Rustic-medieval is the look; a butter churn in the corridor, awe-inspiring Norman armoires, a well-worn kneading trough in a large family room, all remind you that this was a working farm. Off the main restaurant is a large, vaulted, stone-flagged sitting area with a log fire at one end making a perfect spot for after-dinner coffee. The bright breakfast room and terrace face south to catch the morning light. Young and efficient, Isabelle Sileghem and her husband, with help from myriad devoted staff, keep this place humming. Book ahead for the best rooms. Entirely wonderful.

Price	€55–€130. Suites €160–€190.
Rooms	35: 21 twins/doubles, 13 triples. Manoir: 1 suite.
Meals	Breakfast €12. Lunch €24. Dinner €48. Wine €15–€40. Restaurant closed 3-25 January.
Closed	Rarely.
Directions	From Caen exit 7 to Creully on D22 for 19km. Right at church for Arromanches on D65. In Crépon, 1st on right.

Isabelle & Koen Sileghem
Route de Creully, Arromanches,
14480 Crépon, Calvados

Tel	+33 (0)2 31 22 21 73
Email	ranconniere@wanadoo.fr
Web	www.ranconniere.fr

Ivan Vautier

The Vautiers have owned this fabulous hotel since 1994; in 2010 they created a radical new look. Bedrooms are classy and bathrooms spacious. Black artificial ostrich leather covers the large headboards, there are fitted oak-doored cupboards and sleek flat-screens. Views of neighbouring houses are uninspiring but you won't forget the key containing a unique bronze figure to match the room's bronze mobile — custom-made by a local sculptress. This 18th-century building has been a hotel and restaurant for more than 130 years. Now a chic veranda runs along the front; at one end is the lounge, at the other the reception bar, its shelves aglow with regional brandies and specialities. Much of this appears on the menu in the Michelin-starred restaurant where classy tables are divided among three intimate rooms facing a grassed walled courtyard. At dinner, there's refined food and a seven-course 'tasting menu'. At breakfast, homemade jams and local honey. English-speaking Sandrine heads the restaurant staff, unpretentious Ivan cooked for heads of state at the D-Day 60th anniversary celebrations. Gorgeous all round.

Price	€120–€260.
Rooms	19: 10 doubles, 9 twins/doubles.
Meals	Breakfast €15. Dinner €53.
Closed	Rarely.
Directions	Sent on booking.

Ivan Vautier
3 avenue Henry Chéron,
14000 Caen, Calvados

Tel	+33 (0)2 31 73 32 71
Email	info@ivanvautier.com
Web	www.ivanvautier.com

Hôtel & Spa Les Maisons de Léa

You could almost do with a guide to hand, to steer you round the passageways, narrow stairs and twists and turns of this intriguing 16th-century building – once three fishermen's houses and a salt warehouse. Each of the houses, plus three across the way, has its own decorative style – romantic, nautical, Baltimore, country; the attention to detail is exquisite. Imagine dreamy fabrics, limewashed walls, fresh orchids, elegant omelettes on white china, cushions on painted wicker, toys and chairs for children and a booklet for each guest on the treasures of Honfleur. Look forward to fresh snacks when you want them, starred restaurants around the corner, and breakfast laid out in a yellow room with views to the big square and the Church of Sainte Catherine; on Saturdays, the food market leaps into action. Relax in the salons – one with a library, one with a fire – spoil yourself in the spa or the (free) hammam, self-cater in the delicious Petite Maison. No lift – that would spoil the charm – and a car park a few minutes' walk away, but staff will happily ferry bags to the upper floors. A total gem. *Hammam & massage available.*

Price	€120–€210.
	Suites & cottage €210–€320.
Rooms	29 + 1: 24 twins/doubles, 5 suites.
	1 cottage for 5.
Meals	Breakfast €15. Light meals available.
	Restaurants within walking distance.
Closed	Rarely.
Directions	A13 exit Beauzeville; A29 exit Honfleur, right at r'bout with fountains; follow quai Sainte Catherine, cross bridge; left, Rue des Logettes. Private car park on request, €20.

Didier Lassarat
Place Sainte Catherine,
14600 Honfleur, Calvados

Tel	+33 (0)2 31 14 49 49
Email	contact@lesmaisonsdelea.com
Web	www.lesmaisonsdelea.com

La Maison du Parc

The house stands over the town like a venerable French gentleman: tall, handsome, impeccably dressed in a pale wisteria-trimmed suit with olive lapels, flanked by a magnificent pine. A 1760s shipbuilder designed the mansion; he liked to spy – telescope in hand – on Honfleur's pretty port and the estuary, now spanned by the stunning Pont de Normandie. With Parisian owners, this is all about comfort, design and decadence. Sink back on soft four-posters heaped with cushions; walls whirl with vibrant paintings; sculptures stand sentinel in marble fireplaces; oriental rugs compliment flame silks. Tucked under the attic timbers, the suite's bathroom dazzles: a free-falling shower set in the lee of a dormer window – funky! Enter the long graceful dining room to a fanfare of homemade breakfast treats: fruit tarts, smoothies, possibly crêpes or créme caramel. A cider route wends through Normandy's rural villages, there are seafood restaurants, cheesemakers, beaches, boat rides and heaps of Impressionist art. A superb luxury ferry-stop – Caen and Le Havre are half an hour – or a indulgent weekend escape.

Price	€135–€145. Suite €185. Family room for 3, €175.
Rooms	5: 3 doubles, 1 suite for 2, 1 family room for 3.
Meals	Breakfast included. Restaurants 500m.
Closed	January.
Directions	From Caen A13 then A29 to Honfleur. Arriving on D580, 3rd exit at last r'bout before town, up hill 100m; 1st right Rue St Léonard; house on left, green gates.

Annick & Paul Coudrier
76 rue Saint Léonard,
14600 Honfleur, Calvados

Tel	+33 (0)2 31 98 48 77
Mobile	+33 (0)6 01 86 56 80
Email	alamaisonduparc@gmail.com
Web	www.alamaisonduparc-honfleur.com

Hôtel Maison de Lucie

Named after the romantic novelist and poet Lucie Delarue Mardrus, who was born here, the 1850 house in the heart of Honfleur is shielded by a high wall. Sunshine illuminates panelled walls and leather sofas, the parquet'd salon has an Edwardian air and bedrooms, elegantly colour-themed, now expand into an adjoining house; those on the second floor overlook the estuary. Furnishings are immaculate – plum taffeta, burgundy velvet – beds are big and reading lamps won't spoil your eyes. Bathrooms are awash with potions and lotions, there are fresh orchids and vivid rugs, roll top baths and antique chests of drawers, and wide views over rooftops to the sea. Our favourite room is under the eaves, but they're all lovely. In the courtyard, the old caretaker's house is now a suite, its ground-floor sitting area furnished in a deliciously decadent 1930s manner; another room has a small new terraced courtyard area. Soak away your cares in the brick-walled jacuzzi; take your time over a great homemade breakfast of bacon, eggs, fruits, cheese – in bed or in the sun. Muriel's welcome is the candle on the cake. *Spa available.*

Price	€150-€250. Suites €315.
Rooms	12: 9 doubles, 3 suites.
Meals	Breakfast €12-€18. Restaurants 300m.
Closed	Early to mid-December.
Directions	5 minutes from A13, signed from Église Ste Catherine.

Muriel Daridon
44 rue Capucins,
14600 Honfleur, Calvados
Tel +33 (0)2 31 14 40 40
Email info@lamaisondelucie.com
Web www.lamaisondelucie.com

La Petite Folie

Fabulously sited for exploring Honfleur, just steps from the old harbour, these three townhouses are havens from the artistic bustle. The commanding main house (B&B), built for a sea captain in the 1830s, has heavy shutters over grand mansard windows. Its more modest but older neighbour, a gorgeous 14th-century house, contains three double-aspect apartments that march up three floors. Up the street are two more superb apartments with views onto a beautiful listed garden. American-born Penny married Frenchman Thierry and they set out to tailor bedrooms lavishly and beautifully, each an enchanting mix of handsome bedsteads, plump duvets, lacquered armchairs, mahogany chests of drawers and whirls of different tones. Breakfast is a daily treat. The ground-floor sitting room, as wide as the house, offers red suede sofas at one end and a leather chesterfield at the other. The garden is a compact, neatly planted square of charm, its focal point a summerhouse with a Byzantine flourish and belvedere views out to sea. All this, free WiFi, and delightful hosts. *Min. stay two nights. Children over 10 welcome in apartments.*

Price	€145–€175. Apartments €195–€295.
Rooms	5 + 5: 4 doubles, 1 twin.
	5 apartments: 3 for 2, 2 for 1-4.
Meals	Breakfast to apartments on request.
	Restaurants nearby.
Closed	Early-January to mid-February.
Directions	A13 exit A29 Honfleur; towards centre then 'Naturospace'. Over bridge, to rue Haute; road forks, keep right. 100m, on right, green shutters.

Penny & Thierry Vincent
44 rue Haute,
14600 Honfleur, Calvados

Mobile	+33 (0)6 74 39 46 46
Email	info@lapetitefolie-honfleur.com
Web	www.lapetitefolie-honfleur.com

Entry 130   Map 4

Château du Mesnil d'O

The approach to this 18th-century château lifts the spirit. Stone pillars and tall iron gates mark the entrance from the road, a tree-lined avenue set in five hectares of garden and parkland rolls you to the front door: the setting is enchanting. The four bedrooms, one with listed wallpaper from 1905, are on the first floor up a beautiful staircase in white Caen with (listed) wrought-iron handrail and balustrade. A square landing with a long view over the park is the perfect place to spread your newspaper on a lovely old dining table; bookshelves bursting with literature line the length of one wall. Family portraits bring the corridor to life, along with the odd antique; fresh flowers are placed in bedrooms and on landings. A feast for the eye: blue velvet chairs, chevron parquet floor, panelled walls with painted scenes above the doors and a wonderful Louis XVI buffet displaying its collection of old plates – that is the backdrop for buffet breakfast. One might feel overawed by such splendour but the welcome makes the visitor feel instantly at home. *No credit cards.*

Price	€110. Suite €170.
Rooms	4: 3 doubles, 1 suite for 4.
Meals	Restaurants within 5km.
Closed	Rarely.
Directions	From Caen N13 to Paris. In Vimont, right D47 then D40 for St Pierre sur Dives 7km; on right.

Guy de Chabaneix
14270 Vieux Fumé, Calvados

Tel	+33 (0)2 31 20 01 47
Email	lemesnildo@wanadoo.fr
Web	www.lemesnildo.com

Château La Cour

Your hosts are warm and charming and their attention to detail is impressive. Not everyone can take a 13th-century castle, once owned by the Ducs d'Harcourt, and so successfully blend history with comfort. Expect some subtly bold décor and subdued luxury: Lloyd Loom chairs, marble fireplaces, Egyptian cotton. One bedroom has a curved wooden stair up to a superb bathroom; the apartment is stunning; all face south over the garden. Breakfast includes home-grown fruit, homemade yogurt and eggs from the château's happy hens. A house for fine dining, too: English china, damask and candelabra set the table in the lovely dining room. David grows — beautifully — for Lesley to cook — deliciously — and his organic potager is a delightful diversion (seven varieties of potato, 50 of vegetable); high stone walls shelter it from unkind winds, fruit trees shade the lawn, long narrow beds make for easy harvesting. The Cravens are keen conservationists, too; barn owls nest in the end wall and there is good bird watching. The Normandy beaches, Bayeux and its tapestry are within easy reach. *No credit cards. Children over 12 welcome.*

Price	€150. Apartment €750 per week.
Rooms	4 + 1: 3 doubles, 1 twin. Apartment for 2.
Meals	Hosted dinner with wine, €35–€50; book ahead.
Closed	Rarely.
Directions	D562 south from Thury Harcourt for 5km; right onto D133 for Culey le Patry; left onto D166; 2nd right onto D211. Château on right approaching village.

David & Lesley Craven
14220 Culey le Patry, Calvados

Tel	+33 (0)2 31 79 19 37
Email	info@chateaulacour.com
Web	www.chateaulacour.com

Bois Joli

In the middle of a pretty, fashionable and traditional spa town whose waters rise at 24° and whose original boating lake, casino and spa remain intact, Bois Joli was a *pension* built in the mid-1800s for those taking the waters. It sits at the edge of the Andaine forest in a neat, railinged acre of lawn, shrubs and sequoias. Décor is traditional classic French, understated and elegant. In the salon are good chairs, books, newspapers, flowers in pewter and a piano you may play; in the dining room, fine rush-seated chairs and white napery. The food is good-looking and delicious: fresh bread and squeezed orange for breakfast; oysters, pigeon breast and apricot tart for dinner. Slip off your shoes in a carpeted bedroom, immaculate with matching toile de Jouy or pale spriggy wallpaper and fabrics, perhaps an old country wardrobe to add character. That lovely lake is a minute away and the hotel arranges mushroom-picking weekends in the woods. Owners and staff are friendly, discreet and helpful, and you are surrounded by all the benefits of civilisation – golf, swimming, tennis and restaurants aplenty.

Price	€80–€168.
Rooms	20 twins/doubles.
Meals	Breakfast €11.
	Lunch & dinner €21–€69.
Closed	Rarely.
Directions	From Argentan, D916 for Mayenne, follow signs for Bagnoles Lac. Signed.

Yvette & Daniel Mariette
12 avenue Philippe du Rozier,
61140 Bagnoles de l'Orne, Orne

Tel	+33 (0)2 33 37 92 77
Email	boisjoli@wanadoo.fr
Web	www.hotelboisjoli.com

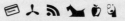

Auberge de la Source

Christine and Serge, a smiling, hard-working couple, used reclaimed beams and stone to build the auberge on the site of his parents' 18th-century apple press – so no more home cider, but they do serve a superb one made just down the road. The dining rooms (mostly for receptions) – one smaller and cosier, the other with huge sliding windows – and the bedrooms were designed to draw in the view down to the lake, the hub of a huge sports complex. Apart from windsurfing and a sailing school, there's riding, a climbing wall, archery, fishing and 'swing-golf', easy to learn, apparently. Children have a play area, pony rides, mini-golf and pedal boats. If you want real nature, you will see huge stags without too much searching in the nearby forest. The neat and tidy auberge has big rooms for families, all with huge beams and a mix of chunky country antiques and more modern furniture. The food is simple, focusing on steaks cooked over a wood fire and fresh farm produce to go with them. A sensible choice for families with small children – or sporty teenagers. *This is a farming family; please book ahead for dinner.*

Price	€58-€98.
Rooms	5: 1 double, 3 family rooms for 3, 1 family room for 4.
Meals	Picnic €10. Lunch & dinner from €17, book ahead. Wine €5-€20.
Closed	Rarely.
Directions	From La Ferté Macé D908 for Domfront Mont St Michel. After 2km right to hotel; signed.

Christine & Serge Volclair
La Peleras,
61600 La Ferté Macé, Orne
Tel   +33 (0)2 33 37 28 23
Email   auberge.lasource@orange.fr
Web   pagesperso-orange.fr/auberge.lasource/

Le Pavillon de Gouffern

More mansion than lodge, Gouffern was built 200 years ago by a wealthy gentleman with plenty of fellow hunters to entertain. But the scale of this elegant 'pavilion' is perfect for today's traveller. It stands in an estate of over 60 hectares and guests can walk, cycle or ride in the private forest in peace and seclusion. Big windows let in lots of soft light to illuminate the newly renovated décor: hunting themes, an Edwardian salon with leather chairs and oak floors, an unfussy elegance that gives a sense of the quiet, comfortable, class of a good country house. Recently renovated bedrooms, some of them in the well-converted outbuildings, are big and eminently striking (smaller on the top floor), new bathrooms have all the necessary bits and meals are served in the handsome dining room – the food has been much praised. In the grounds, the delightful Doll's House, built for children of another age, is now an idyllic suite (honeymoon specials arranged). A nearby stable delivers horses to the door and, if you are lucky, the chef will cook your freshly caught trout.

Price	€75-€200. Cottage €150-€200. All prices per night.
Rooms	19 + 1: 18 doubles, 1 single. Cottage for 2-4.
Meals	Breakfast €12. Picnic available. Lunch & dinner €28-€55.
Closed	24 to 25 December.
Directions	N26 exit Argentan. Hotel 7km from Argentan in forest of Silly en Gouffern; signed.

Karelle Jouaux & Vincent Thomas
61310 Silly en Gouffern, Orne

Tel	+33 (0)2 33 36 64 26
Email	pavillondegouffern@wanadoo.fr
Web	www.pavillondegouffern.com

La Louvière

It's a joy to discover this 18th-century manor house, a classic *gentilhommière* embraced by delicious grounds. Drive up an avenue of lime trees, step under the clematis-strewn pergolas, and enter the hall. Charming hostess Isabelle Groult says the old house has "une ambiance de soie": a chandelier sparkles above lace tablecloths in the dining room, pale chintz dresses elegant windows in the sunny *grand salon*, and the *petit salon*'s fireplace is flanked by charming chairs. Colours and fabrics match beautifully. Take an aperitif on the terrace, get sporty on the tennis court, and dream in the gardens, fragrant with roses and buzzing with bees. Patterned paving leads to a potager in which your dinner vegetables grow. Inside the house, an oak staircase curves up to the first-floor bedrooms, daintily, exquisitely romantic, decorated with fine fabrics and antiques; up again is Chambre d'Aurélie, tucked into the splendid 'charpente'. Chambre d'Alexandre is equally striking – and discreet. Everything you could want for a weekend is here: a heated pool, tennis court, small fishing lake, happiness and peace.

Price	€95-€135. Suite €160.
Rooms	4: 3 doubles, 1 suite for 4.
Meals	Dinner with wine & coffee, €38.
Closed	November to Easter.
Directions	From Alençon N12 west. In St Denis sur Sarthon right; signed La Roche Mabile for 2km to Le Fault. Property signed on right.

Isabelle & Alain Groult
Le Fault,
61420 Saint Denis sur Sarthon, Orne

Tel	+33 (0)2 33 29 25 61
Email	isabelle@louviere.fr
Web	www.louviere.fr

Château de Blavou

Tales of grandeur and history seep from this deep-country castle, embellished with turrets and neo-Gothic flourishes and once home to the Blavou family – friends of Henri IV. Nowadays, the deep vaulted cellars and underground tunnels are the background to happenings both simple and sophisticated; and everything works in this slick, immaculate château. There's tons of space, the grounds span a large estate with grand lawns, handsome outbuildings, neatly clipped hedges and an orchard, while the reception, dining and sitting rooms are impeccably and beautifully furnished: limestone flags underfoot, heavy beams overhead, cane tub dining chairs, theatre posters, upholstered armchairs. Carved four-posters and exquisite rugs and tapestries add traditional luxury to seriously fabulous bedrooms; spacious bathrooms have lovely tubs and park views. Concerts, theatre schooling and language lessons are put on for guests by sociable Nigel, as well as great local food – and the cheese comes from cows fed with the château's own hay. All this and fascinating medieval Bellême nearby – as well as lots of wonderful walking.

Price	€110–€160.
Rooms	5 doubles.
Meals	Dinner €35.
Closed	Rarely.
Directions	From Mortagne au Perche D938 dir. Bellême for 5 km; right to Blavou & Bellavilliers on D210. Entrance on right after 1km.

Nigel Murray
61400 Saint Denis sur Huisne, Orne
Tel   +33 (0)2 33 25 68 90
Email   enquiries@chateaudeblavou.com
Web   www.chateaudeblavou.com

Hôtel de Suhard

On the square of Bellême, a famously beautiful medieval town with street markets, cobbles and restaurants, is a tall, shuttered, oh-so-French mansion with a 16th-century pedigree: note the lovely steep weathered roofs on the garden side. Fastidiously restored, the earthly hued interiors have discreet opulence and a gorgeous unfussiness. Imagine Louis XV fireplaces and sand-blasted beams, satin-smooth stone floors and seriously old doors, gilded antiques and tinkling chandeliers... married with state-of-the-art showers, ethnic sculptures and romantically curtained claw-foot baths. Two bedrooms overlook the walled garden – a sweet setting for breakfasts of fresh fruits and pastries – with views to the countryside beyond; the other three overlook the road and the quaint town. All are divine. From one of three restaurants gourmet dinners may be ordered then served in a dining room on fine china. It's a showcase house in an authentic setting, run by sympathetic Parisian owners with exceptional attention to detail who provide mushroom forays in autumn and three different types of breakfast coffee.

Price	€75–€120.
Rooms	5: 1 double, 2 twins/doubles, 2 suites.
Meals	Restaurant 500m. Catered dinner available.
Closed	December to March.
Directions	From Paris N12 to Mortagne au Perche; D938 to Bellême; in main square, take Rue d'Alençon down from church; house on right halfway down.

Josiane Lenoir
34 rue d'Alençon, 61130 Bellême, Orne

Tel	+33 (0)2 33 83 53 47
Mobile	+33 (0)6 79 64 35 21
Email	contact@hotel-de-suhard.fr
Web	www.hotel-de-suhard.fr

Domaine de Villeray

The château serene on the hill, the auberge-like mill by its ever-rushing race down at the bottom, Villeray is a whole estate that the relaxed and affable Eelsen family are still working hard to bring back to life. The scale of the grand old 16th-century mill is thrilling. The great paddle wheel sits behind a huge window in a dining room that trumpets excellent food and wines, owner Christian's pride. There are age-old flagstones, soft mushroom and fawn fabrics, much cosy beaminess here. A cavernous bread oven has become an open fireplace, the epitome of warm rusticity and symbol of this family's welcome and dedication. And a great new spa complex to top it off. Way above, commanding acres of parkland, stands the utterly French Renaissance château. A splendid stone staircase leads you to rooms in all shapes and sizes that are, *château oblige*, more traditional, united by the easy elegance of Art Deco armchairs, polished boards, faded oriental rugs, the odd four-poster. Enjoy the informality, the remarkable food — up the hill in winter, at the mill in summer — the pool, the spa and the deep country quiet. *Spa on site.*

Price	€95–€295. Suites €205–€395.
Rooms	39: Moulin: 19 twins/doubles, 7 suites. Château: 9 doubles, 4 suites for 2.
Meals	Breakfast €15. Lunch €28–€69. Dinner €38–€69. May to mid-Sept half-board only, €47–€70 extra p.p.
Closed	Never.
Directions	From Chartres, N23 dir. Nogent Le Rotrou. 14km after Montlandon, right on D203 to Condé sur Huisne; D10 dir. Remalard for 3km, left to Villeray. At bottom of hill on right.

Christian Eelsen
Villeray, 61110 Condeau, Orne

Tel	+33 (0)2 33 73 30 22
Email	contact@domainedevilleray.com
Web	www.domainedevilleray.com

Domaine de la Louveterie

From the forested road, the drive descends to glorious views over the hills of the Perche. And there is the house, a 17th-century *longère* in 32 acres of peacefulness, rescued and restored by Carol and Pietro. A charming ex-Parisian couple, well travelled and fluent in several languages, they are enchanted with the slow pace of life here. A gravelled courtyard sets the scene, beyond are two gîtes. Inside is a mixture of rustic and antique with a few exotic notes and no ostentation, simply an overwhelming feeling of comfort and well-being. Pietro oversees pasture and woodland, potager and pool; Carol, a food photographer, stars in the kitchen. Good wines and food are ferried to a room where logs smoulder; hosts join guests for after-dinner coffee and digestifs. And so to bed… the Fifties room is caught in a cosy time warp (in spite of the flat-screen TV), 'Chinoise' and 'Voyage' lie warmly under the eaves, and the suites spread themselves impressively over two floors, the grandest with wooden panelling, choice antiques and a real fire. *No credit cards. Ask about cookery & watercolour courses & riding weekends.*

Price	€95–€115. Suites €140–€165. Apartments €640 per week.
Rooms	5 + 2: 3 doubles, 2 duplex suites for 2. 2 apts: 1 for 2, 1 for 3.
Meals	Dinner, 3–5 courses with wine, €39–€72.
Closed	Rarely.
Directions	From Dreux, D828 & D928 to La Loupe; D920 & D918 to Moutiers au Perche. From village centre for Rémalard; entry on right at sharp bend, 1.3 km after village. Ask for detailed directions.

Carol & Pietro Cossu–Descordes
61110 Moutiers au Perche, Orne

Tel	+33 (0)2 33 73 11 63
Mobile	+33 (0)6 22 47 42 71
Email	domainedelalouveterie@wanadoo.fr
Web	www.domainedelalouveterie.com

Villa Fol Avril

Once a stopover for travellers passing on this peaceful road, the 19th-century staging post became a petrol station some years ago; now it's been rescued by the Sicres. Since leaving Paris, this energetic couple have added modern touches to authentic features and created a beautiful, bright hotel. Sunshine pours in through windows overlooking the pretty village's rosy-coloured roofs, and handcrafted furnishings pop up everywhere. Bedrooms are bold and individual, all with elaborately carved key fobs and something to make you go "ooh!". In one, an oak ladder leads to a high mezzanine – great fun for kids. The exposed timbers upstairs are magnificent and some remnants from the coach house's old life have been given a new lease of life: an ancient hayrack and shutters have become quirky headboards. Bathrooms are equally distinctive, with yellow tiles. Fresh local produce is served in the restaurant or on the garden terrace; look out for snails from the local *escargotière*. Venture into the Perche for plenty of surprises: forested walking tracks, fairy-tale manoirs and the famous Percheron horses.

Price	€70–€130. Family room & triple €110–€160.
Rooms	9: 5 doubles, 2 twins, 1 family room, 1 triple.
Meals	Breakfast €9. Dinner €25–€45. Wine €20–€60. Restaurants 8km.
Closed	Never.
Directions	From Nogent-le-Rotrou D918 dir. L'Aigle for 21km. Hotel in centre of Moutiers au Perche.

Monsieur & Madame Sicre
2 rue des Fers Chauds,
61110 Moutiers au Perche, Orne

Tel	+33 (0)2 33 83 22 67
Email	contact@villafolavril.fr
Web	www.villafolavril.fr

Château de la Puisaye

Cats, dogs, horses, sheep and a fleet of farmyard fowl in 27 acres of countryside heaven. Delightful ex-solicitor Diana moved to France with her French husband to indulge her love of horses. With its scattering of shuttered windows and classically pale façade, this fine château oozes 19th-century elegance. Large airy bedrooms, where genuine English wallpapers are artfully mixed with French antiques, huge mantelpiece mirrors and glass-panelled doors that flood spaces with light; ivory paintwork, marble fireplaces and snowy linen create an ordered calm. The salon and library have elaborate woodwork and the dining room, with its gleaming table and silver candlesticks, invites you to linger over breakfast, a feast of homemade pastries, jams and cooked dishes. Diana, a stylish cook, will prepare a light supper or dinner on request, perhaps foie gras then truffle-stuffed guinea fowl; fruit and veg come from the potager, the 19th-century greenhouse and local markets. Lounge in the library over books, games, WiFi; borrow a bike and pedal the grounds; relax in the infra-red sauna among delicious aromatherapy oils.

Price	€98-€128. Suite €138-€185.
Rooms	5: 3 doubles, 1 twin, 1 suite for 2-4.
Meals	Dinner €33; menu gourmand €55; Normandy platter with cider €16.
Closed	One week in winter.
Directions	From Verneuil sur Avre on D839 to Chartres; D56 dir. Senonches for 1.5km; right onto C19 for château.

Bruno & Diana Costes
Lieu-dit La Puisaye,
27130 Verneuil sur Avre, Eure

Tel   +33 (0)2 32 58 65 35
Email   info@chateaudelapuisaye.com
Web   www.chateaudelapuisaye.com

Château d'Emalleville

An elegant, listed, 18th-century château, Emalleville has it all: perfectly landscaped with formal gardens, vast woodlands for walking (and autumn shooting), a tennis court, an ancient fallen mulberry that has rebuilt itself, a cosy suite in the converted beamed dovecote (a favourite) and fine rooms in the orange-coloured brick and limestone coach house and outbuilding. There is perfect toile de Jouy in some of the rooms and most beds are canopied. Contemporary touches here and there work nicely: photographs and drawings dedicated to the dancer who took Paris by storm in 'Joséphine', a colourful bullfighting theme in 'Seville', while 'Giverny' is floral and feminine. All open directly to the lawns. Tucked away behind the precious vegetable garden and orchard is the heated pool. Breakfast is served in the *salle de chasse*: try the mulberry or wild plum jam. The lady of the manor's exquisite taste has woven a magic from floor to ceiling, from Jouy print to antique wardrobe: you will feel like prince and princess here. And you're only 30 minutes' drive from Giverny.

Price	€100–€150. Suites €140–€230. Cottage €150–€200. Minimum stay 2 nights in cottage.
Rooms	8 + 1: 5 doubles, 1 twin, 2 suites for 2-5. 1 cottage for 2-4.
Meals	Restaurant 8km.
Closed	Never.
Directions	From Evreux, D155 for Louviers & Acquigny. Thro' Boulay Morin, 500m after village, left to Emalleville. 2nd road on right; château opp. church; ring bell.

Arnaud & Frédérique Tourtoulou
17 rue de l'Eglise,
27930 Emalleville, Eure

Tel	+33 (0)2 32 34 01 87
Mobile	+33 (0)6 14 49 24 20
Email	tourtoulou@chateaudemalleville.com
Web	www.chateaudemalleville.com

Le Moulin de Connelles

Bring your boater, hop in a green and red-trimmed flatboat right out of a Monet painting and punt along a quiet arm of the Seine after a morning at Monet's garden (Giverny is 30 minutes). Watery greens, pinks and that scintillating veil of haze that is particular to this part of Normandy intensify the Impressionist mood. Then look up at the extraordinary half-timbered, chequer-boarded, turreted manor house and you will have to pinch yourself, hard. Part of the house is on an island; hidden paths lead through flowering bushes to a private pool; Karine keeps up her father's tradition of quiet hospitality and has refined the park, its flowerbeds and furniture. Bedrooms and restaurant have been renovated with fine materials: oak, mosaics, weathered marble, granite and limestone. Step around to the garden and peek through the kitchen windows at rows of copper pots, reflections of the lovely meals served in the restaurant. Reserve a room with a balcony overlooking the river and its water-kissing willows or splurge on the suite and its jacuzzi for two in the tower. Bring your paintbrushes. *Boats for trips upriver.*

Price	€130–€170. Suites €170–€310.
Rooms	12: 6 doubles, 6 suites.
Meals	Breakfast €15. Lunch & dinner €35–€58. Children's meals €16. Wine from €6.50.
Closed	Sunday evening; Mondays October to April.
Directions	From A13 exit 18 Louviers on N15 towards Pont de l'Arche for 4km; right to St Pierre du Vauvray, Andé & Connelles; signed.

Karine Petiteau
40 route d'Amfreville sous les Monts,
27430 Connelles, Eure

Tel	+33 (0)2 32 59 53 33
Email	moulindeconnelles@wanadoo.fr
Web	www.moulin-de-connelles.fr

Château de Bonnemare

You could almost imagine the Vicomte de Valmont and the Marquise de Merteuil plotting in the *grand salon*! A Renaissance gatehouse leads to a remarkable 16th-century *brique de St Jean* façade as you enter the grounds of this enticing 'monument historique'. Alain and Sylvie, generous and charming, have restored two elegant ground-floor rooms in the north wing, and two suites with listed decoration on the first floor. Breathtaking 'La Parade' announces a velvet swagged four-poster in an ornate alcove, a monumental fireplace and a single-bedded nursery; 'Louis XVI', decorated in 1777, reveals a pure French classical elegance, its exquisitely furnished yellow salon adjoining a vast bedroom with chandeliers and intricate mouldings. Bathrooms are pleasingly lavish — and modern. Breakfast in the vaulted Great Kitchen, its vast fireplace replete with a turbine-driven spit designed by da Vinci, means embroidered napkins, fresh fruits and flowers, pâtisserie and homemade jams. The estate walls enclose a small kingdom: chapel, farm, cider press, bakery, barns and 44 acres of park and woodland. Amazing.

Price	€92–€100. Suites €188–€246.
Rooms	4: 2 doubles (can interconnect), 2 suites for 2-3.
Meals	Restaurant 6km.
Closed	November to January.
Directions	From Paris A15 to Cergy-Pointoise. D14, then D6014 to Rouen. At r'bout in Fleury sur Andelle, dir. Radepont 4km. Exit Radepont, left to château, 3km outside village.

Sylvie Vandecandelaere
990 route de Bacqueville,
27380 Radepont, Eure

Tel	+33 (0)2 32 69 44 33
Mobile	+33 (0)6 03 96 36 53
Email	svdc2@wanadoo.fr
Web	www.bonnemare.com

Château de Saint Maclou la Campagne

Fabulous tales of drama, decadence, travels, travails, wealth and war surround this 17th-century château; these days, the proud brick and limestone mansion is certainly more peaceful than in the past, yet every bit as deliciously luxurious. British hosts Robin and Nicola Gage welcome guests into an elegant wood-panelled drawing room where you can admire porcelains, portraits and family photographs – and snuggle before a winter fire. Similarly graceful is the green dining room with its fine mahogany table; you can have breakfast here or in the cosy semi-cellar amid brick walls and copper utensils. Waft up to generous bedrooms in apple green, mushroom, apricot or sunny yellow, each bearing antiques and an art collection spanning many years and styles. Bathrooms are thoroughly 21st-century. A dry moat encircles the château; beyond lie vast lawns interspersed with neat hedges, an orchard and a dovecote that once boasted 5,000 pigeons; beyond lie Normandy's cider apple countryside and beaches. A fascinating slice of history set in tranquil surroundings – and in the summer months you can rent the whole château.

Price	€150–€200.
	Whole house €5,000–€8,000 per week.
Rooms	4: 1 double, 3 twins/doubles.
	Whole house available.
Meals	Breakfast €12.50. Restaurant 300m.
Closed	Rarely.
Directions	See owner website.

	Robin Gage
	352 rue Émile Desson,
	27210 Saint Maclou, Eure
Tel	+33 (0)2 32 57 26 62
Mobile	+33 (0)6 75 96 87 74
Email	rg@chateaudesaintmaclou.com
Web	www.chateaudesaintmaclou.com

Entry 146   Map 4

La Grange des Marettes

In pure, peaceful countryside, an impeccably renovated hay barn and luxurious small hotel. From the car park it's a sprint to the wide raised terrace, behind which lie four lovely bedrooms. (The fifth – cosy pine-clad 'Noisette' – rests below.) A steel corkscrew stair leads to the family suites on the first floor, sinfully comfortable and inviting. Each has a romantically draped bed and a further single on the mezzanine reached by ladder (perfect for a nimble child). The décor is mix-and-match in contemporary style, the walls are clad in white wood, the furniture is pastel-washed and each room is different. Feel spoiled by big square French pillows, pristine white salad-bowl hand basins, fat duvets, and a couple of saunas to steam up in. Accomplished paintings and engravings add colour and depth and from every upper room there's a beautiful view. Look forward to buffet breakfast in the day room, served until 11am; glimpse the owner's manor house through the sheltering trees. Riverside Rouen is a 20-minute drive; the pretty Château de Clères – with gibbons, geese and exotic birds – is just down the road.

Price	€100. Suites €150 for 2, €180 for 3.
Rooms	5: 1 double, 2 suites, 2 family suites.
Meals	Breakfast included. Guest kitchen. Restaurant 3km.
Closed	Rarely.
Directions	Sent on booking.

Jacques Lernon
Lieu-dit Le Bois Hébert, Les Marettes, 76690 Clères, Seine-Maritime

Tel	+33 (0)2 35 33 24 44
Mobile	+33 (0)6 84 77 21 42
Email	la-grange@les-marettes.fr
Web	www.les-marettes.fr

Brittany

Hôtel La Désirade

Everyone loves an island and this one, with its wild windswept coast, is especially enticing. Battered by storms in winter, it is hot and gorse-scented in summer and the roads are silent. La Désirade, sheltered in its parkland, is made up of a new village of colour-washed houses round a pool. If leafy gardens, comfortable hotelly bedrooms and super bathrooms (white bathrobes, lashings of hot water) don't bring instant relaxation, the spa and massages surely will. Breakfast is served buffet-style in the breakfast room or by the pool; dinner, formal but excellent, is in the hotel restaurant across the lane. The young chef specialises in local dishes and the presentation is impeccable; wines are first-class too. Research the island's possibilities curled up in a wicker chair in the reception salon with its unexpectedly blue fireplace: there are lots of illustrated books. You have 104 kilometres of coastal paths and cycle routes to choose from, while the beaches are a 20-minute walk away. Take your paintbox and you'll be in good company: Monet and Matisse both came to the island to paint.

Price	€142–€180. Family rooms €280–€360.
Rooms	32: 14 doubles, 14 twins, 4 family rooms for 4.
Meals	Breakfast €17. Picnic lunch available. Dinner from €31. Wine €24–€99.
Closed	Early November to early April.
Directions	From Quiberon, ferry to Belle Île (45 min) then taxi or bus (7km). Well signed.

Ethical Collection: Environment; Food.
See page 429 for details

Pierre & Bénédicte Rebour
Le Petit Cosquet, Bangor,
56360 Belle Île en Mer, Morbihan
Tel   +33 (0)2 97 31 70 70
Email   hotel-la-desirade@wanadoo.fr
Web   www.hotel-la-desirade.com

Domaine de Bodeuc

The 19th-century manor stands in its own park surrounded by woodland. Jean and Sylvie, urban escapees, have restored it most glamorously, bringing a taste of Paris to the country. The roomy hall is dominated by a glass chandelier, walls are in warm, earthy colours – mushroom, aubergine – and a bold mix of good antiques with striking modern art gives a dramatic impression. Salons are small, bedrooms are big; whether in the house or stables, they have a quiet, attractive feel: beds large and crisply white with sheets and blankets and colourful spreads; bathrooms elegant and pampering. The new, romantic 'room in a forest glade' in the old ironworker's shop is utterly delectable. Relax with a drink on the small terrace overlooking the park or in the piano bar, dine well on locally sourced produce. It is supremely tranquil here yet you're close to wild beaches, a huge choice of golf courses and excellent shopping in the fortified port of Vannes. Wine tasting and mushroom weekends are planned for the future, along with the development of the organic potager and the original walled garden. *Balneotherapy on request.*

Price	€82-€202. Single €70-€95. Suite & family rooms €140-€220.
Rooms	14: 10 twins/doubles, 1 single, 1 suite, 2 family rooms for 3-4.
Meals	Breakfast €12.50. Dinner €30, book ahead. Wine €19-€59.
Closed	Mid-November to mid-December; mid-January to mid-March.
Directions	N165 from Nantes or Vannes, exit 16 (Nivillac) towards St Dolay. After 3km left in Izernac. From Rennes near Redon, right in Izernac, 4km before La Roche Bernard.

Sylvie & Jean Leterre
Route de Saint Dolay, Nivillac,
56130 La Roche Bernard, Morbihan

Tel	+33 (0)2 99 90 89 63
Email	contact@hotel-bodeuc.com
Web	www.hotel-bodeuc.com

Villa Kerasy Hôtel & Spa

Bamboos and cherry trees, koi carp and stone statues – this hotel in the town centre is an oasis of calm. The East is Jean-Jacques's spiritual home, the Spice Route is his theme, and wonderful antiques are brought back from his travels. The 1914 building, once a factory, is pleasing enough from the outside, but inside it is captivating. From the moment you pass the sentinel stone elephants you are enveloped in tranquillity and luxury. Bedrooms flourish Indonesian carved headboards, Kenzo fabrics, ceremonial shawls and percale linen; each is different, each special. Some overlook the railway, others the minute Japanese garden. Thoughtfulness and attention to detail are apparent throughout – even the buddha has a fresh camellia dropped into his capacious lap. Jean-Jacques knows exactly how to look after you without impinging on your space; and staff are lovely. There's a spa with delicious treatments, breakfasts are fabulous, curry nights are in the offing and you're a ten-minute walk from the centre of Vannes: heaps of good shops and restaurants. Don't miss the Saturday market. *Ayurveda spa.*

Price	€133–€238. Suite €360–€430.
Rooms	15: 7 doubles, 7 twins, 1 suite for 2-4.
Meals	Breakfast €14.
	Restaurants 10-minute walk.
Closed	Mid-November to mid-December; January.
Directions	From N165 exit Vannes centre; follow signs to Hôpital or Gare SNCF; hotel signed.

Jean-Jacques Violo
20 avenue Favrel et Lincy,
56000 Vannes, Morbihan

Tel	+33 (0)2 97 68 36 83
Email	info@villakerasy.com
Web	www.villakerasy.com

Le Parc er Gréo

Fields, woods, sea and the coastal path are just yards away, belying the suburban context. Éric and Sophie built the neat modern building in the 1990s, achieving their aim to stop being clients in boring hotels and do things properly themselves. They and their family are still enthusiastic, though we all know that maintenance is less stimulating than creation. The high north wall at the front may seem forbidding but it shelters house and garden from the wild elements. Warm colours, oriental rugs and fine family pieces sit easily in the smallish salon and dining room; these open onto terrace and garden – great places to relax or play with the children on the big lawn. Éric attentively prepares itineraries for guests: boating, swimming in the sea or in the pool. His father's watercolours lend personality to all the rooms and the unusual candlesticks in the hall and ancestral portraits, including a large Velazquez-style child in a great gilt frame, are most appealing. Snug bedrooms, attractive in shades of red, green and salmon, are functionally furnished. An easy, friendly place to stay.

Price	€72–€147.
Rooms	14: 12 doubles, 2 singles.
Meals	Breakfast €14. Restaurants 3km.
Closed	Mid-November to mid-February (open Christmas).
Directions	From Vannes D101 for Île aux Moines. Ignore left turns to Arradon. Left to Le Moustoir then on to Le Gréo; follow signs.

	Éric & Sophie Bermond
	9 rue Mané Guen, Le Gréo,
	56610 Arradon, Morbihan
Tel	+33 (0)2 97 44 73 03
Email	contact@parcergreo.com
Web	www.parcergreo.com

Hôtel Le Lodge Kerisper

Claudie and her young family moved from Paris to open this chic and charming hotel. Huge mirrors reflect white walls, pale floors and seaside touches as you enter. There is more than a whiff of the 'French Hamptons' about these converted stone buildings perched high above steep little lanes leading down to the harbour; sunhats, toys, kites and beach paraphernalia are the order of the day: the fun-loving owners welcome families but the pool is tiny. The bedrooms in this cleverly adapted building, complete with its giddy, architect designed conservatory on stilts, look into a small, prettily lawned garden and pool; antique gilt chairs chit-chat with modern sofas as you sip your drinks at the ultra smart, zinc-topped bar. Bedrooms, many with terraces, are comfortably understated. Linen and voile curtains float on polished floors, white-painted timber ceilings are discreetly contemporary. A hard day's cycling on the coastal paths (or people watching on a sandy beach) leads, inevitably, to a drink on the stylish little port where fairy lights twinkle, halyards click and yachts bob gently. *Spa & treatments.*

Price	€90–€270. Suites €160–€310.
Rooms	20: 12 doubles, 3 suites, 5 family suites.
Meals	Breakfast €15 (children €8). Restaurant 100m.
Closed	2 to 22 January.
Directions	100m north of main harbour street La Trinité sur Mer. Signed.

Claudie & Philippe Favre
4 rue du Latz,
56470 La Trinité sur Mer, Morbihan

Tel	+33 (0)2 97 52 88 56
Email	contact@lodgekerisper.com
Web	www.lodge-kerisper.com

Château du Launay

A dream of a place, another world, another time. Beside bird-swept pond and quiet woods, Launay marries austere grandeur with simple luxury, fine old stones with contemporary art, rich minimalism with exotica. In the great white hall, a decorated Indian marriage chest shares the Persian rug with two bronze stags. The staircase sweeps up, past fascinating art, to big light-filled rooms where beds are white, bathrooms are plainly, beautifully modern and light and colour are handled with consummate skill. For relaxation, choose the billiard room, the book-filled library or the stupendous drawing room with a piano and many sitting corners. Now mix culture with sport. Endurance horses are bred and trained here: bring your own or, if you are an experienced rider, ride the Launay ponies. Your charming, energetic hosts are just as passionate about sourcing fresh, local food for their mainly vegetarian and fish meals. A house of a million marvels where you take unexpected journeys and may find yourself riding along old Roman roads or pike fishing on the pond, picnicking on mountain bikes or gathering low-cholesterol blue eggs (yes!).

Price	€160–€180. Apartments €125–€140 (€750–€850 per week).
Rooms	8 + 2: 6 doubles, 2 twins. 2 apartments for 2-4.
Meals	Dinner €40. Wine €14–€30. Restaurant 5km.
Closed	January to February.
Directions	From Pontivy, D782 for 21km to Guémené; D1 for Gourin to Toubahado for 9km. Don't go to Ploërdut. In Toubahado right on C3 for Locuon for 3km. Entrance immed. after Launay sign.

Carole & Christophe Bogrand
Launay,
56160 Ploërdut, Morbihan

Tel	+33 (0)2 97 39 46 32
Email	info@chateaudulaunay.fr
Web	www.chateaudulaunay.com

Château de Kerlarec

Leave your modern gadgets at the gate and enter an astonishing 19th-century French experience. In the hall, rare and precious panoramic wallpaper scenes of Swiss mountain lakes and Joan of Arc in stained glass (the original Lorraine-born baron was descended from Joan's brother) date from 1834. The rich and varied rooms are garnished with lace, plush and brocade: George Sand serenely feminine in white, grey and rich pink; Jeanne d'Arc surely more gorgeous and lacey than anything she ever encountered during her short hard life... Take a second-floor suite and revel in your own tower salon. Your hosts, passionate and knowledgeable about interiors of the past, lavish care and attention on every antique, objet and painting – and on their guests. For breakfast, expect excellent English, fresh juices and 37 leaf teas served in porcelain and silver. There's a piano to play, a library and a sitting room with log fires for quiet reading; or retire to the conservatory, a striking glass palace with views over the lovely semi-tropical gardens that trumpet tennis court and pool. Amazing. *No credit cards.*

Price	€115–€160.
Rooms	5 suites: 3 for 2, 2 for 2-3. Two rooms connect.
Meals	Gourmet candlelit dinners by arrangement €30–€50. Wine list. Restaurants nearby.
Closed	Rarely.
Directions	From Quimperlé D22 NE towards Arzano for 6km; château on left – take care on entry.

Françoise & Dominique Avelange
29300 Arzano, Finistère

Tel	+33 (0)2 98 71 75 06
Email	chateau-de-kerlarec@orange.fr
Web	www.chateau-de-kerlarec.com

Manoir du Stang

There is ancient grandeur in this 'hollow place' (*stang*) between the dovecote arch and the wild lakes. On the tamed side: a formal courtyard, a fine rose garden, an avenue of mature magnolias, masterly stonework. The welcome is utterly natural, the highly individual rooms not at all intimidating. The eighth generation of Huberts like you to feel at home in their family mansion with a choice antique here, an original fabric there, a nostalgically pink bathroom (updates are under way) to contrast with a gentle antique chest: solid, reliable comfort and enough space. Views are heart-warming, over courtyard, water and woods, the peace is total, bar the odd quack. Communal rooms are stupendous, as befits the receptions held here: the superb dining room can seat 60 in grey-panelled, pink-curtained splendour, its glass bays looking across to the gleaming lakes. The vast salon, with another wall of windows overlooking that mesmerising water, holds a raft of tables, fleets of high-backed chairs, a couple of sofas – and there's space and monumental fireplaces. World-class sailing at nearby Port la Forêt, too.

Price	€75–€150.
Rooms	19: 15 twins/doubles, 4 apts for 2-4.
Meals	Breakfast €12. Dinner for large groups only. Restaurants 1km.
Closed	20 September to mid-May; open by arrangement for groups only.
Directions	From Quimper N165 exit Concarneau & Fouesnant on D44, then D783 for Quimper. Entrance on left, private road. Parking a little way from hotel.

	Hubert Family
	29940 La Forêt Fouesnant, Finistère
Tel	+33 (0)2 98 56 96 38
Email	contact@manoirdustang.com
Web	www.manoirdustang.com

Château du Guilguiffin

The fairy-tale name of the rough knight who became first Baron in 1010, the fascination of the place in its own swathe of wild Brittany, the vast opulent rooms and the tree-and-daffodil-lined approach, seduced us utterly: it is a magical place, grand rather than intimate, unforgettable. Built with stones from the ruined fortress that originally stood here, the present château is a jewel of 18th-century aristocratic architecture. Philippe Davy loves his ancient family seat, and applies his energy and intelligence to restoring château and park. Panelled painted doors are classic duck-egg blue, dusky pink or deep turquoise, rugs are oriental, fabrics are Pierre Frey; art connoisseurs would be in heaven. A vast fireplace is lit throughout the year to welcome guests to the 12-seater table where morning feasts are served on fine Limoges. You may spread out in this room all day — or in the elegant salon, or the cosy parlour, or sip drinks on the generous terrace with views. But it would be a pity to miss the beautiful old timbered city of Quimper, the markets of Douarnenez, and all those glorious coves and beaches.

Price	€135–€160. Suite €190–€250.
Rooms	5: 4 twins/doubles, 1 suite.
Meals	Breakfast included.
	Restaurants 15-minute drive.
Closed	Rarely.
Directions	D784 Quimper dir. Audierne, left after 12km, follow drive 1km, signed.

Philippe Davy
29710 Landudec, Finistère
Tel   +33 (0)2 98 91 52 11
Email   info@guilguiffin.com
Web   www.guilguiffin.com

La Vinotière

Mature elegance meets modern chic at the 'end of the earth' — that's the feel at this 16th-century merchant's house teetering on the Finistère coast. Around it, Le Conquet bustles: fishermen and ferries sail from the port, boutiques cluster, the market confabs every Tuesday. Inside lies innovation: squeezing bathrooms into all ten bedrooms has required a clever use of light and space and some bathrooms are sectioned from the bedroom by half-glazed walls or low panels. Quirky perhaps, but stylish to a fault: La Vinotière is part-owned by an interior decorator. Exposed stone, customised furniture, neutral colours and oak shutters convey class; bright oil paintings (for sale) add a splash. Most fun is for kids: bunk-bedded 'Petite Vinotière' is like a ship's cabin so little ones can sleep like sailors before paddling on the local beach. You can walk the Kermorvan Peninsula or have fishy fun at Brest's Océanopolis, a shortish drive. No outdoor space but adults can retire to the hotel's Salon de Thé whose comfy confines offer cakes and organic teas — the perfect pick-me-up before more exploring.

Price	€60–€125.
Rooms	10: 7 doubles, 1 twin/double, 1 room with bunkbed, 1 family room for 4.
Meals	Breakfast €10. Light lunch available. Restaurants within walking distance.
Closed	Rarely.
Directions	From Brest D789 to Le Conquet; in village, hotel on corner on left.

Joëlle Tromeur
1 rue Lieutenant Jourden,
29217 Le Conquet, Finistère

Tel	+33 (0)2 98 89 17 79
Email	info@lavinotiere.fr
Web	www.lavinotiere.fr

Grand Hôtel des Bains

Marine purity on the north Brittany coast: it's like a slightly snobby yacht club where you are an old member. The minimalist magician has cast natural spells of cotton, cane, wood, wool, seagrass: nothing synthetic or pompous. Sober lines, little ornamentation and restful colours leave space for the scenery, the sky pours in through walls of glass, the peaceful garden flows into rocks, beach and sea. Moss-green panelling lines the deep-chaired bar where a fire leaps in winter. Smallish, pale grey-panelled bedrooms have dark mushroom carpets and thick cotton stripes and checks, a four-poster here, a balcony there, nearly all have the ever-changing sea view. Bathrooms are due for refurbishment but bathrobes give you that four-star look on your way to the indoor seawater pool and treatment spa. Staff are smiling and easy, the ivory-panelled dining room with its sand-coloured tablecloths is deeply tempting. Spectacular coastal paths, a choice of beaches, yoga and spa retreats, even a writer's workshop — the luxury of space, pure elegant simplicity and personal attention are yours. *Excellent wine cellar. Spa.*

Price	€160–€278.
Rooms	36 twins/doubles.
Meals	Dinner €37–€50.
Closed	Rarely.
Directions	From Rennes-Brest N12 exit Plouégat & Moysan, then Plestin les Grèves; cont. to Locquirec. Hotel in centre. Through gate to private car park.

Madame Nicol
15 bis rue de l'Église,
29241 Locquirec, Finistère

Tel	+33 (0)2 98 67 41 02
Email	reception@grand-hotel-des-bains.com
Web	www.grand-hotel-des-bains.com

Ti al Lannec

Heaps of English antiques yet it is superbly French and fulsome: an Edwardian seaside residence perched on the cliff, its gardens ambling down to rocky coves and sandy beaches; fall asleep to waves and wind in the pines. (The beach club closes at midnight.) Inside, a mellow warmth envelops you in armfuls of drapes, swags and sprigs. Each room is a different shape and size, individually decorated as if in a private country mansion, with a sitting space, a writing table, a pretty bathroom and a view to the cypresses or, most wonderful, the sea. Expect florals, stripes, oriental rugs, white linen. Some bedrooms are big, with well-furnished white loggias, some are made for families with convertible bunk-bed sofas. Salons are cosily arranged with little lamps, mirrors, ornaments, old prints; the restaurant faces the sea and serves some pretty fancy and decorative food. The genuinely charming Jouanny family, immersed in the community and very mindful of their guests' welfare, have created a smart but human hotel with a lovely intimate spa by the indoor pool. Walk, swim, or just lounge in this stunning setting.

Price	€180–€452. Singles €95–€149. Family rooms €206–€572.
Rooms	33: 24 twins/doubles, 2 singles, 7 family rooms for 3-5.
Meals	Breakfast €17. Lunch & dinner €27–€83. Children's meals €16–€24.
Closed	Mid-November to March.
Directions	From N12 Rennes-Brest road, exit 3km west of Guingamp for Lannion onto D767. In Lannion, follow signs to Trébeurden; signed.

Jouanny Family
14 allée de Mezo Guen,
22560 Trébeurden, Côtes-d'Armor

Tel	+33 (0)2 96 15 01 01
Email	contact@tiallannec.com
Web	www.tiallannec.com

Hôtel Manoir de Rigourdaine

At the end of the lane, firm on its hillside, Rigourdaine breathes space, sky, permanence. The square-yarded manor farm, originally a stronghold with moat and all requisite towers, now looks serenely out over wide estuary and rolling pastures, and offers a sheltering embrace. The reception/bar in the converted barn is a good place to meet the friendly, attentive master of the manor, properly pleased with his excellent conversion. A high open fireplace warms a sunken sitting well; the courtyard, a gravelled enclosure overlooking the estuary, is made for lounging in the sun; breakfast is at charming long tables laid with bright mats. Rooms are attractive too, in unfrilly good taste and comfort: Iranian rugs on plain carpets, coordinated contemporary-chic fabrics in pleasing colours, some fine old furniture, pale bathrooms with all essentials. Six ground-floor rooms have private terraces onto the kempt garden – ideal for sundowners. Good clean-cut rooms, atmosphere lent by old timbers and antiques, and always the long limpid view. Great for families, cyclists, sailors, walkers. *Sailing school in Ploüer. Golf 10km.*

Price	€82–€97. Triples €109–€117. Quadruples €129–€137.
Rooms	19: 10 doubles, 4 twins, 3 triples, 2 quadruples.
Meals	Breakfast €9. Snacks & wine can be provided. Restaurants 4km.
Closed	Mid-November to Easter.
Directions	From St Malo N137 for Rennes. Right on N176 for Dinan & St Brieuc; over river Rance. Exit for Ploüer sur Rance for Langrolay for 500m; lane to Rigourdaine.

Patrick Van Valenberg
Route de Langrolay,
22490 Ploüer sur Rance,
Côtes-d'Armor

Tel   +33 (0)2 96 86 89 96
Email   hotel.rigourdaine@wanadoo.fr
Web   www.hotel-rigourdaine.fr

Malouinière le Valmarin

The graceful *malouinière* was built in the early 18th century by a wealthy shipowner. Very near the ferry terminal, and in the centre of town, whence the urban buzz, this hotel has an unexpectedly large rose-filled garden with loungers and tables beneath mature cedars and the copper beech. Most bedrooms – light-filled with high ceilings, tall windows carefully draped to match the bed covers – overlook the garden. Second-floor rooms have sloping ceilings and a cosier feel, with exposed beams, white walls and pale blue carpets. The indefatigable and cheerful Françoise and Bertrand refurbish a couple of rooms each winter. There are lavender bags in the wardrobes, plenty of books in French and English, and breakfast at the small yellow and blue dining tables. Or have your café-au-lait in bed and laze a bit before exploring the fabulous ramparts of the city or sunning on the nearby beaches. There's riding nearby and excellent thalassotherapy spas, or take an ocean ride to one of the Channel Islands (Sark is fascinating). Dinard, the 'Nice of the North', is a very short drive. Great value. *Secure parking available.*

Price	€100–€145. Extra person €25.
Rooms	12: 8 twins/doubles, 4 family rooms for 3–5.
Meals	Breakfast €12. Restaurants nearby.
Closed	Never.
Directions	In St Malo follow signs for St Servan & town centre. Then for the Hotel 'Le Valmarin'.

Françoise Nicolas-Quéric
7 rue Jean XXIII, St Servan,
35400 Saint Malo, Ille-et-Vilaine
Tel   +33 (0)2 99 81 94 76
Email   levalmarin@wanadoo.fr
Web   www.levalmarin.com

Château de la Ballue

Artists say this 1620s château inspires creativity; the moment you spot its graceful two-winged façade you'll fall under its spell. The formal gardens are incredible, so wonderfully recreated they are listed and open to the public, a French reverie of bosquets and paths sprinkled with modern sculptures, gazing out to Mont St Michel. Baroque recitals may ring in the courtyard; inside, Purcell odes may float through elegant wood-panelled rooms, over marble fireplaces, antique paintings, gilded mirrors and orchids. This is no museum, however, but a family home with three young sons, and your hosts are as passionate about it as they are relaxed. Drift off on dreamy canopied beds in rooms that are all different, all fabulous, from bold red 'Victor Hugo' to 'Florence' with its blue fern patterns and feathery toile. Three have tented *cabinets de toilette* rather than separate bathrooms – another period feature. Silver cutlery tinkles over a fine continental spread in the blue-panelled breakfast room; birds sing a glorious hymn in the *bosquet de musique*. Baroque, family-friendly, enchanting.

Price	€190-€215. Suite €240-€295. Triple €280-€335. Extra bed €40.
Rooms	5: 3 doubles, 1 suite for 2-4, 1 triple.
Meals	Breakfast €18. Restaurants 7km.
Closed	Rarely.
Directions	St Malo N137 towards Rennes, after 27km, left to Combourg; D796 to Bazouges la Pérouse. Signed.

Marie-Françoise Mathiot-Mathon
35560 Bazouges la Pérouse,
Ille-et-Vilaine
Tel   +33 (0)2 99 97 47 86
Email   chateau@la-ballue.com
Web   www.laballue.com

La Foltière

Come for your host's pride and joy, the 'parc floral' or botanic gardens. They date from 1847 when the château was built, designed to be fashionably informal. The setting is magical and the architecture lovely, the château has the usual sweeping drive and imposing stone steps and hall, rooms are almost too vast to furnish completely. The feel is of a hushed and faded stately home, yet it's not at all precious and children are welcomed with mazes and bridges, slides and surprises. Tall-windowed bedrooms are big enough to dance in: peachy 'Degas' with its own dressing room, deep-red 'Renoir' (these two interconnect); blue 'Monet' with its original porcelain loo; 'Sisley', a symphony in yellow; 'Pissaro', ideal for wheelchair users. Breakfast on homemade croissants, parma ham, cheese and a neighbour's homemade organic jams. Then seek out the grounds – magnificent from March to October, a delight for all ages. Paths meander round the huge lake and past secret corners bursting with camellias and narcissi, azaleas and rhododendrons, old roses and banks of hydrangea. *Tea room & garden shop open afternoons.*

Price	€158. Suite €178.
Rooms	5: 4 doubles, 1 suite.
Meals	Breakfast €12.50. Restaurants nearby.
Closed	20 to 28 December.
Directions	From Rennes & Caen A84; exit 30 for Fougères; Parc Floral 10km from Fougères towards Mont St Michel & St Malo.

	Alain Jouno
	35133 Le Châtellier,
	Ille-et-Vilaine
Tel	+33 (0)2 99 95 48 32
Email	botanique@me.com
Web	www.jardin-garden.com

Entry 163   Map 3

Château du Pin

The lively, artistic Ruans have renovated their small château with passionate enthusiasm. It's a mix of romantic softness outside – colours faded by weather and sunlight, a ruined chapel in the leafy grounds, old roses climbing – and drama inside. In the magnificent red salon, Catherine's vibrant art sits comfortably with beautifully painted brocante finds, innumerable books tumble from shelves, the latest mags on Brittany lie about. It's great fun and has a thrilling atmosphere. The original staircase curves up to two floors of lovely bedrooms where a warm balance is struck between timeless dreamscape and modern comfort, showers fitting snugly behind a great rafter each. A small cottage with a romantic garden and interior courtyard sits in the big park. Your fascinating hosts love cooking: breakfast is a treat with crêpes, homemade jams and cakes, fruit and yogurt; in the evening, they may share supper and stimulating talk with you. This is a land of legends: Brocéliande forest, for King Arthur & Co, is within easy reach; as are the Emerald coast, the gulf of Morbihan, Dinard and St Malo.

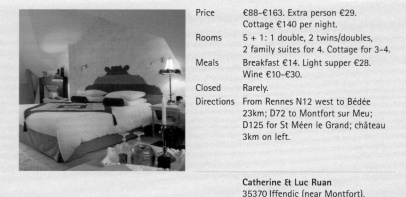

Price	€88–€163. Extra person €29. Cottage €140 per night.
Rooms	5 + 1: 1 double, 2 twins/doubles, 2 family suites for 4. Cottage for 3-4.
Meals	Breakfast €14. Light supper €28. Wine €10–€30.
Closed	Rarely.
Directions	From Rennes N12 west to Bédée 23km; D72 to Montfort sur Meu; D125 for St Méen le Grand; château 3km on left.

Catherine & Luc Ruan
35370 Iffendic (near Montfort),
Ille-et-Vilaine

Tel	+33 (0)2 99 09 34 05
Email	luc.ruan@wanadoo.fr
Web	www.chateaudupin-bretagne.com

Western Loire

Le Château de l'Abbaye

In wide flat countryside, set back from the main road in its own walled grounds, this *castel romantique* had been graciously managed by Danielle Renard for 25 years; now she, her son Renaud-Pierre and daughter-in-law Korakot make a delightful, welcoming trio. Visual enticements greet you as you arrive: bibelots and boxes, photographs and fresh flowers, Korakot's little embroideries, furniture antique and new, even a vintage Belgian stove. Roosters, a family passion, can be found in every medium, shape and size; don't miss the bulging scrapbooks of drawings by guests and their children. Continental breakfast is on the veranda in summer; dinner at candlelit tables reflects the best seasonal produce (French menus by Danielle, Thai by Korakot). In the château, bedrooms, not huge, are decorated to create cocoon-like spaces; extras include children's books and embroidered needlework, typical touches from these thoughtful hosts. Two big rooms in an outbuilding are more modern-oriental with fabulous ceiling lights. All have electronic extras, suites have their own garden and jacuzzi bath. There's a wellness space, too.

Price	€79–€249. Apartment €189. All prices per night.
Rooms	9 + 1: Château: 3 twins/doubles, 2 suites. Le Portal: 1 twin/double, 3 suites. 1 apartment for 2-4.
Meals	Breakfast €14. Dinner €36. Wine €19–€49.
Closed	Rarely.
Directions	A83 exit 7 to La Rochelle; thro' Moreilles, château at end of village with large red gate.

Renard Family
85450 Moreilles, Vendée

Tel	+33 (0)2 51 56 17 56
Email	chateau-moreilles@orange.fr
Web	www.chateau-moreilles.com

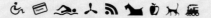

Manoir de Ponsay

The family manor, a listed building, goes back to 1492: note the coat of arms above the door. Now both castle and hotel are run generously, and singlehandedly, by charming young Laurent, who was born here, and his Romanian wife Orelia. Outside is one of the oldest dovecotes in France, and a peaceful pool, a tiny sauna, table tennis and bikes; the grounds are open and safe, the meadows stretch to the horizon. Inside, a dignified room for candlelit feasts, a sitting room with billiards and a tapestry or two, a priest's hole for hiding revolutionaries (should any lurk), and a massive stone stair. This sweeps you up to five characterful suites, historic, traditional, their long windows overlooking the park, their armoires polished to perfection, their chintz bright, their fireplaces lit (when required); the Chambre à Baldaquin has an exquisite four-poster and there's a claw-foot tub in the largest suite. Dinner is prepared, served and taken with your hosts; special wines can be ordered from the cellar. Beyond: the summer extravaganzas at Puy du Fou draw a million spectators a year.

Price	€65–€125.
Rooms	5 suites: 3 for 2, 1 for 3, 1 for 4.
Meals	Breakfast €9. Dinner €34.
Closed	November to April (open only by arrangement).
Directions	From Nantes A83 dir. Bordeaux; exit 6 Chantonnay & Bournezeau. D949B Poitiers to St Mars des Près. Signed.

Laurent de Ponsay
85110 Chantonnay, Vendée

Tel	+33 (0)2 51 46 96 71
Email	manoir.de.ponsay@orange.fr
Web	www.manoirdeponsay.com

Château de la Flocellière

You really need to see La Flocellière from a helicopter. The aerial view is the most striking; the battlement'd castle was built around 1090 and is listed. Guests stay in the château, where bedrooms are vast, gracious and opulent, with huge windows on two sides onto the gardens and park. Overseeing this vast dominion is the Vicomtesse and her meticulous eye misses nothing, from the topiary in the grounds to the maids' attire. All is opulence and beauty and beeswax infuses every room. You can lounge around in the sitting room in the gallery, play a game of billiards, admire the magnificent potager below the ruined walls, visit the library or be taken on a full tour. This is living at its most sedate and children are welcome providing they behave impeccably. The heated pool area (saltwater pool open April to October) is secluded and as smart as the rest ("a terrace, not a beach"). If you choose to dine, tables d'hôtes for ten takes place two to three times a week: your chance to meet the hosts. It's a fabulous place to have a big party and the setting is sensational. Historic, magnificent, hospitable.

Price	€125-€205. Suites €225-€305. Houses €1,000-€2,000 p.w.
Rooms	3 + 3: 1 twin/double, 2 suites for 2-4. 2 houses for 10-14, 1 apt for 6.
Meals	Breakfast included. Dinner with wine, €50; book ahead. Restaurant 500m.
Closed	January & February.
Directions	From Paris A11 for Angers; A87 to La Roche sur Yon; exit 28 Puy du Fou, then Pouzauges until St Michel Mt Mercure. 2nd lights, left to La Flocellière; left on rue du Château.

Vicomte & Vicomtesse Vignial
85700 La Flocellière, Vendée
Tel   +33 (0)2 51 57 22 03
Email flocelliere.chateau@wanadoo.fr
Web   www.chateaudelaflocelliere.com

Château de la Vérie

Impressive but not overwhelming, this small Renaissance château comes with an enclosed courtyard, tall brick chimneys, sweeping slate roofs, long narrow windows and the mandatory tower. Away from any village and far enough from the road for complete silence, it sits in a park of 17 hectares. At the back, an inviting terrace with large green parasols, where meals are served in good weather, overlooks a large expanse of lawn spotted with fragrant lime trees; in the distance are a river and small ponds. This bucolic vision is perfectly framed by the dining room's elegant windows. Sparkles from the chandelier warm pale gold mouldings and matching curtains, bringing out the shine on the crystal and adding a glow to crisp white tablecloths. Food is the thing here, regional cuisine is the focus; one of the chef's signature dishes – roasted duck fillet poached in saffron with a gingered vinegar pear compote – also features the famous potatoes from Noirmoutier (just up the road). Rooms are comfortably classic and big enough to stay a couple of days; those on the second floor, under the eaves, are smaller.

Price	€75-€185. Triples €113-€193. Family room €128-€200.
Rooms	21: 17 doubles/twins, 3 triples, 1 family room for 4.
Meals	Breakfast €15. Lunch €17-€52. Dinner €29-€52 (closed Sun eve, Tues lunch & Mon). Wine from €15. Children's meals €13.
Closed	Rarely. Restaurant closed Christmas, 2 weeks in Feb, 3 weeks in Nov.
Directions	From Challans D69 for St Gilles Croix de Vie. At r'bout 2nd exit. Signed.

Nienke Jansen
Route de Soullans,
85300 Challans, Vendée

Tel	+33 (0)2 51 35 33 44
Email	contact@chateau-de-la-verie.com
Web	www.chateau-de-la-verie.com

Hôtel Fleur de Sel

Noirmoutier has a personality all its own: this group of simple white buildings in its Mediterranean garden is typical, sitting tranquilly between sea and salt marsh, long sandy beach and little yachting harbour. Perfect for family holidays, it has a tennis court, golf driving range, big pool and outdoor hot tub. Bedrooms are good too, some in classic cosy style with country fabrics and teak and pine, others more bracing with ship-shape yew furniture and yachting motifs; several have little ground-floor terraces. The delightful, caring owners have humour and intelligence and their daughter's paintings sit well in several of the rooms. The chef has worked with the very best in Paris and meals are served by courteous waiters in the airy, raftered dining room or on the oleander-lined terrace. It is all clean-cut, sun-warmed, impeccable and welcoming: you will feel sheltered. There is a bridge but try and come by the Passage du Gois causeway, open for three hours at low tide: an unforgettable four-kilometre drive 'through the sea' where shellfish-diggers cluster. The island is naturally very popular in summer.

Price	€100–€220.
Rooms	35: 30 doubles, 5 family rooms.
Meals	Lunch €20. Dinner €31–€41. Wine €16.
Closed	Early November to mid-March.
Directions	From Nantes ring road south-west D723, D751, D758 to Beauvoir sur Mer. Road to Noirmoutier via Le Gois only possible at low tide; otherwise take bridge. Hotel 500m behind church.

Pierrick Wattecamps
Rue des Saulniers,
85330 Noirmoutier en l'Île, Vendée

Tel	+33 (0)2 51 39 09 07
Email	contact@fleurdesel.fr
Web	www.fleurdesel.fr

Château de Cop-Choux

The name, from 'couper la chaux' (cutting lime), refers to the old lime kilns: nothing to do with cabbages. Where to start: the elegant house built just before the French Revolution with towers added in the early 20th century, the 18 hectares of park, the pool, the rolling lawns and ancient trees? Or the 17 marble fireplaces and your friendly hosts? Patrick took over a well-renovated château and has been developing the 'events market,' possibly to the detriment of the B&B rooms. The park is huge, chestnut trees line the approach, a river runs through the grounds, there are lakes and woods for ramblers, rare ferns for plant buffs, farm animals, even dromedaries in summer. The house is full of light, several rooms have windows on three sides and the big bedrooms are dreamy: filmy blue fabric floating at tall windows in 'Violette', exquisite carved twin beds (and an interconnecting room) in 'Romarin'; bathrooms are still good. Breakfast comes with a selection of teas in a pretty panelled room or on the terrace; then amble across the lawns to the pool – or beyond. *Large cottage for six for weekly rental.*

Price	€110-€120. Suite €150.
Rooms	5: 4 twins/doubles, 1 suite for 4.
Meals	Breakfast €8. Dinner with wine €38. Restaurants 12km.
Closed	Rarely.
Directions	A11 exit 20 for Ancenis; N23 for Nantes; D164 towards Nort sur Erdre for 11km, right after Pont Esnault. Signed.

	Patrick Moreau
	44850 Mouzeil, Loire-Atlantique
Tel	+33 (0)2 40 97 28 52
Email	chateau-cop-choux@orange.fr
Web	www.chateau-cop-choux.com

Le Chai de la Paleine

Despite doing all the restoration in the 19th-century manor house, opening an hotel in the old wine warehouse *(chai)* and having five children, Caroline and Philippe are unfailingly relaxed and welcoming. Is their secret that they want everyone to fall in love with La Paleine, as they did? Old buildings are scattered here and there: a hen house with nesting holes in its walls, an old wash-house in the middle of the lawn with a stone trough and fireplace, now a garden salon; all sorts of hideouts in semi-secluded corners of the grounds. The rooms are simple, uncluttered, stylish. The new glass-domed star-gazing cubes are simply brilliant, self-contained with telescope, night-sky map and book. Children love having breakfast inside the enormous *foudres* (wine casks), big enough for six. There are two sitting rooms with soft sofas, bookcases for browsing, a fully fitted kitchen and an honesty bar. It's an interesting village with a good little auberge down the road for supper. Come for a great family atmosphere, homemade jam and yogurt for breakfast and a bag of walnuts to take home.

Price	€69–€89. Singles €50–€55.
Rooms	12: 11 doubles, 1 suite for 4 (some with kitchen).
Meals	Auberge 200m (closed Mondays).
Closed	12 to 20 January.
Directions	From A11 onto A85 exit Saumur for Poitiers; N147 exit Le Puy; 2nd right following Toutes Directions; house opp. stop sign.

Philippe Wadoux
10 place Jules Raimbault,
49260 Le Puy Notre Dame,
Maine-et-Loire

Tel	+33 (0)2 41 38 28 25
Email	lapaleine@wanadoo.fr
Web	www.relais-du-bien-etre.com

Le Domaine de Mestré

History oozes from every corner of Mestré. A Roman road; a cockleshell for the pilgrims en route to Compostella; the remnants of a 12th-century chapel; the mill and tithe barn to remind us that monks farmed here when Mestré was part of Fontevraud Abbey. Most of the present building is 18th century and the family have farmed here for 200 years, keeping the traditions of French country hospitality alive. Monsieur runs the eco-conscious farm, milking by hand; one daughter makes fine natural soaps by sustainable methods, the other manages the estate with its ancient, efficient drainage system. All take pride in their delicious home-grown food (including dairy and meat) and elegant service. Big bedrooms are furnished with lovely family antiques – huge sleigh or brass beds with wool mattresses, fluffy eiderdowns – and no TV; some have views over the wooded valley. The sitting room is a 'Victorian parlour' with dark panelling and red wallpaper; the dining room is simply delightful. A sense of timeless welcome and class enfolds the guest of the Dauge family. Popular with cyclists. *Cash or travellers' euro cheque only.*

Price	€80–€90. Singles €56. Suites €112–€160.
Rooms	11: 6 doubles, 2 triples, 3 suites.
Meals	Breakfast €10. Dinner €26 (closed Thursdays & Sundays); book ahead. Wine €16–€20.
Closed	16 December to March.
Directions	From Saumur D947 for Chinon. Right in Montsoreau for Fontevraud l'Abbaye. 1st right 1.5km after Montsoreau; signed.

Dominique & Rosine Dauge
49590 Fontevraud l'Abbaye,
Maine-et-Loire

Tel	+33 (0)2 41 51 75 87
Email	domaine-de-mestre@wanadoo.fr
Web	www.domaine-de-mestre.com

Hôtel & Spa La Marine de Loire

In a pretty little town on the banks of the Loire, this lovely hotel is casual, stylish and run with superb efficiency. Friendly, elegant Caroline bought the building five years ago and gave it a fabulous new look. With her flair for interior decoration she's clearly had fun: 'Sous la Lune' has glittering stars, 'Reflet' has a floaty airy feel, while driftwood and pebbles adorn others, decorated in chalky colours. There are super bathrooms and many have views over the river or the handsome courtyard. Suites are big and mostly come with mezzanine sleeping areas, although access to one is up some tricky stairs – check before you go. In the large salon you'll find comfy sofas, fresh flowers, lots of plants and a relaxed homey feel. In a long sunny room that gazes over the garden, on the second Sunday of the month, brunch includes heavenly terrine and sweet French treats from the local brocante market. Then off to explore narrow winding streets that take you up to the cliff face for stunning views. You're well placed for cycling, gardens and châteaux abound, cocktails at the bar will tempt you back. *Spa & hammam.*

Price	€150–€190. Suites €250.
Rooms	11: 7 doubles, 4 suites.
Meals	Breakfast €13–€16. Dinner €35. Restaurant 1km.
Closed	Rarely.
Directions	Sent on booking.

Caroline Chagnaud
9 avenue de la Loire, Montsoreau,
49730 Saumur, Maine-et-Loire

Tel	+33 (0)2 41 50 18 21
Email	resa@hotel-lamarinedeloire.com
Web	www.hotel-lamarinedeloire.com

Château de Beaulieu

Set back from the banks of the river Loire lies this characterful château, whose charm matches that of its owners. The Coady-Maguires are Irish, delightful, an animated couple with many interests. Renowned architect Jean Drapeau built the château in 1727 and the décor, traditional and authentic, captures the romance of that earlier age. Five bedrooms lead off an oak-beamed corridor. They range from the dramatic – the Louis XIII with its four-poster bed and bold colour scheme – to the cosy and intimate. Antique armoires, ornate fireplaces and spotless bathrooms await, along with dreamy views of the large, enticing, tree-brimmed garden, with its lily-covered fishpond, lovely heated swimming pool and small, prospering vineyard. Snuggle down into deep-seated sofas with a book from the library or try your hand at billiards – it's all very relaxed. There's wine tasting next door, the historic town of Saumur is a short jaunt up the river and the treasures of the Loire valley are nearby – visit the châteaux on horseback! A magical place; one could stay for the atmosphere and company alone.

Price	€95-€120. Suite €130-€180.
Rooms	5: 4 doubles, 1 suite for 2-4.
Meals	Breakfast included. Restaurants 1km.
Closed	November to Easter.
Directions	From Saumur D947E dir. Montsoreau & Chinon for 2km. Château on right after Gratien & Meyer wine cellars.

Conor & Mary Coady-Maguire
98 route de Montsoreau,
49400 Saumur, Maine-et-Loire

Tel	+33 (0)2 41 50 83 52
Email	info@chateaudebeaulieu.fr
Web	www.chateaudebeaulieu.fr

Château de Verrières

Readers are full of praise for this elegant château, built in 1890 to host balls and grand soirées. In recent years it has been passionately, authentically, lavishly restored. The house stands in huge grounds – unusually so since it is right in the heart of old Saumur – and the charming Valbray-Augers, who speak impeccable English, could not be more welcoming or more helpful. Bedrooms are lofty, lovely and filled with light. Every trace of modern updating – central heating, rewiring – has been artfully concealed, and generous curtains hang at huge windows overlooking the private park. Other rooms overlook the elegant Academy of Cavalry, where aristocratic officers used to hone their equestrian skills, or the Château de Saumur. The décor is classic French at its finest, apart from the contemporary and zen-like top-floor suite. Bathrooms are as luxurious, each one unique. Swim in the heated pool or step into town – don't miss the Saturday market! Yolaine, the lady of the house, is an accomplished cook and makes homemade jams for simple, beautiful breakfasts. Dinners (occasional) are to die for. Worth every sou.

Price	€150–€290.
Rooms	10: 8 doubles, 1 twin, 1 suite.
Meals	Breakfast €15. Restaurant 400m.
Closed	Christmas.
Directions	A85 exit Saumur for Saumur Centre; over 2 r'bouts. Left for Château de Saumur at 2nd lights. Verrières 100m on right.

Yolaine de Valbray-Auger
53 rue d'Alsace, 49400 Saumur,
Maine-et-Loire

Tel	+33 (0)2 41 38 05 15
Email	contact@chateau-verrieres.com
Web	www.chateau-verrieres.com

Château du Plessis Anjou

You can lift off from the grounds in a balloon; some of the finest châteaux and wineries of the Loire are within easy reach. Built in the 16th century, Le Plessis has always been in the family and has been taking guests for years. Though large and very elegant, the château, set in 21 hectares of wooded park, is inviting rather than imposing, with Anjou slate roofs, white walls and creeper-covered shutters. Dinner, at a long table in a rather ornate dining room with scenes from the Roman Empire, could include salmon, duck with apricots, cheese and a crisp fruit tart. Fruit (masses of raspberries) and vegetables come directly from the walled potager. One bedroom is striking with oriental rugs and the bed in a deep alcove; others have lofty beamed ceilings; beds are turned down at night: water and chocolates placed on bedside tables. Children are welcome: the Renouls have two of their own, hence the playground and trampoline as well as rabbits and a goat. There's a small pond brimming with fish and lilies, and a hen house — Madame invites children to gather the eggs. Terra Botanica is a 15-minute drive.

Price	€155–€175. Suites €215–€245.
Rooms	5: 3 doubles, 2 suites.
Meals	Breakfast €12. Hosted dinner €48; book ahead. Wine €20–€240.
Closed	Rarely.
Directions	From A11 exit Durtal on D859 to Châteauneuf sur Sarthe; D770 for Le Lion d'Angers for 18km. Right on N162 for Château Gontier. After 11km right on D189 for La Jaille Yvon.

Valérie & Laurent Renoul
49220 La Jaille Yvon,
Maine-et-Loire

Tel	+33 (0)2 41 95 12 75
Email	plessis.anjou@wanadoo.fr
Web	www.chateau-du-plessis.com

Hôtel Oasis

Efficient anglophile Steve and his young wife Emilie run a happy ship. You couldn't fail to feel well cared for: spotless and well-equipped bedrooms, leather sofas in the bar and a personal trainer in the gym. The cosy, woody reception sets the tone, flaunting all the beams, joists, exposed stones and wafer-brick walls you'd expect from a restored farmhouse with outbuildings. Bedrooms are in the stable wing, some off a raftered corridor upstairs, some at ground level. All have old timbers, attractive repro country furniture, comfy armchairs, writing desks and immaculate bathrooms. The bar, which has an English pubby feel, serves very decent food (there's also a super pizzeria/grill in the courtyard), the lounge is snug with plants, piano and pool table and the breakfast room is a treat: red-clothed tables on a stone floor and a big stone fireplace crackling with logs. A shame to stay just a night, there's so much to see in the area, from the 24-hour race at Le Mans to the 14th-century château at Carrouges. And you could squeeze in a round of mini-golf before breakfast. Friendly people, excellent value.

Price	€48–€120. Family rooms €85–€140.
Rooms	14: 8 doubles, 3 twins, 2 family rooms for 4, 1 family room for 6.
Meals	Breakfast €7.80. Light meals available.
Closed	Never.
Directions	From N12 at Javron, D13 to Villaines la Juhel. On right entering village.

Steve & Émilie Chedor
La Sourderie,
53700 Villaines la Juhel, Mayenne

Tel	+33 (0)2 43 03 28 67
Email	oasis@oasis.fr
Web	www.oasis.fr

Château de Saint Paterne

A 21st-century fairy tale: a 500-year-old château abandoned for 30 years then rediscovered by the heir who promptly left sunny yellow Provence for cool green pastures to resurrect the old shell. He and his wife, a charming couple, have redecorated with refreshing spirit, respecting the style and history of the building, adding a zest of southern colour to panelled, antique-filled rooms, pretty country furniture before ancient fireplaces and rough, hand-rendered finishes – nothing stiff or rigid. Sitting, dining and first-floor bedrooms are in château-style; the Henri IV room (he had a mistress here, of course) has thrillingly painted beams; ancestors and *objets* adorn but don't clutter. The attic floor is fantasy among the rafters: nooks and split levels, a striking green and red bathroom, a bath sunk into the floor. The theatrical new tower room is worth every one of the 52 steps up. Your host, an excellent cook, uses exotic vegetables from his potager and calls his cookery courses 'Liaisons Délicieuses'. A fine mixture of past and present values and superb high-energy hosts.

Price	€140–€170. Suites €210–€250.
Rooms	10: 5 doubles, 5 suites.
Meals	Breakfast €13. Dinner with aperitif & coffee, €47; book ahead. Wine €15–€49. Also their restaurant in Alençon (5-min drive).
Closed	January to March; Christmas week.
Directions	A28 exit 19 for St Paterne then St Paterne centre; signed.

Charles–Henry & Ségolène de Valbray
72610 Saint Paterne,
Sarthe

Tel	+33 (0)2 33 27 54 71
Email	chateaudesaintpaterne@wanadoo.fr
Web	www.chateau-saintpaterne.com

Château de Monhoudou

Your delightful hosts are keeping the ancestral home alive in a dignified manner –
19 generations on. Something special inhabits a place when it has been treasured by the
same family for so long and you'll find it here. It's a jewel set in rolling parkland; sheep
graze under mature trees, there are horses in the paddock, swans on the lake, the
occasional call of peacock, deer or boar, and, now, past the ancient kitchen garden, a lovely
large swimming pool. Endless scope too for biking and hiking. Inside are antiques on
polished parquet, comfortable beds in large lovely rooms, bathrooms and loos in turrets,
billiards and a small library, intriguing alcoves, hunting trophies and a dining room elegant
with family silver. Dinner, prepared by Madame, can be a romantic affair for two or you
can join other guests for home-prepared foie gras, coquilles Saint Jacques, duck with
peaches, braised leeks, apple and calvados sorbet. Then bask in front of the log fire in the
sitting room under the ancestors' gaze. Timeless tranquillity, friendly staff – and a
charming little chapel upstairs.

Price	€110-€180.
Rooms	6: 4 doubles, 1 twin, 1 suite for 3.
Meals	Breakfast included. Dinner with wine, €44.
Closed	Rarely.
Directions	From Alençon N138 S for Le Mans, approx. 14km; at La Hutte left D310 for 10km; right D19 through Courgains; left D132 to Monhoudou; signed.

Michel & Marie-Christine
de Monhoudou
72260 Monhoudou, Sarthe

Tel	+33 (0)2 43 97 40 05
Mobile	+33 (0)6 83 35 39 12
Email	info@monhoudou.com
Web	www.monhoudou.com

Château de l'Enclos

The Guillous welcome you to a grand château in an elegant setting. Proud owners of a red 1933 Citroen, they will happily introduce you to their parkland of fine trees (schools love the tree trail), their lamas, sheep, donkeys and hens. Opt to stay in the treehouse and you find a circular, 40-step staircase to two lovely, cosy, resin-scented rooms and an octagonal deck. Live close to nature and toast the views at sunset; wake to a breakfast basket at the end of a pulley (perhaps even champagne). Back at the château, a staircase sweeps you up to handsome bedrooms of parquet floors and rich carpets and tall windows. Three have balconies. The charming salon opens to a stage-set-perfect garden, and you dine with your hosts in best table d'hôtes style. Brûlon, 'petite cité de caractère', is so close you can stroll there and medieval Le Mans is not much further. A grand house, beautifully furnished and equipped, yet not in the least intimidating, thanks to your hosts who adore English-speaking visitors and will treat you like long lost friends. A lucky find. *No credit cards.*

Price	€120. Treehouse €170. Gypsy caravan €140.
Rooms	5: 2 doubles, 1 twin, 1 treehouse for 2, 1 gypsy caravan for 2.
Meals	Dinner with wine, €45.
Closed	Rarely.
Directions	From A81 Le Mans-Laval; exit 1 to Brûlon. Château on right at end of town. Signed.

Annie-Claude & Jean-Claude Guillou
2 avenue de la Libération,
72350 Brûlon, Sarthe
Tel   +33 (0)2 43 92 17 85
Email   jean-claude.guillou5@orange.fr
Web   www.chateau-enclos.com

Château de Vaulogé

A fairy tale place! The Radinis, from Milan, wanted their children to have an international education, eventually finding Vaulogé. Marisa and her delightful, amusing daughter Micol now run the place, Marisa devoting herself to the garden, her latest project being the horseshoe-shaped potager for fresh dinner produce. The original part of the château, where the family lives, was built in the 15th century. Vaulogé was later remodelled in troubadour style, giving it two circular pepperpot towers; when the shock waves of the Revolution had faded, the aristocracy reclaimed their houses. If it's space you're after, stay in 'Casanova': a huge round tower room, with terracotta floor and amazing, near-vertical beams – excellent for propping books on. (There are plenty of books: Marisa feels a house is not properly furnished without them.) There are other round rooms – 'La Grande Tour' is smaller, and ravishingly pretty. The whole place is enticing with flowers and little nooks and crannies, often put to good use as wardrobes or cupboards. The grounds are lovely, with lilies on the moat and a delicate stone chapel.

Price	€230. Suites €250.
Rooms	5: 1 double, 4 suites for 2.
Meals	Dinner with wine, €70; book ahead.
Closed	2 January to 31 March.
Directions	A11 exit 9 Le Mans Sud. D309 for Noyen via Louplande, Chemiré le Gaudin. 1.5km after Fercé sur Sarthe, right at small chapel.

Marisa Radini & Micol Tassan Din
72430 Fercé sur Sarthe,
Sarthe

Tel	+33 (0)2 43 77 32 81
Email	vauloge@mail.com
Web	www.vauloge.com

Hôtel Haras de la Potardière

François Benoist's mother inherited La Potardière from her father; now her son is entrusted with its keep. François, an architect specialising in restoring old buildings, lives in a creeper-covered wing with his large family; note the family history in the entertaining brochure. François' grandfather built up a successful centre for training show jumpers alongside an established thoroughbred stud; then, in the nineties, after ten years of empty stables, La Potardière began taking in stallions for the summer. Now horsey guests bring steeds from all over France... the very pretty approach includes mares and foals grazing beneath horse chestnut trees. Main house bedrooms are a graceful mix of prettiness and elegance, polished parquet and fresh flowers; those in the stables are less formal, and cosier. What a place for a horse-mad child! though all children will love it here: fields, a safe and secluded pool, billiards, table football, a Wendy house full of toys. There's an honesty bar and relaxed seating, a piano you may play and sociable aperitifs on Saturdays. The welcome is superb.

Price	€90–€130. Suites €130–€185. Triples €130–€150.
Rooms	18: Château: 7 twins/doubles, 3 suites for 4-5, 1 triple. Stables: 4 twins/doubles, 2 suites for 4-5, 1 triple.
Meals	Breakfast €10. Cold platter €23; book ahead. Wine €20. Group dinners by arrangement.
Closed	16 February to 3 March.
Directions	From Paris A11 exit 10; D306 for Sablé la Flèche. Right in village Crosmières; signed.

François & Marie-Yvonne Benoist
Route de Bazouges,
72200 Crosmières, Sarthe

Tel	+33 (0)2 43 45 83 47
Email	haras-de-la-potardiere@wanadoo.fr
Web	www.potardiere.com

Auberge du Port des Roches

If you like the idea of idling with an evening drink by the slow green water, watching out for the odd fish, looking forward to an exceptionally good dinner, this is the place for you. Not grand, not the Loire – the Loir is a sweet, lovely and unsung river – but we can hear you saying: "Oh, what a pretty spot". Valérie and Thierry, who have been here for almost two decades, are young, very friendly, though a touch shy, and full of enthusiasm for their auberge. The lively little restaurant, which seats about 50 people in two rooms, and the riverside terrace heavy with roses and sweet-smelling climbers are the star turns here, but Valérie is justly proud of the effort she has put into the bedrooms, and the way everything sparkles. Rooms are not large but done up in fresh colours with white bedcovers. Those at the back overlook the courtyard, those at the front face the Loir, double glazing separates you from the small road that runs past and peace reigns at night. This is a quiet, very French place to stay, within easy reach of the châteaux. All round superb value – and plenty of choice for vegetarians.

Price	€50–€65.
Rooms	12: 9 doubles, 2 twins, 1 family room for 3.
Meals	Breakfast €8. Picnic available. Lunch & dinner €25–€54. Wine €16–€72. Restaurant closed Sun eve, Mon, & Tues lunchtimes.
Closed	February; 1 week in autumn.
Directions	From La Flèche, N23 to Le Mans for 5km; right on D13 to Luché Pringé. Through village for 2km, right on D214; signed.

Valérie & Thierry Lesiourd
Le Port des Roches,
72800 Luché Pringé, Sarthe
Tel   +33 (0)2 43 45 44 48
Email   leportdesroches@orange.fr

Château de la Barre

Over the cattle grid, down through unfenced fields, to the majesty of this ancient parkland – dotted with ewes and lambs in spring. Continue and you arrive at an enchanting medieval château – in the family since 1404. Your hosts, she English, he French, greet you warmly and usher you into the hall. The portraits and furniture in the *grand salon* are as they were in 1784, a Dutch dresser displays family treasures, there's an honesty bar in the Salon Rose, and young Kakou the parrot keeps his distance (he's shy of strangers!). Comte and Comtesse de Vanssay, known as Guy and Marnie by their guests, instantly make you feel at home. Book in for wonderful dinners served on fine china; tip-toe up an ancient spiral stone stair to bed. Bedrooms have oriental rugs on parquet, rich fabrics and grand oils, pillows dressed in embroidered linen, Roger & Gallet soaps by antique tubs (or new jacuzzis), marble fireplaces and balconies with parkland views. There are summer concerts, and guided tours to the Perche, Le Mans, châteaux and gardens. One of the best. *Wine tastings & motoring treats! Children over eight welcome.*

Price	€180–€360. Suites €380–€480.
Rooms	5: 2 doubles, 3 suites for 3. Whole château available (sleeps 12-18).
Meals	Breakfast €18. Hosted dinner with wine, €95; book ahead. Restaurants 3km & 25km.
Closed	Early January to early March.
Directions	A11 Le Mans & Rennes, exit La Ferté-Bernard. D1 for St Calais. Château 3km before St Calais; right directly off D1.

Comte & Comtesse de Vanssay
72120 Conflans sur Anille, Sarthe

Tel	+33 (0)2 43 35 00 17
Email	info@chateaudelabarre.com
Web	www.chateaudelabarre.com

Ethical Collection: Environment; Community; Food. See page 429 for details

Loire Valley

Château La Touanne

Lush trees and elaborate gates frame the graceful façade. Nicolas and Christine's courteous informality permeates their peaceful 17th-century château. Downstairs, ancestral portraits survey antiques, gilt mirrors and fine porcelain; you have the run of the antler-decked billiard room, panelled green sitting room and chandeliered salon. Breakfast in the stately dining room, where table d'hôtes dinners of locally sourced food and wine are also held. Bedrooms are sumptuous: marble fireplaces, high ceilings, fine oak parquet. One, in imperial purple and white, has a new, regal free-standing bath. Another, gorgeously simple, has been redone in contemporary grey and lime green. A third has ravishing views on three sides and walls papered in a beautiful Jacobean print. The terrace leads into tree-studded parkland, home to the estate farm, chapel, and an orchard concealing the heated pool. Stroll through meadows past the Gothic tower to explore bosky riverside paths, borrow a boat from the boathouse. But come above all for the gracious, relaxing welcome of this authentic family château, just 90 minutes from Paris.

Price	€110–€170.
Rooms	4: 3 doubles, 1 twin/double.
Meals	Dinner with wine, €30.
Closed	Mid-November to March.
Directions	From Orléans A10 dir. Tours, exit 15; left at r'bout onto D2, thro' Le Bardon for 3km dir. Baccon. Château entrance on right.

Nicolas & Christine d'Aboville
45130 Baccon, Loiret

Tel	+33 (0)2 38 46 51 39
Mobile	+33 (0)6 83 20 75 15
Email	chateau-latouanne@orange.fr
Web	www.chateau-latouanne.com

Château des Réaux

Pass the village, dive into the woods and there it stands; a neo-Gothic castle, wonderfully asymmetrical, with a crenellated tower carrying a magnificent staircase. Its new guardians are Michèle and Philippe who gave up the worlds of TV and film for the country – and are loving their new life. Outside are semi-wild grounds where six French hens roam and a vegetable garden flourishes; Philippe is chef so do eat in. Inside is a stunning fusion of classic and contemporary. You'll find a manorial drawing room with a beamed ceiling, furnishings in warm minimalist style and a striking wall of green, a 'smoking room' with comfy sofas, a dining room with white-clothed tables and deep red walls, and, on the first floor, a library/games room to keep you busy. Everything's spacious, generous and that includes the bedrooms, two with sitting rooms, all with gentle colours, soft carpets and great big windows surveying the grounds – blissfully serene. Bathrooms are state of the art. After feasting on *viennoiseries* at the convivial table, visit tiny Apremont up the road and fall in love with its delicate wines.

Price	€100–€220.
Rooms	3: 1 double, 2 suites.
Meals	Dinner €35. Restaurant 10km.
Closed	Rarely.
Directions	Sent on booking.

Michèle Graves
18150 Le Chautay, Cher
Tel +33 (0)2 48 74 93 78
Email lechateaudesreaux@shdnet.fr
Web www.lechateaudesreaux.fr

Château du Boisrenault

Built by a 19th-century aristocrat as a wedding present for his daughter — well overdue, she'd had two sons by the time it was finished — Boisrenault may be turreted, noble and imposing on the outside but it's a family home within. Furniture, objects, pictures, all have a story to tell — and there's no shortage of hunting trophies and stags' heads on the wall. The hostess, Florence, is a gentle soul who leaves sheets of favourite poetry in guests' rooms. Reception rooms are lofty, with huge fireplaces. One sitting room has a baby grand; another, smaller and cosier, is lined with books. As for the bedrooms, each is an adventure in itself. Named after the family's children and grandchildren, they feature a hotchpotch of pieces from different periods, including some excellent antiques; two apartments upstairs have their own fitted kitchens. A delicious pool is discreetly tucked away behind trees in the lovely grounds; table tennis and table football are a godsend on rainy days. Meals, cooked by Florence herself, are served at a vast table in the dining room; be sure to book if you'd like dinner.

Price	€86–€112. Family rooms €112–€150. Apartments €450–€510 per week.
Rooms	7 + 2: 2 doubles, 1 twin, 4 family rooms: 3 for 3, 1 for 4. 2 apartments for 4–5.
Meals	Dinner €25; book ahead. Wine €16.
Closed	Rarely.
Directions	From A20 exit 11 D8 to Levroux; D926 for Buzançais. Château on left 3km before town.

Florence du Manoir
36500 Buzançais, Indre

Tel	+33 (0)2 54 84 03 01
Mobile	+33 (0)6 89 30 44 16
Email	boisrenault@wanadoo.fr
Web	www.chateau-du-boisrenault.com

Relais de la Mothe

Madame de Rochechouart has put her all into creating a delightful and intimate hotel at this once undistinguished inn. The 18th-century staging post sits at the heart of Yzeures sur Creuse, one of the oldest villages in Touraine region. It's neat outside — the courtyard clambered by roses and, hidden away, an enchanting private cloister-garden. However, it's the inside that shines: beyond the rustic salon you'll find bedrooms that are individual retreats of unpretentious sophistication, two ideal for disabled guests. Colours are contemporary — parma violet, muted greens — and details appealing; modernity lights original oak floors and dark beams. Bathrooms are state-of-the-art, one marrying bright orange walls with a smart travertine floor. Breakfast (bread from the next-door baker, homemade jams) is good; lunch and dinner even better — the terracotta and chequerboard dining room, open to non-residents, serves great value versions of steak tartare and rabbit pâté. Still peckish? Use the hotel's bikes to reach Michelin-starred Restaurant de la Promenade in Le Petit Pressigny, just up the road.

Price	€72–€85. Apartment €110–€145.
Rooms	21: 12 doubles, 8 twins, 1 apartment for 4 (no kitchen).
Meals	Breakfast €9. Dinner €19–€28. Restaurant closed Monday & Tuesday evenings.
Closed	Mid-December to early February.
Directions	Sent on booking.

Isabelle de Rochechouart
1 place du 11 Novembre,
37290 Yzeures sur Creuse,
Indre-et-Loire

Tel	+33 (0)2 47 91 49 00
Email	relaisdelamothe@gmail.com
Web	www.relaisdelamothe.com

Hôtel Diderot

Contentment radiates from the very walls of the large sunny courtyard; climbers romp merrily up pergolas, roses peek past olive tree, tables and chairs rest in shady corners. You'll want to linger here over breakfast, and 66 varieties of homemade jam are the perfect excuse. In winter you're in a low-beamed and charming dining room with a vast fireplace lit on cool days – a survivor from the original 15th-century house. Bedrooms feel like beautiful rooms in a family home, each in a different style: Napoleon III, Art Deco, contemporary. All have simple, elegant fabrics, pretty pictures, a good supply of books. Those facing the magical courtyard garden are light and airy, those at the back, darker but cool and appealing, overlook a quiet street. Done in modern, cheerful colours, the ground-floor rooms in the new 'Pavillon' also have good traditional furniture. Françoise, Martine, brother Laurent and Boubi the ginger cat are naturally, delightfully hospitable; having lived in this town for ever, they know its history well. Castle, river, churches and restaurants lie just beyond the door.

Price	€56–€86.
Rooms	23: 15 doubles, 8 twins.
Meals	Breakfast €9.
	Restaurants walking distance.
Closed	Last 2 weeks January; first 2 weeks December.
Directions	From Paris A10 exit 24 after Tours. D751 to Chinon; signed.

Françoise & Laurent Dutheil
4 rue de Buffon & 7 rue Diderot,
37500 Chinon, Indre-et-Loire

Tel	+33 (0)2 47 93 18 87
Email	hoteldiderot@wanadoo.fr
Web	www.hoteldiderot.com

Domaine du Château d'Hommes

No hunting, no shooting on this 178-hectare estate hence lots of deer and birdsong and a posse of tame-wild boar; when we visited, a tit had just nested in the postbox again and Madame was hand-rearing an orphan rook. She also looks after her baby granddaughter, and the donkey and the horses. The courtyard setting is splendid: the moat and the ruins of the old castle, with one little tower still standing, make a thoroughly romantic picture of this great house, originally the tithe barn built just outside the castle wall. Inside, a vast baronial hall and fireplace welcome you. Antiques in the bedrooms (beautifully Italian in one case) go hand in hand with lavish, impeccable bathrooms. Two rooms give onto that fine rather formal courtyard bounded by outbuildings; two look out to open fields and woods. In contrast, honeymoon couples ask for the Tower Room where the view overlooks the moat. Walk out into the countryside or relax on the large lawned area starring a huge walnut tree. There's a new hot tub, too. Peaceful and charming. *Spa & hot tub.*

Price	€99–€129.
Rooms	6: 3 doubles, 2 twins, 1 suite.
Meals	Restaurant 10-minute walk.
Closed	Mid-November to mid-February.
Directions	From Le Mans for Château du Loir & Château La Vallière. Then to Rillé, then Hommes. TD64 for Gizeux. Château on right on leaving village.

	Hardy Family
	37340 Hommes, Indre-et-Loire
Tel	+33 (0)2 47 24 95 13
Email	levieuxchateaudehommes@wanadoo.fr
Web	www.le-vieux-chateau-de-hommes.com

Château de l'Hérissaudière

Park beside the guardian totems, a glimpse of Madame's spirit, then wander through wild cyclamen beneath giant sequoias, take a dip in the elegant heated pool, enjoy a drink on the flowery terrace, play a game of tennis. You could get used to country-house living here, French-style. Madame, charming, cultured, welcomes you as family. Wrapped in 18 acres of parkland, the manor is all light, elegance and fresh flowers. Walls carry old mirrors and bold paintings, tables display intriguing *objets*. Relax in the sunny salon or the splendid library with its books and games table. Bedrooms, over the park, are large, gracious and subtly themed, Empire perhaps, or rich Louis XV. Lovely light 'Chinon' is pretty in pink and white; 'Montlouis', the former hunting room, is wheelchair-friendly. Grand bathrooms have original tiling and marble floors. Tuck into a gourmet breakfast while Madame recommends local restaurants for dinner. The old chapel is now a summer kitchen. Ping-pong, badminton and more are in the grounds, châteaux and golf, riding and cycling trails (bikes to hire) are nearby.

Price	€120-€135. Suites €130-€180.
Rooms	5: 2 doubles, 3 suites.
Meals	Breakfast included. Restaurant 3km.
Closed	Rarely.
Directions	Leave Tours for Angers & Laval. 7km after La Membrolle sur Choisille, left onto D48, dir. Langeais & Pernay.

Claudine Detilleux
37230 Pernay, Indre-et-Loire

Tel	+33 (0)2 47 55 95 28
Mobile	+33 (0)6 03 22 34 45
Email	lherissaudiere@aol.com
Web	www.herissaudiere.com

Hostellerie de la Mère Hamard

Watch the world from your window, the locals clutching their baguettes on their way home. Two pretty townhouses in the centre of a quiet little village, this has been a restaurant-hotel since it was bought in 1903 by a remarkable widow, Madame Hamard, who built up an excellent reputation – Parisian actors loved it and the Duke of Windsor passed by. Here since 1975, Monique and Patrick and their staff still extend a genuinely warm welcome. They have done it up in an attractively modern way with serene and peaceful rooms and bright, crisp bathrooms with pretty friezes. The two big ground-floor rooms have tasteful colour schemes; upstairs there are pale walls and light, bright fabrics; the two smallest rooms under the roof are charming in simple country style; the 'chalet' room over the restaurant is completely different with its wood-slatted walls, and cheerful checked fabrics. Another reason to stay is the seriously good food, traditional with original touches. It's popular with the locals so book your table at weekends. An excellent place to start a family holiday or spend a few days exploring the area.

Price	€80-€110. Extra bed €15.
Rooms	11: 7 twins/doubles, 4 family rooms for 3.
Meals	Breakfast €12.50. Lunch & dinner €29-€65. Restaurant closed Sunday eve & Mondays. Restaurants 5km.
Closed	Early January to mid February.
Directions	From Tours, N138 for Le Mans; left for Semblançay. Hotel in centre of village, opp. church.

Monique & Patrick Pegué
37360 Semblançay,
Indre-et-Loire

Tel	+33 (0)2 47 56 62 04
Email	reservation@lamerehamard.com
Web	www.lamerehamard.com

Château de l'Aubrière

Faded elegance and chaotic charm sums it up. Even before the wonderfully energetic Comtesse greets you, the fairy-tale turrets drop polite hints about aristocracy. Yet the 1864 château has a family feel, its ornate towers good-humouredly at odds with the kids' bikes by the back door – evidence of the Lussacs' five children. Rest assured, it is 'châteauesque' inside. First-floor bedrooms, named after Loire châteaux, are 1870s flamboyant – deep blue and red comfort in enormous 'Chenonceau', a beautiful old elm wardrobe in 'Langeais', a Napoleon III writing desk for composing your cards in 'Villandry'. One bathroom is faux-black marble, some have jet baths. Other, smaller, rooms, heavily atmospheric in their florals, have less bathroom space and superb great views. In the big, swagged and flounced dining room, sit at individual tables beneath some fine portraits for scallop salad, duck confit, vegetables from the garden and lavender ice cream – but save room for green-tomato jam at breakfast. There's plenty to do here: swim in the heated pool, explore the 15 hectares of spectacular grounds…

Price	€100–€170. Single €80. Suites €200–€250. Family suite €250 for 4. Triple €160–€250.
Rooms	13: 4 doubles, 3 twins, 1 single, 3 suites, 1 family suite for 4-5, 1 triple.
Meals	Breakfast €14. Dinner from €40. Wine €10 p.p. Restaurant closed Wednesdays.
Closed	October to end April.
Directions	A10 exit 19 to Tours Nord & Le Mans. Signs for Le Mans on D938; exit La Membrolle sur Choisille. Signed.

Comte & Comtesse Régis de Lussac
Route de Fondettes,
37390 La Membrolle sur Choisille,
Indre-et-Loire

Tel	+33 (0)2 47 51 50 35
Email	aubriere@wanadoo.fr
Web	www.aubriere.fr

Château du Vau

Lanky, relaxed philosopher Bruno has turned his family château into a delightful, harmonious refuge for the world-weary traveller. The cosy, book-lined, deep-chaired sitting room is a place where you find yourself irresistibly drawn into long conversations about music, yoga, art... The sunny breakfast room is charming with its stone-coloured tiles and pretty fabrics. Generations of sliding children have polished the banisters on the stairs leading to the large, light bedrooms that are beautifully but unfussily decorated – splendid brass bedsteads, Turkish rugs on parquet floors, old family furniture, pictures and memorabilia – the spirit of zen can be felt in the search for pure authenticity. A flock of sheep graze peacefully in the newly planted orchard, and there's a dreadlocked donkey called Omega. Deer can often be seen bounding across the meadow. With 118 hectares of grounds it is very hard to imagine that you're only 15 minutes from the centre of Tours. On fine summer evenings you can take a supper tray à la Glyndebourne in a favourite corner of the vast grounds. *Golf course opposite.*

Price	€130.
Rooms	5: 3 doubles, 1 family room, 1 triple.
Meals	Dinner with wine €42.
	Summer buffets in garden €26.
Closed	Rarely.
Directions	From Tours for A85 Saumur; 1st exit for Ballan Miré; signs for Ferme Château du Vau & golf course at motorway exit. Entrance opp. golf course.

Bruno Clément
37510 Ballan Miré, Indre-et-Loire

Tel	+33 (0)2 47 67 84 04
Email	info@chateau-du-vau.com
Web	www.chateau-du-vau.com

Château de Reignac

A remarkably balanced restoration is this four-star hotel, full of elegance and charm, where the 'old' is underplayed and the 'new' is discreet. So many personalities stayed or were connected with this château that Erick decided to theme the rooms adding a portrait or special object – and a biography. 'Lafayette', who inherited the château and visited until 1792, is a small suite with two bathrooms all in subtle greens and yellows with an attractive writing desk for your historical novel and a private terrace for a balmy evenings. 'Axel de Fersen', a Swedish nobleman who swooned for Marie Antoinette, is in pale blues and yellows with a statue of his beloved and a claw-foot bath. Lime and mauve work wonders in the *grand salon* – enormous sparkling mirrors and flower-dressed chimney – while the exotic smoking room/bar – Zanzibar – is in dark browns with cane furniture. Books can be borrowed from the properly sober library where an Egyptian theme runs through the art on the walls. The guests-only restaurant serves a daily changing menu, full of spicy, original touches. We think you will like it here.

Price	€170. Suites €200–€250. Apartment €350.
Rooms	12: 6 doubles, 2 twins, 3 suites for 3, 1 apartment for 4 (without kitchen).
Meals	Buffet breakfast €14. Dinner with wine, from €47.
Closed	January.
Directions	A10 to Bordeaux, exit 23 Tours Sud; N143 to Loches for 22km; Reignac on left; château next to church.

Erick Charrier
19 rue Louis de Barberin,
37310 Reignac sur Indre,
Indre-et-Loire

Tel	+33 (0)2 47 94 14 10
Email	contact@lechateaudereignac.com
Web	www.lechateaudereignac.com

Domaine de la Tortinière

It seems unreal, this pepperpot-towered château on a hill above the Indre, the bird-filled woods where wild cyclamen lay a carpet in autumn and daffodils radiate their light in spring. Then there's the view across to the stony keep of Montbazon; this is an exceptional spot with tennis, a heated pool, fishing or rowing on the river, too. Bedrooms are decorated with flair and imagination, be they in the château or in one of the several outbuildings. The smallest, just renovated, is enchanting in its elegant simplicity and fine fabrics; the orchard pavilion, for playing shepherdesses, is big and beautifully furnished – the desk invites great writings. Bathrooms are luxurious, some smaller than others. For wet nights there's an underground passage to the orangery where you dine – with a dining terrace for summer. Soft lighting, panelled reception rooms, deep comfort and discreet friendliness here in this real family-run hotel: the warm, humorous owners are genuinely attentive, their sole aim to make your stay peaceful and harmonious. Discover the unsung mills and villages of the Indre.

Price	€165–€275. Suites €350–€390.
Rooms	30: 7 doubles, 4 suites. Outbuildings: 16 doubles, 3 suites.
Meals	Breakfast €18. Dinner €50–€75. Restaurant closed Sunday eve November–March.
Closed	Mid-December to March.
Directions	2km north of Montbazon. From Tours D910 south for Poitiers for 10km. In Les Gués, right at 2nd lights; signed.

Xavier & Anne Olivereau
Les Gués de Veigné,
37250 Montbazon, Indre-et-Loire

Tel	+33 (0)2 47 34 35 00
Email	domaine.tortiniere@wanadoo.fr
Web	www.tortiniere.com

Domaine des Bidaùdières

Sylvie and Pascal, she in the house, he in the garden, have made their mark on this classic, pale-stone former wine-grower's property. They now produce a small quantity of wine from their vineyard on the terraced land above the house while cypress trees standing on the hillside behind give it an Italianate feel. Unstuffy and outgoing, this stylish young couple lend sophistication to the place. Bedrooms are fresh and contemporary, each immaculate and carpeted and decorated in Designers Guild fabrics. Some are light, south-facing and have valley views; the cottage suites – one a cave dwelling, the other a gatehouse – are simpler and more rustic. The cosy, den-like sitting room, with its wood-burner in the old fireplace and its billiard table, is hewn out of the rock. Breakfast is served in the sunny stone-flagged conservatory. Guests can idle away the afternoon in the elegant swimming pool on the lower terrace built alongside the carefully restored *orangerie* (you can even reach the pool by the lift in the main house). Sun beds are separated by small bushes for more privacy: every detail is attended to.

Price	From €135. Suite €150. Apartment €170. Cottages €1,000-€1,200 p.w.
Rooms	7 + 2: 4 doubles, 1 twin, 1 suite for 3, 1 apartment for 4-5 with kitchenette; 2 cottages for 4-5.
Meals	Restaurants 2-15km.
Closed	Rarely.
Directions	From Paris A10 exit 20 Vouvray onto N952 for Amboise. In Vouvray D46 for Vernou sur Brenne; 2nd street on left after r'bout.

Pascal & Sylvie Suzanne
Rue du Peu Morier,
37210 Vouvray, Indre-et-Loire
Tel   +33 (0)2 47 52 66 85
Email   contact@bidaudieres.com
Web   www.bidaudieres.com

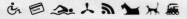

Entry 197   Map 4

Auberge du Bon Laboureur

This little hotel, a stroll from the glorious château of Chenonceau, was a coaching inn in the 18th century. Now in the hands of the fourth generation, it has expanded higgledy-piggledy into adjoining buildings: the old village school and a house with a 1950s tower, known tongue-in-cheek as 'The Manor'. The pool is in a brilliantly secluded garden over the road. Kept in top condition, bedrooms are light, airy and quietly pretty with plenty of space and storage, classic Jouy fabrics, antiques, books and prints. In the original inn, the heart of the hotel, you find three utterly restful sitting rooms and the elegant dining room with a simpler, more relaxed one next to it. In summer, tables with starched white cloths, candles and flowers are set on the terrace under the trees. A good spot for château-seeing; Amboise, Chaumont, Chambord and more are within easy reach, you can make your visits and be back in time for a swim and glass of fine local wine before dinner. A large potager behind the hotel, overseen by Isabelle, supplies vegetables for Antoine's kitchen. Huge character, charming owners, delightful cuisine.

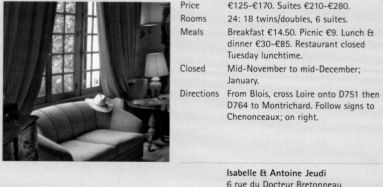

Price	€125–€170. Suites €210–€280.
Rooms	24: 18 twins/doubles, 6 suites.
Meals	Breakfast €14.50. Picnic €9. Lunch & dinner €30–€85. Restaurant closed Tuesday lunchtime.
Closed	Mid-November to mid-December; January.
Directions	From Blois, cross Loire onto D751 then D764 to Montrichard. Follow signs to Chenonceaux; on right.

Isabelle & Antoine Jeudi
6 rue du Docteur Bretonneau,
37150 Chenonceaux, Indre-et-Loire

Tel	+33 (0)2 47 23 90 02
Email	laboureur@wanadoo.fr
Web	www.bonlaboureur.com

Le Vieux Manoir

Imagine visiting Amboise, doing a whistle-stop tour of the magnificent château, a spot of lunch, and then staying in a beautiful manoir from whose wine cellars runs a secret tunnel to the château's very grounds. Gloria ran a wonderful B&B in Boston before resettling in France with her husband to fulfil a dream of restoring a 17th-century jewel. Rooms are filled with fascinating French flea market finds and family antiques, and bedrooms bow to the ladies: Colette is beamed and bright in a red and white theme, Madame de Lafayette's hand basin sits in an antique dresser, bevelled mirrors and hand-made tiles sparkle in the bathrooms. There's a salon, a snooze-friendly library and a convivial conservatory for fine breakfasting which opens onto a cheery French-formal town garden. The little two-storey Maison de Gardien has become an impeccable cottage for four with a sitting room and a kitchen only Americans know how to do — perfect for families with children over five. A second cottage next to the gates, equally special, is suitable for all ages, including couples in search of a romantic escape. Croissants on the house!

Price	€145-€185. Cottages €220-€295.
Rooms	6 + 2: 5 doubles, 1 triple.
	2 cottages for 2-4.
Meals	Restaurants in town.
Closed	November to February. Call for out of season reservations.
Directions	In Amboise, from Quai Général de Gaulle onto Ave des Martyrs at post office. Rue Rabelais left after 150m, one way, narrow.

Gloria & Robert Belknap
13 rue Rabelais, 37400 Amboise,
Indre-et-Loire

Tel	+33 (0)2 47 30 41 27
Email	le_vieux_manoir@yahoo.com
Web	www.le-vieux-manoir.com

Le Manoir Saint Thomas

A bow-shot from the castle in Amboise's historic timbered heart is a turreted manor cushioned by sweeping gardens: a classic French country hotel. Although little remains of the 12th-century priory that stood here, the patterned stonework and leaded, stained-glass windows evoke deep history. Interiors, too, recall another age: finely tiled floors, ornate fireplaces and a charming sitting room with piano, antique globe and hand-painted ceiling. Generous buffet breakfasts are laid in the light, airy dining room, but summer dinners are best enjoyed among the garden's shady limes and bright beds. (A heated pool – discreetly hidden from view – invites a pre-dinner dip.) Ascend to country-classic bedrooms with antique dressers, parquet floors and good modern bathrooms; some have beams and castle views; all are bathed in light. Staff leave hand-written welcome notes and a local fruit liqueur. But it's the setting that wins most hearts: a step away from Amboise's royal château, the river Loire, the Clos Lucé where Leonardo da Vinci lived and died – and an easy drive from superb châteaux and wineries.

Price	€125–€175. Suites €170–€255.
Rooms	10: 8 doubles, 2 suites.
Meals	Breakfast €15. Dinner €27–€33.
Closed	January.
Directions	A10 exit 18 Château Renault/Amboise, to Royal d'Amboise. Right on Rue de la Tour in front of château. Manoir on left.

Ala Socolovschi & Antonella Pautout
1 mail Saint Thomas,
37400 Amboise, Indre-et-Loire
Tel   +33 (0)2 47 23 21 82
Email   info@manoir-saint-thomas.com
Web   www.manoir-saint-thomas.com

Château des Ormeaux

The view's the thing. From the turreted 19th-century château constructed around a 15th-century tower, you take in the glories of 27 hectares. The back of the château is built into the rock face and one of the cave rooms has been turned into a boutique selling, among other things, Éric's delicious home made jam. Corner rooms on two floors – original panelling on the first floor, sloping ceilings on the second – have tiny little boudoirs off the main room in the tower; on the second floor dream yourself into a fairy tale with spiral stairs and miniature turrets. A decent size, bedrooms have elaborate bedcovers and drapes; bathrooms are grand in a turn-of-the-century way. One room, blue and gold, has a marble fireplace and an 'armoire à glace': a wall of mirrors hidden behind an apparently ordinary cupboard; another, decorated in ochre and maroon, a crystal chandelier and plushly canopied bed. Two new rooms have been carefully restored in the 18th-century manoir, with visible beams and lime rendering. Best of all, from wherever you stand (or swim) those valley views are superb. A hugely welcoming place.

Price	€120-€255.
Rooms	8: 5 doubles, 3 twins.
Meals	Restaurants 6km.
Closed	15 January to 15 February.
Directions	From Paris A10 exit 18 Amboise, D31 for Amboise. Right at Autrèche onto D55 to Montreuil en Touraine; D5 to Nazelles; right on D1 for Noizay. Château at end of village after La Bardouillère.

Emmanuel Guénot & Éric Fontbonnat
24 route de Noizay, Nazelles,
37530 Amboise, Indre-et-Loire

Tel   +33 (0)2 47 23 26 51
Email   contact@chateaudesormeaux.fr
Web   www.chateaudesormeaux.fr

Château des Arpentis

This glorious 14th-century château lies just outside town, but after climbing the tree-cloaked drive, you're immersed in countryside: the grounds are vast and secluded. Behind the castle a cliff face is hewn with scruffy caves; to the front: what a view! From a sweeping lawn – constantly mown by robot – and an elegant pool – reached via a tunnel – the eye is drawn to a pond at the bottom of a sloping sward, shrouded by woodland and best explored on the riddle of trails. A sense of the regal pervades the interiors, too. The huge panelled sitting room, its sofas hugging the fireplace, feels fit for royal gatherings; the sunny dining room, leading out to the terrace, is elegant simplicity incarnate, a beautiful backdrop for breakfast; for dinner, you have the restaurants of Amboise. There are just five guest rooms here, one of which is a vast raftered suite with its own tower annexe and stylish in-room tub. All have views over the grounds, newly gleaming bathrooms, gorgeous furnishings. Sylvie Suzanne (the owner, and great fun) spends a lot of time here; unsurprisingly, she can t keep away.

Price	€95–€195. Suite €115–€365.
Rooms	12: 9 doubles, 2 suites for 2-4, 1 suite for 2-3.
Meals	Restaurants 3km.
Closed	Rarely.
Directions	Sent on booking.

Pascal & Sylvie Suzanne
37530 Saint Règle,
Indre-et-Loire

Tel	+33 (0)2 47 23 00 00
Email	contact@chateaudesarpentis.com
Web	www.chateaudesarpentis.com

Le Fleuray Hôtel & Restaurant

The Newington family hotel is a haven of peace surrounded by fields and grazing cows. The basics at Le Fleuray are ideal: a solid, handsome old manor house with duck pond and barns, mature trees and bushes — all that's needed for genuine rest. Then there's the wonderful country-house mood: lightly floral sofas into which you can sink, bookcases, prints and flowers. The rooms in the converted barns are just right for families; slightly cut off from the rest, they have French windows opening onto the garden so each has an individual patio. Those in the main building are a bit smaller but cosy and immaculate, with queen-size or twin beds. In summer, enjoy a heated pool and dining on the terrace. In winter, aperitifs are served in front of a crackling fire. Talented young French chef Romain Grasso, who has a fabulous pedigree, produces a delicately inventive and exquisitely presented cuisine; the restaurant is one of the most popular in the area. Expect a genuine welcome from family and staff; they are constantly improving to make your stay yet more comfortable. *Jacuzzi open all year.*

Price	€70–€145.
	Suites & family rooms €119–€170.
Rooms	23: 9 twins/doubles, 2 suites for 4–6,
	12 family rooms for 2–5.
Meals	Breakfast €15. Children's breakfast €9.
	Dinner €29–€50. Children's meals
	from €17. Wine €18–€24.
Closed	Rarely.
Directions	From A10 exit 18 Amboise & Château
	Renault. D31 to Autrèche. Left on
	D55 to Dame Marie les Bois. Right on
	D74 for Cangey. 8km from exit.

Newington Family
Fleuray, 37530 Cangey-Amboise,
Indre-et-Loire

Tel	+33 (0)2 47 56 09 25
Email	contact@lefleurayhotel.com
Web	www.lefleurayhotel.com

Ethical Collection: Food.
See page 429 for details

Château du Portail

Replete with suave gallic style amid five acres of delicious orchard-cushioned rose gardens, this 14th-century moat-fringed château has been a home to successions of French nobility, and a more recent haunt of contemporary European royals. Five country-best bedrooms range from the cosily inviting Suite de la Tour to the opulent Toile King Room, with matching bedspreads and wallpaper. An abundance of polished Versailles floors, exposed beams, exquisite antiques (your host, the amicable Claude Hubert Le Carpentier, is a connoisseur), baroque furniture, porcelains, thick oriental rugs, heavy curtains and huge marble fireplaces – lit in winter – make for an authentically regal mood in the library, dining room and grand salon. Mod cons such as WiFi and 'American style' bathrooms tether you to the present. Enjoy a peaceful read and aperitif in the shade of weeping willows, picnic on the banks of the Loire, explore the region's vineyards by bike, horse or helicopter, or simply swoon along the 19th-century bridal walk and pretend you're in *Dangerous Liaisons*. Worth every sou.

Price	€160–€190. Suite €265.
Rooms	5: 3 doubles, 1 twin, 1 suite for 2-4.
Meals	Dinner €50, on request. Restaurant 10-minute drive.
Closed	Rarely.
Directions	A10 for Bordeaux; exit Amboise to N152, 25km to Veuves; on to Monteaux. In village follow signs for 'Mesland'. Château 1km after village, green & white sign at entrance on right.

Claude Hubert Le Carpentier
Route de Mesland, 41150 Monteaux,
Loir-et-Cher

Tel	+33 (0)2 54 70 22 88
Email	chateauduportail@orange.fr
Web	www.chateauduportail.com

Poitou – Charentes

Le Logis d'Antan

Blue shutters against pale walls, faded terracotta roofs – the long façade suggests a simple country elegance. Once a wine merchant's house, then part of a farm, it basks in gardens full of beeches and wild poppies, fruit trees and figs. There's even a little pavilion. Bruno and Annie, ex-journalists with a young family, have created a friendly, unpretentious atmosphere – you'll like their style. Meals (Bruno has been on a cookery course) are eaten at a table seating up to 16 in a typically French dining room – or out on the veranda in good weather. Upstairs, where a mezzanine and maze of passageways make for great hide-and-seek, you can prepare picnics in a communal kitchen. Up here, too, are two double rooms, one with a bunk-bedded children's annexe. The triples are on the ground floor: big, traditional rooms, with their own entrances off the drive. Les Pictons, overlooking the front lawn, has exposed stone walls and a grandfather clock; La Pibale, its own terrace. Bruno and Annie work closely with a company called Cycling for Softies, so grab the bikes and explore the country. *No credit cards.*

Price	€69-€87. Suite €105. Family rooms €69-€123.
Rooms	5: 1 double, 1 suite for 4, 3 family rooms: 2 for 3, 1 for 4-5.
Meals	Dinner with wine, €27.
Closed	27 October to 5 November.
Directions	From A10 (Paris-Bordeaux) exit 33. 8km after toll, left to 'Vallans'. Logis on exit dir. Epannes.

Annie & Bruno
Ragouilliaux–Di Battista
140 rue Saint-Louis,
79270 Vallans, Deux Sèvres

Tel   +33 (0)5 49 04 86 75
Email   info@logisdantan.com
Web   www.logisdantan.com

Le Logis Saint Martin

Run with efficiency by Édouard Pellegrin, this 17th-century *gentilhommière* offers that most attractive combination for travellers – solidly comfortable rooms and superb food. It is set conveniently on the outskirts of town, beyond suburbia, in a little wooded valley with a small stream running just outside. The bedrooms are mostly smallish, beamed, traditionally furnished and very comfortable; the bigger rooms, with lovely old rafters, are on the top floor. The tower has been converted into a charming suite with a sitting area downstairs and a smallish stone-walled bedroom up steepish stairs. Food is the thing here – regional, seasonal and served with panache, in the colour-washed restaurant or the pleasantly shaded and tranquil garden. New chef Aline Jarriault has worked with the best and there is an innovative yet classic feel, matched by some tempting wines. Choose between the menu terroir and the menu gourmand – or pull out all the stops and work your way through the menu dégustation! As for Saint Maixent l'École, it's a pretty market town not far from Poitiers and La Rochelle.

Price	€145–€155. Suite €310. Family room €185.
Rooms	12: 9 doubles, 1 twin, 1 suite, 1 family room for 3.
Meals	Breakfast €16. Lunch from €18. Dinner €32–€79. Restaurant closed Sat & Mon lunchtime.
Closed	Never.
Directions	From Poitiers exit 31; N11 until St Maixent l'École; follow signs for Niort, left at 4th set of lights; follow signs. 400m from lights.

Édouard Pellegrin
Chemin de Pissot,
79400 Saint Maixent l'École,
Deux Sèvres

Tel	+33 (0)5 49 05 58 68
Email	contact@logis-saint-martin.com
Web	www.logis-saint-martin.com

Château de Saint Loup sur Thouet

The Black Prince incarcerated John the Good here in 1356 and it was rebuilt in the 17th century by the Marquis of Carabas, whose magnificence inspired the fairy tale author Perrault to write *Puss in Boots*! Charles-Henri visited the château on Christmas Eve 1990, fell in love with it – and bought it ten days later. Saint Loup is a listed monument open to the public and its restoration is a gigantic task. Using 18th-century plans, the count is also working on the 50 hectares of grounds and kitchen garden. Rooms are lofty and light in the château, medieval in the separate keep. The Bishop's room in the château has a splendid canopied bed between two big windows overlooking the garden; in the keep, two huge, hand-carved single beds, in a style befitting the history of the building, grace one of the rooms. It's all a romantic's dream, though a housemaid's nightmare. Enjoy aperitifs in the walled garden or the orangery across the moat; your charming hosts make sure guests meet each other before dinner, delicious and exquisitely prepared. A jewel of a château, a happy and authentic home.

Price	€150–€220.
Rooms	18: 16 doubles, 2 singles. Whole château (& 8-bedroom keep) available.
Meals	Breakfast €15. Dinner with wine, €75. Restaurants nearby.
Closed	Rarely.
Directions	From Airvault D46 to St Loup Lamairé. Château visible on entering village.

Comte Charles-Henri de Bartillat
79600 Saint Loup Lamairé,
Deux Sèvres

Tel	+33 (0)5 49 64 81 73
Mobile	+33 (0)6 80 15 67 36
Email	st-loup@wanadoo.fr
Web	www.chateaudesaint-loup.com

Hôtel Le Pigeonnier du Perron

René Descartes once owned this little *seigneurie*; its deeds are 15th century. More a country guest house than a hotel, it's been in the family for 150 years. Father and son are fully occupied in their wine laboratory in Cahors; Emilie, in her 20s and fresh from hotel school, prepares good simple meals (some organic produce, some fish) and runs it all with Fridda. Family connections guarantee an excellent selection of wines from Cahors, but also from Poitou and the Val de Loire. Sun-ripened tomatoes, courgettes and peppers are home grown along with essential herbs for the kitchen, and you can eat on the the stone-flagged terrace in summer. The modest farm buildings are grouped round a sunny courtyard, hollyhocks surge from every nook and cranny and there's a lovely pool. The smallish bedrooms are simply, pleasantly decorated with the odd splash of colour, their floors pale pine, their walls soft-sponged – or of creamy exposed stone. One in the dovecote has a little balcony, many look over the fields and valley. Good value. *Advanced notice please for vegetarian fare.*

Price	€79–€89. Family rooms €117–€149.
Rooms	14: 11 doubles, 1 twin, 2 family rooms.
Meals	Dinner €19. Wine €20.
Closed	Rarely.
Directions	A10 exit 27 for Châtellerault Sud. 2nd r'bout for Cenon; thro' Cenon for Availles. 1st right after village sign. Signed on right after 1km.

Emilie Thiollet
Le Perron,
86530 Availles en Châtellerault,
Vienne

Tel	+33 (0)5 49 19 76 08
Email	accueil@lepigeonnierduperron.com
Web	www.lepigeonnierduperron.com

Le Relais du Lyon d'Or

The pretty little hotel-restaurant stands in one of France's most beautiful medieval villages. Diana, American, brings her professional experience; Dominique, a fully-fledged French wine expert and dealer, will suggest the perfect bottle be it for dinner or a big event, simple or organic, for connoisseurs or big budgets. The public rooms, rebuilt round old flagstones and beams, are decorated in warm natural colours to enhance the beauty of the original architecture. Bedrooms, some big, some smaller, have intriguing and individual details; rafters for those under the roof, high ceilings and beams or rough terracotta floors for others; none are overdone and all have sparkling bathrooms. The varied menu focuses on traditional dishes and local and seasonal produce, served when possible on the pretty terrace alive with wisteria and roses, hydrangea and geraniums… Masses to see and do: the Valley of the Frescoes with its abbey at St Savin (UNESCO), the markets of medieval Chauvigny and Loches, the superb Parc de la Brenne, for birds, turtles, orchids, Poitiers… or the quiet wonders of nature in the nearby valleys.

Price	€75–€145. Suites €125–€145.
Rooms	10: 8 doubles, 1 suite for 4, 1 suite for 5.
Meals	Breakfast €12. Dinner €25–€40. Wine €22–€500. Lunch for groups by arrangement. Restaurant closed mid-Nov to mid-March.
Closed	Rarely.
Directions	A10 exit Châtellerault Nord D9/D725 east through La Roche Posay; D5 to Angles sur l'Anglin. Hotel in village centre.

Dominique Fuscien & Diana Hager
4 rue d'Enfer,
86260 Angles sur l'Anglin, Vienne

Tel	+33 (0)5 49 48 32 53
Email	contact@lyondor.com
Web	www.lyondor.com

Hôtel Les Orangeries

The long cool pool beneath the trees will convince you that these people have the finest sense of how to treat an old house and its surroundings. A deep wooden deck, rustic stone walls, giant flower baskets, orange trees, candles at night – all create tranquillity and harmony. The young owners (he an architect) fell in love with the place and applied all their talent to blending 18th-century elegance with contemporary charm. Stripped oak doors, exposed stone walls, cool stone floors glow with loving care, like valued old friends. Olivia has given each bedroom its own sense of uncluttered harmony, those facing the main road are double-glazed (earplugs could come in handy, too), the split-level suites are a delight. The Gautiers' passions include the old-fashioned games they have resuscitated for you: croquet and skittles under the trees, two kinds of billiards, backgammon and mahjong. Olivia speaks English and her enthusiasm for house, garden and guests is catching. Food is delicious, local, organic; breakfast, in the garden in summer, is all you'd hope for the price. Exceptional. *Electric bikes & car on request.*

Price	€70–€140. Apartments €115–€185.
Rooms	15: 11 doubles, 4 apartments for 4-5 (without kitchen).
Meals	Breakfast from €12.50. Dinner from €28. Wine from €19.50.
Closed	Rarely.
Directions	From Poitiers N147 for Limoges to Lussac les Châteaux; 35km. Hotel on left on entering town.

Olivia & Jean-Philippe Gautier
12 avenue du Docteur Dupont,
86320 Lussac les Châteaux, Vienne

Tel	+33 (0)5 49 84 07 07
Email	orangeries@wanadoo.fr
Web	www.lesorangeries.fr

Ethical Collection: Environment; Food.
See page 429 for details

Château de Nieuil

François I built this fairy-tale château as a hunting lodge in the 16th century – and went on to create the Château de Chambord. A gambling Count sold Nieuil to the Bodinauds' grandparents; now its hunting days are over and it's become an exciting hotel, paying homage to our feathered friends with a magical bird-spotting walk round the moat. Each room is named after a bird and, if you are not woken by real ones, an alarm will sing 'your' song. A chandelier hung with love letters and a stainless-steel bar bring touches of modern elegance to this country retreat, grand and beautifully decorated. One room has a small children's room up a spiral stair, another a tiny reading room in a turret. Most look onto the ornate gardens at the back, whose newest addition is an eco-cosy star-gazing cabin – book early, it's popular. (There's a gypsy caravan, too.) The breakfast room looks onto the grounds through stained-glass windows, and Madame, a chef in her own right, has trained the young trio who run the restaurant in the old stables: fabulous. Open-hearted, open-armed, these people love what they do, and it shows.

Price	€140-€300. Suites €280-€460. Garden cabin €90. Gîtes from €550 pw. Gypsy caravan €200 pw.
Rooms	16 + 3: 11 twins/doubles, 3 suites, 1 gypsy caravan,1 garden cabin. 3 gîtes.
Meals	Breakfast €15. Lunch €25-€50. Dinner €50-€80. Restaurant closed Sunday eve; Mon & Tues lunch Sept-June.
Closed	November.
Directions	From Angoulême N141 to La Rochefoucauld & Chasseneuil. On for 6.5km; in Suaux, left on D739 to Nieuil.

Monsieur & Madame Bodinaud
16270 Nieuil, Charente

Tel	+33 (0)5 45 71 36 38
Email	chateaunieuilhotel@wanadoo.fr
Web	www.chateaunieuilhotel.com

Logis de Puygâty

Swathed in the rolling greenery of the south Charente, the Logis de Puygâty's rustic 15th-century charms are gilded with a sleek contemporary edge. Once home to an advisor of François I, this ancient fortified manor has become a design masterpiece, its medieval rooms revitalised by the genius of Max and Pierre, your delightful – and creative – hosts. A particular highlight is Maison d'Amis, the cottage in the grounds, its beautiful pale stone fireplace soaring upwards, illuminated by simple naked bulbs. Elsewhere there are cream stone walls, rustic floors, perfect linen. Visit their shop, Sorti de Grange ('found in the barn'), an amazing showcase (with a floating stairs) for Pierre's own designs, displayed alongside regional produce. Outside, white hydrangeas burst from flower beds, horses neigh, donkeys bray, a pool beckons. Dinner is available with 24-hour notice and Pierre champions hearty regional dishes – try the meats doused in cognac and pineau. The next morning he can be found sipping expresso and serving piles of locally made *viennoiseries*. Worth every sou.

Price	€150-€190. Extra bed €40. Cottage €285 (per night).
Rooms	3 + 1: 2 doubles, 1 twin. Cottage for 2.
Meals	Breakfast €13. Dinner with wine, €50.
Closed	Rarely.
Directions	Sent on booking.

Pierre Casteleyn & Max Griffin
16250 Chadurie, Charente

Tel	+33 (0)5 45 21 75 11
Email	info@logisdepuygaty.com
Web	www.logisdepuygaty.com

Relais de Saint Preuil

Madame from Burgundy has lived in Asia and has come home to fulfil a dream: to run her own hotel in the Poitou – Charentes. The Montembaults, in search of a big old property and a business adventure, ended up with a hamlet… Le Relais de St Preuil sits alone at the top of a hill surrounded by vineyards and sky and it's a fabulous setting. Hard work and dedication have resulted in an expertly run holiday complex and some very comfortably dressed rooms (all but one on the ground floor): expect shiny sleigh beds, cheerful fabrics, ethnic themes and a few stunning old rafters. And there's so much to do you could never be bored: a tennis court and big outdoor pool, a pool house with fitness room and sauna, mountain bikes, ping-pong and playground… all has been included, from in-room massages to generous pool towels. This would be a terrific place for a group of friends – or for a sociable family. Meet the guests at table d'hôtes over regional dishes delicately and deliciously flavoured with cognac and pineau des Charentes. The finest cognac vineyards surround you.

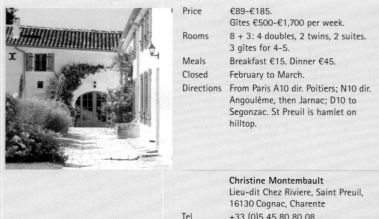

Price	€89-€185.
	Gîtes €500-€1,700 per week.
Rooms	8 + 3: 4 doubles, 2 twins, 2 suites.
	3 gîtes for 4-5.
Meals	Breakfast €15. Dinner €45.
Closed	February to March.
Directions	From Paris A10 dir. Poitiers; N10 dir. Angoulême, then Jarnac; D10 to Segonzac. St Preuil is hamlet on hilltop.

Christine Montembault
Lieu-dit Chez Riviere, Saint Preuil,
16130 Cognac, Charente

Tel	+33 (0)5 45 80 80 08
Email	contact@relais-de-saint-preuil.com
Web	www.relais-de-saint-preuil.com

L'Yeuse

A dazzlingly striped little Charente château with a 'flamboyant' modern extension, L'Yeuse is utterly charming, so near Cognac yet wrapped in parkland with views to the river. Large and light in bold country-house style and with ultra-modern bathrooms, bedrooms are along fun, stencilled corridors in the newer part; book a room over the river. By contrast, the 'old' château has classical proportions, elegant furnishings and traditional comfort. Wallow in the clubby cigar-cognac salon with its deep armchairs and glass-fronted cabinets, work your way through the 100-year-old brews. It's posh frocks for dinner in the chandelier-hung dining room, all stiff white napery and black jacketed waiters. The excitement over chef Pascal Nebout's cuisine is palpable, his wife Maria is the sommelier. Céline, efficient, energetic yet ever calm, will advise on visiting distilleries and festivals; husband Rémy has transformed the gardens for biodiversity (insect hotels…) and delicious produce. They are a close-knit team. Relax by the pool, find a shady terrace or treat yourself to a massage in the hammam. Sophisticated living.

Price	€105–€175. Suites €230–€353.
Rooms	24: 8 doubles, 13 twins/doubles, 3 suites.
Meals	Breakfast €19. Lunch €18–€25. Dinner €50–€85. Rest. closed Mon, Sat lunchtimes; Sunday & Monday eve out of season.
Closed	January.
Directions	From Paris A10 exit 34. Follow signs St Jean d'Angély & Cognac, then for Angoulème; D15 to St Brice & Quartier de l'Échassier.

Céline Desmazières & Pascal Nebout
65 rue de Bellevue, Châteaubernard,
16100 Cognac, Charente

Tel	+33 (0)5 45 36 82 60
Email	reservations@yeuse.fr
Web	www.yeuse.fr

Logis du Fresne

The Butler family came to France a century ago to make cognac and Tone's husband Christophe has been in the business all his life. They bought this old, elegant house and created a refined place to stay with an intimate *chambres d'hôtes* feel. Inside, it's as good as its façade is wonderful. The whole feel is light and fresh in turn-of-the-century Norwegian style (Tone's birthplace): old terracotta, pale beams, a cosy library, an elegant salon. Bedrooms are as serene. Those on the first floor have uncluttered chic: a gilded mirror hangs above an open fire, an oriental rug graces a limed floor. Those above are more modern. The two-room suite has its own stair, bathrooms are beautiful, one in orange-ochre with a treat of a sunken bath. The gardens are a delight, and breakfast on the terraces romantic — expect a fresh cut rose and quintessential silver tea set at tables forged in the village. The grounds, with a stunning hidden pool and a 15th-century tower, look across to terracotta roofs against a cornflower blue sky. Take a picnic supper into the garden and enjoy the sunset over the vines.

Price	€120–€130. Suite €195.
Rooms	11: 10 twins/doubles, 1 suite.
Meals	Breakfast €13. Dinner (min. 8 people, outside caterers) €36. Wine €15–€36. Restaurants 5km.
Closed	November to February. Call for out of season group reservations.
Directions	From Cognac, D24 for Segonzac then D736 for Juillac le Coq. 500m after village on right.

Tone Butler
16130 Juillac le Coq,
Charente

Tel	+33 (0)5 45 32 28 74
Email	logisdufresne@wanadoo.fr
Web	www.logisdufresne.com

Le Logis du Paradis

Mellow stones, chunky beams, sensuous fabrics… there's a timeless feel to the beautifully renovated Logis, where Nick and Sally greet you as old friends. The 18th-century buildings (a *paradis* is where the oldest, finest Cognac was stored) embrace a magnificent oval courtyard. In big luxurious bedrooms you snuggle down in superbly comfortable king-size beds under white linen… and wake in anticipation of a delicious breakfast. There's a pool in the aromatic garden, books on the landings, a tea and coffee kitchen, a bar in the former distillery shared with the other guests. Or you may pootle down empty country roads in one of Nick's classic cars (choose from a selection); what better way to discover Cognac's finest vineyards and the Atlantic beaches than in an old MG? Return to a stroll round the walled *parc* by the pretty river Né before a four-course table d'hôtes dinner, enjoyed on the terrace in summer. Nick and Sally's generous table features market-fresh local produce, fine wines, and a glass of the neighbour's superb XO Cognac to finish with. Highly professional. *Two cottages in grounds.*

Price	€95–€125. Cottages €895–€1,395 p.w.
Rooms	5 + 2: 4 twins/doubles, 1 twin. 2 cottages for 4.
Meals	Lunch €19. Dinner €39, on request. Wine from €12.50. Restaurant 4km.
Closed	Mid-January to end February.
Directions	N10 south from Angoulême dir. Bordeaux. Before Barbezieux, D151 thro' Viville; cross D1 until La Magdeleine. 100m after chapel on left.

Nick & Sally Brimblecombe
La Magdeleine,
16300 Criteuil la Magdeleine,
Charente

Tel	+33 (0)5 45 35 39 43
Email	info@logisduparadis.fr
Web	www.logisduparadis.com

Ethical Collection: Community.
See page 429 for details

Château des Salles

A pretty little château set among vineyards and full of character, Salles was built in 1454 and scarcely touched until 1860, when it was 'adapted to the fashion' (profoundly). A century later, the Couillaud family brought the house, vineyard and farm into the 20th century. Behind the fine old exterior you find light, harmony, colour and elegant informality with spiral stone stairs, boldly painted beams and warm, well-furnished bedrooms bathed in soft colours and gentle wallpapers. Salles has a friendly family feel: adorable and elegantly French, Sylvie runs the house with passion and effortless taste, her brother tends the vines, their mother's watercolours hang in the public rooms and decorate bedroom doors. At dinner, refined food made with local and home-grown produce is served with class and estate wines. Sylvie will help you plan your stay, her advice is invaluable. People return again and again to this congenial, welcoming house. One guest said: "She welcomed us like family and sent us home with goodies from her vineyard". *Château produces wines, pineau & cognac. Accept American Express.*

Price	€88–€153.
Rooms	5: 4 twins/doubles, 1 double.
Meals	Breakfast included. Dinner €29–€38. Wine from €15.
Closed	November to March.
Directions	From A10 exit 27 Mirambeau, then D730 towards Royan. Château is between Lorignac and Brie sous Mortagne; signed at D730/D125 junction.

Sylvie Couillaud
17240 Saint Fort sur Gironde,
Charente-Maritime

Tel	+33 (0)5 46 49 95 10
Email	chateaudessalles@wanadoo.fr
Web	www.chateaudessalles.com

Château de la Tillade

You can tell that Michel and Solange like people, they make you feel instantly at ease in their comfortable, friendly home, even if you're secretly terrified of dropping the fine bone china. Their château sits at the top of an avenue of lime trees alongside the family vineyards that have produced grapes for cognac and pineau des Charentes for over two centuries. The original distillery equipment is well worth a visit. Solange's talents as an artist (she also holds painting courses in her art studio) are reflected in her choice of fabrics. The bedrooms are marvellously individual, less by design than by gradual, natural evolution through the years. Each is like a page out of Michel's memory book, you feel they are steeped in family history. The claw-foot bath is fit for a princess. The corner room has a wonderful balcony overlooking the drive. Meals are a delight (book ahead), with good conversation (in English or French) round the family table while you are waited on lavishly but without stuffiness. An rare opportunity to get to know a couple of relaxed and charming French aristocrats.

Price	€90–€120. Extra bed €23.
Rooms	4: 1 twin, 3 family rooms for 3-4 (one room with wc just outside room).
Meals	Dinner €38; book ahead. Restaurant 12km.
Closed	Rarely.
Directions	From A10 exit 36 right for Gémozac. At r'bout. Gémozac bypass for Royan, right on D6 for Tesson. Entrance approx. 3km on left, signed (château not in village, but on D6).

Vicomte & Vicomtesse Michel de Salvert
Gémozac,
17260 Saint Simon de Pellouaille,
Charente-Maritime
Tel   +33 (0)5 46 90 00 20
Email   contact@la-tillade.com
Web   www.la-tillade.com

Ma Maison de Mer

Sink into a cream sofa with a chilled après-plage beer and soak up the nautical chic. Built in the 1920s in a quiet tree-lined street (150m from a lovely beach, 400m from 'centre ville') Ma Maison has been renovated by bubbly Emma, who lives here with her young family. An intimate bar greets you as you enter and the open-plan living and dining rooms are separated by an elegant archway. Wooden floors are painted white as are the walls, drawing attention to vibrant paintings; further charming touches, from seashell collages and knitted cushions to a model gaff-rigged yacht, decorate every room. The same soothing shades are used in the bedrooms, fresh and inviting with seagrass floors, cane chairs, taupe-coloured bedspreads and white linen. Some of the rooms have mosquito nets, others central ceiling fans. The four-course set menu (summer only) changes daily so expect the freshest seafood – superb. If you need an excuse to stay, take a boat across the Gironde from Royan to sample the Medoc wines. There are summer festivals in lively Saint Palais and unspoilt beaches galore.

Price	€70–€155.
Rooms	5: 4 doubles, 1 twin.
Meals	Dinner with wine, €35, on request (June–September only).
Closed	Rarely.
Directions	From A10 exit 5, Saintes to Royan on N150; in Royan D21 to St Palais; at r'bout, 4th exit, house on right. Signed.

Emma Hutchinson
21 avenue du Platin,
17420 Saint Palais sur Mer,
Charente-Maritime
Tel   +33 (0)5 46 23 64 86
Email   reservations@mamaisondemer.com
Web   www.mamaisondemer.com

Le Moulin de Châlons

The generous, open-hearted Bouquets are a family of perfectionists, and it shows in their beautiful stone mill house sitting gracefully at the water's edge, its sun terrace overlooking the mill race. The restaurant, with its crisp white tables and tankful of lobsters, has earned a huge reputation for finesse; the family hotel is charming. Enter a relaxed salon with a pretty stone fireplace, cosy leather chairs and fresh flowers. Spotless gleaming bedrooms with super sound insulation (against the main road) are traditional; those in the new wing, designed by talented daughter Maud, are ultra-modern and sleek with fluffy tactile touches (faux furs, cushions…). Choose between blue Jouy with bold pebble stencils or elegant antique sofas with rust-and-grey spots and swirls. Bathrooms are immaculate and gorgeous, too; the newest have a serene eastern feel. Neatly tended gardens line the entrance while thoughtful resting places invite you to admire the birds bobbing downstream. Close by are the smart islands of Ré and Oléron; if it's green peace you want, catch a slow boat up the Marais to the Venise Verte.

Price	€115–€130. Suites €145–€165. Family room €145.
Rooms	10: 5 doubles, 2 twins, 2 suites for 2, 1 family room for 3.
Meals	Breakfast €13. Lunch & dinner €29–€50.
Closed	Rarely.
Directions	From Royan on D25; left on D733, right on D241. Moulin 500m after leaving Le Gua.

Bouquet Family
2 rue du Bassin,
17600 Le Gua,
Charente-Maritime

Tel	+33 (0)5 46 22 82 72
Email	moulin-de-chalons@wanadoo.fr
Web	www.moulin-de-chalons.com

Hôtel Napoléon

A boat trip over an island-dotted seascape delivers you to another world – one of simple sophistication, of a love story set in the Roaring Twenties, of historic buildings artfully preserved. In the hotel where Baron Gorgaud and his American lover entertained intellectuals and artists, Martine and Noël now steal the show. They've made it marvellously modern with period furniture and sharp design: a fireside chessboard, Stibley paintings of 1920s scenes, a glass-topped well over a wine cellar, pop art on sober bedroom walls. The restaurant gleams – glass tables, transparent chairs – and the food is as delicious to eat as it is to gaze upon: local oysters, duck with fig jus, Grand-mère's chocolate cake. Chef specials appear at breakfast, on the deck or in your room. There are plans for a pool, but ocean views are ever present; just 250 villagers, and, at sunset, the day visitors depart. Close to La Rochelle but a car-free escape from well-worn tracks: hire bikes or horse-drawn carriage to explore this tiny island, with its museum of Napoleon's last days in France. History, adventure, romance!

Price	€85–€180.
Rooms	18: 13 doubles, 3 twins, 1 triple, 1 suite for 1-4.
Meals	Breakfast €12. Lunch & dinner €22–€26. Wine €12–€35.
Closed	Mid-November to early February.
Directions	See owner website.

Martine & Noël Bourdet
Rue Gourgaud, 17123 Île d'Aix,
Charente-Maritime

Tel	+33 (0)5 46 84 00 77
Email	contact@hotel-ile-aix.com
Web	www.hotel-ile-aix.com

Hôtel de l'Océan

A hotel of contrasts: big yet small; hotel and restaurant; perspex by thick curtains; Mediterranean by the Atlantic. Seasoned travellers, Martine and Noël worked in antiques and interior design but realised, after a spell running a restaurant, that they should be running a hotel – but where? It had to feel like home, it had to be on an island; then they stumbled on a place on the Île de Ré and knew that this was it. Set back from the street in a quiet little town, the Océan has 29 bedrooms in sixes and sevens, each cluster with individual flavour, some round a courtyard pungent with rosemary and lavender, some tiny cottages among the hollyhocks. Children love the curtained cabin bed set in a buttercup-yellow alcove. Two brand new rooms in a wing are large and colonial looking, with super bathrooms and a calm cool feel. Floors are covered in matting; ships, lighthouses and shells are dotted around against soft soothing colours. After your aperitif, dinner will involve fresh fish and herbs. The dining room is another success, with cream-boarded walls and palest green-grey carved chairs. *Beach 15-minute walk.*

Price	€75–€180. Twins €85–€120. Triples €105–€160. Quadruple €165–€200.
Rooms	29: 22 doubles, 4 twins, 2 triples, 1 quadruple.
Meals	Breakfast €10. Lunch & dinner €24–€50. Wine €14–€40. Restaurant closed Weds Oct–March.
Closed	January.
Directions	A10 exit Niort sud; N248 to La Rochelle, then N11 Rocade round La Rochelle for Pont Île de Ré; after bridge, south to Bois Plage. Hotel in town centre.

Martine & Noël Bourdet
172 rue Saint Martin,
17580 Le Bois Plage en Ré (Île de Ré),
Charente-Maritime

Tel	+ 33 (0)5 46 09 23 07
Email	info@re-hotel-ocean.com
Web	www.re-hotel-ocean.com

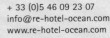

Maison des Algues

In a residential area, behind private gates on the outskirts of Rivedoux Plage, is a modern single-storey hotel, whitewashed, shuttered and impeccably maintained. The design and the décor have been carefully considered and calm reigns supreme. Nothing is too much trouble for delightful Christian and Jocelyne, who will pick you up from the airport and insist on giving you the best: snowy towels for the bathroom, coloured towels for the pool, delicious pâtisseries for tea. Christian is proud to be a founding member of the Île de Ré cricket club – hence the cricket pitch in the garden. Guest bedrooms, which open to a smart wicker-chaired terrace, are roomy, restful, flooded with light. After breakfast at 9am – no earlier please, you're here to unwind – slope off to a cushioned sunbed by the pool, spotlessly clean and heated to 28 degrees. Or spin off on a bike (there are ten, in tip-top condition and free of charge) and acquaint yourself with the island: the hollyhocks and whitewashed houses of villages like La Flotte, the fabulous white sand beaches, the chic shops and markets of St Martin.

Price	€125–€215.
Rooms	5: 3 doubles, 2 suites (2 rooms interconnect).
Meals	Restaurants within walking distance. Guest kitchen.
Closed	Rarely.
Directions	Sent on booking.

Christian & Jocelyne Gatta-Boucard
147 rue des Algues,
17940 Rivedoux (Île de Ré),
Charente-Maritime

Tel	+33 (0)5 46 68 01 23
Email	information@maison-des-algues.com
Web	www.maison-des-algues.com

Hôtel de Toiras

It's the French hotel you dream of but rarely find. Exquisite is the first word, refined is the second, then you stop thinking and let the senses rule. Revel in the soul of this quayside hotel, inspired by the illustrious figure of Jean de Caylar de Saint Bonnet de Toiras who protected the island from the English in 1627. Thus the arts of navigation and hunting set the tone and imbue the rooms with history. Linking the old part with the new is a cool fragrant garden with three palms. Then a reception room that resembles a study, black and white tiles in an elegant living room/library, open fires, a small bar, soothing music, friendly, impeccable staff. Gracious bedrooms, some large, some small, are named after writers, botanists, socialites, sailors; the detail in fabrics, paintings, *objets* and books is both rich and meticulous. The food? It's memorable — and you can shop with the chef for a tailormade dinner. This is an island of big skies and bicycles: 60 miles of cycle paths criss-cross its vineyards and pine forests. Stop off at ocean-side Cabana Jim's for fresh oysters — bliss!

Price	€135–€550. Suites €320–€2,000.
Rooms	29: 15 doubles, 14 suites.
Meals	Breakfast €19–€28. Dinner from €55. Wine €50.
Closed	Never.
Directions	From La Rochelle, over bridge to Île de Ré; on quay. In summer, call for code.

Olivia Le Calvez
1 quai Job Foran,
17410 Saint Martin de Ré (Île de Ré),
Charente-Maritime

Tel	+33 (0)5 46 35 40 32
Email	contact@hotel-de-toiras.com
Web	www.hotel-de-toiras.com

Hôtel & Spa La Baronnie – Domaine du Bien-Être

A step away from the winding streets, through beautiful old iron gates, you enter civilised seclusion. Built as government premises in the 18th century, the "finest house on the island" has a delightful cobbled courtyard where honeysuckle, mint and jasmine scent the air. Inside are fresh flowers, panelling, tiled floors and an ornate iron staircase to sweep you upstairs. Big light bedrooms are finely tuned in gorgeous colours with thick curtains and elegant cushions, pale rugs on stripped wooden floors, good antiques and garden or courtyard views. Next door is the as-inviting Domaine du Bien-Être, its bedrooms exuding a gentle country chic, the quietest facing the gardens. Here, on an achingly beautiful sideboard, you'll find the superb breakfast buffet. The lovely owners, Pierre and Florence, know their island well, its nature and history, its endless beaches, cycle paths, sand dunes and pines: they led the rise of St Martin's popularity. The little town is full of chic shops, restaurants, bars and atmosphere. Fun for a stylish weekend – or more. *Secure parking €15. Osteopath & beauty treatments available.*

Price	€130-€270. Family room €150-€230.
Rooms	17: 12 doubles, 5 family rooms.
Meals	Breakfast €16. Restaurants nearby.
Closed	November to March.
Directions	Over bridge from La Rochelle to St Martin harbour. Street on left going down to port.

Florence Pallardy
17-21 rue Baron de Chantal,
17410 Saint Martin de Ré (Île de Ré),
Charente-Maritime
Tel   +33 (0)5 46 09 21 29
Email   info@hotel-labaronnie.com
Web   www.hotel-labaronnie.com

Hôtel du Donjon

Armelle and Stéphane left Normandy in search of adventure and stumbled across a townhouse in the middle of Aulnay that was in need of love and care, and they are still pouring their heart and soul into it. Olive green woodwork and neatly trimmed privet now announce the entrance. Your hosts are always to hand, the service is simple and friendly, people come and go and everything ticks over harmoniously The downstairs lobby, bustling, bright and scented with fresh-cut garden flowers, has peaceful furnishings and a central stone fireplace. Polished staircases are lit with spots; corridors have pale stone and exposed natural beams on split levels. Some of the quiet, simple bedrooms have views to the pretty walled garden where honeysuckle creeps up the walls; the bedroom for guests with limited mobility is superbly equipped. Wine tasting tours can be arranged and, for animal lovers, there's the Charentais Donkey Protection Society to visit and discover the rare 'dreadlocks' Poitou donkey: one of the region's best-kept secrets. It's a great little place – and excellent value.

Price	€59–€79.
Rooms	10: 7 doubles, 2 triples, 1 family room for 4.
Meals	Breakfast €8. Dinner €14. Wine €11–€15. Restaurant 50m.
Closed	Rarely.
Directions	Paris to Bordeaux on A10, exit Niort Sud or Saint Jean d'Augely. D950 to Poitiers Saintes.

Armelle & Stéphane Gras
4 rue des Hivers,
17470 Aulnay de Saintonge,
Charente-Maritime

Tel	+33 (0)5 46 33 67 67
Email	hoteldudonjon@wanadoo.fr
Web	www.hoteldudonjon.com

Aquitaine

L'Hôtel Particulier

In beautiful Bordeaux – a city abuzz with bistro-brasseries and chic boutiques – it's hard to believe such a place could exist: a sanctum of peace behind closed doors. And what doors! Off the busy street, this classic baroque 19th-century townhouse is entered via imposing barn-style doors that swing open into a quiet lawned quadrangle, a secret world. There are five guest rooms hidden away here, the quietest at the back: opulent boudoirs that ooze style and indulgence. Ornate fireplaces and polished floors line spacious rooms rendered light and bright by long, throw-open windows – nature's air con. One has a leafy balcony and delightful mouldings, another comes with its own conservatory. Philippe Starck had a hand in two of the bathrooms, but all have chunky double basins, downy robes and designer fittings. Breakfast is a flexible, communal affair of fresh fruit and local croissants overseen by generous, humorous Alizée and her daughter. The big traditional living room doesn't serve dinners – yet. But Bordeaux's mind-boggling array of eateries is on the doorstep.

Price	€160–€185. Suites €215–€295.
Rooms	5: 2 doubles, 1 single, 1 suite for 2, 1 suite for 3.
Meals	Breakfast €12. Restaurants nearby.
Closed	Rarely.
Directions	Sent on booking.

	Alizée San José
	44 rue Vital Carles,
	33000 Bordeaux, Gironde
Tel	+33 (0)5 57 88 28 80
Email	alizee.sanjose@gmail.com
Web	www.lhotel-particulier.com

Château Lavergne Dulong

Views over vineyards and award-winning comfort: in the capable hands of Sylvie Dulong this 19th-century mansion has become a sumptuous stopover. Through the neo-Gothic façade you step into a surprising baroque-furnished hall complete with sculptures, exposed stonework and sweeping staircase leading to elegant chocolate-coloured bedrooms. Gilt mirrors, sink-into beds and superb linen heighten your sense of indulgence, as do the neatly placed club chairs, Edwardian-style bathrooms and fresh towels. These are lavish, lovely, expansive rooms in which give yourself up to peace. Sylvie willingly shares her expertise through tasting tours of her cellar and 15-hectare vineyard, and her four-course dinners can be accompanied by a bottle from the estate. In the morning, linger over a breakfast that favours fresh juice and organic ingredients, perhaps surveying the avenue of noble sequoias; then it's a ten-minute drive to the tram that ferries you straight into Bordeaux. Or meander by the summerhouse and spread out lazily on a poolside recliner, until sleep or appetite beckons you away.

Price	€140–€158.
Rooms	4: 2 doubles, 2 suites.
Meals	Breakfast included. Dinner €35. Wine €5.50–€16. Summer kitchen.
Closed	December to February.
Directions	N89 from Libourne dir. Bordeaux; exit 3 route du Courneau. 200m after Allée de Lamotte (on left), up drive on left, signed.

Sylvie Dulong
23 route du Courneau, Montussan,
33450 Bordeaux, Gironde

Tel	+33 (0)5 56 72 19 52
Email	contact@chateau-lavergne-dulong.com
Web	www.chateau-lavergne-dulong.com

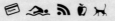

Château Julie

Even if bordeaux is not your favourite tipple, this is a superb place to stay. Viticulture is the business here and if you come at the right time you have a grandstand view. Château Julie is Dutch-owned, run by young Renée and Rinse – a practised cook in his own right, he makes food to match the fine house wine. Rebuilt in the 18th century to charming proportions, the house is surrounded by 80 hectares of land, half of them glistening with vines. Stay in the château, whose rooms are simple and uncluttered, with big bathrooms, views over the park and oodles of towels, or in the self-catering cottage opposite; it sleeps six comfortably, has a big kitchen and two shower rooms. Meals are served in the panelled dining room; coffee and armagnac are taken in the drawing room across the impressive hall. In the day there's tennis, fishing in the lake, exploring the grounds. Rinse can also arrange for you to visit a sister château near Saint-Émilion. A great place for an active break or a lazy afternoon reading in the shade of a tree. *French, Dutch, English & German spoken.*

Price	€80–€135. Family rooms €135. Cottage €650 per week.
Rooms	5 + 1: 3 twins/doubles, 2 family rooms: 1 for 3, 1 for 4. Cottage for 6.
Meals	Dinner €30. Wine €7–€20. Restaurant 6km.
Closed	Rarely.
Directions	A10 Paris & Bordeaux, past toll Virsac. 1st exit towards Angoulême; signed.

Renée & Rinse Sevenster
1 Naudonnet,
33240 Virsac (Nr St André de Cubzac),
Gironde

Tel	+33 (0)5 57 94 08 20
Email	contact@chateau-julie.com
Web	www.chateau-julie.com

Château Richelieu

A five-minute hop from Saint-Émilion, this domaine produces fine wines. Covering the southern slope of the estate are vineyards purchased four centuries ago by Cardinal Richelieu, and the whole team here pursues his winemaking dream. Bedrooms, in an 18th-century wing, are named after characters from Dumas' *Three Musketeers*: Athos, Porthos, Aramis and d'Artagnan lie up the twisting stairs; the ground-floor room, Richelieu, is named after their brilliant and power-hungry arch-enemy. Large, elegantly proportioned and simply done, the rooms are furnished with fabrics that complement plain wooden floorboards and serene walls. Bathrooms are huge, contemporary and spoiling. Tall, elegant doors open onto gardens with quiet leafy glades, clipped lawns and a partly walled swimming pool surrounded by evergreen shrubs. Breakfast out here when the sun shines and, during the winter months, within the thick stone walls of the old chartreuse. Arjen, part-owner and director, lives nearby; Sylvie does the meeting and greeting of guests. A great chance to stay on a high-class Bordeaux vineyard.

Price	€110.
Rooms	5 doubles.
Meals	Restaurant 1km.
Closed	November to March.
Directions	Sent on booking.

Sylvie Perez
1 chemin du Tertre,
33126 Fronsac, Gironde

Tel	+33 (0)5 57 51 13 94
Email	info@chateau-richelieu.com
Web	www.chateau-richelieu.com

Château Lamothe du Prince Noir

Turn off a suburban road into the pages of a fairy tale. A creeper-clad, stone château framed by two towers sits serenely in the middle of a moat. Knights on white chargers, or at the very least Rapunzel, should soon appear… or possibly Edward, the Black Prince, who used it as a medieval hunting lodge. Slip between the trees, over the bridge and be welcomed by the Bastide family. Warm and charismatic, they have given the château a stylish opulence without detracting from its character. Large bedrooms have canopied beds, strong colours, antique bed linen and a rich but comfortable assortment of furniture. One suite has a colonial theme, another, overlooking the moat, has murals of the seasons. Bathrooms are grand with gold taps, Venetian glass, and most have windows. Breakfast on the rose-covered terrace or in the elegant, chandelier-hung salon. Light suppers or, for groups, slap-up dinners with family silver and lacy napery, can be arranged. Visit Bordeaux, beaches, play golf, fish in the moat. You will be treated as family guests and the Bastides can arrange riding, wine tastings, even a massage.

Price	€180–€275. Single €85. Suites €225–€275. Family room €275–€350.
Rooms	8: 2 doubles, 1 single, 3 suites for 2, 1 suite for 3, 1 family room for 3–5.
Meals	Light supper with wine, €35–€45; book ahead. Restaurant 5-minute drive.
Closed	Rarely.
Directions	From Bordeaux N89 exit 5; D13 to St Sulpice. 2nd right across from bakery to stadium. Gate 800m on left. Signed.

Jacques & Luce Bastide
6 route du Stade,
33450 Saint Sulpice et Cameyrac,
Gironde

Tel	+33 (0)5 56 30 82 16
Email	chat.lamothe@wanadoo.fr
Web	www.chateaulamotheprincenoir.com

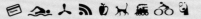

Château de Carbonneau

Big château bedrooms bathed in light, a Napoleon III conservatory for quiet contemplation, gentle pastels over classic dados and big bathrooms gleaming with rich tiles – here is a quiet, self-assured family house and readers are full of praise. Good quality comes naturally, history stalks and there's space aplenty for three young Ferrières and a dozen guests. Outside are delightful grounds with a big fenced pool and 50 hectares of farmland, some of it planted with vines under the appellation Sainte Foy Bordeaux. The rest are used as grazing land for a small herd of Blondes d'Aquitaine cattle. Visit Wilfred's winery and taste the talent handed down by his forebears; you may leave with a case or two. Jacquie, a relaxed but dynamic New Zealander, makes the meals, wields a canny paintbrush and has created a guest sitting room with two smart linen sofas and guidebooks aplenty. Breakfast is served on the main terrace in summer and Jacquie's dinners, enjoyed with the other guests, sound most tempting – salmon in filo with orange and mint dressing, chicken on a bed of courgettes.

Price	€90-€130.
Rooms	5: 2 doubles, 3 twins/doubles.
Meals	Dinner €27. Wine €8-€20.
Closed	December to February.
Directions	D936 to Castillion la Bataille-Bergerac; from Réaux, right to Gensac, Pessac; at r'bout D18 to Ste Foy la Grande; 2km on right.

Jacquie Franc de Ferrière
33890 Pessac sur Dordogne, Gironde

Tel	+33 (0)5 57 47 46 46
Mobile	+33 (0)6 83 30 14 35
Email	carbonneau@orange.fr
Web	www.chateau-carbonneau.com

Château de Sanse

You are in Bordeaux wine country looking at a château more Tuscan than 18th-century French. The stunning entrance hall sets the tone: clean lines and a palette of pale creams and whites set off by splashes of mauve; no fuss, no swags, only the necessary teak desk and wickerwork sofa strewn with white cushions – deeply pleasing. The off-white and oatmeal theme continues upstairs with sisal in the corridor and coir in some of the bedrooms — a play of texture rather than colour. Thought has been given to families – triples can be arranged and some rooms interconnect; there's a child-friendly pool and early suppers for the little ones. Most rooms have private balconies with lovely rural views and are big enough to sit in comfort. A talented and experienced chef reigns in the kitchen and delivers some inventive dishes, nothing overly pretentious or complicated. Enjoy such treats as terrine of foie gras *mi-cuit* with spiced bread and pear chutney, and lemon and ginger crème brûlée. Peaceful seclusion and a special place where quietness is appreciated – book early in season.

Price	€120–€165. Suites €165–€210.
Rooms	16: 12 twins/doubles, 4 suites.
Meals	Breakfast €12. Lunch from €20. Dinner from €32. Wine €18–€145.
Closed	January.
Directions	A10 exit St André de Cubzac for Libourne then Castillon La Bataille; D17 right Pujols; D18 left Gensac; D15 right to Coubeyrac. Hotel signed on right.

Philip Harris
33350 Sainte Radegonde, Gironde
Tel +33 (0)5 57 56 41 10
Email contact@chateaudesanse.com
Web www.chateaudesanse.com

Château des Baudry

Steeped in 500 years of history, the four solid wings of this distinguished château enclose a grand central courtyard where water shimmers and tinkles and tiny fish flit. Entering through the hall, veer to the left for the salon, to the right, through large wood-panelled doors, for the intimate dining room: a room wrapped in blue wallpaper bearing a flower and ribbon motif. Seated at one of the tables, you'll discover that Hélène's wonderful cuisine 'à la grand-mère' is more than delicious, it's a reason to be here. To the north is the Italian-themed orangery where breakfast is served among terracotta and citrus trees; to the south and east, guest rooms are large, traditional, framed by lofty beams and supported by equally solid stone piers. Fireplaces bring out the earthy colours, the glow of antiques and the softness of cotton and quilted coverings. From bedroom windows, views of formal Italianate gardens and a long drive of hornbeam hedges give way to more untouched countryside, even as pillars by the pool guide the eye to vistas of the Dordogne and Bordeaux landscapes beyond.

Ethical Collection: Environment; Food.
See page 429 for details

Price	€120–€150.
Rooms	4: 1 double, 3 twins/doubles.
Meals	Breakfast €12. Dinner €35. Wine €12–€30.
Closed	Rarely.
Directions	From Bergerac D936 for Bordeaux 12km to Gardonne; left D4 to Saussignac 5km, on D4 for Monestier. Château 2km from Saussignac, on left.

Hélène Boulet & François Passebon
24240 Monestier, Dordogne
Tel   +33 (0)5 53 23 46 42
Email   chateaudesbaudry@orange.fr
Web   www.chateaudesbaudry.com

Château La Thuilière

In a quiet setting with distant neighbours, a mid-19th-century château – a landowner's gift to his fiancée – has been transformed into a charming hotel with a heady mix of modern and old. Sweep up the staircase with carved griffons on its banisters to pass a stained-glass window of the original owner resplendent in armour. Sumptuous hall and reception rooms bedecked with tapestries contrast with five huge bedrooms where walls and ceilings are painted in muted tints from the trendy palette of today, and Nespresso is on tap; pull aside lavish curtains for views of rolling parkland dotted with cedars – glorious. It may be a trudge from car park to balustraded steps to front door, especially in wet weather, but there are a dozen umbrellas in the hall: typical of the thoughtfulness that lies behind this venture. If you want privacy, then dinner can be served in the cosy, friendly sofa'd billiard or music room. Communal breakfasts are in the kitchen – perhaps in the company of Spanish owner Jordi and pretty spaniel Patch. The cherry on the cake: your gregarious host is full of ideas of where to go and what to do.

Price	€150–€250.
Rooms	5 twins/doubles.
Meals	Breakfast included. Dinner €35–€48. Wine €20–€80.
Closed	Rarely.
Directions	From Libourne A89 exit 12; D708, D3 for 15km; signed after St Martin l'Astier.

Eduard Díaz
24400 Saint Front de Pradoux,
Dordogne

Mobile	+33 (0)6 45 35 36 82
Email	chateau@lathuiliere.net
Web	www.lathuiliere.net

Château Le Mas de Montet

A nose for fine living brought new owners Paul and Lise to this happy place. At the end of an avenue guarded by plane trees – serenely, gloriously French – is the château, slate-topped and turreted in Renaissance style. Once frequented by Mitterrand and his labradors, it has since been extravagantly restored. Doors open in summer to a big terrace and 50 hectares of parkland with pool, while reception rooms lined with eau-de-nil brocade are sated with auction house finds. Richness and softness bring instant seduction and bedrooms, named after Corneille, Voltaire, Madame de Lafayette, have all you'd hope for the price. The owners do their utmost to make you feel welcome: beds are big and supremely comfortable, four-posters canopied and draped, and bathrooms are Deco-white... the one in the tower has its own chandelier. Paul and Lise are avid gardeners and a potager is on its way, so super-fresh produce will land on your plate; the food, served in the orangery restaurant, is Périgordian and exquisite. Grand yet easy, uncommercial and full of charm, this is a brilliant place for stressed city souls to unwind.

Price	€150–€195. Suites €200–€320. Gîte €1,200 (per week).
Rooms	10 + 2: 4 doubles, 1 twin, 5 suites. 2 gîtes for 2.
Meals	Breakfast €16. Lunch €20. Dinner €45. Wine €28–€135.
Closed	Early to late December.
Directions	A10 then N10 to Angoulême, south towards Libourne, then Montmoreau, then Aubeterre. Signed on D2 & D20 between Aubeterre & Ribérac.

Paul Cavaleiro & Lise Daneels
Petit Bersac, 24600 Ribérac, Dordogne
Tel   +33 (0)5 53 90 08 71
Email   lemasdemontet@gmail.com
Web   www.lemasdemontet.com

Auberge de l'Étang Bleu

The hunting lodge restaurant bursts with French charm. Tables are laid with white cloths and candelabra, a log fire roars in the grate, stuffed squirrels dot the walls and the food is delicious. The 'Inn by the Blue Pond' was dreamed up by Pierre's father who bought ten hectares of wasteland within easy reach of watery Brantôme. The Colas are a sweet and eccentric pair, hugely proud of both hotel and restaurant; Pierre is head chef and Anne, once an English teacher, is front of house. Inside it feels older than it is, with dark oak beams and traditional furniture; bedrooms, not huge, are carpeted and comfortable, those at the front with a balcony, those at the back with park views. But you are here for the food and, in a region famous for its cuisine, this well-established, much-loved restaurant takes it seriously. The garden runs down to the water and you can breakfast on the terrace in summer: a feast of omelettes, croissants, yogurts and homemade jams. Ducks potter, dogs wander, fish lurk in the lake – bring your rods. A refreshing mix of delicious food and memorable eccentricity. *Cable internet available.*

Price	€70–€80.
Rooms	11: 6 doubles, 5 twins.
Meals	Breakfast €10. Dinner €28–€33. Wine €20. Children's meals €15.
Closed	Mid-December to mid-January.
Directions	From Angoulême D939 for Périgueux. After approx. 45km, left on D93 at Vieux-Mareuil. Signed on right.

	Anne & Pierre Colas
	24340 Vieux Mareuil, Dordogne
Tel	+33 (0)5 53 60 92 63
Email	etang.bleu@wanadoo.fr
Web	www.auberge-de-letang-bleu.com

Le Chatenet

Layers of history are here. Brantôme has been home to man since prehistoric times; the grand Benedictine abbey, carved out at the bottom of the cliffs, overlooks the ribbon of the river Dronne that slowly rings the town. Just up the road, a perfect distance from the hustle and bustle, is Le Chatenet, a Périgord-style stone house built at the end of the 17th century. Jane will show you the sundial they found under the roof marked 1688, William will point the way to the hidden canopy of trees over a path which leads to the centre of town in a ten-minute stroll. Or you may just want to sit on the stone veranda and follow the sun as it sinks pinkly over the walnut trees and the green valleys. There are big rooms with stunning fabric on the walls, billiards in the games room, rivers to be canoed and grottoes to be explored. There is even a farm down the street with rabbits, chickens and cows, source of your breakfast eggs and milk. Jane and William are super hosts. Brantôme's bell tower is thought to be one of the oldest in France; they say it must be seen from the inside. Add an extra day, you won't regret it.

Price	€110–€135. Suites €150–€195. Extra bed €25.
Rooms	5: 3 twins/doubles, 2 suites.
Meals	Breakfast €12. Dinner from €30. Wine from €25. Restaurant 1km.
Closed	Mid-October to mid-April.
Directions	From Périgueux, D939 to Brantôme; left on D78 for l'Abbaye dir. Bourdeilles; road looks like it ends but cont. on; Le Chatenet 1km out of town. Signed.

Jane & William Laxton
Lieu-dit Le Chatenet, 24310 Brantôme, Dordogne

Tel   +33 (0)5 53 05 81 08
Email lechatenet@gmail.com
Web   www.lechatenet.com

Hostellerie Les Griffons

The setting is impossibly lovely. Discover a handsome 17th-century house by a medieval bridge over the Dronne, with an irresistibly inviting face and village and château views that tip the dream beyond reality. One look at the website and you want to be there. Many of the old features have been nurtured – the magnificent stone fireplaces, the lovely old windows; every beautifully decorated room has a rich medieval flavour. The mood on the first floor is a touch sombre, as befits a grand old mansion, though the colours are fashionably bold; on the second, windows and amazing roof timbers are white. From most bedrooms the views, to river, château and mill, are unique; bathrooms are fine. You dine and breakfast stylishly by the river's edge in summer (you would long to picnic here if you were just passing through). The restaurant is superb and local paintings add personality. Bourdeilles, downriver from lovely, summer-touristy Brantôme – 'the Venice of the Périgord' – is enchanting. Come to be spoiled by Jacques, Frédérique and their excellent staff who all treat guests as valued friends.

Price	€92–€115. Family rooms €145.
Rooms	10: 6 doubles, 2 twins, 2 family rooms for 3.
Meals	Breakfast €12. Lunch & dinner €34–€40. Wine €23–€60.
Closed	November to 31 March.
Directions	From Périgueux for Angoulême; just before Brantôme, left for Bourdeilles (medieval village) for 5km. Hotel in village centre.

Frédérique & Jacques Dauba
24310 Bourdeilles, Dordogne

Tel	+33 (0)5 53 45 45 35
Email	info@griffons.fr
Web	www.griffons.fr

Château de Villars

View it from a teak sunlounger, iced drink in hand: the Château de Villars sits in a bubble of calm, set apart from the world by a beautiful buffer of parkland and forest. Unbroken views swoop to forests as far as the eye can see and church bells from the village occasionally break the pastoral quiet – as do the sploshing of swimmers and the rustling of the poolside barbecue. Light pours into the neo-Gothic building, where guests drift between library, terrace-bar, sitting room, gym and massage treatment salon. Of the immaculate bedrooms, Auvezère is one favourite; outside, tucked between the trees, the splendid Russian dacha summerhouse with its own veranda is ideal for self-caterers. In the main house is a long banqueting table for breakfast, while dinner (marvellous value) is served three days a week: organic veg from the garden and gluten-free dishes if required. There are heaps of restaurants in nearby Brantôme. At the end of a leafy drive of horse-chestnut trees, managed by these charming and attentive owners, this is one lovely retreat. *Ask about cookery & art courses.*

Price	€105–€150. Gîte €875–€1,125 p.w. Studio €135–€165 per night.
Rooms	5 + 2: 5 doubles. Gîte for 4. Studio for 2.
Meals	Breakfast included. Dinner €26–€29. Wine €11–€35. Restaurant 5-minute drive.
Closed	November to mid-April.
Directions	Sent on booking.

Bill Davies & Kevin Saunders
Près de la Cure, 24530 Villars, Dordogne

Tel	+33 (0)5 53 03 41 58
Mobile	+33 (0)6 83 26 03 95
Email	Chateauvillars@aol.com
Web	www.chateaudevillars.com

La Commanderie

The setting is very special. Off a medieval street in a charming hamlet, through the stone archway and the lightly-tree'd gardens, into the steep-roofed *commanderie*. The Commanders of the Order of Malta put up here 700 years ago en route to Santiago de Compostella and a low curved toll passage still forms part of the house. This is not so much a hotel as a houseful of guests overseen by diminutive Madame, a correct but considerate hostess. An uncontrived collection of antiques warms the friendly bedrooms, each with its own personality — convent-white walls are set off by touches of dark blue, ceilings soar, floors of varying ages and diverse patterns are softened by Indian rugs. Downstairs, guests gather at round tables set with antique cane chairs, flowery curtains hang at tall windows and you get two choices per gastronomic course — just right for this unassuming but atmospheric place. There's a delicious little pool in the shade of the cedars and the Lascaux Caves are a mile down the road. Great value for what you get, and that includes very good, classic French food.

Price	€85.
Rooms	7: 5 doubles, 2 twins.
Meals	Breakfast €10. Lunch €20–€45. Dinner €25–€48. Restaurant closed Mondays.
Closed	Rarely.
Directions	N89 between Brive & Périgueux. At x-roads at Lardin, towards Condat, right to La Commanderie. Hotel 50m after church.

Madame Annick Roux
1 place du Verdier,
24570 Condat sur Vézère, Dordogne

Tel	+33 (0)5 53 51 26 49
Email	hotellacommanderie@wanadoo.fr
Web	www.hotel-lacommanderie.com

Auberge de Castel Merle

On the edge of a charming hamlet, a hidden paradise, a small inn atop a limestone knob that once held a castle of the Knights Templar. It has been in Anita's family for five generations; her archaeologist grandfather added stones from his own digs (Les Eyzies, the capital of prehistory, is nearby). Husband Christopher is also devoted to this atmospheric place and they have renovated the old buildings with consummate care, keeping the traditional look and using walnut from their land to restore bedheads and doors. Christopher is an enthusiastic truffle hunter and head chef; this is wild boar country and *sanglier* is one of his specialities. Flowery curtains, pelmets and painted flowers on the walls prettify the dining room; bedrooms have an unfussy country look: Provençal prints, stone walls. Some rooms overlook the courtyard, others the woods. As for the views: the glory of the place is its position, high above the valley of the Vézère with river, forests and castles beyond – best admired from a check-clothed table on the large leafy terrace. Hiking in the forests is a joy. *French lessons on request.*

Price	€73.
Rooms	8: 7 doubles, 1 twin.
Meals	Breakfast €8. Dinner €16–€28. Wine €17–€25. Restaurant closed lunchtimes. Half-board only in August.
Closed	October to March.
Directions	A89 to Montignac, then D706 for Les Eyzies. At Thonac left over bridge then right to Sergeac; signed.

	Anita Castanet & Christopher Millinship
	24290 Sergeac, Dordogne
Tel	+33 (0)5 53 50 70 08
Email	hotelcastelmerle@yahoo.fr
Web	www.hotelcastelmerle.com

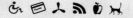

Hotel Aquitaine

La Roseraie

Built as the country residence for a Parisian family, it is now a sparkling hotel. Experienced, enthusiastic hoteliers, the Nourrissons brought their good chef with them. Pretty dining rooms dotted with yellow-clothed tables and posies set the scene for celery and truffle millefeuille and braised guinea fowl with pumpkin and chestnuts; such is their devotion to food there is an 'Initiation à la Gourmandise' menu for children. In summer you spill onto a terrace edged with clipped box… which leads to a garden of mature trees, roses and 19th-century formality, and a delicious palm-fringed pool. The gardens edge the river, prone to flood in winter (one good reason why La Roseraie closes in November). Bedrooms, comfortably pattern-carpeted with traditional furniture soon to be updated, have sweet river and garden views, while two apartments sit privately across the square revealing an unusual mix of the rustic and the frou-frou: fine old beams, stone walls, rococo-style chairs and a fancy four-poster. Medieval Montignac has it all – including the caves at Lascaux.

Price	€78-€130. Family rooms €140-€200. Apartments €270. Half-board €80-€150 p.p.
Rooms	16: 7 doubles, 3 twins, 4 family rooms for 4, 2 apartments for 4.
Meals	Breakfast €14. Lunch from €27. Dinner €27-€53. Wine €18-€75. Half-board mandatory July/August.
Closed	November to Easter.
Directions	A20 & A89 to La Bachellerie; take road to Montignac to town centre.

Vincent & Isabelle Nourrisson
11 place d'Armes,
24290 Montignac Lascaux, Dordogne
Tel +33 (0)5 53 50 53 92
Email hotelroseraie@wanadoo.fr
Web www.laroseraie-hotel.com

Le Relais du Touron

Such a nice approach up the drive lined with box hedges and spiræa, past lawns and handsome trees. The reception is in the family house, all rooms and the dining room are in the converted barn and stable block, with the pool just below. A fireplace in the dining area keeps a cheery flame but in summer everyone gathers on the terrace under an open-sided timbered roof; the pool and garden beyond are flooded with light in the evening. Brothers married to sisters, Philippe and Chantal, Roland and Monique have built up a solid reputation for good, interesting food; choose the five-course half-board menu or go à la carte. Bedrooms with park and pool views are decorated in straightforward style: plain carpets, bright furnishings, decent lighting; sparkling new bathrooms have handsome basins. The nearby road is well screened by thick trees and shrubs; indeed, the three-hectare garden, which also contains a small pond, is a great asset with lots of private corners to be explored. A delightful six-kilometre path will take you by foot or by bike right into Sarlat. Low-key, excellent value with a wonderful family welcome.

Price	€55-€80. Family room €98-€145.
Rooms	18: 12 doubles, 5 twins, 1 family room for 4.
Meals	Breakfast €9. Lunch & dinner €19.50-€38.
Closed	Early November to March.
Directions	From Sarlat D704 to Gourdon. Hotel signed on right before Carsac.

Viala Family
Le Touron, 24200 Carsac Aillac, Dordogne

Tel	+33 (0)5 53 28 16 70
Email	contact@lerelaisdutouron.com
Web	www.lerelaisdutouron.com

La Villa Romaine

The 19th-century farmhouse and its two outbuildings are planted solidly in the ground; their neatly-pointed limestone walls glow in the sun. They partially surround a vast courtyard that leads down to an infinity pool – and a wow of a view that sweeps the eye over Druid forests, green hills and a perched village on a cliff across the way. Plumb in the middle of the courtyard is an open-sided structure, once called the Halle aux Saumons, the salmon market; we now can only imagine the river running below flowing silver with fish. Fine dining here, on fish or fowl, is the attraction, as well as the restaurant itself. It's a long, airy, beamed and timbered room with a bar and a comfortable little sitting area where armchairs beckon, some draped in pale linen, at the far end. Crisp white tablecloths set off sparkling table settings; French windows bring light and lead to a large terrace. Bedrooms, some in the outbuildings, some above the restaurant, are huge; the family suite with two bedrooms sleeps six. A choice of eight breakfast teas might give a clue to what is in store.

Price	€110-€160. Duplex €185-€250. Family suite €220-€300. Triples €160-€190.
Rooms	17: 12 twins/doubles, 1 duplex for 2-4, 1 family suite for 4-6, 3 triples.
Meals	Breakfast €13-€15. Dinner from €32. Restaurant closed mid-November to April.
Closed	Never.
Directions	From Sarlat to Gourdon & Cahors 6km. Signed.

David Vacelet & Emilie Velut
Saint Rome, 24200 Carsac Aillac, Dordogne

Tel   +33 (0)5 53 28 52 07
Email   contact@lavillaromaine.com
Web   www.lavillaromaine.com

Entry 245   Map 9

Auberge de la Salvetat

In ancient times La Salvetat was a 'safe haven': the 12th-century church ruins on the estate pre-date the nearby Cadouin cloisters, now a UNESCO heritage site. With sublime views from its terrace across woods and pastures, not another building in sight, the old presbytery contains some bedrooms and the restaurant. Now overseen by Ann, who still makes the puddings, it has a local reputation for refined cuisine with a modern touch. Steve and Ann are loving their change of career and everything is done with a smile; there's not a trace of pomposity here. Bedrooms – not huge – have terraces and are perfectly comfortable; those in the main house are the best and the one with the mezzanine is great for families. The good-sized infinity pool is the place for just lounging by the water, or you can relax with a book under the trees in the pretty garden. Six of 'France's most beautiful villages' lie within a short drive, there are some exciting water sports nearby and a different market almost every day. Walkers and cyclists will be happy, too: routes run from the door. Then return to perfect peace.

Price	€79–€115.
Rooms	14: 7 doubles, 3 twins, 4 family rooms for 3.
Meals	Breakfast €11. Lunch & dinner €24.50–€35.50. Wine €15–€30. Restaurant open evenings & Sun lunchtime.
Closed	Mid-October to April.
Directions	Sent on booking.

Steven & Ann Jordan
Route de Belvès, 24480 Cadouin, Dordogne
Tel   +33 (0)5 53 63 42 79
Email   contact@lasalvetat.com
Web   www.lasalvetat.com

Auberge Lou Peyrol

In a perfect village, opposite a honeystone church, a perfect restaurant with rooms. The old épicerie/bar, the hub of St Marcel, has become this delicious auberge. As Philippe works his magic in the kitchen his wife meets and greets charmingly: the restaurant is intimate and friendly, and the tone is set by Fiona. Food lovers travel miles for this chef's take on foie gras, girolles and local produce – those who've stayed say the food is a joy – and an exceptional attention to detail runs throughout, from the tables set with white Limoges porcelain to the log fires on winter nights. Now they've added two bedrooms under the eaves – both large, both lovely. Chunky old rafters have been given a new lease of life, floors are wooden, beds are king-size, mattresses are enveloped in neat white linen and bathrooms are indulgent. Both rooms have sofabeds for children, both have tables and chairs for breakfast; in summer you can munch your croissants on the shaded terrace and listen to the birds. Leave the immaculate grass verges of the village behind for the woods and walks of the Dordogne. *Cookery courses in low season.*

Price	€90.	
Rooms	2: 1 double; 1 double with sofabed.	
Meals	Breakfast €5.50–€16. Dinner €35. Wine €11–€68. Restaurant limited opening in winter.	
Closed	Rarely.	
Directions	D32 from Bergerac, 20km to St Marcel du Périgord; auberge in village opp. church.	

Fiona & Philippe Wavrin
Le Bourg,
24510 Saint Marcel du Périgord,
Dordogne

Tel	+33 (0)5 53 24 09 71
Email	lou.peyrol@orange.fr
Web	www.loupeyrol.com

Entry 247   Map 9

Château Les Merles

The 19th-century French façade conceals an interior of Dutch minimalism suffused with light. Old and stylish new march hand in hand and the chef brings exceptional finesse to the cooking: great spit roasts, Bergerac wines, fresh vegetables from the organic garden and a sumptuous tasting menu. The staff are lovely, full of hospitality and charm. A rustic-chic bistro (Philippe Starck chairs on charming old flags), a restaurant in the stables, two light-streamed sitting rooms, a bucolic nine-hole golf course to one side… A golfers' haven it is, but we would all love it here. This family-run hotel brims with generosity and professionalism. A black and white theme runs throughout — matt-black beds, white bedspreads, black frames, white lamp shades, black towels, white roses — the austerity offset by a rich gilt-framed mirror or a fuchsia fauteuil. Outside is a vast gravelled courtyard with striking white dining chairs and black parasols, a terrace looks south to the shimmering pool (with a direct line to reception!) and the hills are braided with vines. Fabulous. *Daytime childminding available by arrangement.*

Price	€125–€180. Single €105–€160. Suites €150–€240. Apartment €220–€340.
Rooms	15: 11 twins/doubles, 1 single, 2 suites, 1 apartment for 4.
Meals	Breakfast €15. Lunch & dinner €22.50–€49. Wine from €16.
Closed	Never.
Directions	From Bergerac D660 for Sarlat. At Tuilières, left onto D36 for Pressignac. Château 800m.

Jan Van Grinsven
Tuilières, 24520 Mouleydier, Dordogne
Tel   +33 (0)5 53 63 13 42
Email   info@lesmerles.com
Web   www.lesmerles.com

La Métairie

If you love horses you'll be in your element: you can relax on the terrace and watch them in the next field. You can also ride close by. La Métairie was built as a farm at the beginning of the last century and converted into a 'boutique' hotel some 40 years ago, a U-shaped building smothered in wisteria and Virginia creeper. There's no road in sight and you really do feel away from it all – yet the Dordogne and its clifftop villages are minutes away. Borrow bikes if you're feeling energetic! Bedrooms are charming, cheerful and full of sunshiney yellows and huge beds. They have room for a couple of comfy chairs, too. Bathrooms match – big and bright – and three ground-floor rooms have French windows and a semi-private patio. The pool is big enough for a proper swim and when you come out you can read under the trees that are waiting for you by the pool. In summer you can eat out here, or on the flowery terrace. The dining room has black and white floors, washed stone walls and well-spaced tables. Go ahead, indulge, order the four-course *menu périgourdin*. You can swim it off later. Delightful staff, too.

Price	€135–€185. Suite €195–€310. Half-board €54 extra p.p. (mandatory in high season).
Rooms	10: 9 doubles, 1 suite.
Meals	Breakfast €18. Lunch €18–€50. Dinner €43–€58; Perigordian menu €55. Wine €25–€100.
Closed	November to March.
Directions	From Lalinde, D703 for Le Bugue. At Sauveboeuf, D31 through Mauzac; signed.

R. & H. Johner & C. Bertschy
24150 Mauzac & Grand Castang,
Dordogne

Tel	+33 (0)5 53 22 50 47
Email	metairie.la@wanadoo.fr
Web	www.la-metairie.com

Hôtel Edward 1er

Some people lie around the pool on their honeymoon; Arjan and Marije went hotel hunting on theirs. And they found one: a handsome 19th-century townhouse in a village voted one of the most beautiful in France. Now they are settled in nicely. Herbs are from the garden, vegetables and fruit are local, fish hales from Bordeaux and Arcachon; all is homemade here except bread and ice cream, and these are supplied by artisans. Marije creates the menus and has chosen mostly regional wines – Bergerac, Cahors, Monbazillac – to accompany the foie gras and duck cuisine. After you have explored the miraculously preserved 13th-century village, the four-sided fortress round a central square, the surrounding houses corbelled out with arches, the perfectly straight streets leading from each side, you may want to compare Monpazier with the other medieval bastides; there are a dozen or so. Arjan has prepared bicycle itineraries and can point out the best place to paddle a canoe. Or you may just want to lounge around the pool, honeymoon-style! Romantic rooms await.

Price	€68–€188.
Rooms	12: 6 doubles, 6 twins.
Meals	Breakfast €12. Dinner €29.50–€39.50. Wine €19–€50.
Closed	Mid-November to mid-March.
Directions	From St Cyprien D703 dir. Bergerac; left on D710 to Belvès; D53 to Monpazier.

Arjan & Marije Capelle
5 rue Saint Pierre, 24540 Monpazier,
Dordogne

Tel   +33 (0)5 53 22 44 00
Email   info@hoteledward1er.com
Web   www.hoteledward1er.com

Hôtel de Bois

This interesting dwelling started life as a simple country house and has since undergone extensive demolition to make it what it is today – un Dump grand-classe. Lured by the divine views of the scrubby grass and the plentiful wood from the trees that surround it, hotelier Monsieur le Porcine-Cochon painstakingly built his hotel stick by stick. Art lovers will adore the approach with what at first sight may appear to be a load of old rubbish and well-trodden straw piled around… this is in fact an installation by the little-known Pierre Poubelle. Inside is gloomy, compact and comes with an unusual but familiar odour. Meals are served on the terrace year round, so breakfast on stale bread and join Madame in the evening for an hors d'œuvre of fermented apple or a confit de potato peel: nothing goes to waste here. If you do decide to stay, a word of warning, there's a nasty old wolf who lives nearby and sometimes pops over to huff and puff; he's already done the eco build, straw-bale place next door. Those of a nervous disposition may prefer the Hôtel de Briques up the road.

Price	Poor value.
Rooms	Not really.
Meals	Doubt it.
Closed	Always.
Directions	You don't need to know.

Monsieur le Porcine-Cochon
Timide du Loup, Dordogne

Tel	Awaiting reinstallation
Email	As if
Web	www.huffnillpuff.fr

Le Prieuré du Château de Biron

The imposing Château de Biron, tossed back and forth between the English and the French for centuries, sits regally atop the highest point of the village, visible from miles around. Behind and below it is the church which gazes over the little village and hidden behind that, this 16th-century priory. Through the gate, across a tiny cobblestone courtyard, an ornate knocker on the nail-studded door sets a tone of enchantment. Under a low beamed ceiling, the original stone floor in the hall leads to an elegant curved staircase. You can still see the original stone cooker and sink, too, in the delightfully cosy living area; a door leads to the garden with heavenly views across the fields. Fireplaces take pride of place in the huge rooms on the first floor, along with exposed stone walls, the glow of antiques, fine linens and subtle colours of powder blue and pale gold. Rafters fly through the mostly white rooms under the roof, the views are stunning as are the bathrooms, double sinks and fluffy robes throughout. Harmonious and rich, elegant and welcoming, this is not to be missed.

Price	€120–€160.
	Apartment €950–€1,130 per week.
Rooms	5 + 1: 3 suites, 2 family suites for 3.
	Apartment for 3.
Meals	Breakfast €10 for self-caterers.
	Dinner €30. Restaurant 50m.
Closed	Mid-November to February.
Directions	From St Cyprien D703 for Bergerac;
	left D710 to Belvès; D53 to
	Monpazier; D2 for Villeréal 5km, left
	D53 to Biron. Parking below château.

Élisabeth Vedier
Le Bourg, 24540 Biron, Dordogne

Tel	+33 (0)5 53 61 93 03
Mobile	+33 (0)6 84 31 38 38
Email	leprieurebiron@gmail.com
Web	www.leprieurebiron.com

Domaine du Moulin de Labique

Ducks on the pond, goats in the greenhouse and food *à la grand-mère* on the plate – the lovely Moulin de Labique glows with warmth and good humour. Shutters are painted with *bleu de pastel* and the 13th-century interiors have lost none of their charm. The Belgian owners, Christine and Patrick, share dinners (seasonal, local, delicious) in wonderfully relaxed fashion. Bedrooms are a match for the rest of the place and are divided between those in the main building above a vaulted *salle d'armes*, those in the barn, reached via a grand stone stair, and a suite in the old bread and prune-drying ovens. There are chunky roof beams, seagrass mats on ancient tiles, lovely old iron bedsteads, antique mirrors and papers sprigged in raspberry and jade green. One room has a balcony, the apartment in the barn has a terrace, and some bathrooms have Portuguese tiles: there's much to captivate and delight. Outside, old French roses, young alleys of trees, a bamboo-fringed stream and an exquisite, child-safe pool. Book a long stay, and make time for tastings at the Monbazillac domaines. *Cookery courses in winter.*

Price	€110–€135. Suite €190.
Rooms	6: 3 doubles, 2 twins, 1 suite for 4.
Meals	Dinner €27. Wine €16–€30.
Closed	Rarely.
Directions	From N21 at Cancon D124 for Monflanquin 5.5km; left D153 through St Vivien; on right 1km after St Vivien.

Patrick & Christine Hendricx
Saint Vivien, 47210 Villeréal,
Lot-et-Garonne

Tel	+33 (0)5 53 01 63 90
Email	moulin-de-labique@wanadoo.fr
Web	www.moulin-de-labique.net

Domaine de Pine

Hidden among 52 acres of fields and sweeping woodland lies a beautifully proportioned manor house and two self-catering cottages. Built for a baron 200 years ago, it's been transformed by an easy-going English couple with impeccable taste into a haven of luxurious modern comfort and period style. Cathy looks after the 'arts de la table': served among flowers and fine china, her breakfasts are fresh and tasty. Five elegant bedrooms (some air-conditioned) are large and light (two interconnect to make a family suite) with beamed ceilings and great views; soft creams and whites dominate. In the bathrooms you'll find fluffy towels and dressing gowns. Springtime calls for lazing on sumptuous wicker loungers, spoiled by divine poolside nibbles and cocktails, and a delicious dinner of locally-sourced specialities on the view-filled terrace – all meals can be enjoyed by self-caterers, too. In winter, cosy up by a roaring fire, enjoy candlelit suppers in the blue and white dining room. Step out for medieval town markets or music festivals, or cycle around the estate – tons of choice. *New heated pool.*

Price	€80–€195.
Rooms	5 doubles (2 interconnect as family suite).
Meals	Breakfast €15. Lunch & dinner from €35; book ahead (euro cheques or cash only). Restaurants 2-minute drive.
Closed	Rarely.
Directions	D656 between Agen and Cahors; 2.5km from St Victor, signed Pine; house 1km down road.

Marcus & Cathy Becker
47470 Blaymont, Lot-et-Garonne

Tel	+33 (0)5 53 66 44 93
Mobile	+44 (0)7831 115599
Email	ddp@qmh.co.uk
Web	www.domainedepine.com

Château de Lamothe

Historic surroundings, breathtaking views, decadent bedrooms and a swimming pool in a secluded area, Lamothe is an idyll of indulgence whose grandiose interior makes you feel like royalty but whose playful touches make you feel at home. Romantic window dressings and lavish Designer Guild décor complement flat-screen TVs and walk-in showers, while the family room has a more neutral loft theme. Those thick, soft carpets and heavenly beds are utterly inviting, but don't miss breakfast in a dining room of gilt mouldings and candelabras — you could even spoil yourself with champagne. Later, explore the expansive gardens with Pyrenean backdrops, the fabulous pool and the exercise suite. Lie by the stream — or relax in the billiard room, the home cinema, the plush aubergine salon: all yours. Your charming Dutch hosts Laurent and Christine will happily prepare evening meals drawing on local specialities and their global travels. They're always ready to share their passion for the region and will advise on visits as well as good wine. A beguiling place that you'll long to return to — again and again.

Price	From €225.
Rooms	5: 4 doubles, 1 family room for 4–6.
Meals	Breakfast included. Dinner €40. Restaurant 5km.
Closed	Rarely.
Directions	From Oloron Ste Marie D936, left into Moumour. Right at church.

Laurent Nederlof
64400 Moumour, Pyrénées-Atlantiques
Mobile   +33 (0)6 88 28 38 61
Email   laurentnederlof@gmail.com
Web   www.chateau-de-lamothe.eu

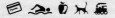

Château de Méracq

Madame will give you a warm welcome in excellent English and is always happy to help or just to chat. She is very proud of her château, her dog, her hens and her husband's cooking. He has established a menu that combines the south-west's predilection for foie gras and duck with exotic sprinklings of spices and rose petals. If you take the half-board option, you can juggle your meals around as you like: even by eating more the next day if you miss one. The pretty château is at the end of a long and inviting driveway through large grounds with chairs under shady trees. One oak is 200 years old, perhaps planted by the proud new owners of the day. The eight bedrooms are an unusual mix: some in fresh stripes or flowers, others with bold turquoise or rose walls, with contemporary patterns on the beds. The first-floor rooms are grander, with bath and shower; those on the second floor are simpler but each has its own shower. Rooms have lace-trimmed sheets and bowls of fruit and flowers – and un-numbered doors. As Madame says, "it wouldn't feel like home", which it does.

Price	€100–€135. Suites €200-235.
Rooms	8: 5 doubles, 1 twin, 1 suite for 3, 1 suite for 4.
Meals	Breakfast €14–€17. Lunch or dinner €32–€55; book ahead. Wine €19–€150.
Closed	15 to 30 December.
Directions	From Pau D834 north for Aire sur l'Adour 17km; left D944 through Thèze; 1st right. Château on edge of Méracq.

Monsieur & Madame
Guérin-Recoussine
64410 Méracq Arzacq,
Pyrénées-Atlantiques

Tel	+33 (0)5 59 04 53 01
Email	chateau-meracq@wanadoo.fr
Web	www.chateau-meracq.com

Château de Bouillon

The arrow slits remain, the ancient and uneven limestone walls have kept their golden hue but this once tremendously fortified 14th-century 'donjon' has softened over the years. Now, in the restoring hands of British couple Rory and Mini, it is a charming wisteria-draped family home. The grandeur begins at the wrought-iron gates and tree-lined avenue, continues to the formal gardens and topiaries, retreats inside to the elegant 18th-century salon and culminates in the stately dining room, where breakfast is served beneath the ancestors. But there's intimacy too, particularly in the lavender garden and along the narrow paths that lead to the wilder meadows, where Blonde d'Aquitaine cattle graze. Generations of farmers have worked this land, so throw open the shutters of (preferably) one of the grand double bedrooms – blessed by antique beds, dark oak parquet floors and Arudy marble bathrooms – and breathe in the peace. Mini is one of only 290 people in the world to hold the prestigious status of 'master of wine'; you will appreciate this over a glass on the terrace, gazing towards the snow-capped Pyrenees.

Price	€80–€130.
Rooms	3: 2 doubles, 1 twin. Extra beds available.
Meals	Breakfast included. Dinner €25. Wine €12–€60. Restaurant 4km.
Closed	November to March (open by arrangement).
Directions	Sent on booking.

Rory & Mini Constant
8 chemin des Berges du Luy,
64410 Bouillon, Pyrénées-Atlantiques

Tel   +33 (0)5 59 81 40 95
Email   info@chateaubedbreakfast.com
Web   www.chateaubedbreakfast.com

Château d'Urtubie

Urtubie is old, very old: built in 1341 with permission from Edward III. The keep is still intact, though the roof was changed in 1654 to resemble Versailles. Your host Laurent, generous, charming, passionate about Urtubie, is a direct descendant of Martin de Tartas who built the castle, which is listed. It's even a (fascinating) museum: the Antiques Roadshow could run an entire series here. Laurent opened his château hotel in 1996. The whole place is friendly and elegant, and that includes the stunningly renovated rooms, reached by stair or discreet lift. The first-floor 'prestige' rooms are light and airy, grand and imposing, in keeping with the building's age and style. The smaller second-floor 'charm' bedrooms are equally inviting. On the outskirts of this pretty little Basque town, a hop from the (audible) motorway and five minutes from the beach, Urtubie is a sweet retreat in fine gardens with a super pool. Don't imagine it's stuffy: Laurent couldn't be easier or more welcoming. His wife is the mayor, his brother and sister-in-law have a Michelin-forked restaurant 500 metres away.

Price	€80–€160.
Rooms	10: 1 double, 8 twins/doubles, 1 single.
Meals	Breakfast €11. Restaurant 500m.
Closed	November to March.
Directions	A63 Bayonne & St Sebastien, exit St Jean de Luz Sud; 1st on left, N10 for Urrugne. Right just before r'bout entering Urrugne. 3km from St Jean de Luz.

Laurent de Coral
Urrugne, 64122 Saint Jean de Luz,
Pyrénées-Atlantiques

Tel	+33 (0)5 59 54 31 15
Email	info@chateaudurtubie.fr
Web	www.chateaudurtubie.fr

Arguibel

Guéthary is one of the best-kept Basque secrets — at least, out of season. The beaches are charming, the coastal walks breathtaking, there are friendly bars and an artistic history; Debussy, Ravel and Chaplin spent heady summers here. A mile outside the village (with restaurants — but you will need a car), behind a conventional and modest façade, is this surprisingly theatrical hotel, whose boutiquey flourishes are the right side of kitsch and whose bathrooms are pure works of art. Art Deco furniture, 18th-century toile de Jouy, 21st-century sculpture and rock 'n' roll memorabilia inhabit the same space, yet create an astonishingly harmonious whole. Each large bedroom and suite (four reached via the sweeping stair) has its own cocooning luxury (iPods etc) and a balcony with an unbroken view, of rolling hills and mountains beyond. In spite of the vast salon, the chic library/bar, the separate tables at breakfast, there's a personal mood. Fifteen minutes up the coast is grand old Biarritz, paradise for surfers and chic shoppers; south, the atmospheric 'vieille ville' of the port of St Jean de Luz.

Price	€120–€210. Suites €200–€285.
Rooms	5: 3 doubles, 2 suites.
Meals	Breakfast €16. Restaurants 400m.
Closed	5 January to 13 February.
Directions	From Biarritz airport, D810 for St Jean de Luz. At Guéthary head for 'La Table des Frères Ibarboure'. Entrance to Arguibel 50m after 'La Table...' on right.

François Blasselle
1146 chemin de Laharraga,
64210 Guéthary, Pyrénées-Atlantiques

Tel	+33 (0)5 59 41 90 46
Mobile	+33 (0)6 75 68 68 06
Email	contact@arguibel.fr
Web	www.arguibel.fr

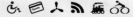

Hôtel Villa Catarie

Guéthary is extraordinary: between September and May as quiet as can be, bursting at the seams in summer. Two beaches, a little harbour, chic shops, cafés and big sister Biarritz... so many reasons to come. Now there's another: this tall stately Basque townhouse (once a pension, now a hotel) idyllically sited in the centre of town. From the cool shaded terrace you enter a sitting room/reception with sunny stippled walls, silk drapes and Louis XV sofas: a décor that's rococo and refined. A little lift ferries you up to one of three floors and bedrooms categorised by size and orientation – find new painted armoires, comfortable new mattresses and seascapes on the walls. Towelling bathrobes are also provided, handy for trips across the car park to the pool which is safely fenced and a good size. It's delightful to breakfast off white china on tables dressed in striped Basque linen, or out on the terrace in fine weather watching the world go by – to the markets at weekends (brocante on Saturday, food stalls on Sunday) and the surf and sand in summer. Spanish guests are sometimes served as late as midday!

Price	€130-€220. Suites €200-€265.
Rooms	16: 14 doubles, 2 suites.
Meals	Breakfast €12. Restaurants 50m.
Closed	Never.
Directions	A64 exit 1 Bayonne; A63 for Biarritz; exit 3 for Guéthary; along D810, left onto Avenue Général de Gaulle. Hotel past post office on left.

Peggy Alday
Avenue du Général de Gaulle,
64210 Guéthary, Pyrénées-Atlantiques

Tel	+33 (0)5 59 47 59 00
Email	hotel@villa-catarie.com
Web	www.villa-catarie.com

Maison Garnier

In the playground of royalty and stars, a jewel of sophisticated simplicity. Pure white bathrooms have monsoon showers, bedrooms are luminous white, eggshell, cocoa and coffee and the occasional flourish of brilliant colour. The bright breakfast room has original floorboards, pale walls, red and white stripes; white linen is a perfect foil for lovely regional tableware in a red and green stripe, and light pours in from great (double-glazed) windows. In 1999 the former boarding house was turned into this smart, hospitable little hotel. There's no reception desk in the hall, just a gorgeous wrought-iron stair rail, a 1930s-feel salon with deep sofa, original fireplace and huge oriental carpet – the tone is set the moment you arrive. In 2008, delightful new owners arrived, he quietly courteous, she chatty and interested, who always dreamed of a seaside hotel. And a superb position in lively Rue Gambetta, the hub of Biarritz's market life and a five-minute walk from the famous surfing beaches, walking distance to everything. A calm, poised retreat from the noisy street. Book early.

Price	€100–€180.
Rooms	7: 5 doubles, 2 twins.
Meals	Breakfast €10-18. Restaurants 50m.
Closed	Rarely.
Directions	From A63 exit Biarritz & La Négresse for Centre Ville & Place Clémenceau. Straight ahead for large, white bank building with clock; left onto Rue Gambetta. Free parking on side street.

Joanne Veillot & Patrick Chacoris
29 rue Gambetta,
64200 Biarritz, Pyrénées-Atlantiques

Tel   +33 (0)5 59 01 60 70
Email   maison-garnier@hotel-biarritz.com
Web   www.hotel-biarritz.com

Villa le Goëland

Every room has an ocean view, the wonderful family bedroom has "the finest view in Biarritz". Villa le Goëland is lush, lavish and inviting. Dominating the ocean, yards from the beaches of glamorous Biarritz, the only privately owned villa of its kind to have resisted commercial redevelopment has opened its arms to guests. Turrets were added in 1903; Paul's family took possession in 1934; now he and his wife, young, charming, professional, are its inspired guardians and restorers. They live in an apartment upstairs and know all there is to know about the pleasures of Biarritz: casino, museums, boutiques, golf, surf, spa. Oak floors, magnificent stairs and sunshine-filled balconies that go on for ever; the salon and dining room each have one so fling open the tall French windows. Bedrooms, not cosy but lofty, are panelled and parquet'd, beds are king-size, two have terraces, bathrooms date from the 1900s to the 1960s, and every window watches the waves. Breakfasts bring *viennoiseries*, served by Paul with a smile. The final touch: a private parking space for every guest, a godsend in this town.

Price	€150–€270.
Rooms	4: 3 doubles, 1 suite for 3.
Meals	Free breakfast on presentation of a Sawday guide. Restaurant 20m.
Closed	November to February.
Directions	From Place Clémençeau in Biarritz centre follow signs for place Ste Eugénie by Rue Mazagran; after pharmacy 1st right Rue des Goélands. House between antique shop & bar, narrow street.

Paul & Élisabeth Daraignez
12 plateau de l'Atalaye, 64200 Biarritz, Pyrénées-Atlantiques

Tel	+33 (0)5 59 24 25 76
Mobile	+33 (0)6 87 66 22 19
Web	www.villagoeland.com

Hôtel Laminak

Smiling and relaxed, Philippe and Chantal are enchanted with their simple little hotel, the result of a long-cherished dream (the name means Basque pixies). You should be too: it is intimate and stylish in its delightful setting, with all the lush greenery of the Basque country at your feet, and mountain views. On a quiet road outside the village of Arbonne, it has a few discreetly screened neighbours and a big handsome garden full of mature shrubs and trees; it's lovely to be served breakfast outside in summer. Rooms are crisp and fresh, a pleasing mix of antique and modern, with harmonious colours and bright walls; we especially like the three garden rooms. Use the splendid sauna, settle by the pool in summer, by the open fire in winter where you sink into a big bright cushion-strewn sofa. Above all, the owners' friendliness and sense of humour bring a light-hearted atmosphere. It's a ten-minute hop to the best surfing coast in Europe and the heady charm of Biarritz, or the antiques fair at Ahetze, or a championship golf course — and the mountains are worth a week's effort in themselves.

Price	€75–€105. Children under 2 free.
Rooms	12 twins/doubles.
Meals	Breakfast €11. Light supper €11–€17; book ahead.
Closed	Rarely.
Directions	A63 exit 4 La Négresse & follow signs to Arbonne; signed.

Philippe & Chantal Basin
Route de Saint Pée, 64210 Arbonne,
Pyrénées-Atlantiques

Tel	+33 (0)5 59 41 95 40
Email	info@hotel-laminak.com
Web	www.hotel-laminak.com

Hôtel 202

No Room 101, this! Hôtel 202 is spanking new and full of personality. In a secluded spot among the pines and mimosas of Hossegor – mecca for surfers and golfers – this Art Nouveau/contemporary Basque-style building is 50 metres from the golf course and a short hop to the beach. Inside, all is effortlessly chic – edges curve, white surfaces gleam, light floods through arched windows. Owner Jérôme runs the place with a passion for detail, a charming 'hands-on' attitude, a love for this region. Bedrooms have crisp white linen, furry throws and good-sized balconies that overlook the pool or the pines. Funky canvas message-paintings hang above the bed: 'Surf's up', 'Hello world!'. A breakfast buffet and fresh smoothies are served on the wooden decking or in the bright spacious bar area and there are plenty of restaurants for dinner nearby – just ask. Surf competitions run during the summer and a shuttle bus ferries you from the hotel in peak season (July/August) to the lake. Run by friendly and efficient staff, this is a cool and quirky place from which to explore Les Landes. Fabulous. *Accept American Express.*

Price	€95–€230. Suites €125–€410.
Rooms	25: 23 doubles/twins, 2 suites.
Meals	Breakfast €14. Restaurants 2km.
Closed	Early January to early February.
Directions	A63 dir. Hossegor exit Benesse Maremne; hotel next to Golf Club.

Jérôme Lacroix
202 avenue du Golf,
40150 Hossegor, Landes
Tel   +33 (0)5 58 43 22 02
Email   contact@hotel202.fr
Web   www.hotel202.fr

Ó Anne Lanta / Pays ACT

Domaine de Sengresse

The characterful entrance hall sets the tone: raw silk dressing windows, a Steinway on a sparkling floor, oil paintings from Michèle's mother. This ravishing 17th-century domaine exudes a rare combination of elegance and rustic charm and, in the manner of the best country hotels, the owners' personality. Michèle and Rob, who moved from Somerset to the Landes in 2005, are there to look after you – but never intrude – and happily share their houseful of riches. You'll love the bedrooms of luxury and light, the calm colours and the exposed beams, the peaceful gardens with hammocks and hidden corners, the elegant breakfasts on the terrace, the candlelit dinners beneath an ecclesiastical chandelier. The food is organic, home-grown, bountiful and delicious (and you may eat romantically à deux if you prefer). Breathtaking parkland surrounds you, there's a long avenue of trees, a pool by the beautiful stone barn and a children's library under the stairs. All this and the lovely Landes, with its markets for foodies and brocanteurs, its surfing dunes for beach bums and its small châteaux at Gaujacq and Amou.

Price	€95–€130.
Rooms	4 + 1: 3 doubles, 1 twin. House for 2-6.
Meals	Dinner with wine, from €30.
Closed	Rarely.
Directions	12km from N124 Dax & Mont de Marsan; exit Tartas for Mugron D924, 4km, right Mugron D332; right at junc. D3 to Mugron. 2nd right Gouts D18; entrance on right after Cap Blanc Kiwi sign.

Ó Anne Lanta / Pays ACT

Michèle & Rob McLusky
& Sasha Ibbotson
Route de Gouts,
40250 Souprosse, Landes

Tel	+33 (0)5 58 97 78 34
Email	sengresse@hotmail.fr
Web	www.sengresse.com

Limousin & Auvergne

La Maison des Chanoines

Built for the canons (chanoines) of Turenne, this ancient hotel-restaurant has been in Claude's family for 300 years. No wonder the family held on to it: the 16th-century, mellow-stoned house with its steep slate roof is one of the loveliest in a very lovely village. Chantal, charming and gracious, takes care of guests from dawn to dusk, always with a smile. The pretty bedrooms, freshly decorated and sparkled up, are scattered among outbuildings, one of them approached via a little bridge from the garden. Well lit, they have parquet floors and white walls; bathrooms ooze fluffy towels. The stone-flagged breakfast room feels ancient and airy. Dining takes place in the cosy old cellar whose ceiling vaults over just six white-clothed tables — nicely intimate — or under a fairy-lit pergola in the garden amid honeysuckle and roses where you are asked to "pour your ice-bucket water onto the tomatoes". The food is a delight; Claude is the chef and will use only the freshest, most local produce for his much-praised regional dishes. Ask about their three-day gourmet stay. Great value.

Price	€85–€155.
Rooms	5: 2 doubles, 1 twin/double, 1 family room for 4, 1 suite for 2-3.
Meals	Breakfast €10. Dinner €35-€50.
Closed	Wednesdays, except during school holidays.
Directions	From Brive D38 to Monplaisir, then D8 for 8km to Turenne. Left uphill following château sign; hotel on left before church (private parking for guests).

Chantal & Claude Cheyroux
Route de l'Église, 19500 Turenne,
Corrèze

Tel	+33 (0)5 55 85 93 43
Email	maisondeschanoines@wanadoo.fr
Web	www.maison-des-chanoines.com

Au Rendez-Vous des Pêcheurs/Fabry

It isn't called 'Fishermen's Lodge' for nothing and there's a spectacular, steep winding descent to the house and the exquisite riverside setting to which it is intimately linked. Fifty years ago, the Fabrys built a house on the banks of the Dordogne; at the same time a dam was started just upstream. Madame opened a kitchen for the site workers – and the house became an inn. This being the Corrèze, food looms as large as the river. The restaurant, a fine room full of light and plants and Limoges china, overlooks the view reaching off to the distant wooded hills of the gorge. The chef is masterly: "I had a set menu of homemade aperitif nibbles, a *mise en bouche*, perch in ginger and lemongrass with fabulous mushroom-stuffed potatoes, and four types of chocolate dessert that defy description," said a reader. Smallish bedrooms, five with river views, are decorated in simple, pleasing country style with excellent if slightly dated bathrooms. The terrace is generous, the garden pretty, the view to treasure. A really special place in one of the gentlest, loveliest, most secret parts of France. Tremendous value, too.

Price	€47–€52. Half-board mandatory in summer €49 p.p.
Rooms	8: 5 doubles, 1 twin, 2 triples.
Meals	Breakfast €8. Picnic available. Lunch & dinner €16–€45. Restaurant closed Sun eve, Tues lunch & Mon in low season.
Closed	Mid-November to mid-February.
Directions	42km east of Tulle; D978 to St Merd de Lapleau via Marcillac la Croisille, then D13 to lieu-dit Pont du Chambon.

Madame Fabry
Pont du Chambon,
19320 Saint Merd de Lapleau, Corrèze
Tel   +33 (0)5 55 27 88 39
Email   contact@rest-fabry.com
Web   www.rest-fabry.com

Auberge de Concasty

Half a mile high lies the river-ploughed plateau: strong air, wild country, vast space. Built 300 years ago, the family mansion stands prouder than ever, and clever, delightful Martine has brought everything thoroughly up to date: jacuzzi, hammam, organic or local food (veg from her brother's farm next door) to keep you blooming. The dining room, with its vast inglenook fireplace, and the covered patio overlooking the pool and the view, are the stage for lovingly prepared shows of foie gras and asparagus, scallops and confits (you can watch: Martine chats happily while cooking), the supporting cast an impressive choice of wines; great breakfasts, too. Bedrooms – in the main house, the restored barn or the newly renovated chestnut dryer – are stylishly rustic with space, good floral fabrics and an evocative name each – nothing standard here, except for that view. The magnificent new family room in ivory and soft blue is the height of sophistication. You will love the smiling, attentive staff, the warm family atmosphere they generate, the freedom in the air. *Some rooms with balcony or terrace.*

Price	€64–€136. Suite €140–€168. Extra person €16–€18.
Rooms	12: 11 doubles, 1 suite.
Meals	Breakfast €9.50. Brunch €17. Dinner €40–€48. Half-board option (min. 2 nights). Restaurant 10km.
Closed	December to March.
Directions	From Aurillac, N122 for Figeac, left to Manhès on D64. From Figeac, N122, then D17 after Maurs.

Martine Causse
15600 Boisset,
Cantal

Tel	+33 (0)4 71 62 21 16
Email	info@auberge-concasty.com
Web	www.auberge-concasty.com

Château de Sédaiges

An old creeper-strewn château such as children dream of, Sédaiges has it all: 15th-century turrets and crenellations, stairs and corridors galore, a crazily high neo-Gothic hammer-beamed hall built to house the tapestries given by Louis XVI, elegant 18th-century drawing rooms, open to the public, where Marie-Antoinette's lookalike holds court. Delightful Bab tells the tales with all her passion for this microcosm of a vanishing way of life – the remote Auvergne is more unspoilt than any other part of old France, as the family chapel bears witness. In the creaky old warren upstairs, beneath aristocratic ceilings, are the endearingly unpretentious family-château bedrooms, two of them refurbished: marble and muslin, florals and plush frame some fine old pieces. Bathrooms, too, vary from 60s to modern. A simple, damask-clothed, silver-served coffee and croissant breakfast among gleaming copper pans in the old kitchen is as atmospheric as it gets. Don't miss the antique toys, all retrieved from the château's cupboards, or the wonderful botanical walk through the park with its stupendously towering specimen trees.

Price	€110–€150. Extra bed €20.
Rooms	5: 3 doubles, 1 suite for 3, 1 room for 4. Overflow room for children.
Meals	Restaurant in village.
Closed	October to April.
Directions	From Aurillac D922 for Mauriac 10km. At Jussac right onto D59 to Marmanhac; signed.

	Bab & Patrice de Varax
	15250 Marmanhac,
	Cantal
Tel	+33 (0)4 71 47 30 01
Email	chateau15@free.fr
Web	www.chateausedaiges.com

Instants d'Absolu – Écolodge du Lac du Pêcher

Sledge with dogs through the forest, ride horses at night and hear stags 'bark', cook with wild plants, fish for trout, snow-shoe in winter – tempting! Peace and serenity reign supreme, at this remote eco-lodge by the Lac du Pêcher, a 17th-century farmhouse originally built of lava and wood, now extensively and invitingly remodelled. The owners, generous and thoughtful, are committed to the happiness of their guests. It's a place for those who love wild nature, wholesome pampering and food in tune with the seasons. It's bliss to retire to harmonious bedrooms, each evoking the spirit of nature: they have sheep and goat skins for carpets; stylish basins of wood, marble, granite or lava; and huge views of forest, volcano or lake. In the sitting room, sofas wear fur cushions, a chandelier drips with glass, a fire crackles, an 'indoor garden' brings the outside in. In the restaurant, curtains are changed according to the seasons: linen for summer, virgin wool for winter. There's a spa for reiki, shiatsu, reflexology, massage with lava stones… and a garden with outdoor 'pillows' by the lake.

Price	€115 p.p half-board. Suite €180 p.p half-board. Min. 2 nights; 4 nights July/Aug; 7 nights Christmas-New Year.
Rooms	12: 4 doubles, 1 single, 7 suites.
Meals	Half-board April-Nov; full-board Dec-Mar. Restaurant 4km.
Closed	Mid-November to mid-December; mid-March to Easter.
Directions	Sent on booking.

Laurence Costa
Lac du Pêcher,
15300 Chavagnac, Cantal

Tel	+33 (0)4 71 20 83 09
Email	info@ecolodge-france.com
Web	www.ecolodge-france.com

Auberge de Chassignolles

The old village lay untouched in the pure green air, its 1930s inn decaying gently behind the medieval church; then along came two charming, colourful young Londoners, bringing oodles of talent and baby Fred (a little sister has since arrived). The place now hums with good looks and seriously delicious food. It is simplicity incarnate: upstairs, light from tall windows falls on old parquet, bounces off white walls onto warm old furniture – a 1930s carved and inlaid bedroom suite dressed in pure white linen, a deep and friendly armchair; Ali's artistic eye sees to all the details. Bathrooms come with good extras. One room above the restaurant is a library/sitting room and there's a meadow with fruit trees over the road. The pretty, old-style restaurant – country furniture, checked cloths, crinkly lamps, a fascinating mixture of old crockery – is the ideal frame for Harry's finely honed *cuisine de terroir*, all fresh local produce and taste. An antidote to urban frenzy, with a small grocery shop by the bar, this is a perfect focus for revived community life and a boon for travellers.

Price	€45–€65. Extra bed €15.
Rooms	8: 6 doubles, 1 family room for 4; 1 twin sharing bathroom.
Meals	Breakfast €7.50. Lunch €24 (Sunday only). Dinner €24 (except Mon). Wine €7.50–€80. Picnic €8.
Closed	Early October to early June.
Directions	From A75 exit 17, left under m'way dir. Jumeaux onto Auzon; D5 for 8km, left onto D52 to Chassignolles. Auberge in main square.

Ethical Collection: Environment; Community; Food. See page 429 for details

Harry Lester & Ali Johnson
Le Bourg,
43440 Chassignolles, Haute-Loire
Tel   +33 (0)4 71 76 32 36
Email info@aubergedechassignolles.com
Web   www.aubergedechassignolles.com

Domaine de Gaudon – Le Château

The contrast could scarcely be greater. In the wilds of deepest Auvergne with nature bounding free all round, you find new Medici urns lining the edges of a great park. Inside the 19th-century splendour of glossy oak panelling, mouldings and original wall coverings, this totally natural, endearing couple have created a glamorous backdrop, all brass and satin, gilt and quilting, for their superb French antiques show. Gleaming luxuriously, big bathrooms are in keeping. Alain is a dab hand at wall panels and mouldings, Monique knows exactly what she likes in fabrics and colour combinations (Prussian blue and gold, canary yellow and gold, green and orange), they simply love having guests and breakfast is designed to dazzle you as your bedroom did. Gaudon is a Gîte Panda in a wildlife conservation area with some superb specimen trees, a young arboretum, a wetland observation spot and innumerable frogs, bats, birds and insects (there are samples in frames indoors). Herons fish in the pond, woods invite explorers, children love the place, and a well-being centre is in the making. Astonishing.

Price	€110. Suite €130. Extra bed €25.
Rooms	5: 3 doubles, 1 twin, 1 suite.
Meals	Supper trays available. Restaurant 4km.
Closed	Rarely.
Directions	A75 from Montpellier exit 9; D229 then D996 to St Dier d'Auvergne. At end of village D6 for Domaize 3km. Right for Ceilloux 1km.

Alain & Monique Bozzo
63520 Ceilloux,
Puy-de-Dôme

Tel	+33 (0)4 73 70 76 25
Email	domainedegaudon@wanadoo.fr
Web	www.domainedegaudon.fr

Château Royal de Saint-Saturnin

Oodles of atmosphere, rooks aplenty, and views over one of Auvergne's wonderful romanesque churches. A volcanic region is the perfect cradle for this magnificently turreted and castellated fortress, high on the forested fringes of one of France's most beautiful villages, Saint Saturnin. A stone spiral, worn with age and history, leads to five sumptuous bedrooms – regal four-posters and an inspired blend of antique and modern furniture – in the oldest wing of the 13th-century 'monument historique'. The Louis XIII suite, its bathroom tucked into a tower, spans the castle's width; views are to tumbling rooftops and romanesque church, and to gardens and parkland behind (heaven for weddings). The vaulted dining room, decked with gleaming coppers, is the background for relaxed breakfast spreads. Redolent with royal history, the château has been lovingly, painstakingly returned to its original glory, yet, thanks to friendly, well-travelled Emmanuel and Christine, is in no way intimidating. Catherine de Médicis and La Reine Margot were once owners and now Château Royal is open to the public.

Price	€160-€195. Suites €195-€230.
Rooms	5: 2 doubles, 3 suites.
Meals	Breakfast €14. Restaurant 1.5km.
Closed	Mid-November to end March.
Directions	From Clermont-Ferrand, A75 for Issoire & Montpellier; exit 5 for Aydat for 6km; left for St Saturnin; left Rue de la Chantelle; at fountain square, gate on right.

Emmanuel & Christine Pénicaud
Place de l'Ormeau,
63450 Saint Saturnin, Puy-de-Dôme

Tel	+33 (0)4 73 39 39 64
Email	chateaudesaintsaturnin@yahoo.fr
Web	www.chateaudesaintsaturnin.com

Château de Maulmont

This extraordinary place, built in 1830 by Louis Philippe for his sister Adélaïde, has long views and architecture: medieval crenellations, 16th-century brick patterning, Loire-Valley slate roofs, neo-Gothic windows, even real Templar ruins – a cornucopia of character. The owners provide activities on 23 hectares of parkland (a golf driving range, fishing, sauna, swimming pools outdoors and in, riding nearby) and cultivate a certain 'formal informality'. They have preserved original features – carved inside shutters, the original spit in the kitchen, the panelled banqueting hall with its stained-glass portraits of Adélaïde in various moods – and collected some impressive furniture. Bedrooms are spacious, all are individually decorated and there's a wonderfully romantic room in the tower reached via a spiral stair. All have very smart bathrooms. The well-established restaurant where classical piped music plays is wood-panelled from top to toe, staff are alert and friendly, and you can arrive by helicopter if you choose. A destination place for grand events, and a super family hotel.

Price	€135-€195. Suites €195-€240. Apartments €200-€290. All prices per night.
Rooms	19 + 2: 9 doubles, 7 twins, 1 suite for 2, 2 family suites for 3-4. 2 apartments for 4-6.
Meals	Breakfast €15-€17. Lunch & dinner €30-€55. Wine €30-€150.
Closed	Early November to end March.
Directions	N209 for Vichy; D131 for Hauterive; there, right to St Priest Bramefant; D55 then right at r'bout on D59 to Randan.

Ian & Maartje Lawrie
Saint Priest Bramefant, 63310 Randan,
Puy-de-Dôme

Tel	+33 (0)4 70 59 14 95
Email	info@chateau-maulmont.com
Web	www.chateau-maulmont.com

Château Neureux

In unspoilt France, with bucolic views to hills, pastures, lake and stream, is a perfect little 18th-century getaway. Once country home to Louis XV's finance minister, it is now owned by an interesting pair: a Dutch film director and an American ballerina, ex-prima of the Dutch National Ballet. Quietly attentive, hospitable, delightful, Roeland and Valerie give you big inviting bedrooms with an elegant décor that mixes French classicism with Dutch sobriety. Up the splendid wooden stair, past deep-red walls and a fabulous beaded Deco chandelier, are superb mattresses on beds of mahogany and cherry, sweeping polished boards and oriental rugs, ornate wallpapers and louvered French shutters – and bathrooms that ooze towels, soaps and bubbles. As you tuck into breakfast's pâtisseries, gaze through tall windows to the vast estate where proud peacocks and friendly donkeys roam, wild deer and foxes saunter, and a swimming pool, shared with the gîte guests, awaits behind orchard walls. Rent bikes, stride into the hills, fish on the lake… and polish off the day with a delicious meal in Neure.

Price	€110-€130.
Rooms	5: 2 doubles, 2 twins/doubles, 1 suite for 2-4.
Meals	Breakfast included. Restaurant 1km.
Closed	Rarely.
Directions	From Paris A6 to A77 dir. Nevers, exit St Pierre le Moutier; D978A for Lurcy Lévis; 2km after Neure, signed.

Roeland Kerbosch
& Valerie Valentine
03320 Lurcy Lévis, Allier

Tel	+33 (0)9 64 41 55 30
Email	info@chateauneureux.com
Web	www.chateauneureux.com

Midi – Pyrénées

Le Domaine de la Borie Grande

The 18th-century house in two hectares of parkland combines understatedly elegant luxury with a country-house B&B mood – delightful. It is a beautifully kept home of friendly proportions where you will find artistic flair, a love of cooking (the neighbour's vegetables in season, local wines) and stimulating company. Alain's lovingly collected antiques (he has some beautiful pieces) and works of art add sparkle to a palette of taupe, cream and dove grey. Enter a square hall off which lead three reception rooms: a cosy one for contemplation, a tranquil drawing room for tea and a grand salon for aperitifs and conversation. A stunning carved armoire takes pride of place, the deep cream sofa could seat a dozen, a big pale rug softens a terracotta floor and Cordes is perched high on the hill with its magical view. You will be guided up a sweeping stair to large and luminous bedrooms where antique rugs strew polished parquet, crisp linen enfolds new beds and white bathrooms have big mirrors and oodles of towels. The raised garden is lovely and you may share bikes, tennis court and saltwater pool. *Cash or cheque only.*

Price	€125–€135. Suites €135–€180.
Rooms	4: 1 double, 1 twin, 2 suites.
Meals	Dinner with wine, €40.
Closed	Rarely.
Directions	From Cordes sur Ciel for Laguépie. Right at bend at bottom of hill leaving Cordes; 1km to church in Campes; left for St Amans. On left, 500m from church.

Alain Guyomarch
Saint Marcel Campes,
81170 Cordes sur Ciel, Tarn
Tel   +33 (0)5 63 56 58 24
Email   laboriegrande@wanadoo.fr
Web   www.laboriegrande.com

Château de Brametourte

Just outside jewel-like Lautrec, this great ramble of a place holds fine English antiques and French château décor inside 1,000 years of solid history: Cathars, Templars and Toulouse-Lautrec's ancestors all left their marks. Paul and Alison, high-flying business folk, fled the corporate world for five happy, hard-working years in bucolic France learning the crafts and restoring Brametourte, their neglected pile, with reclaimed materials and eco-caring methods, discreet modernisation (reversible underfloor heating by heat-pump) and the latest thing in bathrooms. Reed-bed filter systems lie above the spring-fed, three-tiered forest garden (orchard trees, soft-fruit bushes, vegetables) that aims for permaculture. This is Liz's domain. Three years ago, she came for a week — and stayed to create two ambitious organic kitchen gardens and resuscitate the formal terrace. Bedrooms are unpretentiously classy. The welcome is as big as the stones, tree-trunk beams and giant fireplaces that give the house such a safe feel. Paul cooks lovingly, especially vegetarian, Alison runs the B&B, the area brims with things to do.

Price	€60–€120. Extra bed €29.
Rooms	5 doubles. Extra beds available & overflow dormitory.
Meals	Dinner with wine €12–€25. Restaurants nearby.
Closed	Rarely.
Directions	From A68 exit 7 on D12/D631 thro' Giroussens to Graulhet. Right D83 to Lautrec; at r'bout, right D92 for Vielmur 1km; by Aquaval, right for Brametourte holiday centre 1km; 2nd track on right. Château at end on left.

Paul Hunter & Alison Ward
81440 Lautrec, Tarn

Tel	+33 (0)5 63 75 01 25
Email	enquiries@brametourte.com
Web	www.brametourte.com

Hôtel Cuq en Terrasses

Come to the Pays de Cocagne, the brochure says. Where is that, you ask, have I drunk that wine? It is an imaginary land of pleasure in the once prosperous pastel-producing Tarn. Philippe and Andonis gave up good jobs in Paris to buy this 18th-century presbytery after falling in love with the region. Perched in mouthwatering gardens on the side of a hill, the multi-level mellow stone edifice looks – and is – utterly inviting. All the rooms, including the two-floor suite by the saltwater pool, exude character and finesse. All are different, with original terracotta floors, hand-finished plaster, exposed beams, a Chinese vase here, an antique bed there. It is worth staying just for the bathrooms, lovely with hand-painted tiles. Evening meals, on the terrace in summer, are a delight for eye and palate: something different each day, fresh from the market, beautifully balanced by wines from the region. Readers are full of praise, for the food and the gardens, the pool and waterfall, the blissful views, the wonderful hosts. We cannot fault it.

Price	€95–€160. Suite €210. Half-board €192–€282 for 2 (min. 4 nights).
Rooms	8: 3 doubles, 3 twins/doubles, 2 suites.
Meals	Breakfast €15. Snacks available. Hosted dinner €36; book ahead. Wine €14–€25.
Closed	November to Easter.
Directions	N126 to Cuq Toulza then D45 towards Revel. After 2km on left at top of hill in old village.

Philippe Gallice & Andonis Vassalos
Cuq le Château,
81470 Cuq Toulza, Tarn

Tel	+33 (0)5 63 82 54 00
Email	cuq-en-terrasses@wanadoo.fr
Web	www.cuqenterrasses.com

Domaine de Rasigous

The drawing room is the magnet of this exceptional house: gentle colours, fabulous fabrics and, in autumn, a log fire in a marble fireplace. The soft yellow and white dining room is full of light, its tables beautifully dressed for good-looking varied food and local wines (especially the delicious Gaillac). Lots of super art on the walls, too. Naturally pale bare floorboards with fine rugs or thick plain carpets give that country-house feel to heavenly bedrooms, sensitively decorated with rich colours and French and Spanish antiques. The three suites are luxuriously unfrilly. Superb bathrooms have been ingeniously fitted into odd spaces – the free-standing bath is most handsome. Even the single room, with its sleigh bed, lovely linen and bathroom in a walk-in cupboard, is on the 'noble' floor, not in the attic. The courtyard is ideal for summer dining. Gaze at the water lilies in the water garden, eight different types of frog will sing and jump for you; in the park, huge sculptures by a local artist will draw your eye. Analia's warmth, flair and hospitality make this a wonderful place to stay. And now a spa.

Price	€170. Single €80. Suites €200-€230.	
Rooms	8: 4 twins/doubles, 1 single, 3 suites for 2.	
Meals	Breakfast €12. Dinner €29 (except Wednesdays). Wine €18-€65. Restaurant nearby.	
Closed	15 November to 15 March.	
Directions	From Mazamet D621 for Soual for 16km; left on D85 to St Affrique les Montagnes. On for 2km on D85; green sign on left.	

Emile & Analia Navas
81290 Saint Affrique les Montagnes, Tarn

Tel	+33 (0)5 63 73 30 50
Email	info@domainederasigous.com
Web	www.domainederasigous.com

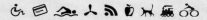

Château de Séguenville

A dream of a 13th-century French family château, Séguenville was rebuilt in 1653 and has been in the family for many years; Marie can tell you all about both house and region. Restoring it is a perpetual labour of love for her and it still has oodles of character – plus a newly discovered treasure of a painted ceiling. She is an enthusiastic cook and loves wine, so will happily prepare a gastronomic menu if you ask in advance. Galleried bedrooms with marble fireplaces and creaky floors charm, big bathrooms combine the old with the new, the 'salon chinois' has black leather sofas, centuries-old trees stand in the vast park. It's still crumbling in places but you'll love the slightly frayed charm, and Marie, who has children of her own, enjoys having families to stay. Decoration is simple yet elegant and full of original personality, like the owner. Outside are a swimming pool and a terrace for breakfast with glorious views. In the summer, spin off on a bike – or visit the château's windmill, open to visitors and still grinding flour. In stunning countryside – and within easy reach of the airport.

Price	€120-€135.
Rooms	5: 3 doubles, 1 suite, 1 family room for 4.
Meals	Dinner, 3 courses, €30. Wine from €7.
Closed	15 December to 15 January.
Directions	From Toulouse dir. Blagnac Airport; Cornebarrieu & Cadours; on to Cox, 3rd road on right. Signed 5km after Cox.

Marie Lareng
Région de Toulouse,
31480 Cabanac Séguenville,
Haute-Garonne
Tel   +33 (0)5 62 13 42 67
Email   info@chateau-de-seguenville.com
Web   www.chateau-de-seguenville.com

Château de Beauregard

The château – actually, a big country house grafted onto a 17th-century dairy farm in 1820 – was in woeful condition when Paul, trained chef and entrepreneur, bought it. With intuition, imagination and reclamation, he then created something memorable. He even found some massive old radiators so the new central heating looks perfectly at home. The château rooms and suites are full of appeal and interest, their reclaimed furniture and fabrics having just enough shabby chic to look as though they've been there forever. But the two new Californian-style rooms in the fully refurbished stables are in another league: vast, double-height to the great roof carpentry, beautifully pointed stone walls, a balcony each, oak floors and, contrasting with all these natural materials, super-contemporary furnishings and 21st-century, black and white, rain-shower bathrooms. Breakfast is served in the pretty winter garden or, in hot weather, out under the shade of the wisteria. Dining at the Auberge d'Antan is a treat and you can watch the (very good) Gascon-style food being cooked over a wood fire. The spa is a proper one, too.

Price	€60–€100. Suites €80–€120. Balcony rooms €180–€220. Apartment €460–€900 per week. Half board €72–€152 p.p.
Rooms	10 + 1: 4 twins/doubles, 4 suites, 2 balcony rooms. Apartment for 6.
Meals	Breakfast €13. Dinner €28–€33. Wine from €16. Restaurant 2km.
Closed	November.
Directions	From Toulouse to Tarbes, A20 exit 20 to Salies du Salat; D117 to Saint Girons, Massat.

Paul Fontvieille
L'Auberge d'Antan,
Avenue de la Résistance,
09200 Saint Girons, Ariège
Tel +33 (0)5 61 66 66 64
Email contact@chateaubeauregard.net
Web www.chateaubeauregard.net

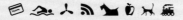

Entry 281 Map 14

L'Abbaye Château de Camon

Camon… the name carries images of pious folk, wrapped in sackcloth and arriving by donkey. Art history buffs will swoon trying to find which bits were built when, but it was first recorded as a Benedictine Abbey in 928. Now Peter, who managed luxurious Samling Hotel in Cumbria, and his wife Katie, an interior designer turned young mother, run the place hands-on like a B&B (though breakfast is extra). They give you monks' bedrooms with vaulted ceilings, tiny glistening floor tiles and tall 28-pane windows looking south to the hills; rooms on the second floor are squarer; all have soft colours, lovely fabrics, spoiling bathrooms. Relax in the huge salon with its exquisite 18th-century plasterwork and floral ceiling, or take tea in the sheltered cloister garden. Breakfast is served, most elegantly, on a long high terrace running the length of the château and overlooking formal gardens with lawns, mature trees and swimming pool. The refined *menu dégustation* is a memorable dining experience, the wine list is superb and you are in the heart of Cathar country, near the medieval delights of Mirepoix.

Price	€130–€190. Suites €250–€270.
Rooms	11: 9 doubles, 2 suites for 4.
Meals	Breakfast €18. Dinner €40. Wine €16–€44.
Closed	November to 15 March.
Directions	From Carcassonne, N13 to Bram; D4 to Fanjeaux; D119 south to Mirepoix; D625 towards Laroque; D7 for Camon. Signed.

Katie & Peter Lawton
09500 Camon, Ariège

Tel	+33 (0)5 61 60 31 23
Email	katie@chateaudecamon.com
Web	www.chateaudecamon.com

Hôtel Restaurant Relais Royal

Arrive on a summer afternoon and you'll pass the courtyard tables set for tea. Then through the Renaissance-style gate and into the lobby where terracotta gleams, the grandfather clock ticks away the hours and pretty arched doors lead to a second courtyard and small pool. The lofty dining room has a touch of gilt here and there and is a suitable setting for some serious dining (menus include one for young gourmets!). Service is very friendly and unobtrusive. Dine in winter in front of a fire in the old kitchen, its walls lined with copper pans; retire to the clubby Blue Room. Then up the grand ironwork staircase to bedrooms with a modern décor that allows the original features to shine: glorious 18th-century windows and Nespresso machines, high ceilings and beams painted fashionably white. Fabrics are coordinated and bathrooms are large and luxy, some with roll tops. The Pyrenees provide a beautiful (hiking and biking) backdrop to this sweet cathedral town, its medieval square full of tempting cafés, and there's a great pâtisserie round the corner. Fascinating Carcassonne is worth at least a day.

Price	€199–€299. Suites €299–€399.
Rooms	9: 5 twins/doubles, 4 suites for 2-4.
Meals	Breakfast €20. Lunch €20–€50. Dinner €50 (except Mon & Tues). Children's meals €18. Wine €20.
Closed	Early January to early February.
Directions	From Toulouse A66 to Foix. Exit Pamiers, Mirepoix & Carcassonne. D20 to Mirepoix & Bram. In centre of Mirepoix, near post office.

Gerwin Rutten &
Rogier Van Den Biggelaar
8 rue Maréchal Clauzel,
09500 Mirepoix, Ariège

Tel	+33 (0)5 61 60 19 19
Email	relaisroyal@relaischateaux.com
Web	www.relaisroyal.com

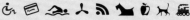

Le Mûrier de Viels

You won't meet a soul on the drive to get here, except possibly a wild deer. This intimate hotel, made up of a sprinkling of 18th-century buildings on several lush levels, hides among the oak woods and gazes down on the river with beautiful views of the valley. Come for a smiling welcome and an atmosphere of relaxed comfort: Joséphine and Oz left stressful lives in Britain to realise their dream of owning a small hotel and bringing up a family in France. The layout is charming, with reception, restaurant and guest rooms scattered among terraces and secret corners. The pool area has a great view, as do most of the rooms; there's space and blissful tranquillity. In the bedrooms where rustic stone walls rub shoulders with white plaster you'll find stylish modern French furniture and soothing colours, big walk-in showers, good reading lamps and fat pillows. The suite has a fitted wardrobe with antique doors, a comfy raffia sofa and a stunning view through a huge window. Every room is pristine. Treat yourself to Oz's beautiful cooking on the terrace or in a dining room bright with yellow leather chairs.

Price	€65–€105. Singles €50–€70. Duplex suite €105–€130. Family rooms €75–€105. Cottage €450–€750 p.w.
Rooms	7 + 1: 3 doubles, 1 twin, 1 duplex suite for 3, 2 family rooms for 3. Cottage for 4.
Meals	Breakfast €9.50. Picnic on request. Dinner €25–€30. Wine €10–€27.
Closed	13 November to 28 February.
Directions	From Figeac to Villefranche de Rouergue, cross river then immed. right onto D86 to Cajac. 2km, follow signs.

Joséphine & Oz
12700 Causse et Diège, Aveyron

Tel	+33 (0)5 65 80 89 82
Email	mail@le-murier.com
Web	www.le-murier.com

Château de Labro

In a large park with vast pastures, woods and every imaginable tree, this fine 16th-century château has all the ingredients for a magical stay. A tree-lined drive leads to an old gated entrance beyond which a walled vineyard hides a huge pool and a lawn. Nearly all the bedrooms are large, with fine parquet floors and views to slate roofs, the garden or the foothills of the Massif Central. Those in the main house are dedicated to local artists, others, off a stone-flagged courtyard, have four-posters; one, the delectable treehouse, complete with chandelier, sits in the branches of an ancient oak tree. A generous breakfast is laid on elegantly dressed tables in the old pigsty and there's a large salon with chesterfield sofas behind the fine wooden bar. Check out the magnificent wine rack (sample their 'Marcillac'); indulge in special food in a gorgeous setting. Local folk Giselle and Sylvain look after it all with ease and charm, owner Monsieur Rouquet pops in from time to time. Take a trip to the Gorges du Tarn or the Roquefort cheese caves, hike or bike in the wonderful Aubrac. Enchanting. *Weddings. Spa.*

Price	€110–€250.
Rooms	17: 12 doubles, 1 twin, 3 triples, 1 treehouse for 2.
Meals	Breakfast €10. Dinner €20–€30. Wine €12–€28.
Closed	Rarely.
Directions	From A75 exit 42 Séverac le Château for Rodez and Decazeville; after viaduct right on D901 for 4km; left for Onet le Château. Signed.

Jean & Nizou Rouquet
12850 Labro, Aveyron

Tel	+33 (0)5 65 67 90 62
Email	j.rouquet@wanadoo.fr
Web	www.chateaulabro.fr

Hôtel Relais Sainte Anne

In the centre of beautifully preserved Martel, step in from the quiet street, take a deep breath, feel the still magic of the place. The fabulous garden has endless secret corners and pathways running through high box-edged lanes. The several buildings that house the bedrooms were once a girls' school, the delightful covered terrace was their playground, the old school house is now an oriental suite exuding opulence and space. Warm old stones and terracotta, fine fabrics and heavy rugs abound. We loved the lighter rooms, too, and the simpler yet pretty rooms for smaller budgets: such a friendly touch. Bathrooms are original and fun: black and terracotta, a bit of gilt or candy stripe, a flowery frieze. All this, a perfectly lovely family (Madame still says "I'm so happy here," and gets a kick out of each new decorative idea) and innovative cuisine, served on the terrace or in the intimate dining room by a big open fire. A 'lovers' table' dressed with roses and candles can be set under the porch of the little chapel. Sophistication without self-consciousness – a rare treat.

Price	€85–€185. Suites €155–€275.
Rooms	16: 7 doubles, 4 twins, 1 single, 4 suites.
Meals	Breakfast €13–€15. Lunch & dinner €16–€35. Wine €19–€90. Restaurant closed Monday lunchtime.
Closed	Mid-November to mid-March.
Directions	From Brive A20 for Cahors exit 54 for Martel; Rue du Pourtanel; hotel on right at town entrance.

Ghislaine Rimet-Mignon
Rue du Pourtanel,
46600 Martel, Lot
Tel   +33 (0)5 65 37 40 56
Email   relais.sainteanne@wanadoo.fr
Web   www.relais-sainte-anne.com

Manoir de Malagorse

You get more than you pay for here, so enjoy it to the hilt. The refined manoir in the idyllic setting was once a farmhouse whose occupants fell on hard times. Now the place smiles again, thanks to Anna and Abel's loving restoration. Off the central staircase, spread over two floors, the bedrooms are statements of simple luxury and the great kitchen is a wonder to behold: a massive fireplace, a vaulted ceiling. This is where you dine at one long table – unless you choose the privacy of the dining room, or the terrace among the immaculate pom-pom hedges. Anna's table decorations are a match for Abel's exquisite food: napkins tied with twine, candles tall and dramatic. Now this delightful pair have twins of their own; they love the idea of entertaining families and have created two contemporary suites in an outbuilding. Colours are muted, bed covers quilted, your hosts are unintrusively present and Anna can offer a professional massage after Abel's demanding wine-tastings. There are cookery courses in summer; in winter they run an Alpine restaurant. Special. *Truffle weekends. Wine tasting. Massage.*

Price	€130–€185. Suites €220–€310. Extra bed available.
Rooms	6: 4 doubles, 2 suites.
Meals	À la carte lunch, from €20. Dinner €42. Wine from €20.
Closed	Weekdays December to February; March-April.
Directions	From Souillac 6km, N20 for Cressensac. On dual c'way, 1st right to Cuzance & Église de Rignac; 1st right in Rignac, signed; check directions before you go.

Anna & Abel Congratel
46600 Cuzance, Lot

Tel	+33 (0)5 65 27 14 83
Mobile	+33 (0)6 76 74 86 08
Email	acongratel@manoir-de-malagorse.fr
Web	www.manoir-de-malagorse.fr

Hôtel Restaurant Le Vert

The alchemy of family tradition – three generations and 30 years for this Belgo-German couple – has rubbed off onto the very stones of their beautiful, authentic country inn where Bernard's skills shine from the kitchen. It feels like a private house: fresh flowers, glowing silverware and old flagstones leading you from the small lobby to the dining room. Glance at the blackboard for the day's special to get your appetite going and, if the weather is right, head for a table on the flowered terrace. The local foodies are greeted as friends here, always an auspicious sign. Ingredients are vital to Bernard – organic and local whenever possible – and he works wonders with them. This is Cahors wine territory: delightful, chatty Eva will advise. The rooms in the garden annexe are big, cool and elegant with beamed ceilings, stone walls and antique furniture lightened by simple white curtains and delicate bedspreads. The pool is hidden on the far side of the green and shady garden. In a country where politicians are authors and cooks are philosophers, Bernard's ivory tower is in the kitchen.

Price	€85-€130.
Rooms	6 twins/doubles.
Meals	Breakfast €10. Dinner €28-€40. Wine €5-€100.
Closed	November to March.
Directions	From Villeneuve sur Lot, D811 for Fumel; south of Fumel D139 for Montayral. Past Mauroux towards Puy l'Évêque for approx. 1km. Hotel on right.

Bernard & Eva Philippe
Le Vert, 46700 Mauroux, Lot
Tel   +33 (0)5 65 36 51 36
Email   info@hotellevert.com
Web   www.hotellevert.com

Hostellerie du Manoir de Saint Jean

Hats off to Anne-Marie who has impressed the locals (we asked around) with her renovations and cuisine. This might not have been so difficult for a native of the little town but she is a transplant from Nice, the big city, and an ex-antique dealer to boot. The dining room is outstanding in soft yellow and cream, full of enormous gilt-framed mirrors and beautiful curtains at huge windows. The terrace is particularly lovely and overlooks the colourful, flower-filled formal garden and the side of the pool. Anne-Marie is the cook: her 'menu of the day' is based on seasonal produce and offers two choices for each course. She hand-picks her wine suppliers, too, and now sources only 100% organic food and wine. Enjoy space and more space – from the entrance hall to the corridors to the big bedrooms where well-chosen antiques rest in just the right places adding warmth and colour. Bathrooms are bright and airy. This hotel and restaurant are an image of their owner, who is definitely a people person, relaxed, efficient and quietly, warmly comfortable: she makes the place.

Price	€100–€130. Suites €150–€200.
Rooms	10: 1 double, 9 suites for 2-4.
Meals	Breakfast €13.
	Lunch & dinner €38–€70.
	Restaurant closed Sunday eve &
	Mondays. Wine €38–€75.
Closed	November.
Directions	A62 exit 9; in Moissac, D7 to Bourg de Visa. 9km; well signed.

Anne-Marie Morgadès
Saint Jean de Cornac,
82400 Saint Paul d'Espis,
Tarn-et-Garonne

Tel	+33 (0)5 63 05 02 34
Email	info@manoirsaintjean.com
Web	www.manoirsaintjean.com

Hôtel Lous Grits

This extremely elegant, refined and comfortable house was built from scratch yet reflects the local architecture in every loving detail. Note the pointed stone-clad tower, the traditional rows of pantiles below the tiled roofs, adding grandeur but not ostentation, and the most noble, mason-laid, golden-hued stone. The hotel gazes in on itself from charming balconies; neat courtyard gardens are studded with olive trees in urns, flowering abelia and box plants, and shady, well-furnished sitting spots. Gorgeous, refined rooms are light, spacious and airy, their beige and cream schemes topped with touches of faded pink, lavender and manganese red. Dreamy. Fine contemporary curtains, antique lampshades and lovely bedcovers and cushions provide texture, while antique pieces – Directoire, Napoleon III, Provençal – create a mood of serenity and harmony, right down to the blue woad soaps and oils in the intimate bathrooms. Your gracious, informed hosts are Martine and Marie Pitron, a brilliant mother and daughter team with superlative style. Take time to explore this hauntingly beautiful area, the Tuscany of France.

Price	€205–€310.
Rooms	6: 3 doubles, 1 twin, 2 family suites.
Meals	Breakfast €20. Dinner €42, book ahead. Wine from €40.
Closed	Rarely.
Directions	D7 from Condom or Lectoure onto D166 to Marsolan; hotel in village, on left.

Martine Pitron
Le Village, 32700 Marsolan, Gers

Tel	+33 (0)5 62 28 37 10
Email	contact@hotel-lousgrits.com
Web	www.hotel-lousgrits.com

Castelnau des Fieumarcon

Castelnau is rare pearl. Built in the 13th century by local feudal lords – who, during the Hundred Year War, pledged allegiance to the English crown – this glorious fortified village within a village was left to crumble until 25 years ago when the owners moved in. Pass through a Renaissance portal to find restored ramparts and 13 renovated houses, each with its own half-wild garden. Trees abound, much of the creeper-clad stone has been left untouched, and there's a surprise around every corner. A unique combination of grandeur and simplicity adds fascination: a Louis XV armoire or a tapestry, framed dried herbs on painted walls, fairylight baldaquins, books, art and antique Gascony treasures. Touches of surreal influence mingle with a love of 'arte povera'; humour and inventiveness are ever present. Castelnau is on high ground so the views from the pool – indeed, from every window – are astounding. A timeless haze glows from fields and low-lying Pyrenean hills. Stendhal, who called it the French Tuscany, would be at home here – no cars, no TVs, no telephones – and staff take service to new levels. *Ask about weddings.*

Price	€95–€428 (€1,250–€3,000 p.w.). B&B option also.
Rooms	13 houses for 2-11.
Meals	Breakfast €15. Restaurant 4km.
Closed	Rarely.
Directions	A61 exit for Auch on N2. From Astaffort right onto D266 after police station; D266 until Castelnau. After 1km left to Lagarde Fieumarcon, on 4.5km; on right after church; ring gong.

Frédéric Coustols
32700 Lagarde Fieumarcon, Gers

Tel	+33 (0)5 62 68 99 30
Email	office@lagarde.org
Web	www.gascony.org

Château de Projan

Fascinating, the story of how this eccentric traveller and painter restored an 18th-century château to house his art collection. Eclectic and convincing, the mix of antiques – mirrors, chests and armoires – with paintings, tapestries and sculpture from the pre-Raphaelite, Cubist and Art Deco periods; most special, the inlaid marble floor at the foot of the staircase. First-floor bedrooms have wide oak boards, tomette tiles and antique writing desks. One great room has a 15-metre ceiling with its original mouldings, others still have their timber frames. Most astonishing are the recent panelled bathrooms, doubtless built for a king's ransom to harmonise with the rooms: sparkling white china, modern taps, massive mirrors, huge showers. There are two dining terraces with views across to the Pyrenees, a hall-cum-piano room and fireplaces for chilly evenings. The kitchen opens to the ground-floor hall so you can watch Richard prepare his Gascon specialities for dinner. He is helping promote the excellent local wines, too. He and Christine are lovely hosts. Perfect for the jazz festival in Marciac.

Price	€130-€200.
Rooms	7: 6 doubles, 1 family room for 4.
Meals	Breakfast €13.50. Dinner €37-€57.
Closed	February; week before All Saints' Day; 21-28 December.
Directions	From Pau; exit 7 (Garlin). From Bordeaux; exit 8 (aire sur l'adour sud) D646 to Riscle, St Mont & Projan. Signed.

Christine & Richard Poullain
32400 Projan,
Gers

Tel	+33 (0)5 62 09 46 21
Email	infos@chateau-de-projan.com
Web	www.chateau-de-projan.com

Le Relais de Saux

Three to five hundred years old, high on a hill facing Lourdes and some dazzling Pyrenean peaks, the house still has a few unregenerate arrow slits, left over from sterner days. You come in through the multi-coloured garden that spreads across lawns and terraces with corners for reading or painting. Bernard Hères inherited Saux from his parents and, with the help of his late wife's flair and energy, opened it to guests. He knows the area thoroughly and can guide you to fine walks, climbs or visits. Return to deep armchairs in the dark old-beamed salon with its peaceful garden view (some traffic hum outside). Bedrooms with carpeted bathrooms are in the same traditional, elegant mood with draped bedheads and darkish plush or flock-papered walls. One has no fewer than four tall windows, another has an old fireplace, the two second-floor rooms are big yet cosy beneath their lower ceilings. Lourdes' torchlit Marian Procession — praying the rosary in all the languages — is a moving experience. But a word of warning: be careful on leaving the dual carriageway on your return.

Price	€96–€103.
Rooms	5: 3 doubles, 2 twins/doubles.
Meals	Restaurant 2km.
Closed	Occasionally.
Directions	Left 3km north of Lourdes. Signed but difficult to spot; 1st property 100m from main road.

Bernard Hères
Route de Tarbes, Le Hameau de Saux,
65100 Lourdes, Hautes-Pyrénées

Tel +33 (0)5 62 94 29 61
Email contacts@lourdes-relais.com
Web www.lourdes-relais.com

Languedoc – Roussillon

La Lozerette

In September 1878, Robert Louis Stevenson set off from Le Monastier, with Modestine the donkey, to walk the 220 kilometres to St Jean du Gard. Towards the end of his journey he stopped off at the Cévennes village of Cocurès, on the river Tarn, just above the National Park. Here, Pierrette runs the country inn started by her grandmother and passed on to her by her parents. Laid-back staff, warm and friendly, handle all comers to this busy hotel. Pierrette herself is hands-on, running the reception, taking orders in the (excellent) restaurant, managing the wine cellar: a trained sommelier, she will pick you out just the right bottle; her cheeseboard is to die for. Bedrooms, mostly a good size, colour coordinated but not twee, have wooden floors, oh-so-comfortable beds and stripey, checked or flowery décor. The small bar with its cheerful bucket chairs is charming, the gardens pretty, the balconies bright with flowers. The whole hotel shines. Take a drink into the garden or play boules, walk in the National Park, follow Stevenson's trail – on foot, donkey or horseback. Good value, one of the best.

Price	€63–€92. Half-board €62–€76 p.p.
Rooms	20: 12 twins/doubles; 8 family rooms for 4.
Meals	Breakfast €8.80. Lunch & dinner €17–€47. Children's meals €10.50. Restaurant closed Tues & Wed lunch out of season.
Closed	November to Easter.
Directions	From Florac, N106 for Mende; right on D998 for Le Pont de Montvert. After 4km hotel on left, signed.

Pierrette Agulhon
Cocurès, 48400 Florac, Lozère

Tel	+33 (0)4 66 45 06 04
Email	lalozerette@wanadoo.fr
Web	www.lalozerette.com

La Maison d'Ulysse

Behind high walls, off a small sleepy village square, is a 15th-century silk farm full of surprises. Spiritual, tranquil and with a wonderful Mediterranean garden that opens to the public once a year, it's a national treasure. Guy works in Paris during the week, Gauthier is here full time: he gardens, cooks like a dream and looks after guests with aplomb. Inside is as striking as can be. The bones of the suites are Provençal but the furniture is Danish and Italian, beds wear Indian bedspreads and Alpaca blankets, chic shower tiles are darkly iridescent, towels are black and fluffy, and there are few paintings: bold walls and modernist pieces are statements in themselves. Bedrooms range from big to vast, one with an open fire, one with a terrace, all with bathrooms in the rooms (wc's are separate). Wake to the prospect of breakfast in the shaded courtyard, or inside when the Mistral blows, the glass doors flung open. Jams (Gauthier's) and cheeses (local) change every day: the attention to detail is wonderful. Thrill to Uzès, Nîmes, the Pont du Gard, spin off on horseback or bike, return to a delicious decked pool.

Price	€110–€190. Suites €150–€240.
Rooms	5: 2 doubles, 3 suites.
Meals	Lunch €12–€16.
	Dinner, 3 courses, €35.
	Wine €19–€40. Restaurant 300m.
Closed	Rarely.
Directions	Sent on booking.

Guy & Gauthier Vandendriessche
Place Ulysse Dumas, Baron,
30700 Uzès, Gard

Tel	+33 (0)4 66 81 38 41
Mobile	+33 (0)6 48 77 67 70
Email	contact@lamaisondulysse.com
Web	www.lamaisondulysse.com

Domaine de Marsault

At the end of an avenue of fine plane trees is this most elegant family mansion, joyfully revived by Jean-Pierre Salle. Step into a stone-flagged hallway and a vast salon, awash with light from high windows overlooking the garden beyond. Red-check armchairs and a fire make this room a winter retreat; for summer there's an Empire 'salon d'été'. Two bedrooms sharing a big bathroom with a wonderful old bath are equally plush – one floral with a huge half-tester bed, the other with a draped four-poster – while the big boldly coloured suites have dressing rooms and marble fireplaces, gleaming armoires and pretty daybeds. Antoine serves a generous, delicious and languorous breakfast at round tables under parasols or at the big polished dining table. As for the garden, it's large, walled and wonderfully made of green swards, sweet roses and a graciously round saltwater pool with the cypress standing guard. The cherry on the cake? Lovely honey-stoned Uzès awaits at the end of a well-used track through the vines: in 20 minutes you are in *le centre ville*. *Wine tasting & Uzès tours. Minimum stay two nights.*

Price	€190. Suites €230.
Rooms	5: 2 doubles, 2 suites; 1 double sharing bathroom (let to same party only).
Meals	Restaurants 2km.
Closed	Mid-October to mid-March, except Truffle Fair in January.
Directions	A9 exit Rémoulins dir. Uzès; thro' Uzès dir. Alès; 1km, 1st right at r'bout onto Rue Landry; left after 400m; 200m, right at driveway with plane trees. Car park on left.

	Jean-Pierre Salle
	30700 Uzès, Gard
Tel	+33 (0)4 66 22 53 92
Email	info@domainedemarsault.com
Web	www.domainedemarsault.com

Château Saint Victor

This frightfully grand-looking 1880s building, all towered and pillared and Escher-like stone-staired, is actually most friendly and welcoming on the inside. Run as a proper family business, it has a smaller, cosier feel than you might imagine, with the two brothers and Stéphane's wife taking great care of you in hotel and kitchen. A salon with lovely antiques and paintings has space for mingling extroverts as well as corners for quiet chats; the dining area has an arched ceiling, an open fire and big wicker chairs in which to linger. Bedrooms on the first floor are château-grand, with upholstered chairs, views over the park and generous bathrooms, some tower-shaped with bidets like thrones; the rooms above are simpler and more contemporary, with rope carpeting, lighter colours and excellent bedding. Fresh, generous food is beautifully prepared and presented; afterwards you can wander through doors to the garden with its old palm trees and parasols, sloping lawns and silent lily pond. Children will adore the space to run around and you're near Uzès with its stunning market – and Roman Orange.

Price	€90-€150. Suites €180-€240.
Rooms	17: 7 doubles, 4 twins, 6 suites.
Meals	Breakfast €18. Lunch €25. Dinner €39-€45. Wine €20-€40. Restaurant closed Sun evening.
Closed	October to March (except weekends).
Directions	From Uzès D982 to Bagnol sur Cèze for 6km; right on D125 to Saint Victor des Oules. Signed.

Stéphane & Renaud Vieljeux
Place du Château,
30700 Saint Victor des Oules, Gard
Tel   +33 (0)4 66 81 90 47
Email   info@villasaintvictor.com
Web   www.villasaintvictor.com

Domaine du Moulin

Looking for the little luxuries of a good hotel and the personality of a B&B? Come to Antoinette's 12th-century mill. She and Otto, both Dutch and multi-lingual, have respected its age and style, reviving old parquet floors and doors, polishing the wooden stair to glow. Big modern flower paintings and a Belgian tapestry look good on the walls. The river Nizon flows beneath the house and through the many hectares of grounds – a frog-sung mill pond flanked by cherry trees (spectacular in spring), an alley of poplars, a lavender field, a pool. And swings and slides for the grandchildren, which yours may share. Breakfast is a Dutch feast of hams, cheeses and cherry jams, served at the big table under the tented pergola or in the all-white dining room with chandelier. Antoinette is lovely and fills the place with flowers. Bedrooms, named after her daughters, have piles of pillows and fine English florals; all are air conditioned, one has a sun terrace of its own. Bathrooms are swish with big showers or two basins. There's a fine, quiet library full of books, and you and the chef choose the menu for dinner.

Price	€80–€185. Apartment €1,200–€2,200 per week.
Rooms	4 + 1: 4 twins/doubles. Apartment for 7.
Meals	Breakfast €15. Dinner by arrangement. Restaurants nearby.
Closed	Rarely.
Directions	A9 exit 22, Roquemaure for Bagnols sur Cèze. After 4km continue past left turn for St Laurent des Arbres. Left at Rubis, follow road.

Antoinette Keulen &
Otto Van Eikema Hommes
Chemin de la Bégude,
30126 Saint Laurent des Arbres, Gard
Tel   +33 (0)4 66 50 22 67
Email   laurentdesarbres@aol.com
Web   www.domaine-du-moulin.com

Entry 298   Map 16

L'Enclos des Lauriers Roses

The tiny reception gives no clue as to what lies beyond; a hamlet within a village. Step across a sunny dining room, through French windows – and blink. Scattered around three swimming pools is a cluster of cottage rooms. Newly built of pantile and stone recovered from old village houses, most have a private terrace or garden. Large, airy and prettily furnished with painted Provençal pieces and fabulous mattresses, each has a different charm – Mimosa has a finely upholstered yellow bed, Amarilys has big chunky terracotta tiles. Walls are white, ceilings neatly beamed, there might be a bed tucked under a stone arch or extra beds for children on the mezzanine. Bathrooms are modern and marbled and a fridge keeps drinks chilled. Madame Bargeton runs the excellent restaurant, Monsieur does the wine – 500 bottles in the cellar – and their sons take care of the buildings and garden. Eat on the terrace or in the dining room; the locals love the cooking, too. Nîmes, Avignon and beaches are less than an hour, swim in the Gorges du Gardon, walk among the pines. As for the village, it's charming.

Price	€80–€120. Triples €105–€130. Family rooms €120–€190. Half-board €140–€200 for 2.
Rooms	23: 11 twins/doubles, 2 triples, 10 family rooms.
Meals	Breakfast €15. Lunch & dinner €24–€45.
Closed	10 November to 10 March.
Directions	A9 exit 24 for N86 to Remoulins. After 3.5km left to St Gervasy for Cabrières. In village centre, signed.

Bargeton Family
71 rue du 14 Juillet,
30210 Cabrières, Gard

Tel	+33 (0)4 66 75 25 42
Email	reception@hotel-lauriersroses.com
Web	www.hotel-lauriersroses.co.uk

Domaine des Clos

When Sandrine and David returned to their Beaucaire roots, they found a worthy vessel for their creativity in an 18th-century wine domaine. All has been authentically and lovingly restored. Every room has a view to the vineyards or the central courtyard lawn, the pool is large and the family – with three children – truly charming. The beautifully designed interiors reveal lots of old beams, vibrant splashes of colour in curtains, bedspreads and tapestries and artefacts galore, many collected during the Aussets' Tunisian travels. Outside are exquisite Italianate gardens and the best of Provence... from among the olive trees, jasmine and bougainvillea, shady stone pergolas and relaxing sitting spots emerge. Consider an aperitif or, in summer, a meal on the terrace of the old écurie; in winter, keep warm by the fireplace in the communal salon, delightful with its deep fuchsia walls and ceilings hung with handcrafted fixtures. It is hugely original, wonderfully artistic, and the information booklet includes enough markets to keep the picnic bags brimming. Be as active or as idle as you like.

Price	€95-€175. Apartments €550-€1,800 per week.
Rooms	8 + 5: 5 doubles, 3 family rooms for 4. 5 apartments for 2-5.
Meals	Dinner with wine, €28, twice weekly in summer; book ahead. Restaurant 6km.
Closed	January.
Directions	Exit A9 at Remoulins to Beaucaire. On entering Beaucaire 2nd exit at large r'bout, then D38 to St Gilles for 6km. Domaine on left.

Sandrine & David Ausset
911 chemin du Mas de la Tour,
30300 Beaucaire, Gard

Tel	+33 (0)4 66 01 14 61
Mobile	+33 (0)6 22 30 79 50
Email	contact@domaine-des-clos.com
Web	www.domaine-des-clos.com

L'Auberge du Cèdre

No wonder guests return to this big, bustling, ethically-run house. Lively, charming Françoise and her multi-lingual husband Lutz welcome walkers, climbers, cyclists and families. There's a special space for workshop groups, too, separate from the big comfy sitting room. Bedrooms are plain, beamy, white, with the odd splash of ethnic colour and terracotta floors that gleam. Beds, beautifully designed by Lutz and made by local craftsmen, are all twins/doubles. Only a few bathrooms are now shared but the wonderful atmosphere of good humour and laughter has not been affected by the improvements and this is still not a place for luxury-seekers. Art exhibitions are constant, everywhere something beautiful catches the eye. Meals of local and organic produce are chosen from a blackboard menu. It's perfect for families: a swimming pool, space to run around in, boules under the chestnut trees before you turn in for the night. The auberge sits in the middle of the Pic Saint Loup vineyard, one of the best in the Languedoc and Lutz's excellent wine cellar is another reason to prolong your stay.

Price	€58–€144. Half-board €86–€172. Apartment €790–€1,290 per week.
Rooms	19 + 1: 7 twins/doubles, 4 suites; 5 twins/doubles, 2 triples, 1 quad, all sharing 5 shower rooms and 4 wcs. 1 apt for 6.
Meals	Breakfast included. Light lunch €12. À la carte €28–€41(weekends). Wine €9–€88.
Closed	Mid-November to mid-March.
Directions	D17 from Montpellier for Quissac. 6km north of St Mathieu de Tréviers, left to Lauret, 1km. Thro' village; signed.

Françoise Antonin & Lutz Engelmann
Domaine de Cazeneuve,
34270 Lauret, Hérault

Tel	+33 (0)4 67 59 02 02
Email	welcome@auberge-du-cedre.com
Web	www.auberge-du-cedre.com

Hôtel de Baudon de Mauny

A 'château in the city', this classical 18th-century building — majestic stuccoed ceilings, stone floors, vast windows — has been quite dramatically furnished with contemporary dashes of furniture, lighting and wallpapers alongside elegant silken drapes and the occasional ancestor in oils. Some bedrooms have private salons and super new shower rooms, each is a separate poem in style. A refined continental breakfast is served in the enormous light-filled sitting-dining room and the generous hall has more chairs and tables. The young family, whose passion for this house has informed the quiet, pure sophistication of the décor, live on the top floor. It is Alain's family home and his naturally courteous reserve is reflected in the sobriety of line and light and the attention to detail. You will be looked after beautifully, and do take his advice on where to eat, he really knows. Outside the door is grand old Montpellier with its exciting young energy: dance and music festivals, sleek designer trams, a car-free historic centre, a rich collection of art in the newly-restored Musée Fabre. *Minimum stay two nights.*

Price	€165–€275.
Rooms	5: 1 double, 4 suites.
Meals	Breakfast €15. Restaurants nearby.
Closed	Rarely.
Directions	From north A9, exit Montpellier Centre; follow signs for Le Corum (park here). Hotel 200m walk: right out car park, left up Rue Montpellieret, right Rue de l'Aiguillerie, right, 1st left.

Alain de Bordas
1 rue de la Carbonnerie,
34000 Montpellier, Hérault

Tel	+33 (0)4 67 02 21 77
Email	contact@baudondemauny.com
Web	www.baudondemauny.com

15 Grand Rue

Imagine a shade-dappled, flower-scented secret garden and an elegant 1880s residence in the heart of an old Languedoc market town ringed by vineyards. The house has been updated by your hospitable English hosts with the utmost sensitivity. French antiques, paintings and oriental rugs glow to a backdrop of high moulded ceilings, marble fireplaces and dove-grey panelled walls. A stone staircase spirals up to two generous suites, each with an antique bed dressed in hand-embroidered sheets and silk blankets, balconied views over higgledy rooftops and a separate sitting area; a third ground-floor bedroom, once the library, opens to the garden. Breakfast on warm croissants and Abigail's daily 'special' among the palms, acacias, banksia roses and jasmine – gorgeous – or settle under the salon's gilded ceiling. Medieval Caux's narrow tangled streets hide bars, bakeries and wine caves while livelier Pézenas has the restaurants – as well as many shopping delights. Explore Montpellier, roam the Haut Languedoc's mountainous playground or take your beach basket to the golden coast, a 25-minute drive.

Price	€125–€150. Whole house available.
Rooms	5: 3 suites, 2 doubles/twin.
Meals	Restaurants 4-8km. Chef available when whole house rented.
Closed	Mid-December to February.
Directions	A75 exit 60 to Pézenas; D13 dir. Roujan then right to Caux; house on Grand Rue in centre of Caux opp. la Mairie.

Abigail Turner
Caux,
34720 Pézenas, Hérault

Tel	+33 (0)4 67 37 50 61
Email	info@15grandrue.com
Web	www.15grandrue.com

Le Clos de Maussanne

Surrounded by vineyards just off the road, the unusual 17th-century house with the clock tower is smaller inside than it looks. Just one room deep, it is nonetheless elegant – and furnished with panache. The lovely salon, the heart of the place, looks onto noble old plane trees and a beautiful walled garden; there's a covered terrace full of tables and a super restaurant kitchen downstairs: their reputation for good food (Bruno's domain) is spreading far and wide, with no menu and each night a surprise. They do cookery classes, too. Irwin and his staff are delightful. The bedrooms, which overlook the garden, are gorgeous with their sober cream walls, chunky modern furniture, big beds, quilted spreads. The largest room has limewashed timbers to the roof and a pale floor that sweeps out to the terrace. The ground-floor room has the necessary window bars but, looking inward, is the most beautifully done space. The final flourish? Élisabeth Baysset's atmospheric paintings. Visit the lovely pedestrianised old quarter of Pézenas and return to a plant-fringed pool. And the motorway so convenient.

Price	€120–€150.
Rooms	5 doubles.
Meals	Breakfast included. Dinner from €28. Wine €17–€115.
Closed	Rarely.
Directions	A9 exit 35 dir. Béziers. 1st r'bout, 2nd exit dir. Pézenas; 2nd r'bout, 1st exit dir. Pézenas. 2km on right.

Bruno Saurel & Irwin Scott-Davidson
Route de Pézenas,
34500 Béziers, Hérault
Tel   +33 (0)4 67 39 31 81
Email contact@leclosdemaussanne.com
Web   www.leclosdemaussanne.com

Petit Hôtel

Imagine southern light, a timeless French fishing port and a soft yellow townhouse whose cool hall opens to a peaceful walled garden and a private pool. Le Petit Hôtel is gloriously discreet. Its ancient stone stairs spiral up to big restful rooms while living spaces are contemporary open-plan, their polished plaster walls punctuated by bright artwork. Birgit has enhanced the enticing sense of seclusion, ensuring each cool, uncluttered, refreshing room has its own balcony or terrace overlooking garden or street, choice piece of art and walk-in shower. Neighbouring trees and the distant glimmering sea frame a terrace and garden with climbing jasmine, thoughtfully placed furniture and several shady spots, perfect for lazy reading or sipping the local Noilly Prat (visit the cellars nearby). Alternatively, explore art galleries, markets and vibrant Montpellier; windsurf; kayak down the Hérault river; sup on fresh oysters then stroll home to rooftop views and a night-lit pool. The welcoming, interesting Zuckers have had a complete lifestyle change and are enjoying their new life immensely.

Price	€130–€195.
Rooms	5: 2 doubles, 3 twins/doubles.
Meals	Breakfast included.
	Restaurants 5-minute walk.
Closed	Rarely.
Directions	Sent on booking.

Birgit Zucker
5 boulevard Lamartine,
34340 Marseillan, Hérault

Mobile	+33 (0)6 85 88 95 63
Email	contact@petithotel-marseillan.com
Web	www.petithotel-marseillan.com

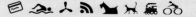

La Chamberte

The engaging new owners are revelling in living with their two sons in this old wine store, fabulously converted by their predecessors. Communal spaces are huge, ceilings high, colours Mediterranean and floors of pigmented polished cement. Refreshingly simple bedrooms have no telly, big beds (some with a step up), beautiful quilts and warm colours; shower rooms are in ochres and muted pinks, some with pebbles set in cement; thick walls keep you cool in high summer. Vivian was born into a local family of chefs and he and Caroline ran a well-known restaurant for years, buying fresh from the markets, specialising in fish and pastries. In summer you dine on the inner patio, a glorious plant-filled space that reaches up to the original barn roof, stunning at night by candlelight; in winter you are treated to a dining room with an open fire and stylishly vibrant little tables: one menu, four courses, each delicious. Villeneuve is a pretty little town surrounded by vineyards, crossed by the Canal du Midi. Historic old Béziers is just five minutes away. Wonderful beaches beckon. *Cash only.*

Price	€72–€98.
	Half-board €960 for 2 per week.
Rooms	5: 3 doubles; 1 twin/double, 1 triple.
Meals	Dinner €25.
	Restaurant 5-minute drive.
Closed	Rarely.
Directions	A9 exit 35 Béziers Est for Villeneuve lès Béziers; over canal to town centre; 2nd left after Hotel Cigale; green gate on right.

Caroline & Vivian Kaesbach
10 rue de la Source,
34420 Villeneuve lès Béziers, Hérault
Tel +33 (0)4 67 39 84 83
Email contact@lachamberte.com
Web www.lachamberte.com

Château de la Prade

Lost among the cool shadows of tall sunlit trees, beside the languid waters of the Canal du Midi, is a place of quiet elegance and refinement – and so much space. Sitting in 12 acres, the fine old building is more country house than château, though the vineyards have long gone and formal hedges, ornamental railings and impressive gates link house to grounds. Swiss Roland runs the house, George looks after the gardens: generous, kind-hearted, discreetly attentive, they are wonderful hosts. Served on beautifully dressed tables in a light, airy room with a crystal chandelier, dinner is a mix of Swiss, French and Italian cuisine, and breakfast a delicious treat (croissants with George's homemade preserves, exquisitely prepared fruit salads). Superb bedrooms have tall windows, polished floors and uncluttered taste; be charmed by traditional armchairs and footstools, huge beds and fresh flowers, white bathrooms with towels to match. You are a half mile from the main road to Carcassonne and yet there's a feeling of rare calm here – interrupted only by the peacocks calling from the balustrades, most vocal in late spring!

Price	€95–€115.
Rooms	4 twins/doubles.
Meals	Dinner €26. Wine €17.50–€23.
Closed	Mid-November to mid-March.
Directions	From A61 exit 22; thro' Bram 2.5km; left D6113 for Villepinte; house signed on left.

Roland Kurt
11150 Bram, Aude
Tel   +33 (0)4 68 78 03 99
Email   chateaulaprade@wanadoo.fr
Web   www.chateaulaprade.eu

Château de Cavanac

A peaceful place where birdsong serenades you. The château, dated 1612 and full of twists, turns and crannies, has been in the family for six generations. Quiet and friendly, it has much comfort and an easy feel. Louis runs a small vineyard, too, so you can drink of the vines that surround you. It's a convivial place with a big rustic restaurant in the old stables — hops hanging from ancient beams and an open fire where they cook the grills; in summer you dine under the stars. Aided by their son, Louis and Anne are justly proud of their food, and breakfasts are delicious. The older bedrooms, with oriental rugs on terracotta tiles, are somewhat dated but the most recently renovated are positively delightful: dramatic canopies, pretty, colourful fabrics, parquet floors, a colonial feel. (Note that some rooms are reached via the breakfast room, unlit after hours.) There's a super pool area and a very pretty sunny terrace dotted with sun-loungers. Beyond the smart wrought-iron gates, the Languedoc waits to beguile you: horses to ride, cellars to visit, Viollet-le-Duc's Carcassonne close by.

Price	€85–€120. Singles €65–€95. Suites €150–€155. Triples €160.
Rooms	28: 19 doubles, 2 singles, 4 suites, 3 triples.
Meals	Breakfast €12. Dinner with wine from €42 (except Mondays). Restaurants 3km.
Closed	January to February; 2 weeks in November.
Directions	From Toulouse, exit Carcassonne Ouest for Centre Hospitalier, then Route de St Hilaire. Signed. Park in restaurant car park.

	Anne & Louis Gobin 11570 Cavanac, Aude
Tel	+33 (0)4 68 79 61 04
Email	infos@chateau-de-cavanac.fr
Web	www.chateau-de-cavanac.fr

Montfaucon

A gracious spot for peace and quiet by the river Aude (strolling couples, quacking ducks) yet a short walk from lovely, lively Limoux – a pull for musicians and artists. Enter the huge beautiful doors to this ancient house, parts of which go back to 1324, to discover a fabulous conversion. Delightful staff welcome you in, to a stylish entrance lobby with stone walls, marble floors and a staircase in turned wood that takes you up three floors. The dining room has beautiful beams, wrought-iron wall lights and huge French windows through which light floods; the terrace, romantically lit at night, overlooks river and town. Cycle to historic villages through rolling vineyards and fields of sunflowers, return to leisurely lunches and candlelit dinners. The atmosphere is one of relaxed indulgence, where individually designed bedrooms in 19th-century style have floral or striped bedcovers and curtains and the best come with a river view. Sleep deeply in a vast bed with monogrammed sheets; wake to gleaming marble, Persian rugs and walk-in showers. An absolute treat. *Minimum stay two nights.*

Price	€185–€235.
Rooms	5: 2 doubles, 2 twins, 1 suite for 2.
Meals	Restaurants 5-minute walk.
Closed	24 December to 5 January.
Directions	Sent on booking.

	Joanne Payan
	11 rue Blanquerie,
	11300 Limoux, Aude
Tel	+33 (0)4 68 69 48 40
Email	joanne@montfaucontours.com
Web	www.montfaucontours.com

Château des Ducs de Joyeuse

The drive up is impressive, the castle even more so: 1500s and fortified, part Gothic, part Renaissance, standing in its own patch of land on the banks of the Aude. A large rectangular courtyard is jolly with summer tables and parasols, the stately dining room has snowy linen cloths and fresh flowers, the staff are truly charming and helpful, and the menu changes daily according to what is fresh. Vaulted ceilings and well-trodden stone spiral stairs lead to formal bedrooms with heavy wooden furniture, some beamed and with stone fireplaces; there's a heraldic feel with narrow high windows, studded doors and smart bedspreads in navy blue and bright red. Ask for a room with a watery view. Bathrooms glow with tiled floors, bright lights and stone walls – some up to two metres thick: perfect sound insulation. Historical information about the building is on display everywhere, manager Philippe is full of ideas and can help you plan your trips out. Hearty souls can knock a ball around the tennis court then cool off in the outdoor pool – or brave that lovely river. Good value.

Price	€95–€135.
	Suites & family rooms €155–€235.
Rooms	35: 10 doubles, 11 twins, 12 suites for 2,
	2 family rooms for 4–5.
Meals	Breakfast €14. Dinner €29–€54.
	Wine €15–€45.
Closed	Mid-November to mid-March.
Directions	A61 exit 23 Carcassonne Ouest.
	D118, left D52.

Dominique & Alain Avelange
Allée du Château,
11190 Couiza, Aude

Tel	+33 (0)4 68 74 23 50
Email	reception@chateau-des-ducs.com
Web	www.chateau-des-ducs.com

La Fargo

Pluck a handful of cherries on the way to breakfast; gather up the scents of rosemary and thyme. This centuries-old converted forge sits effortlessly in the unspoilt Corbières countryside. Christophe and Dominique, a gentle, delightful couple, lived the good life rearing goats before rescuing the building years ago. Large, light bedrooms have a charming and simple colonial style – white or stone walls, tiled floors, dark teak, bright ikat bedcovers – and the new block (six huge rooms and a sitting room) is a credit to the craftsmen. Bathrooms are mosaic'd, showers are like rainstorms. Breakfast – just homemade jams and brioches – is on the terrace beneath the kiwi fruit vines. Dine here or in the restaurant where clean modern lines blend with rustic stonework and food is a fabulous mix of Mediterranean and Asian. Corbières is a natural de-stresser: come for birdwatching, walking, fishing, vineyards, Cathar castles, medieval abbeys. Or wander around La Fargo's potager and orchard, pluck some fruit and lie back in one of dozens of wooden loungers. A serene place – and the infinity pool is a dream.

Price	€90–€140. Family rooms €150–€187. Extra bed €20.
Rooms	12: 8 doubles, 2 twins, 2 family rooms for 2-4.
Meals	Breakfast €10. Lunch & dinner €30–€50. Wine €15–€35.
Closed	15 November to 15 March.
Directions	A61 exit Lézignan-Corbières, D611 to Fabrezan; D212 to Lagrasse, then St Pierre des Champs. Fargo on right on leaving village.

Christophe & Dominique Morellet
11220 Saint Pierre des Champs, Aude

Tel	+33 (0)4 68 43 12 78
Email	contact@lafargo.fr
Web	www.lafargo.fr

Le Mas Trilles

Marie-France and Laszlo have renovated their rambling, honey-coloured 17th-century farmhouse well, with some old-fashioned touches, and their personal welcome makes it feel more like home than hotel. First to greet you are the sounds of birdsong and rushing water, then, perhaps the head-spinning scent of orange or cherry blossom from the lovely scented garden. There are two comfortable sitting rooms, one with its original beams, both with cool terracotta tiles and places to read and relax; some of Marie-France's paintings hang here. Many bedrooms, larger in the main house, are reached by unexpected ups and downs; all have shower-in-bath systems. There are some fine antiques, a few little terraces, and woods and mountains beyond. The largest room has magnificent views of the Canigou mountain, the spiritual home of the Catalan nation (cheaper rooms are quite small). Breakfast on the sweet terrace with homemade fig or apricot jam or in front of a crackling fire on chilly days. Down by the river there are fine views of the mountains and an intoxicating feeling of space.

Price	€95–€156.
	Triples & suites €175–€219.
Rooms	10: 3 doubles, 5 triples, 2 suites.
Meals	Breakfast €13. Light meals €15, on request. Restaurant 200m.
Closed	Early October to late April.
Directions	Exit 43 for Boulou, D115 for Céret but do not enter town. House 2km after Céret towards Amélie les Bains.

Marie-France & Laszlo Bukk
Le Pont de Reynès,
66400 Céret, Pyrénées-Orientales
Tel   +33 (0)4 68 87 38 37
Email   mastrilles@free.fr
Web   www.le-mas-trilles.com

Relais des Chartreuses

Up in the wooded hills above Le Boulou is a French farmhouse hotel with a young modern interior and astonishingly good food. Every evening is a culinary adventure so prepare yourself for a seasonal chalked-up set menu and a beautiful list of Languedoc-Roussillon wines. You enter via a pretty terraced garden, one of several: you can chase the sun (or the shade) all day. Friendly staff usher you up and down steps to calm, restful and chic bedrooms – each one creatively inspired, each different from the last. Prices reflect – fairly – the differences in size, so the priciest is Le Pigeonnier, a secluded suite with the luxuries of air con and a private terrace. Splashes of colour lift greys, taupes and whites, reclaimed materials and quirky artefacts abound, and some bathrooms have his and her showers. It's a brilliant place for forays to Spain and the south coast; dreamy Collioure, beloved of Matisse, is 20 minutes away, Céret, Picasso's favourite, is even closer – seek out the Musée d'Art Moderne and the Saturday market. Return to a stylish lounger, slip into a cool pool.

Price	€65–€235. Suite €196–€240.
Rooms	14: 9 doubles, 3 twins/doubles, 1 family room for 4–5. Pigeonnier: 1 suite.
Meals	Dinner, 3 courses, €35. Wine €16–€76. Restaurant 5km.
Closed	Rarely.
Directions	Sent on booking.

Anne Besset Lissorgue
106 avenue d'en Carbonner,
66160 Le Boulou, Pyrénées-Orientales

Tel	+33 (0)4 68 83 15 88
Email	relaisdeschartreuses@gmail.com
Web	www.relais-des-chartreuses.fr

Rhône Valley – Alps

Le Clos du Châtelet

Washed in barely-there pink, with soft blue shutters, the house was built as a country retreat towards the end of the 18th century by a silk merchant who loved trees. Overlooking the valley of the Saône, with immaculate sweeping lawns, the garden is full of sequoias, cedars, chestnuts and magnolias. To one side of the house, an open outbuilding, home to a collection of antique bird cages, is smothered in flowers. Bedrooms are peaceful havens of elegantly muted colours: 'Joubert' in pink-ochre, its twin wrought-iron four-posters dressed in toile de Jouy; 'Lamartine' in palest aqua with grey and lilac hangings. All have polished wooden floors and gently sober bathrooms. There's much comfort here: an open fire in the sitting room, period furniture, prints, deer antlers on the wall and an delicious air of calm. A harp stands in the corner of the elegant drawing room — we are not sure if it is played but this is the sort of place where it might be. Dinner is by candlelight in an atmospheric dining room with an old terracotta floor and a fountain in the wall. Conveniently close to Bourgogne. *No credit cards.*

Price	€98–€115.
Rooms	4: 3 doubles; 1 double with separate bath.
Meals	Dinner €32. Wine €20–€35.
Closed	Rarely.
Directions	A6 exit Tournus for Bourg en Bresse, then to Cuisery. Right at Cuisery for Sermoyer & Pont de Vaux. In Sermoyer follow chambres d'hôtes signs.

Madame Durand-Pont
01190 Sermoyer,
Ain

Tel	+33 (0)3 85 51 84 37
Email	leclosduchatelet@free.fr
Web	www.leclosduchatelet.com

Hôtel Le Cottage Bise

Not many hotels are blessed with such an eye-capturing lakeside position; gazing from the terrace at the sun setting over the Roc de Chère, you could be in a Wagner opera. The three buildings that make up this friendly, supremely well-run hotel resemble – quelle surprise! – Alpine chalets; what's more, they are set in well-planted gardens with a classy pool and perfectly gravelled pathways. Jean-Claude and Christine run their relaxed and not-so-small hotel with quiet Savoyard efficiency which, at its heart, has a proper concern for your comfort. Rooms, each one different, come in two styles: traditional, with floral papers and antique paintings, or contemporary with paler walls and modern art; all are big with excellent bathrooms; the balconied suites are splendid, with views to lake and mountains. The food, in the restaurant or on the wonderful lake-view terrace, is first class, though half-boarders have less choice. You are away from the bustle of Annecy but close enough to dabble if you wish: the old town is a delight. Sail, windsurf, waterski, pedalo – the lake laps at your feet. *Ask about wellness centre.*

Price	€100–€250.
	Suites €300–€450.
Rooms	31: 25 twins/doubles, 6 suites for 2-4.
Meals	Breakfast €18. Lunch €27–€60.
	Dinner €48–€75. Wine €25–€70.
	Restaurants within walking distance.
Closed	10 October to April.
Directions	In Annecy dir. Bord du Lac for Thônes D909. At Veyrier du Lac, D909A to Talloires. Signed in Talloires.

Jean-Claude & Christine Bise
Au Bord du Lac, 74290 Talloires,
Haute-Savoie

Tel	+33 (0)4 50 60 71 10
Email	cottagebise@wanadoo.fr
Web	www.cottagebise.com

Auberge Le Chalet des Troncs

Some people get everything right, without making a lot of noise about it, and Christine bends over backwards for her guests. The old chalet and its outbuildings, built around 1780, have been skilfully renovated in rustic style with contemporary design. In the two wood-lined sitting rooms, an old sledge has become a coffee table with a nice scatter of antiques and bric-a-brac around; the design of the handsome sofas in front of the big fire is original; so are the open timber bedroom dividers: bathrooms grow seamlessly out of the wooden frame; cleverly fashioned lamps, made of branches, keep the light subdued. Christine is busy in the potager or gathering the wild herbs she uses in her excellent cooking: her famous pot-au-feu is prepared over the open fire. The indoor pool feels outside with its huge picture window onto the mountain and the new infinity hot tub is sheer sybaritic delight. Cross-country ski from the door or catch a free bus 800 metres away for the Grand Bornand. Perfectly quiet, with a lovely rambling garden – grass, shrubs, moss, wild flowers – this place is hard to fault.

Price	€160–€458.
Rooms	5: 3 twins, 1 suite, 1 family room for 3.
Meals	Breakfast €15. Picnic lunch €10–€20. Dinner from €40.
Closed	Rarely.
Directions	At church in La Grand Bornand, straight on 5km dir. Vallée du Bouchet. In Les Plans, right at little chapel for Les Troncs.

Christine Heckler-Charbonnier
Les Troncs, Vallée du Bouchet,
74450 Le Grand Bornand,
Haute-Savoie

Tel   +33 (0)4 50 02 28 50
Email   contact@chaletdestroncs.com
Web   www.chaletdestroncs.com

Au Coin du Feu-Chilly Powder

The homeward piste takes you to the door; the cable car, opposite, sweeps you to the peaks. The chalet is named after its magnificent central fireplace... on one side gleaming leather sofas, on the other, red dining chairs at a long table. Everything feels generous here: great beams span the chalet's length, windows look up to the cliffs of the Hauts Forts, high ceilings give a sense of space. There's a reading room on the mezzanine above the living area with books, internet, antique globe and worn leather armchairs, and a small bar made of English oak by a carpenter friend. Bedrooms are Alpine-swish and themed: there's the Toy Room for families, the English Room that sports a bowler hat. The carpets are sisal, one room's four-poster is veiled in muslin and the bathrooms have luxury bathrobes and shower heads as big as plates. The chef produces the best of country cooking, and Paul and Francesca can organise everything, including torchlight descents. There's massage, a sauna, a hot tub outside, DVDs to cheer wet days – even an in-house crèche. A great spot for families. *New four-bedroom chalet next door.*

Price	€90. Family rooms €120. Family suite €140. Half-board mandatory in winter (€765-€1,295 p.p. per week).
Rooms	17: 9 twins/doubles, 7 family rooms, 1 family suite.
Meals	Picnic lunch €10. Dinner with wine, €45.
Closed	Rarely.
Directions	From Morzine, signs to Avoriaz, then Les Prodains; 2.8 km. On right, just before cable car.

Paul & Francesca Eyre
2740 rue des Ardoisières,
74110 Morzine, Haute-Savoie

Tel	+33 (0)4 50 74 75 21
Email	paul@chillypowder.com
Web	www.chillypowder.com

Ethical Collection: Community.
See page 429 for details

The Farmhouse

The day starts with a breakfast spread in the cattle shed – now a deeply atmospheric dining room – and ends with a slap-up dinner hosted by Dorrien. Many years ago he gave up England for the oldest farmhouse in Morzine – the lovely, steeply pitched Mas de la Coutettaz at the peaceful end of town. Push open the mellow carved door to find a 1771 interior of dark chunky beams, huge Morzine slate flags and patina'd pine doors with original mouldings. Big, characterful, comfortable bedrooms, whose bathrooms promise white robes and lavish lotions, are reached via a central stone stair; some have mountain views. At the end of the garden is an exquisite little mazot, its bedroom up a steep outside stair. Morzine is the perfect staging post for the Avoriaz and Portes du Soleil, so come for hiking, biking, swimming in the lakes; in winter, a 'ski host' at the farmhouse introduces you to the runs, and dinners are lively. Return to a hot toddy in the bar and a crackling log fire, lit at the merest hint of chill, even in summer. Final proof (as if you needed it) that you will adore The Farmhouse and long to return.

Price	€90–€260. Singles €45–€140. Triples €216–€312. Half-board €125–€221 p.p.
Rooms	11: 4 doubles, 3 twins/doubles, 1 suite for 6, 3 triples.
Meals	Dinner, 4 courses with wine, €30–€40. Half-board mandatory Dec-April, on weekly basis.
Closed	May; October to November.
Directions	From Morzine for Avoriaz. On Ave Joux Plan, left after Nicholas Sport, then right. 200m on left, signed.

Dorrien Ricardo
Le Mas de la Coutettaz,
74110 Morzine, Haute-Savoie

Tel	+33 (0)4 50 79 08 26
Mobile	+33 (0)6 80 91 63 21
Email	info@thefarmhouse.co.uk
Web	www.thefarmhouse.co.uk

Chalet Odysseus

Chalet Odysseus has the comfort of soft sofas, bright rugs and an open fire, the hi-techness of satellite, sauna and small gym, and English hosts who spoil you rotten. Meet the dogs: they also breed, train and show border collie sheepdogs; one is even a television star. Kate and Barry lived in the village for 17 years, then built this beautifully solid chalet. They are on the ground floor, you live above, and it's the sort of place where you'd be happy in all weathers. Cheerfully simple, pretty bedrooms come with the requisite pine garb, beds are covered in quilts hand-made by Kate, two rooms have balconies that catch the sun, and the tiniest comes with bunk beds for kids. The shower rooms and bathroom are airy and light. As for Les Carroz, most skiers pass it by on their way to high-rise Flaine – a shame, for the village has heaps of character and several fine places to eat. Your own 4x4 gets you to the lifts in minutes, tying you in with the whole of the Grand Massif. Kate's dinners are four-course and there's a *grole* night to boot. Great for a family break, whatever the season.

Price	€90. Half-board €100 p.p.
Rooms	5: 3 doubles, 2 twins.
Meals	Dinner with wine, €40.
Closed	Rarely.
Directions	From A40 exit 19 to Cluses; N205 for Sallanches; left D106. 2km before Les Carroz at red & white-shuttered chalet on left; signed.

Kate & Barry Joyce
210 route de Lachat,
74300 Les Carroz d'Araches,
Haute-Savoie
Tel +33 (0)4 50 90 66 00
Email chaletodysseus@wanadoo.fr
Web www.chaletodysseuslachat.com

Hôtel Slalom

Right by the Olympic Kandahar run, and opposite the start of the famous Tour du Mont Blanc, is a sparkling hotel. It reopened in 2006 under the inspired stewardship of Tracey Spraggs, whose dream it had been to have a place of her own. Plain on the outside, it is super-stylish within, designer modern but with personality. Bedrooms have fresh white walls, cream carpets and space; curtain-free windows pull in beautiful views. There's a swish little bar, all chrome and polished leather, heaps of restaurants outside the door and a bus a two-minute walk. Best of all, you're 30 metres from the cable car and can ski back to the door. Although this area offers the best tree skiing in the region, the little town of Les Houches – ten minutes from touristy Chamonix – is charming all year round. Take a picnic to the pine-fringed Lac des Chavants and a step back in time on the Mont Blanc Tramway (it opened in 1904 and is still going strong). Sporty types can climb, trek, mountain bike, paraglide, play tennis, have a round of golf and there are good spas nearby, too. Warm, stylish, friendly. *Transfers can be arranged.*

Price	€86–€178.
Rooms	10 twins/doubles.
Meals	Breakfast €10. Restaurants nearby.
Closed	May & November.
Directions	From Geneva A401 to Chamonix. N205 & E25 exit Les Houches, right on D213, right on Rue de Bellevue.

Tracey Spraggs
44 rue de Bellevue,
74310 Les Houches, Haute-Savoie

Tel	+33 (0)4 50 54 40 60
Mobile	+33 (0)6 22 68 20 80
Email	info@hotelslalom.net
Web	www.hotelslalom.net

Château de la Commanderie

Grand it appears, and some of the makers of that grandeur – Knights Templar, princes and prime ministers – gaze down on you in the dining room, a favourite restaurant for the discerning palates of Grenoble. Yet the atmosphere is of an intimate family hotel. The whole place is awash with antiques and heirlooms, breakfast is delicious, good taste prevails and flowers add that touch of life and genuine attention. And there are massages galore in the sumptuous spa. Bedrooms are in four buildings, old and new, adding to the sense of intimacy. Rooms in château and chalet are traditional with carved wooden beds and gilt-framed mirrors, though some of them give onto a small road. The Orangerie's rooms (as you'll discover once you have negotiated the rather plain corridors) look out over fine parkland, and are deliciously peaceful. The least expensive rooms are in the Petit Pavillon, on the roadside. But whichever you choose, you will be beautifully looked after by the Beaumont brothers – they grew up here – in this smart suburb of Grenoble. *Signs for 'La Commanderie' indicate an area of town, not the château.*

Price	€102–€190. Singles €92–€180.
Rooms	42 twins/doubles.
Meals	Buffet breakfast €15. Lunch & dinner €27–€70. Wine €30–€50. Restaurant closed Mondays, Saturday lunch & Sundays, & 1–15 August lunch.
Closed	20 December to 3 January.
Directions	From Grenoble, exit 5 Rocade Sud for Eybens, 1st lights right for Le Bourg; right after Esso garage. Entrance to hotel 300m on left.

	Monsieur de Beaumont
	17 avenue d'Echirolles,
	Eybens,
	38230 Grenoble, Isère
Tel	+33 (0)4 76 25 34 58
Email	resa@commanderie.fr
Web	www.commanderie.fr

Michel Chabran

Michel Chabran is a delightful man and a prince among restaurateurs, and his little hotel, 50 miles south of Lyon, is in France's gastronomic heart. In elegant, luxurious surroundings, before a real fire, be seduced by potato purée with Sevruga caviar, poularde de Bresse, hot soufflé of Grand Marnier – food that has won Michel accolades. The à la carte menu stretches to four pages, the set menu two, there are 400 wines and the service is exemplary. It all started in 1937 when Michel's grandfather supplied sandwiches to workers heading south on the first paid holidays to the sun; the rest is history. Bedrooms are deliciously cosy and soundproofed; some face the main road, others the garden, an oasis of beauty and calm. The restaurant and veranda too overlook the lawns, the plane trees, the flowers, the maples. Come for a truffle weekend from November to March; Michel explains the 'black diamonds', then sits you down to a six-course meal. Work it all off the next day in the Vercors National Park – or visit Chave, producer of those Hermitage wines that will have delighted you the night before. €10 supplement for pets.

Price	€110–€175. Suite €295.
Rooms	9: 8 doubles, 1 suite.
Meals	Breakfast €23.
	Lunch & dinner €35–€159.
	Wine from €25.
Closed	Rarely.
Directions	A7 south of Lyon exit Tain l'Hermitage or Valence North to N7 for Pont de l'Isère. Restaurant & hotel on main street opp. town hall.

Monsieur & Madame Chabran
29 avenue du 45ème Parallèle,
26600 Pont de l'Isère, Drôme

Tel	+33 (0)4 75 84 60 09
Email	chabran@michelchabran.fr
Web	www.michelchabran.fr

La Treille Muscate

It's love at first sight with this jewel of a 17th-century Provençal mas, set in a classified village where pottery and antiques abound. Inside are stone walls, exposed beams, vaulted ceilings and a magnificent ancient fireplace. The views over the Rhône valley and adjoining forests are breathtaking; two of the salons, some of the bedrooms and the highly popular dining terrace all have them. There's also an exquisite enclosed garden for quiet moments. Rooms – four with private terraces – are an inviting and elegant blend of traditional and comfy modern, with choice antiques much in evidence and lots of colour variations, offset by bursts of dazzlingly pure white. The traditional indoor sitting and dining areas are equally welcoming, against a backdrop of stonework and earth tones, and the cuisine regularly gets rave reviews from France's top sources, with the décor sharing the billing. Owner Katy, a former language teacher in France and England, clearly loves her work and greets her guests like old friends. Hiking, horse riding, golf, great markets and summer festivals round out the menu.

Price	€65-€130. Suite €120-€150.	
Rooms	12: 8 doubles, 3 twins/doubles, 1 suite.	
Meals	Breakfast €11. Dinner €29. Wine €18-€82.	
Closed	7 December to 12 February.	
Directions	From north exit A7 Loriol, south on N7 for Montélimar for 1.5km; left on D57, after approx. 3km, D554 to Cliousclat.	

Katy Delaitre
26270 Cliousclat, Drôme

Tel	+33 (0)4 75 63 13 10
Email	latreillemuscate@wanadoo.fr
Web	www.latreillemuscate.com

Le Castel du Mont Boisé

Set in a park of fine old trees above a small Provençal village, the château comes with stunning views that drop to rooftops and rolling hills. Bedrooms are all large and pretty in a non-frilly way, each with a theme and a delightful hand-painted frieze; a chain of Arlesian dancers lights up 'Esprit de Provence', it's enchanting. Some have local-style country furniture, others antique wardrobes. Each of two round medieval tower rooms, with private terraces and a delicate mix of turquoise and white, is perfect for a romantic weekend. Elegance lingers over breakfast and dinner, often to the tunes of a pianist in the evenings. This is a family affair. Regional or Mediterranean dishes are excellently cooked by Philippe; visit between November and March and delectable truffle menus will be on offer. Colette's touch lies in the decoration; Lionel serves in the restaurant – and gives Ayurvedic massage in a gently-lit Indian room upstairs; Yolanda is your charming, multi-lingual hostess. Come for amazing rock climbing, themed wine weekends, music festivals, and nougat in nearby Montelimar. Wonderful. *Golf 1km.*

Price	€90–€150.
Rooms	6: 4 doubles, 2 suites.
Meals	Breakfast €7.50.
	Dinner with wine, €35.
Closed	Rarely.
Directions	Sent on booking.

Yolanda Rousselet
1 rue du Château,
26740 Montboucher sur Jabron, Drôme

Tel	+33 (0)4 75 46 12 23
Mobile	+33 (0)6 88 50 55 38
Email	yolanda@castel-montboise.com
Web	www.castel-montboise.com

Le Clair de la Plume

Set in a sea of lavender, laden with literature, history and flowers, Grignan is a treat of a little town. So is this welcoming hotel within its sheltering walls (some rooms are in another charming house 100m away). Push the heavy gates of the pink *maison de maître* onto a special place. Jean-Luc Valadeau has created a warm hospitable "home with all the comforts of a hotel". He and his staff are a community, ushering you through deliciously elegant rooms where antique pieces catch your eye, and the small terraced garden has a natural pool and a lovely view over the town. Peaceful bedrooms are divided between the main and the second house. A combination of great taste and authenticity mixes Louis Philippe wardrobes, country-style wicker, luxurious bathrooms, washed or ragged walls, original tiles and shining oak planks. After a generous breakfast, walk into town or borrow bikes and explore the picture-perfect villages. Then return to the organic garden restaurant for exotic selections of teas and mouthwatering pâtisseries among the roses or a delectable dinner in the main restaurant – or both.

Price	€99–€195.
Rooms	15: 2 doubles, 10 twins/doubles, 3 family suites.
Meals	Breakfast €14.50. Lunch & dinner €19.50–€49.50. Jardin Restaurant (lunch & tea May–Sept) €20.
Closed	Rarely.
Directions	From Lyon A7 exit 18 Montélimar Sud for Nyons; D133 then D541 to Grignan; signed.

Jean–Luc Valadeau
Place de Mail,
26230 Grignan,
Drôme

Tel	+33 (0)4 75 91 81 30
Email	info@clairplume.com
Web	www.clairplume.com

Château Clément

On a wooded hill filled with birds and views, overlooking the spa town of Vals les Bains and the valley beyond, this ornate 19th-century château once saw service as a wartime prison and a holiday centre. Constantly renovated by Éric and Marie-Antoinette, it is now both luxurious eco-hotel and young-family home. An extraordinary wooden staircase sweeps you up to airy bedrooms of understated elegance and contemporary details that complement original glowing parquet, antiques, tall views to gardens and the undulating Ardèche. 'Le loft' is a must for families. Magnificent new garden-level rooms in exciting contemporary style have designer furniture, subtle LED lighting, jacuzzi baths, private terraces. House and setting may be grand but the young Chabots are as welcoming as can be, grow their own fruit and veg and dine with their guests. Éric, an experienced cook and pâtissier-chocolatier, works his magic at dinner. Breakfasts are fabulous too. Let yourself be enticed from the rose-rich garden and the elegant salons to the summer pool on the sunny south terrace. A cocoon for the senses, a magical place.

Price	€167–€200. Suites €250–€550. Apt €2,000–€2,800 p.w.; 'Le loft' €2,500–€3,800 p.w.
Rooms	5 + 2: 2 doubles, 3 suites (1 for 2-6). Apt for 4. Loft for 8-10.
Meals	Dinner with wine, €65–€70.
Closed	January to March.
Directions	A7 exit Le Pouzin for Privas; thro' St Privat; right D578 to Vals les Bains town centre; right at casino, left T-junc., right after hospital; signs to château; gate on left.

Marie-Antoinette & Éric Chabot
La Châtaigneraie,
07600 Vals les Bains, Ardèche

Tel	+33 (0)4 75 87 40 13
Mobile	+33 (0)6 72 75 03 36
Email	contact@chateauclement.com
Web	www.chateauclement.com

Collège Hôtel

Who would have thought that a school-themed hotel could be so exhilarating? Combine it with sleek new design and you have one of Lyon's most exciting places to stay, built in the 30s in Art Deco style on the edge of the charming old quarter. The new renovation has introduced a quirky kind of cool and at night optical fibres light the façade all colours of the rainbow. The lobby has lovely 'old school' touches, a huge painting of a classroom and a vintage TV running cult school classics. Room prices are chalked on a blackboard; the reception desk was made from a vaulting horse; the brown breakfast room glows with polished wooden tables, leather benches and glass-fronted bookcases. Take the lift, clad in school assembly photographs, to black and white corridors to 'les dortoirs'… The smallish bedrooms (standard double beds) are pure symphonies in white (walls, beds, leather armchairs), bathrooms are stylish, some with big corner bathtubs. A green-clothed terrace graces the roof, jutting like the prow of an ocean liner. The funky new Baràgones wine bar next door is the place for aperitifs and savouries.

Price	€125–€155.
Rooms	40 twins/doubles.
Meals	Breakfast €12. Restaurants nearby.
Closed	Rarely.
Directions	A6 Paris-Lyon exit Vieux Lyon; after Fourière tunnel, immediate left to follow river on Quai Fulchiron & Quai Bondy; left at Pont La Feuillée to Pl. St Paul, opp. station. Hotel on left corner (parking €15).

	Chantal Corgier
	5 place Saint Paul,
	69005 Lyon, Rhône
Tel	+33 (0)4 72 10 05 05
Email	contact@college-hotel.com
Web	www.college-hotel.com

L'Ermitage Hôtel Cuisine-à-manger

An ultra-modern sister for Lyon's centrally sited Collège Hotel, 20 minutes away by car. The architecture may be different but the swish interiors are just as cool: pale blonde wood, walls exposed brick or bright white, mocha leather sofas, a crisp dining room, beautifully designed chairs. But the big plus here is the panorama: views sweep over the city to the green foothills beyond and locals negotiate the twisty road up just for the view; catch it from the terrace with its shady trees and lime green seating, or from the all-weather pool with immaculate decking. The old streets of Lyon teem with good restaurants but you have a couple here, too, one with sliding glass doors to a terrace; we hear good reports of the food. Indulge in a gentle game of boules, puff around the fitness trail, return to minimalist bedrooms short on decoration, just oak floors, excellent mattresses, flat-screen TVs… and retro fridges in the corridors. Some rooms look onto the street; others have the stunning views – at their most dramatic during the Festival of Light, when Lyon's monuments and bridges are floodlit.

Price	€145–€195. Suite €235.
Rooms	28: 27 doubles, 1 suite for 4.
Meals	Breakfast €12.
	Lunch & dinner from €33.
	Wine €29–€63.
Closed	Never.
Directions	From Paris A6 exit 33; follow signs for Limonest; Route de la Garde, Route du Mont Verdun, Route du Mont Thou, Route des Crètes. Free parking.

Nicolas Vainchtock
Chemin de L'Ermitage,
69450 Saint Cyr au Mont d'Or,
Rhône

Tel	+33 (0)4 72 19 69 69
Email	contact@ermitage-college-hotel.com
Web	www.ermitage-college-hotel.com

Château de la Charmeraie

Hidden in the deep quiet of the Lyonnais hills, this 19th-century estate welcomes you with fine craftsmanship into reception rooms panelled in walnut and wild cherry and exquisite, even down to the silver door handles. The outside is beguilingly simple in deep apricot and ochre-pink. A long sun terrace unfolds, furnished in appealing wicker and forming a neat lip above the pool. On fine days breakfast with homemade jams, breads and pastries is served here. From its seat in a dell, the house enjoys a marvellous vista, way over to the Jura, of private lake, park and tree-flanked drive. Bedrooms are sumptuous, traditional and feminine in style, matching enticing beds and perfectly upholstered armchairs, with marble or brass-framed log fires, ingeniously paired at eye-level with flat-screen televisions. One comes with a pretty conservatory, one with an Eiffel-like iron ceiling, another with a bed swathed in fluffy apple-green netting – wondrously amorous. Bathrooms have sheer class. It's easy to get caught up in Brigitte's enthusiasm for her château, particularly while enjoying her fine and tasty cooking.

Price	€76–€128.
Rooms	5: 3 doubles, 2 suites for 2-4.
Meals	Dinner with wine, €30. Restaurant 5km.
Closed	Never.
Directions	A6 from Paris exit Portes de Lyon dir. Rouanne, L'Arbresle, Clermont-Ferrand. Entering St. Laurent de Chamousset, r'bout 4th exit dir. 'Complexe sportif'. Right at Virgin Mary statue; 1st left,1st right.

Brigitte & René Trégouët
Domaine de la Bâtie,
69930 Saint Laurent de Chamousset,
Rhône

Tel	+33 (0)4 74 70 50 70
Email	contact@chateaudelacharmeraie.com
Web	www.chateaudelacharmeraie.com

Château de Pramenoux

Climb into the Monts du Beaujolais above Lyon for a stunning panorama. Rivers pulse down on either side and great Douglas pines clean the air. As you round a curve, a pair of Gothic pepperpot turrets pop surprisingly into view. The château sits in a natural clearing, views from the terrace and bedrooms sweep splendidly down the valley, a small pond in front anchors the eye. Emmanuel, an escapee from the corporate world, charming, engaging and passionate about this place, will point out the bits that date from the 10th century up to the Renaissance. Much patching and painting later, rooms are big, hugely comfortable and have simple, elegant bathrooms. Recline in the panelled room with its gold and white striped bed and Louis XVI chairs in eau-de-nil; dream in a bed canopied in blue and gold fleur-de-lys, a textile re-created by Emmanuel with the weavers of Lyon. Sheer beauty, sweet seclusion, wonderful dinners, cooked (using local organic produce) and hosted by Emmanuel, and summer recitals in the vast reception hall. It is utterly peaceful – and unforgettable. *Cash or cheque only.*

Price	€125–€140.
Rooms	5 doubles.
Meals	Hosted dinner with wine & aperitif, €45; book ahead.
Closed	Rarely.
Directions	From A6 exit Belleville D37 for Beaujeu to St Vincent; left D9 to Quincié, Marchampt, Lamure; at end of Lamure, lane opp. 'terrain de sport' for Pramenoux.

Emmanuel Baudoin
69870 Lamure sur Azergues, Rhône
Tel +33 (0)4 74 03 16 43
Email emmanuel@pramenoux.com
Web www.pramenoux.com

Château de la Motte

Expect a classical décor and a cordial welcome at this fairy-tale castle near Roanne – a small town known for the legendary Troisgros restaurant (you must book weeks in advance). A sure and discerning touch has transformed this light-filled château where gleaming old floors, stained glass and antiques rest easily with deep sofas and unexpectedly modern, and surreal, art. The grounds are not floral but grassy and spreading, with some very fine trees. There's a pool to dip into, a fitness room to work out in, and a sauna and jacuzzi to help you unwind. But best of all is the food. After a sociable aperitif in the salon, guests are ushered into an elegant grey dining room where Alain, your unflustered host, ferries well-presented dishes to hushed soft-lit tables. On a spring evening we were treated to smoked salmon and citrus salad, roast guinea fowl with a balsamic and cream sauce, gratin dauphinois and homemade apple tart, and some of the fine local wine. The final touch: soft music and a turn in the orchard before you climb the creaking old stairs to an excellent bedroom and a delicious bed.

Price	€88–€118.
Rooms	4: 3 doubles, 1 suite for 4.
Meals	Breakfast included.
	Dinner with wine, €28. Restaurant 5km.
Closed	Mid-November to mid-February.
Directions	From Roanne D482 to Pouilly sous Charlieu; D4 left through Briennon; just before Noailly, château on left.

Anny & Alain Froumajou
42640 Noailly, Loire

Tel	+33 (0)4 77 66 64 60
Email	chateaudelamotte@wanadoo.fr
Web	www.chateaudelamotte.net

Provence – Alps – Riviera

Le Mas de Peint

In the heart of the Camargue, book in for an energetic, gastronomic short break and live as a 'cowboy'! Lucille and son Frédéric are warm, kind and proud of their beautiful farm – 250 bulls, 15 horses and swathes of arable land. Lucille creates a sober, elegant French country-farmhouse feel – no flounces or flummery, just impeccable style. They both miss Jacques, husband and father: a legend in the area, he died in 2010. Bedrooms are deep green or old rose; generous curtains are checked dove-grey; floors come tiled or wool-carpeted. There's eye-catching quirkery everywhere – a collection of fine pencil sketches, an antique commode – and some rooms with mezzanine bathrooms under old rafters. Breakfast royally in the big family kitchen or on the wisteria-draped terrace, then drift over the serene canal to the secluded pool, encircled by teak loungers, scented with jasmine. We recommend half-board: the fabulous, innovative chef delivers light, elegant regional food under a muslin canopy at tables aglow with Moroccan lamps. Follow with coffee and cognac in the clubby cigar room or the seductive salon.

Price	€235–€315. Suites €375–€435. Half-board €72 extra p.p.
Rooms	12: 2 doubles, 6 twins/doubles, 3 suites for 2, 1 suite for 3, 1 suite for 3-4.
Meals	Breakfast €12–€22. Lunch, à la carte €39–€55. Dinner €55. Restaurant closed Thurs.
Closed	Early Jan to mid-March; mid-Nov to mid-Dec.
Directions	Arles to St Marie de la Mer D570; 2km after 2nd r'bout, D36 for Salin de Giraud & Le Sambuc. On left 2km after Le Sambuc; signed.

Lucille & Frédéric Bon
Le Sambuc, 13200 Arles,
Bouches-du-Rhône

Tel	+33 (0)4 90 97 20 62
Email	hotel@masdepeint.net
Web	www.masdepeint.com

Grand Hôtel Nord Pinus

An Arlesian legend, where Spain meets France and ancient Rome meets the 21st century, the hotel is hugely atmospheric. Built in 1865 on Roman vaults, it came to fame in the 1950s when a clown and a cabaret singer owned it: famous bullfighters dressed here before entering the ring and the arty crowd flocked (Cocteau, Picasso, Hemingway…). Anne Igou keeps the drama alive today with her strong personality and cinema, fashion and photography folk – and bullfighters still have 'their' superb Spanish Rococo room. The style is vibrant at this show of Art Deco furniture and fittings, corrida posters and costumes, North African carpets and artefacts, fabulous Provençal colours and ironwork. Colour and light are deftly used to create a soft, nostalgic atmosphere where you feel both warm and cool, smart and artistic. Rooms are big or less big, determinedly ornamented or strictly modern, the top-floor suite has a terrace and rooftop views, bathrooms are fittingly old-fashioned. As Cocteau said: "an hotel with a soul" – and delightful staff contribute hugely to its formidable reputation today.

Price	€180–€240. Suites €310. Apartment €570.
Rooms	26: 9 doubles, 9 twins, 6 suites for 2, 1 suite for 4, 1 apartment for 4 (without kitchen).
Meals	Breakfast €18–€22. Lunch & dinner from €35. Restaurant 50m.
Closed	Mid-November to mid-March.
Directions	From A54 exit Arles Centre for Centre Ancien. Boulevard des Lices at main post office; left Rue Jean Jaurès; right Rue Cloître, right to Place du Forum.

Anne Igou
Place du Forum,
13200 Arles,
Bouches-du-Rhône

Tel	+33 (0)4 90 93 44 44
Email	info@nord-pinus.com
Web	www.nord-pinus.com

Le Mas Saint Florent

Legend has it the Minister of Communications installed France's first telephone in this grandiose mansion, an ensemble of stone balustrades and shuttered windows set among olives, plane trees, chestnuts, a rose garden and bamboo. And there are art exhibitions, a small lake and a pool, with pool house and barbecue. Bedrooms are sumptuous; sink back on a mountain of cushions amid period furniture, oriental rugs, sculptures, mirrors, lamps. Most are big and Les Lauriers is immense, with billowing red curtains and velvet sofa; some have fireplaces; one has a terrace and claw-foot bath. It's a wow of a place – a fantasy fulfilled for Gilbert and his partner – but it's Mother who sews the soft furnishings and who greets you on arrival. Theatre sweeps through the common rooms: antique chairs, Chinese rugs, photographs, flowers, fireplaces, a black baby grand, chess board, fossil sculptures, cubic art… even the flooring is remarkable! You can dine in if you wish, or pop into Roman Arles or perhaps Avignon, 35 minutes away; in Camargue there are village festivals, markets, walking and wildlife galore.

Price	€115–€220.
Rooms	6: 3 doubles, 2 family rooms for 3, 1 suite for 4.
Meals	Breakfast €15. Dinner €36. Wine €18–€38.
Closed	Rarely.
Directions	From Avignon D570N to Arles, N113 dir. Salon; exit St Raphèle-lès-Arles; left in village onto D453 dir. Arles 1km. Entrance on right.

Gilbert Poirier
Route de la Crau,
13280 Raphèle lès Arles,
Bouches-du-Rhône

Tel	+33 (0)4 90 97 02 79
Email	massaintflorent@orange.fr
Web	www.le-mas-saint-florent.com

Entry 334   Map 16

Mas des Comtes de Provence

Homesick for the south of France, looking for a life change after a busy career in Paris, Pierre fell for this historic hunting lodge and settled in happily after a huge restoration. The mellow-stone *mas* belonged to King René whose château is up the road; some say the Germans blocked the underground tunnel that connected them. A soberly elegant stone exterior dating from the 15th century protects a large interior courtyard overlooked by pretty shuttered windows. As for the bedrooms, they are regal and awesomely huge – the Royal Suite measures 100m². Roi René comes dressed in tones of ivory, brown and beige, Garance is in terracottas and yellows; bathrooms have huge towels. The vast pool, with *plage*, heated by the Provence sun, is well hidden in the two-hectare park, majestically tree'd with 300-year-old planes, pines, cypresses and cedars; swings and authentic boulodrome, too. Pierre may prepare a barbecue here, but there's a different menu every day. Hiking, cycling, riding – all are minutes away. A lovely property full of history, charm and cachet. *Weddings & seminars can be catered for.*

Price	€145–€210. Suites €205–€400.
Rooms	9: 6 twins/doubles, 3 suites for 4–6. Extra beds available.
Meals	Breakfast €12.50. Lunch €20–€45. Dinner with coffee, €27.50–€45. Wine €20–€47.50. Children's meals €10–€15.
Closed	Rarely.
Directions	From Tarascon D970 for Arles. 200m after Tarascon, D35 on right 'Petite Route d'Arles'; on 800m, road on left. Mas 600m on left.

Pierre Valo
Petite Route d'Arles,
13150 Tarascon,
Bouches-du-Rhône
Tel   +33 (0)4 90 91 00 13
Email   valo@mas-provence.com
Web   www.mas-provence.com

Mas de l'Oulivié

The olive groves, lavender fields and chalky hillsides of Les Baux are a dream of a setting for a new Provence-style hotel, roofed with reclaimed terracotta, sheltered by cypress and oleander (plants are labelled for garden buffs). The owners' taste is impeccable and every detail has been carefully crafted: local oak furniture, painted and waxed walls, homemade tiles round the pool. And what a pool! Curvaceous and spectacular, it has a gentle slope for little ones and a hot tub. Furnishings are fresh, local, designed for deep comfort. Bedrooms are gorgeously coloured, country-style with an elegant twist, some have their own grassy sitting area, the suite has a private patio, the road is discreet. Filled with flowers in the summer, the bright and cosy living-room has a rustic fireplace. The Achards love to provide guests and their children with the best and that includes a superb well-being and massage room and delicious lunches by the pool; they sell their own lavender and oil and Isabelle is ever-helpful. One of the crème de la crème of Provence's small, modern country hotels – near oh-so-pretty Les Baux.

Price	€130-€315. Suites €490. Extra bed €35.
Rooms	27: 25 doubles, 2 suites.
Meals	Breakfast €16. Poolside lunch €9-€35 (booking advisable). Wine €15-€36. Restaurants 2km.
Closed	Mid-November to mid-March.
Directions	From north A7 exit 24 for St Rémy de Provence & Les Baux. Mas 2km from Les Baux on D78F towards Fontvieille.

Emmanuel & Isabelle Achard
Les Arcoules,
13520 Les Baux de Provence,
Bouches-du-Rhône
Tel   +33 (0)4 90 54 35 78
Email   contact@masdeloulivie.com
Web   www.masdeloulivie.com

Entry 336   Map 16

La Bastide de Boulbon

It will fire your imagination. Leave the main road for a secret, dead-end village. There, on the hill, are windmills and a huge castle, old houses line the quaint narrow streets that climb to the summit. In the middle, is this impressive 200-year-old mansion. Jan and Marie-Claire came from Belgium three years ago and have already made their mark by combining proper professional skills with genuine pleasure in receiving guests. They have put their heart and soul into the renovation and decoration and have done a fabulous landscaping job on the garden. Four huge taupe parasols marry the dining patio to the elegant façade with its same-coloured shutters; the giant centuries-old plane trees and trickling stone fountain teach a gentler sense of time. Inside, elegant proportions, clean lines, modern simplicity and the subtlest palette of neutral and dusky tones, with the occasional bold piece of art, make for restful spaces. Be prepared to eat well: Marie-Claire grew up in one of Brussels' best restaurants and has taken on a new French chef. The scene is set for a luxurious, relaxing stay.

Price	€115–€155.
Rooms	10: 5 doubles, 5 twins/doubles.
Meals	Breakfast €15. Dinner from €29. Wine €23–€60.
Closed	November to March.
Directions	Sent on booking.

Jan De Mulder & Marie-Claire Callens
Rue de l'Hôtel de Ville,
13150 Boulbon, Bouches-du-Rhône
Tel   +33 (0)4 90 93 11 11
Email   contact@labastidedeboulbon.com
Web   www.labastidedeboulbon.com

Hôtel Le Cadran Solaire

A soft clear light filters through the house, the light of the south pushing past the windows to stroke the light-handed, rich-pastelled décor where Provençal furniture, stencil motifs and natural materials — cotton, linen and seagrass — give the instant feel of a well-loved family home. A splendid portrait of 'grand-mère' hangs on the landing, below it sit her old trunk and suitcase. The simplicity of a pastel slipcover over a chair, a modern wrought-iron bed frame and an authentic 'boutis' quilt is refreshing and restful — and the house stays deliciously cool in summer. The solid old staging post has stood here, with its thick walls, for 400 years. Its face is as pretty as ever, calmly set in its gentle garden of happy flowers where guests can always find a quiet corner for their deckchairs. You can have delicious breakfast on the shrubby, sun-dappled terrace or in the attractive dining room where a fine big mirror overlooks the smart red-on-white tables. A wonderful atmosphere, relaxed, smiling staff, all family. Linden, olives, figs and roses in the garden, and a great little restaurant in the village.

Price	€72–€120. Family suite €155.
Rooms	12: 5 doubles, 3 twins/doubles, 1 twin, 2 triples, 1 family suite (1 double, 1 twin).
Meals	Breakfast €9. Restaurants in village.
Closed	November to March. Call for out of season reservations.
Directions	A7 exit Avignon Sud for Châteaurenard; D28 to Graveson. 1st right to village; continue almost to end; small sign on right. Right for 200m to end of 1st block; gates on right.

Elisa & Jean-Claude Rastoin
5 rue du Cabaret Neuf,
13690 Graveson, Bouches-du-Rhône

Tel	+33 (0)4 90 95 71 79
Email	cadransolaire@wanadoo.fr
Web	www.hotel-en-provence.com

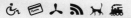

La Maison du Paradou

Those lucky enough to wash up at this honey-stone mas in sleepy Paradou will find intimacy and luxury combined. This charmingly converted coaching inn has a stupendous vaulted salon with a roaring fire and books galore, making it one for all seasons; in good weather you decamp onto the terrace for delicious communal breakfasts. You'll find a boules pitch, two rather swish pools, white sun loungers and a super garden. As for the rooms, expect the best: fabulous linen on the comfiest beds, delicious colours to keep you smiling (emerald, fuchsia, lemon) and bathrooms that go the whole way. A computer in each room is packed with music and movies, but downstairs walls are crammed with art, some of it sensational: Nick's father was a collector. Communal dinners are served twice weekly, and the legendary Bistro du Paradou (Terrance Conran's favourite restaurant) is around the corner. Michelin stars aplenty wait up the hill. Arles is close for all things Van Gogh, as is St Remy for its ever-popular market, and don't miss the magical Cathédrale d'Images at Les Baux. Special place, special people.

Price	€265–€285.
Rooms	5 doubles.
Meals	Breakfast included. Lunch €35. Dinner with wine, €75. Restaurants nearby.
Closed	Rarely.
Directions	From Nice, A8 to A7 north; 1st exit after toll station at Lançon de Provence; A54, 1st exit dir. St Martin de Crau. Right at major junc. in St Martin to Les Baux; on for 7km. Signed.

Andrea & Nick Morris
Route de Saint Roch,
13520 Paradou,
Bouches-du-Rhône

Tel	+33 (0)4 90 54 65 46
Email	reservations@maisonduparadou.com
Web	www.maisonduparadou.com

Hôtel Gounod

Experienced hoteliers, your enthusiastic hosts are rightly proud of their smart little hotel. On the main square, Hôtel Gounod lies at the very heart of lively, artistic Saint Rémy. The oldest hotel in town, it takes its name from the composer Charles Gounod. Helped by gifts of statues and relics from guests, his work informs the entire hotel. His music plays softly in the elegant communal areas, a statue of the Virgin Mary reminds us of his many religious pieces, and each very different bedroom, reached along a labyrinth of corridors, has been decorated to reflect a phase of his life. The effect is theatrical, colourful, diverting and eccentric, bordering at times on the kitsch – and rather vulnerable to energetic children. Beds are voluptuous and the quietest rooms look onto the garden, an oasis of calm with its lazy pool. For a gastronomic treat, pad over to the Salon de Thé where Marilyn – an excellent pâtissière – serves her masterful creations, and delicious bruschettas, too. A very pleasant place in which to hang your Provençal hat. Make sure you're around on a Wednesday, it's market day.

Price	€145–€195. Duplex & suites €230.
Rooms	34: 20 doubles (10 with terrace), 10 twins, 1 duplex, 3 suites.
Meals	Tea room snacks & light supper, from €13.
Closed	Rarely.
Directions	A7 exit Cavaillon to St Rémy, signs for 'centre ville'. On main square opp. church. Free taxi service to local station/airport.

Igor & Marilyn Maurin
18 place de la République,
13210 Saint Rémy de Provence,
Bouches-du-Rhône

Tel	+33 (0)4 90 92 06 14
Email	contact@hotel-gounod.com
Web	www.hotel-gounod.com

Le Mas des Carassins

The charming *mas* settles gently into its leafy cocoon, a massive garden bursting with oleanders, lavender, lemons and fine pieces by local designers and Balinese artists. There are now two pools, one by the new annexe specifically for relaxation and peace. After a swim, there are boules, badminton or bikes (to hire) – fascinating St Rémy is no distance. This is Van Gogh country and an ancient land: the hotel lies within the conservation area of Roman Glanum. In the pretty dining room, oil paintings by a friend add a splash to white walls and meals are a fine feast of market produce accompanied by excellent local wines. Bedrooms in the old *mas* are dreamy, washed in smoky-blue or ochre shades; dark wrought-iron beds are dressed in oatmeal linens and white quilts; ground-floor rooms open to small gardens or wooden decks. In contrast, the new rooms are done with contemporary furniture, Parisian and Balinese art, and pebble-floored showers. The young owners have thought of everything: pick-up from the airport or train, car hire, tickets for local events. Perfect. *Summer/winter pool. Children over 12 welcome.*

Price	€99–€205. Suites €190–€230.
Rooms	22: 19 twins/doubles, 3 suites.
Meals	Breakfast €14. Dinner €32.50. Half-board €28 extra p.p. Wine €18–€65. Restaurants 5-minute walk.
Closed	January to early March, 2 weeks in December.
Directions	From St Rémy de Provence centre, over Canal des Alpilles on Ave Van Gogh, then right into Ave J. d'Arbaud. Hotel entrance on left after 180m.

Michel Dimeux & Pierre Ticot
1 chemin Gaulois,
13210 Saint Rémy de Provence,
Bouches-du-Rhône

Tel	+33 (0)4 90 92 15 48
Email	info@masdescarassins.com
Web	www.masdescarassins.com

Mas du Vigueirat

A small pool cascading into a larger pool, a walled garden with quiet corners, wisteria, honeysuckle, trees of all sorts... and nothing to disturb the view but meadows, woods and horses. You'll find it impossible to leave this tranquil, scented spot – although St Rémy (galleries, Van Gogh museum) is just up the road, and Arles, Avignon, the lavender fields and olive groves of Baux de Provence are not much further. High plane trees flank the drive to the dusky pink, grey-shuttered Provençal farmhouse and inside all is light, simplicity and gentle elegance. Bedrooms are uncluttered spaces of bleached colours, limed walls and terracotta floors. Views are over the beautiful garden or meadows; ground-floor Maillane has a private terrace. The high-beamed dining room/salon is a calm white space with a corner for sofas and books. If the weather's warm you'll take breakfast under the plane tree; after a dip in the pool or a jaunt on the bike, enjoy one of Catherine's delicious lunches, fresh from the vegetable garden. No suppers, but the helpful Jeanniards will recommend local places.

Price	€130–€155.
	Suite €185 (July/August only).
Rooms	4: 3 doubles, 1 suite.
Meals	Picnic available. Poolside meals in summer €15–€20. Restaurants 3km.
Closed	Christmas.
Directions	From Lyon A7 exit Avignon Sud to Noves. In St Rémy, right at 5th r'bout to Maillane. After 3km, right at sign for Pepinières Vigueirat.

Catherine Jeanniard
1977 chemin du Grand Bourbourel,
13210 Saint Rémy de Provence,
Bouches-du-Rhône

Tel	+33 (0)4 90 92 56 07
Email	contact@mas-du-vigueirat.com
Web	www.mas-du-vigueirat.com

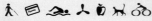

Château de la Barben

The castle, all towers, turrets and terraces, is majestic; as is its position, high on impregnable rock, overlooking a lush valley. Join the museum visitors and enter to discover guardrooms, subterranean passages and watchtowers with pulleys, arrow slits, coats of arms and innumerable tapestried rooms. Madame is as elegant as you would hope her to be, Monsieur looks after the guests, with charm, and their daughter, a talented cook, delivers dinners to the big table in the 11th-century kitchen, shared with your hosts – or to the balustraded terrace for dinner à deux. Bedrooms range from Diane, a (relatively) modest symphony in celestial blue, to the Suite des Amours in the tower, its four-poster dating from the Renaissance, its canopies of cream linen, its stone fireplace vast... take a bottle of bubbly to the private terrace and toast that exceptional view. Bathrooms are mostly huge, and scattered with L'Occitane potions. Heaps to do, from exploring the *orangeries*, topiaries and ornamental ponds in the gloriously historic grounds to discovering the sights, tastes and smells of delicious Provence.

Price	€140–€250.
Rooms	5: 3 doubles, 2 suites.
Meals	Dinner, 4 courses, with wine, €50.
Closed	December to February.
Directions	A7 then A54 exit 15 (Pélisanne); D572 to La Barben village.

Bertrand Pillivuyt
Route du Château,
13330 La Barben,
Bouches-du-Rhône

Tel	+33 (0)4 90 55 25 41
Email	info@chateau-de-la-barben.fr
Web	www.chateaudelabarben.fr

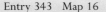

Mas de la Rabassière

Fanfares of lilies at the door, Haydn inside and Michael smiling in his chef's apron. Rabassière means 'where truffles are found' and his epicurean dinners are a must; wines from the neighbouring vineyard and a sculpted dancer also grace the terrace table. Cookery classes using home-produced olive oil and advice on what to see and where to go, jogging companionship and airport pick-ups are all part of Michael's unflagging hospitality; nobly aided by Thévi, his Singaporean assistant. Michael was posted to France by a multi-national and on his retirement slipped into this unusually lush corner of Provence. The proximity of the canal keeps everything green: revel in the well-tree'd park with its grassy olive grove, roses galore, lilies, jasmine, and white and blue wisteria. There's a large library in English and French, and bedrooms and drawing room are comfortable in English country-house style: generous beds, erudite books, a tuned piano, fine etchings and oils, Provençal antiques. Come savour this charmingly generous house – and Michael's homemade croissants and fig jam on the shady veranda. *No credit cards.*

Price	€145.
Rooms	2 doubles.
Meals	Dinner with wine, €50.
Closed	Rarely.
Directions	A54 exit 13 to Grans on D19; right D16 to St Chamas; just before r'way bridge, left for Cornillon, up hill 2km; house on right before tennis court. Map sent on request.

Michael Frost
2137 chemin de la Rabassière,
13250 Saint Chamas,
Bouches-du-Rhône
Tel   +33 (0)4 90 50 70 40
Email   michaelfrost@wanadoo.fr
Web   www.rabassiere.com

Ethical Collection: Environment; Food.
See page 429 for details

Entry 344   Map 16

La Bastide de Cabriès

On its lofty hillside, this 15th-century bastide stands tall with its little pepperpot watchtower, seemingly proud of its many lives: it once produced herbal tea and legend has it that German officers hid treasure (yet to be found) in the cellars during WWII. Now it spends its days well-placed in the hands of the friendly, polite Pédurands with their backgrounds in marketing luxury hotels (Valérie) and catering (Xavier). Some of the bedrooms aren't huge but all are super comfy, decked with scatter cushions, giant beanbags, fluffy duvets. They're great fun: think funky pop art and slick shabby-chic. Bathrooms have boiled sweet-bright flourishes (and a few await their revamp). Downstairs, big rooms are open to all and are equally stylish. Panoramic views to Provençal rooftops and lavender-lined walls accompany your breakfast in the handsome dining room. Come back to dinner and tuck into specialities such as seared red mullet and squid. Plane trees shade the pretty terrace – wonderful in summer; there are festivals in nearby Aix and Marseille, and walks and cycle tracks abound. A good place.

Price	€100–€140.
Rooms	12: 8 doubles, 4 twins/doubles. Extra beds available.
Meals	Breakfast €13. Dinner €35–€80. Restaurant closed Sat lunch, Sunday, Christmas & August. Wine €28–€450.
Closed	Rarely.
Directions	From Marseille A7 for Aix en Provence 19km; exit Marignane for Vitrolles-Griffon onto D9 for Aix en Provence, 9km; right to Calas & Cabriès. Signed.

Valérie & Xavier Pédurand
Rue du Lac, Domaine du Lac Bleu,
13480 Cabriès, Bouches-du-Rhône

Tel	+33 (0)4 42 69 07 81
Email	info@bastidecabries.com
Web	www.bastidecabries.com

Maison°9

A beautifully restored, impeccably decorated 19th-century winemaker's farmhouse on the side of a vineyard-braided hill, Maison °9 is an elegant ochre-pink with faded-green shutters under a flat curved-tile roof. The bedrooms, all different, all plush, are on the 'outskirts' of the main house, while the suite is at a discreet distance down a little path screened by bamboo. Expect big double beds, excellent linen, cool pink and weathered satin-finish terracotta floors, Italianate dipped-floor monsoon-head showers and small terrace gardens: simple, chic perfection. Paved paths lead through a delicious little garden bursting with pots of rosemary, thyme, lavender, sage, pebble beds of kentia palms and olive trees in wooden containers, to the centrepiece: a raised limestone pool lined with cotton loungers and surrounded by a sleek overflow wall with views across wooded hills to the grandiose 'Charlemagne's Crown' cliff face. A spectacular breakfast served in the main house sets you up for a ten-minute traipse to the beach, or you can just chill to the clonk of pétanque. Intimate, spoiling, special.

Price	€195–€245.
Rooms	4 doubles (1 with sofabed).
Meals	Breakfast included. Restaurant 2km.
Closed	November to March.
Directions	From Marseille A50 exit 7 to Cassis; left past Peugeot garage; right at r'bout to rue du Docteur Yves Bourde; thro' tunnel, right at crossroads; 1st house on left.

Cynthia Kayser-Maus
9 avenue du Docteur Yves Bourde,
13260 Cassis, Bouches-du-Rhône

Tel	+33 (0)4 42 08 35 86
Email	contact@maison9.net
Web	www.maison9.net

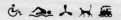

Entry 346   Map 16

La Bastide du Bois Bréant

Step into a corner of paradise. This is a jewel of a 19th-century truffle farm, renovated with equal parts of imagination and stylish good taste. Viviane and Philippe spoil you with a big welcome, and more: superb cuisine Provençal, grounds filled with flowers, rooms aglow with antiques, and a delicious décor. Some rooms have fireplaces, one has a terrace, the garden views are dreamy and there's every mod con. White 'boutis' quilts and diaphanous bed curtains provide the perfect background for chocolate throws, and other contemporary shades. Time seems to stand still as you wander the vast heavily tree'd park and its gardens, laze on one of several terraces, take a plunge in the heated pool. The wood-beamed dining room is bright and spacious, with garden views on two sides; for quiet evenings you have two comfy sitting rooms, with piano, library and fireplaces. The Lubéron bursts with markets every day of the week, Avignon's summer festival is one of many and there's sport for all – cycling, rock climbing, golf, guided walks. Just ask the advice of your hosts. No wonder guests book months in advance.

Price	€128–€215. Suite €215. Treehouses €110–€145.
Rooms	16: 8 doubles, 5 twins/doubles, 1 suite for 4, 2 treehouses for 2.
Meals	Dinner €28; book ahead. Wine €14–€26. Restaurants 200m.
Closed	Early November to mid-March.
Directions	From A7 exit Avignon Sud dir. Apt; on to Coustellet; right at lights to Cavaillon; left after 2km. Hotel signed.

Ethical Collection: Environment .
See page 429 for details

Viviane & Philippe Duminy
501 chemin du Puits du Grandaou,
84660 Maubec en Lubéron, Vaucluse
Tel   +33 (0)4 90 05 86 78
Email   contact@hotel-bastide-bois-breant.com
Web   www.hotel-bastide-bois-breant.com

Lumani

Tucked into the medieval ramparts near the Pope's Palace and the mythical Pont d'Avignon is this handsome 19th-century house. Walk off the street into a cool, lush oasis with venerable plane trees, hammocks, deck chairs, sculptures and shady spots for reading or contemplating; it is beautifully designed and blissfully peaceful (just a fountain splashing, birds chirruping). Inside are light-filled, minimalist rooms with abstract paintings on white or vibrant walls, tiled floors, clever lighting, natural fabrics, all informed by the principles of Feng Shui. Bedrooms overlook the garden and are just as beautifully restful. Your marvellous hosts, Élisabeth, an artist, and Jean, an architect, encourage creative pursuits, giving you a sound-proofed music studio, providing tours and guidebooks on architecture and art and offering cookery classes. Allow them to look after you in the ochre-red salon… or you may rent the whole house and do your own cooking. You are in the heart of Provence so stride past the lavender fields into the hills, visit the delightful villages and their markets. Peaceful, creative, special.

Price	€90–€140. Suites €140–€170. Whole house available.
Rooms	5: 2 twins/doubles, 1 single, 2 suites for 2-4.
Meals	Restaurants 3-minute walk.
Closed	November to mid-March.
Directions	A7 exit north for town centre; left at ramparts. Right at Café Lazare. Under portway to St Lazare, immediately right onto Rempart St Lazare for 200m. Signed.

Élisabeth & Jean Béraud-Hirschi
37 rue du Rempart Saint Lazare,
84000 Avignon, Vaucluse

Tel	+33 (0)4 90 82 94 11
Email	lux@avignon-lumani.com
Web	www.avignon-lumani.com

Couleur Lavande

"Don't work hard when the cicadas sing" reads the pretty stencilling in 'La Provençale' – and how could one, with miles of gentle countryside, village markets and vineyards to discover? Peeping through lavender shutters at sweeping landscaped gardens, this rejuvenated Provençal house fuses hotel comforts and clockwork efficiency with the warmth and personality of a B&B. Take a dip in the natural rock pool, arrange a massage in the garden, wander the orchard, the organic vegetable garden, olive grove and chicken run, gather for a game of boules, help yourself to a cool drink by the fire before dinner – a self-service main dish, or table d'hôtes with your engaging Swiss hosts. He is an architect into sustainable development; she is a hotelier who loves to cook. Bedrooms bear her generous, meticulous touch: plump pillows, lavender lotions, a 70s-style round bed, a free-standing bath, palettes of rich reds or lime greens to match the garden views. Ask for a picnic box and strike out: to Avignon (20 mins), the Camargue with the binoculars or the local market on a bicycle. Your heart – like the cicadas – will sing.

Price	€180.
Rooms	4: 2 doubles, 2 twins/doubles.
Meals	Picnic lunch €12.
	Dinner with wine, €15–€30.
Closed	Rarely.
Directions	A7 exit 24 for Isle sur la Sorgue, on D900. At Vignères left on D98. Signed.

Jacqueline & Axel Renaud
2056 Route des Vignères,
84250 Le Thor, Vaucluse

Mobile	+33 (0)6 30 00 62 04
Email	info@couleurlavande.com
Web	www.couleurlavande.com

Bastide Le Mourre

Victorine is as warmly attentive to guests as she is to her hidden Lubéron paradise, a lovely 17th-century bastide encircled by vines, olives, jasmine and roses. The uninterrupted views up to historic Oppède le Vieux are magical. The silkworm house, the wine stores, the pigeonnier and the two barns are near the house; at the top of the garden, secluded and shaded by an ancient oak, is the little Moulin for two. Each has its own entrance and terrace where breakfast is served, all are filled with light and colour, all will delight you. Imagine big sisal rugs on ancient terracotta floors, fine Provençal ceilings and painted wooden doors, open stone fireplaces and whitewashed stone walls, a piqué cotton cover on a canopied bed, a dove-grey dresser in a sweet, chic kitchen. Victorine was an interior designer and her love of texture, patina and modern art shine through. The generous pool is set discreetly on a lower level away from the house, the grounds are large and open with seductive views, the peace is a balm, the fruit trees yours to harvest. Heavenly place, delightful owner. *Minimum stay three nights.*

Price	€185–€280 (€980–€1,950 per week).
Rooms	6 houses, each with kitchen: 2 for 2, 3 for 4, 1 for 5-6.
Meals	Breakfast €15. Restaurants 5km.
Closed	Rarely.
Directions	Sent on booking.

Victorine Canac
84580 Oppède, Vaucluse
Tel   +33 (0)4 90 76 99 31
Email   lemourre@aol.com
Web   www.lemourre.com

Auberge du Presbytère

They say "when the wind blows at Saignon, tiles fly off in Avignon": the Mistral can blow fiercely down from the mountains to the Mediterranean. Like a well-kept secret, this fairy-tale, 11th-century, pure-Provence village of 300 inhabitants lies deep in the Lubéron hills and lavender fields; the auberge sits deep in Saignon, half hidden behind an ancient tree near the village's statue-topped fountain. Delicious meals are served under that tree, or in a pretty terraced garden, glassed in for the winter months. The bedrooms are simply charming, colour-washed walls, country pieces, no TVs but high class soaps in lovely bathrooms with Italian stone block tiles. One room has a huge fireplace and a stone terrace looking out onto the hills… views from some of the rooms are breathtaking. A log fire burns on chilly days in the informal arched stone sitting area. Gerhard is faithful to the youthful spirit of this ancient hotel and loves the whole Provençal scene. A splendid place from which to visit the hill towns. Or, if you are fit, rent a bike and follow the cycling signs. Outstanding value.

Price	€65–€155.
Rooms	16: 14 twins/doubles; 2 twins/doubles with separate shower/bath. Some rooms interconnect.
Meals	Breakfast €12. Lunch & dinner €20–€38. Half-board €40 p.p. Wine €9–€55. Restaurant closed Wednesdays.
Closed	Mid-January to mid-February.
Directions	From Apt D900, D48 to Saignon. About 1km before village, hotel signed on left. Hotel in centre of old village, signed 'riverains' to Place de la Fontaine.

Anne-Cécile & Gerhard Rose
Place de la Fontaine,
84400 Saignon, Vaucluse

Tel	+33 (0)9 70 44 64 56
Email	reception@auberge-presbytere.com
Web	www.auberge-presbytere.com

Le Clos du Buis

The gorgeous hilltop village of Bonnieux is deservedly renowned. Le Clos sits on one of its lower terraces, looking north to the surrounding hills and the legendary Mont Ventoux, a stunning view. Part of the building used to be the town bakery; the original front and the oven remain. Time and loving care have been distributed without restraint – Monsieur, a charming man, longed to return here – and everything appears to have been just so forever: Provençal country cupboards that rise to the ceiling, ancient patterned cement tiles, a stone staircase with an iron bannister leading to crisp, clean, uncluttered bedrooms, another bannister leading to the garden – a lovely surprise of a shady green oasis within the village. Provence is here on all sides, from the pretty quilts on the beds to the excellent food (by arrangement), served by Monsieur. The beautiful garden frames the large, delightful terrace, pool and summer kitchen. If wine or weather keep you from the hills, days can be spent browsing the books by the old stone hearth – or playing the baby grand. Tremendous value.

Price	€92–€138. Family rooms €117–€135. Extra bed €15.
Rooms	8: 2 doubles, 4 twins/doubles, 2 family rooms for 3.
Meals	Dinner €28. Restaurants within walking distance.
Closed	Mid-November to early March.
Directions	A7 to Aix exit 24 Avignon Sud; D973 to Cavaillon; left onto D22 which becomes D900 for Apt 30km; right on D36. In village centre.

	Monsieur & Madame Maurin
	Rue Victor Hugo,
	84480 Bonnieux, Vaucluse
Tel	+33 (0)4 90 75 88 48
Email	le-clos-du-buis@wanadoo.fr
Web	www.leclosdubuis.fr

The Silk Farm

Drift through lavender fields and olive groves to an 18th-century farmhouse, more home than hotel, that will set your heart aflutter. Behind the gate lies a magical walled courtyard: an enormous outdoor living area for dining and unwinding. Talented architects, Christine and Peter have blended rustic Provençal with modern Italian and added dashes of the Far East: wooden Chinese screens and Thai carvings in big beamed bedrooms with delicious bathrooms. Make yourselves thoroughly at home. Breakfast outside on a generous buffet, lap up views of the Lubéron hills, play croquet in the beautiful garden, cool off in the pool. In the evening, dine in house-party style or opt for a quiet tête-à-tête as wholesome dishes are cooked outside using produce from local farmers; a slither of black truffle is a must. Steal off to the library with its log fire and sofas or to the bright, light living room. Nothing is too much trouble for your young hosts and all feels beautifully serene. There are medieval villages to discover, festivals galore and, in summer, a home cinema under the stars. *Ask about cookery & fitness courses.*

Price	€200–€280.
Rooms	4: 2 doubles, 1 twin, 1 family suite for 4.
Meals	Dinner with aperitif €35. Restaurants 10-minute drive.
Closed	Rarely.
Directions	Sent on booking.

Christine Harvey
Mas de la Calandre,
84480 Bonnieux, Vaucluse

Tel	+33 (0)4 90 05 86 35
Mobile	+33 (0)6 42 99 08 10
Email	info@thesilkfarm.co.uk
Web	www.thesilkfarm.co.uk

La Bastide de Voulonne

Looking utterly Provençal, the bastide sits in splendid isolation in lavender fields spread beneath the ancient hilltop villages of the Lubéron range. As you swing into the circular drive, there are ancient plane trees, wisps of tamarisk, tufts of lavender and blue shutters against golden ochre walls. Glorious – and a genuine family-friendly place, too: family suites, early children's suppers, DVDs galore, safe pool and lawn areas. The heart of this 18th-century farmhouse is a courtyard where you can breakfast to soft fountain music. Bedrooms (and beds) are huge, done in natural local colours, with tiled or parquet floors. The garden – it's more like a park – is vast, with a big pool not far from the house. The owners have refreshed the herb garden for the kitchen and menus focus on local food, while cherries, apricots, pears, figs and raspberries come from their orchards. After a convivial aperitif, dinner is served at separate tables, or at a communal one, in a big dining hall whose centrepiece is the carefully restored bread oven. *Courses on truffles, mushrooms or wine in winter.*

Price	€125-€150. Family suites €180-€265.
Rooms	13: 10 twins/doubles, 3 family suites for 3-5.
Meals	Breakfast €12. Dinner €34. Wine €30.
Closed	Mid-November to December (open Jan & Feb by arrangement).
Directions	From south exit A7 Cavaillon; at Coustellet D2 to Gordes for 1km; right after white fence of Ets Kerry La Cigalette; 600m on left. Not in the village of Cabrières d'Avignon.

Penny & Julien Hemery
Cabrières d'Avignon,
84220 Gordes,
Vaucluse

Tel   +33 (0)4 90 76 77 55
Email contact@bastide-voulonne.com
Web   www.bastide-voulonne.com

Entry 354   Map 16

Le Mas des Romarins

Michel and Pierre, delightful hosts, bought this hotel, overlooking one of France's most beautiful villages, in 2002. Forget the buildings and little roads on either side, the secluded pool and pretty garden will tug you away from it all and there's a private path into town (ten minutes). That fabulous hilltop view of Gordes, with its distant misty-blue mountains and surrounding plains, will ensure you linger long over a delicious buffet breakfast. The sitting room is comfortable without being over-lavish. The ochres and smoky rusts of the bedrooms sit well with the oatmeals and creams of the two-tone walls, Parisian linens and soft furnishings link arms with traditional cotton prints. The bedrooms, each with a terrace, or a garden or a valley view, are small, cool, comfortable and quiet. Best of all is the food, extremely good five-course dinners served on the terrace or at pretty white-clothed tables inside. Should you happen to stay when the kitchen is closed, the friendly staff will book you a table in Gordes. Great walking, fine dining, easy living. And don't miss medieval Sénanque abbey.

Price	€99–€208. Quadruples €182–€214.
Rooms	13: 11 twins/doubles, 2 quadruples.
Meals	Dinner €32.50 (except Tues, Thurs & Sun). Wine €18–€50. Restaurants 10-minute walk.
Closed	Early January to early March; late Nov to early Dec.
Directions	From Avignon, east on N7; left onto N100 for Apt; left to Gordes. Route de Sénanque on left entering Gordes. Hotel 200m on right.

Michel Dimeux & Pierre Ticot
Route de Sénanque,
84220 Gordes, Vaucluse
Tel   +33 (0)4 90 72 12 13
Email   info@masromarins.com
Web   www.masromarins.com

Château La Roque

Look an eagle in the eye, up here on the edge of the Lubéron, safe in the stony arms of the great fortress. Its history starts with the 8th-century Saracen invasion. Peace came at last in 1741 and, blissfully, still reigns, interrupted only by bees buzzing in the lime tree; the glorious views still stretch over the tranquil valley. Kind and interesting, Jean can tell you about the golden ratio used to build the castle; delightful Chantal speaks good English, too. The highly original rock-face pool will enchant you. Bedrooms, uncluttered but never cold, are huge, comfortable and furnished with carefully-chosen antiques, top-quality bedding and unostentatious designer fabrics. One has a deep-coral bed under vaulted ceilings and genuine 13th-century wardrobe doors. Each handsome, roomy bathroom, be it high-modern or new-old, is done with the best fittings. After visiting a pretty Provençal town or famous vineyard (Gigondas, Châteauneuf…), return to dinner of, for example, monkfish with a saffron sauce on a bed of green asparagus served on the vine-dappled terrace or in the garden. *Children over 11 welcome.*

Price	€150–€190. Suites €280.
Rooms	5: 2 doubles, 3 suites.
Meals	Breakfast €20.
	Dinner, 4 courses €44 (except Sun, Mon & Tues); book ahead.
	Wine €26–€600.
Closed	4 January to 10 February.
Directions	From Lyon, A7 exit Orange Sud for Carpentras; on to Pernes les Fontaines, then St Didier, then La Roque 2km.

Chantal & Jean Tomasino
263 chemin du Château,
84210 La Roque sur Pernes, Vaucluse

Tel	+33 (0)4 90 61 68 77
Email	chateaularoque@wanadoo.fr
Web	www.chateaularoque.com

Entry 356 Map 16

Le Mas des Grès

A party atmosphere reigns at this spotless roadside hotel that the attentive owners – German-Swiss Nina and Franco-Italian Thierry – run with clockwork precision and sustainability in mind. Nina looks after you and Thierry conjures up superb food: inspiration from his Italian grandmother. Join in the preparations or sit and enjoy it all in the big beamed dining room or, in summer, under the soaring plane trees on a terrace lit by twinkling lights and candles. Children eat and then potter to their hearts' content. Plainish bedrooms vary in size, with neat quilts on firm beds and views over fields; bathrooms, some with superb Italian showers, are tiled top to toe. Nina knows everyone and can rustle up almost any local delight, from Châteauneuf du Pape wine tastings to Lubéron bike trips, trout fishing with the family or golf at one of 15 courses. A favourite is a guided nature hike to gather culinary plants and herbs; for collectors of brocante, popular L'Isle sur la Sorgue is up the road. Return to a kids' playground and a family-happy roadside pool. *Cookery classes for children (& adults on request).*

Price	€80–€230. Suites €210. Half-board €90–€145 p.p.
Rooms	14: 12 doubles, 2 suites for 4. Some rooms interconnect.
Meals	Breakfast €12. Picnic lunch €15. Buffet lunch €20 (July & August only). Dinner €36. Wine €15–€100.
Closed	11 November to 15 March.
Directions	A7 Apt & Avignon Sud, D33 for 13km; cross Petit Palais on D24. At T-junc. of D901, right to Apt. Hotel after 600m on right.

Nina & Thierry Crovara
1651 route d'Apt, 84800 Lagnes,
Vaucluse

Tel	+33 (0)4 90 20 32 85
Email	info@masdesgres.com
Web	www.masdesgres.com

Le Château de Mazan

The Marquis de Sade's father and uncle were born here, an unexpected connection, given the luminosity inside. Though the infamous Marquis preferred Paris, he often stayed at Mazan, organising France's first theatre festival here in 1772. The château sits in an appealing little town at the foot of Mont Ventoux. Floors are tiled in white-and-terracotta squares that would drown a smaller space, ceilings are lofty, windows are huge with the lightest curtains. This is a family hotel and Frédéric, who speaks good English, runs a smooth team while mother does the fabulous décor, each room an ethereal delight: pale pink walls, a velvet sofa, a touch of apricot taffeta, a flash of red. Ground-floor bedrooms have French windows to a private sitting area; a couple of the rooms in the annexe across the road have their own terraces. There are frondy palms and secluded spots in the garden – doze in the shade of the mulberry trees – and a beautiful terrace for dinner; the chef has worked in starred restaurants and is keen to win his own. Stay on a Friday and catch Carpentras market. Altogether wonderful. *Car park down hill.*

Price	€105–€280. Suites €330–€410. Family rooms €145–€280. Extra bed €30.
Rooms	31: 14 doubles, 3 suites for 4, 14 family rooms for 3-4.
Meals	Breakfast €17. Lunch & dinner from €37. Restaurant closed Tuesdays; Mondays out of season. Wine from €19.
Closed	January to February.
Directions	From Carpentras D942 for Sault & Ventoux, 7km. In Mazan, 1st right near town hall, then left. Signed.

Danièle & Frédéric Lhermie
Place Napoléon,
84380 Mazan, Vaucluse

Tel	+33 (0)4 90 69 62 61
Email	reservation@chateaudemazan.com
Web	www.chateaudemazan.fr

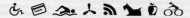

Château Juvenal

From the hall, peep through the double doorways at the sitting and dining rooms. Splendour! With two glorious chandeliers reflecting in the gilt-framed mirrors at each end of this long reception suite, you are transported back a couple of centuries. Surely the chamber orchestra will be tuning up soon, sending notes floating over the exquisite period furniture, high ceilings, tall windows? Yet this 19th-century gem is lived in and loved every day, thanks to delightful Anne-Marie and Bernard, who also produce an award-winning wine and delicious olive oil from their 600 trees. They nurture some superb specimen trees, too, out in the park. The traditional bedrooms are all on the first floor and range from cosy to spacious: 'Iris' the smallest in pure white and grey, 'Cerise', larger, with deep pink spread, 'Raisin' with Louis XIII chairs and marble-top dresser, 'Les Genêts', sunny yellow with a roll top bath. Grab your shopping basket and visit the local market, there is a summer kitchen next to the pool. There are wine visits, a pony for the kids, annual tango events, a spa and two lovely apartments for longer stays.

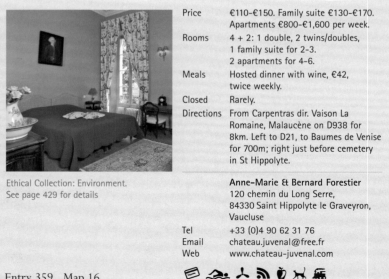

Price	€110–€150. Family suite €130–€170. Apartments €800–€1,600 per week.
Rooms	4 + 2: 1 double, 2 twins/doubles, 1 family suite for 2–3. 2 apartments for 4–6.
Meals	Hosted dinner with wine, €42, twice weekly.
Closed	Rarely.
Directions	From Carpentras dir. Vaison La Romaine, Malaucène on D938 for 8km. Left to D21, to Baumes de Venise for 700m; right just before cemetery in St Hippolyte.

Ethical Collection: Environment.
See page 429 for details

Anne-Marie & Bernard Forestier
120 chemin du Long Serre,
84330 Saint Hippolyte le Graveyron,
Vaucluse
Tel   +33 (0)4 90 62 31 76
Email   chateau.juvenal@free.fr
Web   www.chateau-juvenal.com

Les Florets

The setting is magical, the greeting from the Bernard family is heartfelt and the walks are outstanding. Les Florets sits at the foot of the majestic Dentelles de Montmirail, a small range of mountains crested with long, delicate stone fingers in the middle of Côtes du Rhône country. Over 40km of clearly marked paths call you, so appetites build for sublime food served beneath plane, chestnut and lime trees on the almost theatrical terrace; the low stone walls are bright with busy lizzies and the peonies were blooming in March. You'll also sample some of the wines that the family has been producing since the 1880s. Bright blue and yellow corridors lead to well-organised, well-renovated rooms, some with traditional floral décor, others in soft taupe and ivory, all with big tiled bathrooms but without mozzie meshes or air con. We liked the quirky ceramic soup tureens in reception, the scintillating collection of glass carafes in the warm red dining room and the beautiful new hillside pool. All this, and the wine list a work of art. Book well ahead, people return year after year. *Ask about wine tours & tennis.*

Price	€70–€165. Suite €91–€165.
Rooms	15: 10 doubles, 4 twins, 1 suite.
Meals	Breakfast €15.
	Lunch & dinner €25–€48.
	Half-board available.
	Restaurant closed Wednesdays.
Closed	January to mid-March.
Directions	From Carpentras, D7 for Vacqueyras.
	Right on D7 to Gigondas for 2km;
	signed.

Thierry & Dominique Bernard
Route des Dentelles, 84190 Gigondas,
Vaucluse

Tel	+33 (0)4 90 65 85 01
Email	accueil@hotel-lesflorets.com
Web	www.hotel-lesflorets.com

L'A Propos

It's like stepping through the looking glass into another world, one of refined French taste and modern elegance, where heels click on polished parquet and the smell of fresh coffee drifts through salons warmed by log fires. If the house weren't so full of 19th-century period features you'd say parts were wacky – such as the walls clothed in black-and-white postcard blow-ups of the town. In other parts white predominates, softened by earthy fabrics and oil paintings. The fantasy continues into three private parks through which one wanders in the shade of ancient cypresses and palms. Discover a heated pool, a balneotherapy area, a boules pitch, a buddha to encourage peace and harmony. There's harmony in the bedrooms, too: spacious, beautifully arranged rooms, with fabulous bathrooms attached. All feels classic yet contemporary. Take afternoon tea or a glass of Rhône wine, savour lunch or dinner in the popular restaurant. If only the dream didn't have to end… but beyond are ancient ruins and vibrant markets, canoeing on the Ardèche and wine tastings in Châteauneuf-du-Pape vineyards. Perfection in Orange.

Price	€112–€160. Suites €180–€250.
Rooms	5: 1 double, 4 suites for 1-4.
Meals	Lunch €16. Dinner à la carte, €30; book ahead. Wine €18–€80. Restaurants 150m.
Closed	Rarely.
Directions	Exit A7 at Orange Centre. Follow signs for Vaison la Romaine Hospital; left at corner with Police station. Bear left, hotel 150m on right.

Estelle Godefroy-Mourier
15 avenue Frédéric Mistral,
84100 Orange, Vaucluse

Tel	+33 (0)4 90 34 54 91
Mobile	+33 (0)6 10 33 06 32
Email	info@lapropos.com
Web	www.lapropos.com

Villa Noria

The garden sets the scene, a delightfully secluded enclave of mature cedars, palms, cherries, roses and manicured lawn. Within it is an elegant 18th-century house run by run by the thoroughly delightful Philippe and Sylvie who look after guests with immaculate professionalism. She ushers you up the stone farmhouse stair to beautiful bedrooms decorated in gloriously colourful Provençal style, the finest on the first floor. Cool tiles underfoot, beams overhead, walls colour-washed cerise, blue and raspberry, beds opulently swathed in white linen and bathrooms boldly, diagonally tiled. You breakfast in an elegant, wraparound conservatory, there's a salon with fauteuils dressed in red and white checks, and the long oval dining table sits beneath a huge weeping fern. In summer you're under the trees. Philippe is an experienced chef: don't miss his hosted dinners. Noria is on the edge of the peaceful village of Modène, near several burgeoning villas, and the views sweep over vineyards to mountains beyond; recline by the saltwater pool on a handsome wooden lounger and drink them in. A stylish retreat. *No credit cards.*

Price	€70–€120. Suite €140–€160. Extra bed €30.
Rooms	5: 3 doubles, 1 twin, 1 suite for 4.
Meals	Hosted dinner with wine, €35. Restaurant 3km.
Closed	Rarely.
Directions	D974 Carpentras to Bedoin; after 7.5km, left onto D84 to Modène. House on left on entrance to village. Signed.

Philippe Monti
84330 Modène, Vaucluse

Tel	+33 (0)4 90 62 50 66
Email	post@villa-noria.com
Web	www.villa-noria.com

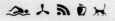

Hostellerie du Val de Sault

This landscape has been called a 'sea of corn gold and lavender blue': from your terrace here you can contemplate the familiar shape of Mont Ventoux, the painter's peak, beyond. The charming, chatty Yves has gathered all possible information, knows everyone there is to know on the Provence scene and is full of good guidance. He creates menus featuring truffles or lavender or spelt, or game with mushrooms for the autumn, beautifully served in the formal atmosphere of the light, airy restaurant. And children can eat earlier, allowing the grown-ups to savour their meal in peace. Perched just above the woods in a big garden is a group of modern one-storey buildings, one housing the bedrooms. Wooden floors and pine-slatted walls bring live warmth, soft colour schemes have oriental flashes, baths in the suites have jets. Each room feels like a very private space with its own terrace (the suites have loungers on theirs): the pool, bar and restaurant are there for conviviality; the fitness room, tennis court and boules pitch for exercise; the jacuzzi space for chilling out. *Ask for a room with a view. Spa.*

Price	€75–€140. Suites €195–€290. Half-board approx. €60 p.p.
Rooms	20: 11 twins/doubles, 9 suites.
Meals	Breakfast €17. Lunch & dinner €45–€99. Wine from €12. Half-board only in July-August for twins/doubles.
Closed	November to March.
Directions	A7 exit 23; D942 for Carpentras Mazan Sault, then for St Trinit & Fourcalquier. Left after r'bout, by fire station.

Yves Gattechaut
Route de Saint Trinit,
Ancien chemin d'Aurel,
84390 Sault, Vaucluse

Tel	+33 (0)4 90 64 01 41
Email	valdesault@aol.com
Web	www.valdesault.com

Auberge de Reillanne

The solid loveliness of this 18th-century house, so typical of the area, reassures you, invites you in. And you will not be disappointed: it feels good to be here, even if you can't quite define the source of the positive energy. Monique is clearly connected to the spirit of the place and has used all her flair and good taste to transform the old inn into a very special place to stay. Large, airy bedrooms are done in cool restful colours with big cupboards and rattan furniture. There are beams, properly whitewashed walls and books. Bathrooms are big and simple too. Downstairs, the sitting and dining areas are decorated in warm, embracing colours with terracotta tiles and flame-coloured curtains. On several levels of stream-fed rolling lawns and tree'd borders, the tranquil garden has hammocks and statues. This would be a place for a quiet holiday with long meditative walks in the hills, a place to come and write that novel under the shade of the ancient trees, or simply to get to know the gentle, delicate, smiling owner who loves nothing better than to receive people in her magical house. One of our favourites.

Price	€75–€78. Singles €60. Half-board €72–€88 p.p.
Rooms	6: 4 doubles, 2 triples.
Meals	Breakfast €8.50. Dinner €25. Wine €16–€26.
Closed	Mid-October to early April.
Directions	N100 through Apt & Céreste. Approx. 8km after Céreste, left on D214 to Reillanne. Hotel on right.

Monique Balmand
04110 Reillanne,
Alpes-de-Haute-Provence
Tel   +33 (0)4 92 76 45 95
Email   monique.balmand@wanadoo.fr
Web   www.auberge-de-reillanne.com

Château d'Esparron

Wallow in the stunning setting, bask in the charm of your laid-back hosts. Bernard inherited the château from his uncle, a 'monument historique' whose 13th-century towers, spiral stone stairs and hand-blown window panes remain wonderfully intact. Charlotte-Anne – as English as a Gainsborough painting – attends to everything and everyone: children, dogs, garden, guests. There are fine bits of furniture and lovely paintings, everything is well cared for and improvements are constantly being made. The garden is pretty, peaceful and private, the bedrooms are simple, elegant and spacious. But best of all are the setting and the views, sweeping over large plane trees and sloping fields to the beautiful, deep-blue lake. Fishing, watersporting and swimming are on the spot, and there's a sailing club for children. The treats continue at table – a big polished round one in a cavernous kitchen where breakfasts of fresh fruits, local sheep cheeses, sausages, eggs and delicious organic apple juice set you up for the day. Return to a library of English books, a wonderful family and dinner in the village.

Price	€150-€260.
Rooms	5: 3 doubles, 1 twin, 1 suite.
Meals	Restaurant 5-minute walk.
Closed	November to March.
Directions	From Aix en Provence A51 exit 18 on D907; D82 to Gréoux les Bains; D952 & D315 to Esparron. Stop & ring at gates (once past, it's impossible to turn).

Bernard & Charlotte-Anne de Castellane
04800 Esparron de Verdon,
Alpes-de-Haute-Provence

Mobile	+33 (0)6 64 65 17 00
Email	chateau.esparron@gmail.com
Web	www.chateau-esparron.com

Villa Morelia

In a delightful Alpine village with breathtaking views, Robert and Marie-Christine, a charming couple who know quite a bit about cuisine, welcome you to their intimate restaurant-hotel. It is a sumptuous and award-winning place to stay, run by people whose hospitality could not be more generous or sincere. You will love everything inside: high airy ceilings, walnut windows and doors, bathrooms with multi-jet showers and all the right touches, big bedrooms that manage to look elegant and welcoming at the same time, and views over big beautiful grounds. Robert is chef, a poet with a magic touch, transforming the freshest market ingredients into pure delight; our dessert consisted of three dishes based on three red fruits in season. Table linens are impeccable, wines are wonderful, the service is exceptional and Robert will pick you up if you don't want to drive. It is, in his words, "une grande maison de famille". In other words, not just a place to hang your hat for a couple of days. Great hiking and biking, and Italy a hop over the pass. *Cookery courses & spa.*

Price	€150-€210. Single €120. Suites €240-€350.
Rooms	24: 20 doubles, 1 single, 3 suites.
Meals	Breakfast €22. Picnic lunch available. Dinner €54. Wine €45-€600.
Closed	12 November to 27 December; April.
Directions	7km from Barcelonnette on D900 Gap-Cuneo road. In centre of village.

Marie-Christine & Robert Boudard
04850 Jausiers,
Alpes-de-Haute-Provence

Tel	+33 (0)4 92 84 67 78
Email	direction@villa-morelia.com
Web	www.villa-morelia.com

Entry 366   Map 16

Le Moulin du Château

A sleepy place – come to doze, your silence broken only by the call of the sparrowhawk or the distant rumble of a car. This 17th-century olive mill once belonged to the château and stands at the foot of a venerable grove; the vast press is now a reception area where modern art hangs on ancient walls. The Moulin, a long, low, stone building with lavender-blue shutters and the odd climbing vine, stands in its own gardens surrounded by lavender and fruit trees. In the bedrooms light filters though voile curtains, shadows dance upon the walls. The feel is uncluttered, cool, breezy, with vibrant colours: turquoise, lilac, lime – luminous yet restful. This is an easy-going 'green' hotel where the emphasis is on the simple things of life. Edith and Nicolas use regional and organic food, boules is played under the cherry tree, poppies grow on an old crumbling stone staircase and views stretch across fields to village and château. There are great walks, bikes for gentle country excursions, a swimming and boating lake nearby, and further afield are the Cistercian abbey of Le Thoronet, the Verdon Canyon and Digne Les Bains.

Price	€118–€142.
	Half-board €178–€202 for 2.
Rooms	10: 5 doubles, 2 twins, 1 triple,
	1 quadruple, 1 suite.
Meals	Breakfast included. Picnic lunch €10.
	Dinner €30 (except Mon & Thurs).
	Wine €6–€40. Restaurants nearby.
Closed	November to March.
Directions	From Gréoux les Bains D952 to Riez,
	then D11 for Quinson; head for St
	Laurent du Verdon; take road after
	château. Signed.

Ethical Collection: Environment; Food.
See page 429 for details

Edith & Nicolas Stämpfli-Faoro
04500 Saint Laurent du Verdon,
Alpes-de-Haute-Provence

Tel	+33 (0)4 92 74 02 47
Email	info@moulin-du-chateau.com
Web	www.moulin-du-chateau.com

La Bastide du Pin

Such a glamorous drive from Nice, straight through the Massif des Maures; you'll need Gucci sunglasses and a soft-top motor. This gorgeous hideaway, reached through a wide gate and a drive bordered by ancient cypresses, is set among gardens of lavender, gravelled paths, sculptures, pool and views as far as the eye can see. It is utterly, peacefully beautiful, and the shady patio, as much Tuscany as Provence, is a delicious place to laze away a hot afternoon with only the fountain to disturb you. (For lazy evenings in, there's billiards, books and WiFi.) Bedrooms, all upstairs, are spacious and elegant with an understated feel: dark wood and terracotta hues in one; long lemon curtains, dove-grey wardrobe and sparkly chandelier in another. Cushions coordinate with bed linen and bathrooms are fresh with bathrobes and soaps. Best of all are Edith and Pierre, your friendly, interesting, attentive hosts, who give you gorgeous breakfasts in their big dining room and host dinner once a week in high season. Walk to Lorgues with the lovely Thoronet abbey, buzzing summer market, shops and bars, all equally alluring in spring.

Price	€85–€155. Family room €95–€135 for 2, €120–€160 for 3.
Rooms	6: 4 doubles, 1 twin/double, 1 family room for 3.
Meals	Occasional summer dinner with wine, €30–€40. Restaurants in Lorgues, 2km.
Closed	Rarely.
Directions	Sent on booking.

Pierre Gissinger & Edith Chemel
1017 route de Salernes,
83510 Lorgues, Var
Tel   +33 (0)4 94 73 90 38
Email   contact@bastidedupin.com
Web   www.bastidedupin.com

Entry 368   Map 16

Une Campagne en Provence

In spring, water gushes through the 400-acre estate: the 12th-century Knights Templar created myriad irrigation channels, the life-source of Une Campagne en Provence. The stunning bastide keeps it fortress-like proportions and bags of character and charm. Martina and Claude love it all, have planted 3,750 trees, and their sense of fun makes a stay a real treat. The main house is arranged around a central patio, with stairs leading to the bedrooms above. Simple Provençal furnishings are lit by huge windows, floors are terracotta, there are cosy 'boutis' quilts and sumptuous towels and linen, and bathrooms cleverly worked around original features. Breakfasts are scrumptious, and fun; dinners – meet lots of other guests – put the accent on excellent local produce and their own wine. In the cellar find music and a mini cinema – great for kids; there's table football and a pool with a view (open May to October), a sauna, a Turkish bath, and a well-stocked library. Beyond are tracks to the hills, and Provençal villages. An isolated paradise for all ages, overseen by a charming young family, two geese and one dear dog.

Price	€95–€115. Suite €110–€120. Studio €110–€130.
Rooms	5: 3 doubles, 1 suite, 1 studio for 2 with kitchenette.
Meals	Hosted dinner with wine, €34. Restaurant 3km.
Closed	January to mid-March.
Directions	A8 Aix-Nice exit St Maximin la Ste Baume; D28 to Bras; after 7km, right & follow signs.

Ethical Collection: Environment; Food.
See page 429 for details

Martina & Claude Fussler
Domaine le Peyrourier,
83149 Bras, Var
Tel   +33 (0)4 98 05 10 20
Email   info@provence4u.com
Web   www.provence4u.com

Bastide Avellanne

Deep comfort and incredible quiet await you in this beautifully renovated bastide with its 1616 build-date carved in stone; private grounds, vineyards and glorious views over the Var surround you. Inside find a huge living and dining area with stone walls and fireplace, arched windows, red leather sofas and interesting paintings; eat here at large wooden tables or on the pretty front terrace. Dinner includes regional specialities mixed with Italian, French and Mediterranean dishes, with the emphasis always on fresh and wholesome. Bedrooms (some upstairs, some down) are truly sumptuous, all a good size with ancient beams, local furniture and fabrics, tiled floors, fresh flowers, clouds of soft pillows and views over the gardens, front or back. Shower rooms are immaculate and luxurious with mosaic floors, coordinated towels and sprigs of lavender; all feels spacious and light. Friendly Steve and Valentina throw open their bougainvillea-scented grounds (also to gîte guests): find a lovely pool, blue sunbeds, boules, tennis courts and a giant chess set under the shade of a 500-year-old oak tree. It's charming.

Price	€140–€240. Suites €200–€240.
	Gîtes €650–€1,480. Apts €450–€900.
Rooms	5 + 4: 3 twins/doubles, 2 suites.
	2 gîtes for 4, 2 apartments for 2.
Meals	Dinner, 3 courses, €30. Restaurant 3km.
	Wine from €20.
Closed	Rarely.
Directions	Sent on booking.

	Steve & Valentina Dixon
	83890 Besse sur Issole, Var
Tel	+33 (0)4 94 69 89 91
Email	info@bastideavellanne.com
Web	www.bastideavellanne.com

Hostellerie Bérard & Spa

Bags of atmosphere, stunning gardens, exquisite gastronomy, a magical spa and possibly the best breakfasts in France. René's son Jean-François in now head chef of the Michelin-starred restaurant; Danièle is an expert in local wines. In both restaurant and bistro the emphasis is on Provençal gastronomy using organic seasonal produce from the kitchen garden; save up for a sumptuous treat. Madame and Monsieur are true belongers, who grew up in this hilltop village, opened in 1969 and have respectfully restored a complex of highly evocative buildings, an 11th-century monastery; a blue-shuttered bastide, a *maison bourgeoise*, an artist's pavilion. The views are framed visions of olive groves, of vines in their serried choreography and Templar strongholds on mountain tops in the distance. Each bedroom is a lovely French surprise – a delicate wrought-iron four-poster, a snowy counterpane, curtains in toile de Jouy – and the small spa is a delight; book in for a treatment. Daughter Sandra, full of friendly enthusiasm, handles the day-to-day running of this charming restaurant-hotel. *Ask about cookery courses with René.*

Price	€99–€195. Suites €251–€299.
Rooms	40: 36 doubles, 4 suites for 4.
Meals	Buffet breakfast €21. Lunch & dinner €48–€154. Wine from €27.
Closed	Early January to early February.
Directions	A50 towards Toulon exit 11; follow signs to Cadière d'Azur. Hotel in centre of village.

Bérard Family
Rue Gabriel Péri,
83740 La Cadière d'Azur, Var

Tel	+33 (0)4 94 90 11 43
Email	berard@hotel-berard.com
Web	www.hotel-berard.com

Hôtel Notre Dame

On the edge of cobbled Collobrières, with wonderful views of the Massif des Maures, is a 18th-century staging post, a delicious modern hotel. Its inspired creators, Nili and Olivier – émigrés from the worlds of fashion and wine – speak several languages, embrace all nationalities and love what they do. They have named each bedroom after a precious stone – sapphire, jade, coral; guests, on booking, are encouraged to pick the colour of their choice. Imagine cool floor tiles, glowing paintings, thick cream curtains, repro Louis XIV tables, bright mosaic'd showers and beautiful stone ceilings washed in white. The Pearl Suite has three windows and is full of light, and some rooms have divans that double up as child beds (families are welcomed with open arms). Outside are a lovely tranquil terrace and an eco-friendly pool, fenced and safe for children. As for the food, there are four different kinds of breakfast – from Scandinavian to continental – served until late, the best ingredients at dinner, and wines from the famous bio vineyards of Correns. What to discover? The palms and sands of Le Lavandou!

Price	€65–€95. Single €65–€89.
	Suite €105–€230. Family room €145.
Rooms	10: 5 doubles, 1 single, 3 suites,
	1 family room.
Meals	Breakfast €12–€25.
	Dinner, 2-3 courses, €22–€28.
	Wine €18.50–€109. Restaurant 1km.
Closed	5 January to mid-March.
Directions	Sent on booking.

Olivier Faivre
15 avenue de la Libération,
83610 Collobrières, Var

Tel	+33 (0)4 94 48 07 13
Email	hotelnotredame@gmail.com
Web	www.hotel-notre-dame.eu

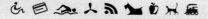

Le Pré aux Marguerites

No bell, no sign, but don't give up: the place is a gem. Built in the 1950s in Provençal style, the house was the family's holiday home when Frédéric was a child. Your captivating, cultured, well-travelled host was an interior designer in New York; now he is passionately engaged in the region, as well as running this exquisitely positioned cliffside B&B, bang in front of the sea. Breakfasts are convivial and copious, served on the terrace or by the pool. And what a pool! Under the pines, free of chemicals, overlooking the sea. You could spend all day here, up among the mimosas and palms, the benches and pathways; there's a small playground too and, best of all, a path that meanders down to a totally private beach. The largest suite, facing the sea, has a big bed enveloped in fawn cotton, a beautiful antique day bed and a matching armoire, and a bathroom with bright blue tiles. Cosier 'Colombier' comes with a sloped beamed ceiling and a sprinkling of as-lovely antiques. Escape Cavalaire, upscale family resort with a huge marina, to hilltop villages Ramatuelle and Gassin – popular with visitors but ever enchanting.

Price	€150-€300.
Rooms	2 suites, each with kitchenette.
Meals	Dinner €45. Wine from €15.
Closed	January to March.
Directions	Ave des Alliers, 1st left Ave Neptune, 1st right Ave des Amphores, 1st left Ave des Triton, 1st right Ave du Corail.

Frédéric Jochem
1 avenue du Corail,
83240 Cavalaire, Var

Tel	+33 (0)4 94 89 11 20
Email	fjochem@aol.com
Web	www.bonporto.com

La Ferme d'Augustin

A 13th-century gateway heralds your arrival to the olive farm that opened to guests (just a few wanderers and celebrities) in the early days of Brigitte Bardot… she still lives nearby. Fifty years on: fabrics from Provence, tiles from Salernes and *objets* stylishly scattered by owner Ninette. The décor is wonderfully relaxed, the pool is discreet and the place is filled with garden roses. The farm rests in a relatively untouched spot of this legendary peninsula, a minute from Tahiti Beach and two miles from St Tropez, reached by a road known only to the locals, or a 15-mile coastal path: the position is among the best on the Riviera. Couples, families, foodies flock. Organic veg from the potager, wines from the vines, fruits from the orchard and their own olive oil structure a cuisine that is as authentic as it is simple; savour the flavours of Provence from the terrace or the pergola. Their very own bath soaps and gels express the same Provençal spirit; bedrooms in apartments are cosy and characterful, some with whirlpool baths and sea views. A rich, relaxed Riviera retreat. *Hydrotherapy pool.*

Price	€150–€800.
Rooms	46: 16 doubles, 28 suites, 2 apartments for 2-4.
Meals	Breakfast €15. Lunch à la carte €15–€50. Dinner à la carte €30–€60.
Closed	Mid-October to April.
Directions	From Nice, exit Le Muy for St Tropez; on to Chemin de la Belle Isnarde. Hotel on road before Tahiti Beach on left. Secure parking.

Vallet Family
Route de Tahiti, Saint Tropez,
83350 Ramatuelle, Var

Tel	+33 (0)4 94 55 97 00
Email	info@fermeaugustin.com
Web	www.fermeaugustin.com

Ethical Collection: Food.
See page 429 for details

Hôtel des Deux Rocs

Crowning an enchanting little hillside town – Seillans is a gem – a lovely old French townhouse bursting with personality and family friendliness. Julie and Nicolas, a young and talented team, spent time in the company of the greats – Paul Bocuse, Michel Troigros, Michel Guérard; you eat well here. The interiors too are a delight, with polished antiques and portraits of noble heads up the stairs; note the rich fabrics on 18th-century chairs, the 17th-century sedan chair, a well-travelled suitcase here and there. Bathrooms are in ageless British style: white porcelain basins, reissued vintage fittings, roll top tubs… perfection. Flowers grown around the village and used by the region's celebrated perfume makers inspired the name of each differently decorated room. Some overlook the valley, others the wide spread of a splendid terrace with a cinematographic view. Rooms, from small to large, have family furniture and cosy Provençal quilts. The splashing of the fountain accompanies fabulous food served under majestic plane trees; candlelit tables are set with small bouquets of rose, lilac and hortensia.

Price	€75-€135. Family rooms €125-€165.
Rooms	14: 11 doubles, 2 family rooms for 3, 1 for 4.
Meals	Breakfast €13. Lunch & dinner €40-€67. Wine from €24. Restaurant closed Sun eve, all day Mon & Tues lunchtimes Oct-April.
Closed	3 January to 14 February.
Directions	From A8 exit 39 Les Adrets; follow signs to Fayence, then Seillans. Hotel at top of village.

Julie & Nicolas Malzac-Heimermann
Place Font d'Amont,
83440 Seillans, Var

Tel	+33 (0)4 94 76 87 32
Email	hoteldeuxrocs@wanadoo.fr
Web	www.hoteldeuxrocs.com

Bastide Saint Mathieu

A house-party hotel set in the hills – near enough for a stroll along the Croisette, far enough from the hordes. Roadside wrought-iron gates open to a stunning 18th-century bastide with gardens and a huge park, fully tree'd and brimful with exotica; the outside terraces, replete with a *cuisine d'été*, are ideal for opulent receptions and weddings. Of massive stone and elegantly shuttered, the bastide overlooks fields and hills of olive and lemon trees. Serene surroundings combine with prime pampering inside and bathrooms are decadently gorgeous, never flashy. Fragrances and soaps may be from Molinard, Fragonard or Galimard. The look is luxury-rustic: sumptuous paintings and fabrics, cashmere blankets, DVDs, a contemporary four-poster facing the window to catch the morning sun. Breakfast, watched over by a painted angel by the lit fireplace (or on the terrace) is as late as you like, and sensational: the juiciest fruits, amazing jams, wonderful French cheeses. Be seduced by a huge heavenly pool, a boules piste, spa treatments on request. And their own opera festival.

Price	€270–€330. Suites €330–€380. Whole house €8,000–€16,000 per week.
Rooms	7: 1 twin/double, 3 doubles, 1 single, 2 suites.
Meals	Restaurants nearby.
Closed	Rarely.

Stop Press
Property sold

Hôtel Le Cavendish

Civilised and convivial, the Cavendish is a joy, offering a drink on arrival and a complimentary bar in the evening. Set back from the bustle of Cannes, this splendid rebirth of a Napoleon III mansion displays Madame Welter's talents. Subtle modern comforts and splendid rooms, some with balcony or terrace, are the frame. Sensuous, exuberant, almost edible choices of fabric and colour that are never overdone – crunchy raspberry taffeta, tasselled pistachio green, twilight mauve – clothe the frame. Quirky old-fashioned charm enfolds it all. It's like being a guest in the grand house of a *grand homme*, such as its namesake, Lord Cavendish. How attentive to offer leaf teas for breakfast, how sexy to dress the curvy Carrara marble staircase with candles at dusk, how delightful to slip between lavender-scented sheets at night. Freshly baked croissants, cakes and crumbles, homemade jams and cheerful staff make mornings easy, especially if you are attending one of the events at the Festival Hall, ten minutes away. Superb. *Private beach nearby, €20 p.p. Valet parking €25.*

Price	€130–€295.
Rooms	35: 23 doubles, 12 twins.
Meals	Breakfast €20 (included for Sawday guests). Complimentary bar 6-9pm.
Closed	Mid-December to mid-January.
Directions	From Nice A8; left at r'bout on Boulevard Carnot; follow signs for Palais des Festivals. Signed.

Christine & Guy Welter
11 boulevard Carnot,
06400 Cannes, Alpes-Maritimes

Tel	+33 (0)4 97 06 26 00
Email	reservation@cavendish-cannes.com
Web	www.cavendish-cannes.com

Hôtel La Jabotte

What makes La Jabotte special? Is it the courtyard scented with oranges or the bedrooms the colours of jewels? Or is it Claude and Yves, Belgians who came to the Cap one summer and fell for a small faded hotel. Today it is an explosion of colour, beautifully clean and inviting. Yves is the artistic one, Claude oversees all, both are generous and kind. Down a small side street, 60 metres from the beach, are polished stone floors and cherry-red walls, pots of roses and bright parakeets, Tommy the wagging white Westie, lavender and champagne. Pass the deep aubergine sofa, enter the gliding wall of glass and find the enchanting pebbled courtyard off which lie the bedrooms. Each has its table and chairs outside the door and pots of plants lovingly labelled; it feels more home than hotel and you get to know your neighbours. Bedrooms – Lavender, Citron – are small but charming, shower rooms have delicious lotions and fulsome towels, though no shower screens. After fresh jams, oranges and croissants, saunter into Old Antibes – or drift down to the free sandy beach and your own parasol. *Limited parking, book ahead.*

Price	€95-€128. Suite €139-€180.
Rooms	10: 9 twins/doubles, 1 suite for 2-4.
Meals	Breakfast included. Restaurants within walking distance.
Closed	November to mid-February.
Directions	Follow signs for Antibes Centre then Cap d'Antibes, Les Plages, La Salis. In small street 60m from La Salis beach.

Yves April & Claude Mora
13 avenue Max Maurey,
06160 Cap d'Antibes, Alpes-Maritimes
Tel   +33 (0)4 93 61 45 89
Email   info@jabotte.com
Web   www.jabotte.com

Entry 378   Map 16

Villa Saint Maxime

On a site facing hilltop St Paul de Vence is a retreat of white spaces, a contemporary gem. The house was built by a British architect during the first Gulf War and, in a modern echo of eastern dwellings, the main atrium has a retractable roof allowing breezes to waft through – and thrilling night-sky views, too. Be wowed by bold sweeping lines, pale marble and gleaming terracotta, pillared halls and, in the central stairwell, a broken-glass garden that sparkles like Ali Baba's jewels. Each air-conditioned room has a balcony or terrace to make the most of the views, the bath and shower rooms are spectacular, and you lounge beneath exotic palms and parasols by a very large pool. Ann and John spent their early married life in this summer-busy village beloved of Picasso, Miro, Chagall. Ann collects modern art; there's a piece or two in your room, more in that great centre of art, Fondation Maeght. Breakfast, with sabre-opened champagne if you wish, is any time at all, while an orange aperitif here sets the mood for dinner at the legendary Colombe d'Or up the hill. Fabulous. *Unsupervised pool. Children over 12 welcome.*

Price	€155–€255. Suites €190–€380.
Rooms	6: 4 doubles, 2 suites.
Meals	Breakfast included.
	Restaurants within walking distance.
Closed	6 November to 28 February.
Directions	A8 exit Cagnes sur Mer for Vence then St Paul. Nearing village, left at blue sign for villa. At end of road, blue gate, on left.

Ann & John Goldenberg
390 route de la Colle,
06570 Saint Paul de Vence,
Alpes-Maritimes

Tel	+33 (0)4 93 32 76 00
Email	riviera@villa-st-maxime.com
Web	www.villa-st-maxime.com

Hôtel Windsor

A 1930s Riviera hotel with a pool in a palm grove and exotic birds in cages – a lush escape in the heart of Nice. Indoors, Hôtel Windsor has introduced the thirties to the 21st century by asking contemporary artists to decorate some of the rooms. The result is gifts of wit, provocation, flights of fancy and minimalist sobriety: Joan Mas's *Cage à Mouches*, cosmopolitan Ben's writing on the walls, Antoine Beaudoin's frescoes of Venice, Egypt, India – and Tintin, all-time favourite. Plain white beds have contrasting cushions or quilts, furniture is minimal but interesting, little bathrooms are delightful and one room is painted in glimmering gold. Clear bright colours everywhere, including the richly exotic public areas; the charming Odile is passionate about contemporary art and chooses a different artist every year to reinvent the lobby. Outside, a tropical garden gives space for reflection among bamboo, fruiting trees and bougainvillea. Light filters through onto warmly smiling staff who prepare sumptuous buffet breakfasts under the palms in summer and run a superb spa, with gym, on the fifth floor.

Price	€95–€190.
Rooms	57 twins/doubles.
Meals	Breakfast €6–€13. Dinner à la carte €29–€40. Wine from €21. Restaurant closed Sundays.
Closed	Rarely.
Directions	In centre of Nice, 10-min walk from train station. A8 exit Promenade des Anglais. Left at museum on Rue Meyerbeer; right on Rue de France; 1st left Rue Dalpozzo.

Odile Redolfi-Payen
11 rue Dalpozzo,
06000 Nice, Alpes-Maritimes

Tel	+33 (0)4 93 88 59 35
Email	contact@hotelwindsornice.com
Web	www.hotelwindsornice.com

Hôtel Les Deux Frères

Only the rich and famous have this view so go ahead, be brave, rise at the crack of dawn and wonder at the glory of the light coming up over the ocean: it is ethereal. All terrace dining tables have views but you will be able to pick a favourite for hot coffee and croissants and linger even more. Willem, the Dutch owner who combines Provençal comfort – books, paintings, statues, magazines – with seven languages and an innovative cuisine – the restaurant is gorgeous – is full of ideas. Lieve runs a popular tea room next door – you may not be able to resist the sweet treats on offer. There's a 10th-century castle in the town, and Monaco and Menton are short drives along the coast. The hotel was a school in the 1850s and there are views of the coastline, mountainside or old village square from every small sparkling room, the best of which are at the front; choose between an oriental blue and gold ceiling, a stylish lime green or a nautical blue. After parking in the village you follow a short, fairly steep path – ideal for the young and fleet of foot. The rooms may be small, but the views are enormous.

Price	€100–€110. Singles €75.
Rooms	9 doubles.
Meals	Breakfast €9. Lunch from €28. Dinner from €48. Rest. closed Mon & Tues lunch in summer; Sun eve; mid-Nov to mid-Dec.
Closed	Rarely.
Directions	From Nice A8 exit 57 La Turbie then Roquebrune Cap Martin. Left at Roquebrune & Vieux Village. Stop at municipal car park & walk, 50m.

Willem & Lieve Bonestroo
Place des Deux Frères,
06190 Roquebrune Cap Martin,
Alpes-Maritimes
Tel   +33 (0)4 93 28 99 00
Email   info@lesdeuxfreres.com
Web   www.lesdeuxfreres.com

Many of you may want to stay in environmentally friendly places. You may be passionate about local, organic or home-grown food. Or perhaps you want to know that the place you are staying in contributes to the community? The Collection is made up of places going the extra mile, and taking the steps that most people have not yet taken, in one or more of the following areas:

• Environment Those making great efforts to reduce the environmental impact of their Special Place. We expect more than energy-saving light bulbs and recycling – in this part of the Collection you might find owners who make their own natural cleaning products, properties with solar hot water and biomass boilers, the odd green roof and a good measure of green elbow grease.

• Community Given to owners who use their property to play a positive role in their local and wider community. For example, by making a contribution from every guest's bill to a local fund, or running pond-dipping courses for local school children on their farm.

• Food Awarded to owners who make a real effort to source local or organic food, or to grow their own. We look for those who have gone out of their way to strike up relationships with local producers or to seek out organic suppliers. It is easier for an owner on a farm to produce their own eggs than for someone in the middle of a city, so we take this into account.

How it works
To become part of our Ethical Collection owners fill in a detailed questionnaire asking demanding questions about their activities in the chosen areas.

We then review each questionnaire carefully before deciding whether or not to give the award(s). The final decision is subjective; it is based not only on whether an owner ticks 'yes' to a question but also on the detailed explanation that accompanies each 'yes' or 'no' answer.

We have tried to be as rigorous as possible and have made sure the questions are demanding. We have not checked out the claims of owners before making our decisions, but we do trust them to be honest. We are only human, as are they, so please let us know if you think we have made any mistakes.

Ethical Collection in this book
A list of places in our Ethical Collection is shown below, by entry number.

Environment 24 • 101 • 148 • 184 • 210 • 234 • 271 • 344 • 347 • 359 • 367 • 369

Community 24 • 184 • 216 • 271 • 317

Food 20 • 24 • 120 • 148 • 184 • 203 • 210 • 234 • 271 • 344 • 367 • 369 • 374

Ethical Collection online
There is stacks more information on our website, www.sawdays.co.uk/about_us_ethical_collection/faq/

Alastair
Sawday's
Self-catering collection

Time away with your friends or family is precious, and when you are booking a whole week or more in one place you dare not get it wrong. The web is awash with advice from strangers but you can trust us to lead you somewhere special. We have visited each place on our site, and written about it honestly ourselves. Find original, quirky, beautiful, memorable properties in Britain, France, Ireland, Italy, Spain & Portugal.

Discover handsome châteaux, city apartments, cosy cottages, gorgeous gîtes, manor houses, tipis and more

Wheelchair-accessible

These places have at least one bedroom and bathroom accessible for wheelchair users. Some châteaux and hotels are keen to accept wheelchair users into their hotels and have made provision for them. However, this does not mean that wheelchair users will always be met with a perfect landscape, nor does it indicate that they have been officially assessed for such a status. You may encounter ramps, a shallow step, graveled paths, alternative routes into some rooms, a bathroom (not a wet room), perhaps even a lift. In short, there may be the odd hindrance and we urge you to call and make sure you will get what you need.

Quick reference index

For many years Alastair Sawday Publishing has been 'greening' the business in different ways. Our aim is to reduce our environmental footprint as far as possible and with almost everything we do we have environmental implications in mind. In recognition of our efforts we won a Business Commitment to the Environment Award in 2005, a Queen's Award for Enterprise in the Sustainable Development category in 2006, and the Independent Publishers Guild Environmental Award in 2008.

The buildings

Beautiful as they were, our old offices leaked heat, used electricity to heat water and rooms, flooded spaces with light to illuminate one person, and were not ours to alter.

So in 2005 we created our own eco offices by converting some old barns to create a low-emissions building. Heating and

lighting the building, which houses over 30 employees, now produces only 0.28 tonnes of carbon dioxide per year – a reduction of 35%. Not bad when you compare this with the six tonnes emitted by the average UK household. We achieved this through a variety of innovative and energy-saving building techniques, some of which are described below.

Insulation By laying insulating board 90mm thick immediately under the roof tiles and on the floor, and lining the inside of the building with plastic sheeting, we are now insulated even for Arctic weather, and almost totally air-tight.

Heating We installed a wood pellet boiler from Austria in order to be largely fossil-fuel free. The heat is conveyed by water to all corners of the building via an underfloor system.

Water We installed a 6,000-litre tank to collect rainwater from the roofs. This is pumped back, via an ultra-violet filter, to lavatories, shower and basins. There are also two solar thermal panels on the roof providing heat to the one hot-water cylinder.

Lighting We have a mix of low-energy lighting – task lighting and up lighting – and have installed three sun pipes.

Electricity Our electricity has long come from the Good Energy Company and is 100% renewable.

Photo above: Tom Germain
Photo opposite: Jackie King

Materials Virtually all materials are non-toxic or natural, and our carpets are made from (80%) Herdwick sheep wool from National Trust farms in the Lake District.

Doors and windows Outside doors and new windows are wooden, double-glazed and beautifully constructed in Norway. Old windows have been double-glazed.

More greenery

Besides having a building we are proud of, and which is pretty impressive visually, too, we work in a number of other ways to reduce the company's overall environmental footprint.

- office travel is logged as part of a carbon sequestration programme, and money for compensatory tree planting donated to SCAD in India for a tree-planting and development project
- we avoid flying and take the train for business trips wherever possible
- car sharing and the use of a company pool car (LPG fuelled) are part of company policy
- organic and Fair Trade basic provisions are used in the staff kitchen and organic and/or local food is provided by the company at all in-house events
- green cleaning products are used throughout
- kitchen waste is composted on our allotment
- the allotment is part of a community garden — alongside which we keep a small family of pigs and hens

However, becoming 'green' is a journey and, although we began long before most companies, we realise we still have a long way to go.

Alastair Sawday has been publishing books since 1994 finding Special Places to Stay in Britain and abroad. All our properties are inspected by us and are chosen for their charm and individuality and now with 25 titles to choose from there are plenty of places to explore. You can buy any of our books direct at a reader discount of 25%* on the RRP.

www.sawdays.co.uk/bookshop

List of titles:	RRP	Discount price
British Bed & Breakfast	£15.99	£11.99
British Bed & Breakfast for Garden Lovers	£19.99	£14.99
British Hotels and Inns	£15.99	£11.99
Pubs & Inns of England & Wales	£15.99	£11.99
Venues	£11.99	£8.99
Cotswolds	£9.99	£7.49
Devon & Cornwall	£9.99	£7.49
Wales	£9.99	£7.49
Dog-friendly Breaks in Britain	£14.99	£11.24
Ireland	£12.99	£9.74
French Bed & Breakfast	£15.99	£11.99
French Self-catering	£14.99	£11.24
French Châteaux & Hotels	£15.99	£11.99
French Vineyards	£19.99	£14.99
Paris	£9.99	£7.49
Green Europe	£11.99	£8.99
Italy	£15.99	£11.99
Portugal	£12.99	£9.74
Spain	£15.99	£11.99
Morocco	£9.99	£7.49
India	£11.99	£8.99
Go Slow England & Wales	£19.99	£14.99
Go Slow France	£19.99	£14.99
Go Slow Italy	£19.99	£14.99
Eat Slow Britain	£19.99	£14.99

*postage and packaging is added to each order

How to order:

You can order online at: www.sawdays.co.uk/bookshop/

or call: **+44(0)1275 395431**

① Lorraine B&B **②**

③ Château d'Alteville

④ Within exploring distance of Strasbourg, Nancy and Metz, the château has more than a whiff of history. It was built for one of Napoleon's generals and the two paintings that hang in the Louis XVI salon were gifts from the Emperor. David's family has farmed here for five generations; now he and Agnieszka welcome guests with huge kindness and eco-awareness. Bedrooms are authentically French and solidly traditional, with carved armoires, Voltaire armchairs, perhaps a draped bedhead or a small chandelier. Parkland views float in through the windows and bathrooms have recently been updated. Downstairs is more stylish: a library/billiard room, a many-windowed salon hung with portraits, a majestic dining room where splendid candlelit dinners are served several nights a week in the company of your lively, interesting hosts (book ahead). Laze on the terrace at the back, admiring the château grounds, or pull on your hiking boots and follow your nose through the woods and round the ponds. Agnieszka fills the place with children and flowers. It's homely, well priced and definitely special. *No credit cards.*

Price	€68–€91.
Rooms	5: 4 doubles, 1 twin.
Meals	Breakfast included.
	Dinner €31–€38.50 by reservation.
	Wine €5–€15.
Closed	Mid-October to mid-April.
Directions	From Nancy N74 for Sarreguemines
	& Château Salins. At Burthecourt
	x-roads, D38 to Dieuze; D999 south
	5km; left on D199F; right D199G
	to château.

⑤ **⑥** **⑦** **⑧** **⑨**

⑩ Ethical Collection: Environment; Community; Food. See page 429 for details

David & Agnieszka Barthélémy
Tarquimpol,
57260 Dieuze, Moselle
Tel   +33 (0)3 87 05 46 63
Mobile +33 (0)6 72 07 56 05
Email   chateau.alteville@free.fr

⑪ Entry 24   Map 7   **⑫**